COUNSELS TO PARENTS, TEACHERS, AND STUDENTS

COUNSELS

TO

Parents, Teachers, and Students

REGARDING

Christian Education

by
ELLEN G. WHITE

AUTHOR OF

Christ's Object Lessons, The Ministry of Healing,
Thoughts From the Mount of Blessing,
Education, Steps to Christ

"TRUE KNOWLEDGE IS DIVINE"

Nampa, Idaho

ISBN 978-0-8163-2543-6

To accurately convey the nineteenth-century intent of
the author, the word "intercourse" on page 338 has been
replaced with the word "fellowship."

April 2016

PREFACE

As early as 1872, counsel and instruction regarding Christian education began to come from the pen of Ellen G. White to Seventh-day Adventists. The first comprehensive article on this subject, entitled "Proper Education," is found in *Testimonies for the Church,* volume 3, pages 131-160. In the thirty pages of this article may be found, in embryo or in well-developed form, every fundamental principle which should govern the training and instruction of children and youth. Revolutionary as some of the views expressed may have seemed to be at the time of writing, they are today recognized and advocated by progressive educational thinkers. Seventh-day Adventists may justly regard themselves as highly favored in that such a fundamental outline of educational principles appeared so early in their literature.

That brief yet comprehensive outline, given to lead us into right educational paths, has been followed through the years by further, more detailed counsels, reiterating the principles first set forth, expanding their application, and urging their adoption. *Christian Education* and *Special Testimonies on Education,* two small works published in the nineties, carried these messages to the people.

Finally, in 1903, *Education,* a masterpiece in the field of character education, was presented to the general reading public by Ellen G. White, and through many printings and translations it has conveyed its helpful messages to thousands in this and in other lands. But the special detailed instruction, specifically addressed to Seventh-day Adventists, could not well be included in this popular volume intended for more general distribution; and the earlier works having passed out of print, much of the wealth of specific counsel of great value to us was no longer available. To provide this, together with later and fuller writings on certain phases of the topic, this work, *Counsels to Parents, Teachers, and Students,* was published in 1913.

Brought to view in this volume are the principles and methods of presenting an education which "includes not only mental discipline, but that training which will secure sound morals and correct deportment"—that education which will "fit men and women for service by developing and bringing into active exercise all their faculties."

As the subject is developed, there are clearly set forth the responsibilities and duties of parents, heartening counsel to guide the teachers in their work, and practical instruction to those who devote the years of their youth in preparing for a life of service.

At the close of each section, a page under the title "For Further Study" presents references to other E. G. White books containing related instruction. With the publication of the four volumes, *Fundamentals of Christian Education* (1923), *Messages to Young People* (1930), *The Adventist Home* (1952), and *Child Guidance* (1954), the sources of available related E. G. White materials is greatly expanded. In this printing the references on the "For Further Study" pages have been broadened to include these helpful sources.

That this volume may serve yet more fully as a guide to parents and teachers in advancing "the most delicate work ever entrusted to mortals," that of bringing "man back into harmony with God," is the earnest desire of the publishers and

THE TRUSTEES OF THE
ELLEN G. WHITE PUBLICATIONS.

CONTENTS

THE HIGHER EDUCATION

The most essential lessons for teachers and students to learn, are those which point, not to the world, but from the world to the cross of Christ.

THE ESSENTIAL KNOWLEDGE

Higher education is an experimental knowledge of the plan of salvation, and this knowledge is secured by earnest and diligent study of the Scriptures. Such an education will renew the mind and transform the character, restoring the image of God in the soul. It will fortify the mind against the deceptive whisperings of the adversary, and enable us to understand the voice of God. It will teach the learner to become a co-worker with Jesus Christ, to dispel the moral darkness about him, and bring light and knowledge to men. It is the simplicity of true godliness—our passport from the preparatory school of earth to the higher school above.

There is no education to be gained higher than that given to the early disciples, and which is revealed to us through the word of God. To gain the higher education means to follow this word implicitly; it means to walk in the footsteps of Christ, to practice His virtues. It means to give up selfishness and to devote the life to the service of God. Higher education calls for something greater, something more divine, than the knowledge to be obtained merely from books. It means a personal, experimental knowledge of Christ; it means emancipation from ideas, from habits and practices, that have been gained in the school of the prince of darkness, and which are opposed to loyalty to God. It means to overcome stubbornness, pride, selfishness, worldly ambition, and unbelief. It is the message of deliverance from sin.

Age after age the curiosity of men has led them to seek for the tree of knowledge, and often they think they are plucking fruit most essential, when in reality it is vanity and nothingness in comparison with that science of true holiness which would open to them the gates of the city of God. Human ambition seeks for knowledge that will bring to them glory, and self-exaltation, and supremacy. Thus Adam and Eve were influenced by Satan until God's restraint was snapped asunder, and their education under the teacher of lies began. They gained the knowledge which God had refused them—to know the consequences of transgression.

The tree of knowledge, so-called, has become an instrument of death. Satan has artfully woven his dogmas, his false theories, into the instruction given. From the tree of knowledge he speaks the most pleasing flattery in regard to the higher education. Thousands partake of the fruit of this tree, but it means death to them. Christ says, "Ye spend money for that which is not bread." Isaiah 55:2. You are using your heaven-entrusted talents to secure an education which God pronounces foolishness.

Upon the mind of every student should be impressed the thought that education is a failure unless the understanding has learned to grasp the truths of divine revelation, and unless the heart accepts the teachings of the gospel of Christ. The student who, in the place of the broad principles of the word of God, will accept common ideas, and will allow the time and attention to be absorbed in commonplace, trivial matters, will find his mind becoming dwarfed and enfeebled. He will lose the power of growth. The mind must be trained to comprehend the important truths that concern eternal life.

I am instructed that we are to carry the minds of our students higher than is now thought to be possible. Heart and mind are to be trained to preserve their purity by receiving daily supplies from the fountain of eternal truth. The education gained from a study of God's word will enlarge the narrow confines of human scholarship, and present before the mind a far deeper knowledge to be obtained through a vital connection with God. It will bring every student who is a doer of the word into a broader field of thought, and secure to him a wealth of learning that is imperishable. Without this knowledge it is certain that man will lose eternal life; possessing it, he will be fitted to become a companion of the saints in light.

The divine mind and hand have preserved through the ages the record of creation in its purity. It is the word of God alone that gives to us an authentic account of the creation of our world. This word is to be the chief study in our schools. In it we may learn what our redemption has cost Him who from the beginning was equal with the Father, and who sacrificed His life that a people might stand before Him redeemed from everything earthly, renewed in the image of God.

God's appointments and grants in our behalf are without limit. The throne of grace is itself the highest attraction, because occupied by One who permits us to call Him Father. But Jehovah did not deem the plan of salvation complete while invested only with His love. He has placed at His altar an Advocate clothed in His nature. As our intercessor, Christ's office work is to introduce us to God as His sons and daughters. He intercedes in behalf of those who receive Him. With His own blood He has paid their ransom. By virtue of His own merits He gives them power to become members of the royal family, children of the heavenly King. And the Father demonstrates His infinite love for Christ by receiving and welcoming Christ's friends as His friends. He is satisfied with the atonement made. He is glorified by the incarnation, the life, death, and mediation, of His Son.

The science of salvation, the science of true godliness, the knowledge which has been revealed from eternity, which enters into the purpose of God, expresses His mind, and reveals His purpose—this Heaven deems all-important. If our youth obtain this knowledge, they will be able to gain all else that is essential; but if not, all the knowledge they may acquire from the world will not place them in the ranks of the Lord. They may gather all the knowledge that books can give, and yet be ignorant of the first principles of that righteousness which will give them characters approved of God.

The Peril in Worldly Education

To many who place their children in our schools, strong temptations will come because they desire them to secure what the world regards as the most essential education. To these I would say, Bring your children to the simplicity of the word, and they will be safe. This Book is the foundation of all true knowledge. The highest education they can receive is to learn how to add to their "faith virtue; and to virtue knowledge; and to knowledge temperance; and to temperance patience; and to patience godliness; and to godliness brotherly kindness; and to brotherly kindness charity." "If these things be in you, and abound," the word of God declares, "they make you that ye shall neither be barren nor unfruitful in the knowledge of our Lord Jesus Christ. . . . If ye do these things, ye shall never fall: for so an entrance shall be ministered unto you abundantly into the everlasting kingdom of our Lord and Saviour Jesus Christ." 2 Peter 1:5-11.

When the word of God is laid aside for books that lead away from God, and that confuse the understanding regarding the principles of the kingdom of heaven, the education given is a perversion of the name. Unless the student has pure mental food, thoroughly winnowed from the so-called "higher education," which is mingled with infidel sentiments, he cannot truly know God. Only those who co-operate with heaven in the plan of salvation can know what true education in its simplicity means.

Those who seek the education that the world esteems

so highly are gradually led farther and farther from the principles of truth, until they become educated worldlings. At what a price have they gained their education! They have parted with the Holy Spirit of God. They have chosen to accept what the world calls knowledge in the place of the truths which God has committed to men through his ministers and apostles and prophets.

And there are some who, having secured this worldly education, think that they can introduce it into our schools. There is constant danger that those who labor in our schools and sanitariums will entertain the idea that they must get in line with the world, study the things the world studies, and become familiar with the things the world becomes familiar with. We shall make grave mistakes unless we give special attention to the searching of the word. The Bible should not be brought into our schools to be sandwiched between infidelity. God's word must be made the groundwork and subject matter of education. It is true that we know much more of this word than we knew in the past, but there is still much to be learned.

_____

The true higher education is that imparted by Him with whom is "wisdom and strength," out of whose mouth "cometh knowledge and understanding." Job 12:13; Proverbs 2:6. In a knowledge of God all true knowledge and real development have their source. Wherever we turn, in the mental, the physical, or the spiritual realm; in whatever we behold, apart from the blight of sin, this knowledge is revealed. Whatever line of investigation we pursue with a sincere purpose to arrive at truth, we are brought in touch with the unseen, mighty Intelligence that is working in and through all. The mind of man is brought into communion with the mind of God, the finite with the Infinite. The effect of such communion on body and mind and soul is beyond estimate.—*Education,* page 14.

In the Teacher sent from God all true educational work finds its center. Of this work today, as verily as of the work He established eighteen hundred years ago, the Saviour speaks in the words, "I am the first and the last, and the Living One." "I am the Alpha and the Omega, the beginning and the end." Revelation 1:17, 18; 21:6, R.V.

In the presence of such a Teacher, with such opportunity for divine education, what worse than folly is it to seek an education apart from Him—to seek to be wise apart from Wisdom; to be true while rejecting Truth; to seek illumination apart from Light, and existence without the Life; to turn from the Fountain of living waters, and hew out broken cisterns, that can hold no water!—*Education,* page 83.

Dear teacher, as you consider your need of strength and guidance,—need that no human source can supply,— I bid you consider the promises of Him who is the wonderful Counselor. "Behold," He says, "I have set before thee an open door, and no man can shut it." Revelation 3:8. "Call unto Me, and I will answer thee." Jeremiah 33:3. "I will instruct thee and teach thee in the way which thou shalt go: I will guide thee with Mine eye." Psalm 32:8. "Even unto the end of the world," "I am with you." Matthew 28:20.

As the highest preparation for your work I point you to the words, the life, the methods, of the Prince of teachers. I bid you consider Him. Here is your true ideal. Behold it, dwell upon it, until the Spirit of the divine Teacher shall take possession of your heart and life. "Reflecting as a mirror the glory of the Lord," you will be "transformed into the same image." 2 Corinthians 3:18, R.V.—*Education,* page 282.

Advancement in true education does not harmonize with selfishness. True knowledge comes from God and returns to God. His children are to receive that they may give again. Those who through the grace of God have received intellectual and spiritual benefits, are to draw others with them as they advance to a higher excellence. And this work, done to promote the good of others, will have the co-operation of unseen agencies. As we faithfully continue the work, we shall have high aspirations for righteousness, holiness, and a perfect knowledge of God. In this life we become complete in Christ, and our increased capabilities we shall take with us to the courts above.

THE FIRST OF SCIENCES

A knowledge of true science is power, and it is the purpose of God that this knowledge shall be taught in our schools as a preparation for the work that is to precede the closing scenes of this earth's history. The truth is to be carried to the remotest bounds of earth, through agents trained for the work.

But while the knowledge of science is power, the knowledge that Jesus came in person to impart is still greater power. The science of salvation is the most important science to be learned in the preparatory school of earth. The wisdom of Solomon is desirable, but the wisdom of Christ is far more desirable and more essential. We cannot reach Christ through a mere intellectual training; but through Him we can reach the highest round of the ladder of intellectual greatness. While the pursuit of knowledge in art, in literature, and in trades should not be discouraged, the student should first secure an experimental knowledge of God and His will.

The opportunity of learning the science of salvation is placed within the reach of all. By abiding in Christ, by doing His will, by exercising simple faith in His word, even those unlearned in the wisdom of the world may have this knowledge. To the humble, trusting soul the Lord reveals that all true knowledge leads heavenward.

Mastering the Science

There is a science of Christianity to be mastered—a science as much deeper, broader, higher, than any human science as the heavens are higher than the earth. The mind is to be disciplined, educated, trained; for men are to do service for God in ways that are not in harmony with inborn inclination. Often the training and education of a lifetime must be discarded, that one may become a learner in the school of Christ. The heart must be educated to become steadfast in God. Old and young are to form habits of thought that will enable them to resist temptation. They must learn to look upward. The principles of the word of God—principles that are as high as heaven and that compass eternity—are to be understood in their bearing on the daily life. Every act, every word, every thought, is to be in accord with these principles.

No other science is equal to that which develops in the life of the student the character of God. Those who become followers of Christ find that new motives of action are supplied, new thoughts arise, and new actions must result. But they can make advancement only through conflict; for there is an enemy who ever contends against them, presenting temptations to cause the soul to doubt and sin. There are hereditary and cultivated tendencies to evil that must be overcome. Appetite and passion must be brought under the control of the Holy Spirit. There is no end to the warfare this side of eternity. But while there are constant battles to fight, there are also precious victories to gain; and the triumph over self and sin is of more value than the mind can estimate.

True Success in Education

True success in education, as in everything else, is found in keeping the future life in view. The human family have scarcely begun to live when they begin to die, and the world's incessant labor ends in nothingness unless a true knowledge in regard to eternal life is gained. He who appreciates probationary time as the preparatory school of life will use it to secure to himself a title to the heavenly mansions, a membership in the higher school. For this school the youth are to be educated, disciplined, and trained by forming such characters as God will approve.

If students are led to understand that the object of their creation is to honor God and to bless their fellow men; if they recognize the tender love which the Father in heaven has manifested toward them, and the high destiny for which the discipline of this life is to prepare them,—the dignity and honor of becoming the sons of God,—thousands will turn from the low and selfish aims and the frivolous pleasures which have hitherto engrossed them. They will learn to hate sin and to shun it, not merely for hope of reward or from fear of punishment, but from a sense of its inherent baseness—because it is degrading to their God-given powers, a stain upon their manhood. The elements of character that make a man successful and honored among men—the irrepressible desire for some greater good, the indomitable will, the strenuous exertion, the untiring perseverance—will not be crushed out. By the grace of God they will be directed to objects as much higher than mere selfish and temporal interests as the heavens are higher than the earth.

"God hath from the beginning chosen you to salvation," the apostle Paul writes, "through sanctification of the Spirit and belief of the truth." 2 Thessalonians 2:13. In this text the two agencies in the work of salvation are revealed—the divine influence, and the strong, living faith of those who follow Christ. It is through the sanctification of the Spirit and belief of the truth that we become laborers together with God. Christ waits for the co-operation of His church. He does not design to add a new element of efficiency to His word; He has done His great work in giving His inspiration to the word. The blood of Jesus Christ, the Holy Spirit, the divine word, are ours. The object of all this provision of heaven is before us— the salvation of the souls for whom Christ died; and it depends upon us to lay hold on the promises God has given, and become laborers together with Him. Divine and human agencies must co-operate in the work.

"Everyone that is of the truth," Christ declared, "heareth My voice." John 18:37. Having stood in the counsels of God, having dwelt in the everlasting heights of the sanctuary, all elements of truth were in Him and of Him. He was one with God. It means more than finite minds can comprehend to present in every missionary effort Christ and Him crucified. "He was wounded for our transgressions, He was bruised for our iniquities: the chastisement of our peace was upon Him; and with His stripes we are healed." Isaiah 53:5. "He hath made Him to be sin for us, who knew no sin; that we might be made the righteousness of God in Him." 2 Corinthians 5:21. Christ crucified for our sins; Christ risen from the dead; Christ ascended on high as our intercessor—this is the science of salvation that we need to learn and to teach. This is to be the burden of our work.

The cross of Christ—teach it to every student over and over again. How many believe it to be what it is? How many bring it into their studies and know its true significance? Could there be a Christian in our world without the cross of Christ? Then keep the cross upheld in your school as the foundation of true education. The cross of Christ is just as near our teachers, and should be as perfectly understood by them, as it was by Paul, who could say, "God forbid that I should glory, save in the cross of our Lord Jesus Christ, by whom the world is crucified unto me, and I unto the world." Galatians 6:14.

Let teachers, from the highest to the lowest, seek to understand what it means to glory in the cross of Christ. Then by precept and example they can teach their students the blessings it brings to those who bear it manfully and bravely. The Saviour declares, "If any man will come after Me, let him deny himself, and take up his cross, and follow Me." Matthew 16:24. And to all who lift it and bear it after Christ, the cross is a pledge of the crown of immortality that they will receive.

Educators who will not work in this line are not worthy of the name they bear. Teachers, turn from the example of the world, cease to extol professedly great men; turn the minds of your students from the glory of everything save the cross of Christ. The crucified Mes-

siah is the central point of all Christianity. The most
essential lessons for teachers and students to learn are
those which point, not to the world, but from the world
to the cross of Calvary.

———————

Godliness—Godlikeness—is the goal to be reached. Before the student there is opened a path of continual progress. He has an object to achieve, a standard to attain, that
includes everything good, and pure, and noble. He will
advance as fast and as far as possible in every branch of
true knowledge. But his efforts will be directed to objects
as much higher than mere selfish and temporal interests
as the heavens are higher than the earth.

He who co-operates with the divine purpose in imparting to the youth a knowledge of God, and molding the
character into harmony with His, does a high and noble
work. As he awakens a desire to reach God's ideal, he
presents an education that is as high as heaven and as
broad as the universe; an education that cannot be com-
pleted in this life, but that will be continued in the life to
come; an education that secures to the successful student
his passport from the preparatory school of earth to the
higher grade, the school above.—*Education*, pages 18, 19.

THE TEACHER OF TRUTH THE ONLY
SAFE EDUCATOR

There are two classes of educators in the world. One class is made up of those whom God makes channels of light; the other of those whom Satan uses as his agents, who are wise to do evil. One class contemplate the character of God, and increase in the knowledge of Jesus. This class become wholly given up to those things which bring heavenly enlightenment, heavenly wisdom, to the uplifting of the soul. Every capability of their nature is submitted to God; even their thoughts are brought into captivity to Christ. The other class are in league with the prince of darkness, who is ever on the alert that he may find an opportunity to teach others the knowledge of evil, and who, if place is made for him, will not be slow to press his way into heart and mind.

There is great need of elevating the standard of righteousness in our schools, of giving instruction that is after God's order. Should Christ enter our institutions for the education of the youth, He would cleanse them as He cleansed the temple, banishing many things that have a defiling influence. Many of the books which the youth study would be expelled, and their places filled with others that would inculcate substantial knowledge, and would abound in sentiments which might be treasured in the heart, and in precepts that might safely govern the conduct.

Is it the Lord's purpose that false principles, false reasoning, and the sophistries of Satan should be kept before the minds of our youth and children? Shall pagan and infidel sentiments be presented to our students as valuable additions to their store of knowledge? The works of the most intellectual skeptic are the works of a mind prostituted to the service of the enemy; and shall those who claim to be reformers, who seek to lead the children and youth in the right way, in the path cast up for the ransomed of the Lord to walk in, imagine that God would have them present to the youth for their study that which will misrepresent His character and place Him in a false light? Shall the sentiments of unbelievers, the expressions of dissolute men, be advocated as worthy of the student's attention, because they are the productions of men whom the world admires as great thinkers? Shall men professing to believe in God gather from these unsanctified authors their expressions and sentiments, and treasure them up as precious jewels to be stored away among the riches of the mind? God forbid!

The Lord bestowed upon these men whom the world admires, priceless intellectual gifts; He endowed them with master minds; but they did not use their powers to the glory of God. They separated themselves from Him, as did Satan; but while they separated themselves from Him, they still retained many of the precious gems of thought which He had given them. These they have placed in a framework of error, to give luster to their own human sentiments, to make attractive the utterances inspired by the prince of evil.

It is true that in the writings of pagans and infidels there are found thoughts of an elevated character, which are attractive to the mind. But there is a reason for this. Was not Satan the light bearer, the sharer of God's glory in heaven, and next to Jesus in power and majesty? In the words of Inspiration he is described as one who sealeth up the sum, "full of wisdom, and perfect in beauty." The prophet declares, "Thou art the anointed cherub that covereth; and I have set thee so: thou wast upon the holy mountain of God; thou hast walked up and down in the midst of the stones of fire. Thou wast perfect in thy ways from the day that thou wast created, till iniquity was found in thee." Ezekiel 28:12, 14, 15. . . .

The greatness and power with which the Creator endowed Lucifer, he has perverted; yet when it suits his purpose, he can impart to men sentiments that are enchanting. Satan can inspire his agents with thoughts that appear elevating and noble. Did he not come to Christ with quotations of Scripture when he designed to overthrow Him with specious temptations? It is thus that he comes to men, disguising his temptations under an appearance of goodness and making them believe him to be the friend rather than the enemy of humanity. In this way he has deceived and seduced the race, beguiling them with subtle temptations, bewildering them with specious deceptions.

God Misrepresented

Satan has ascribed to God all the evils to which flesh is heir. He has represented Him as a God who delights in the sufferings of His creatures, who is revengeful and implacable. It was Satan who originated the doctrine of eternal torment as a punishment for sin, because in this way he could lead men into infidelity and rebellion, distract souls, and dethrone human reason.

Heaven, looking down and seeing the delusions into which men were led, knew that a divine Instructor must come to the earth. Through the misrepresentations of the enemy, many were so deceived that they worshiped a false god, clothed with the attributes of the satanic character. Those in ignorance and moral darkness must have light, spiritual light; for the world knew not God, and He must be revealed to their understanding. Truth looked down from heaven and saw not the reflection of her image; for dense clouds of spiritual darkness and gloom enveloped the world. The Lord Jesus alone was able to roll back the clouds; for He is the light of the world. By His presence He could dissipate the gloomy shadow that Satan had cast between man and God.—First published Nov. 17, 1891.

A True Representation

The Son of God came to this earth to reveal the character of the Father to men, that they might learn to worship Him in spirit and in truth. He came to sow the world with truth. He held the keys of all the treasures of wisdom, and was able to open doors to science, and to reveal undiscovered stores of knowledge, were it essential to salvation. The Light that lighteth every man that cometh into the world, every phase of truth was evident to Him.

In the days of Christ the established teachers instructed men in the traditions of the fathers, in childish fables, with which were mingled the opinions of those who were thought to be high authorities. Yet neither high nor low could find light or strength in their teaching.

Jesus spake as never man spake. He poured out to men the whole treasure of heaven in wisdom and knowledge. He had not come to utter uncertain sentiments and opinions, but to speak truth established on eternal principles. He could have made disclosures in the sciences that would have placed the discoveries of the greatest men in the background as utter littleness; but this was not His mission or His work. He had come to seek and to save the lost, and He would not permit Himself to be turned from His object. He revealed truths that had been buried under the rubbish of error, and He freed them from the exactions and traditions of men, and bade them stand fast forever. He rescued truth from its obscurity, and set it in its proper framework, that it might shine with its original luster. What wonder that crowds followed in the footsteps of the Lord and gave Him homage as they listened to His words!

Christ presented to men that which was entirely contrary to the representations of the enemy in regard to the character of God, and sought to impress upon men the love of the Father, who "so loved the world, that He gave His only-begotten Son, that whosoever believeth in Him should not perish, but have everlasting life." John 3:16. He urged upon men the necessity of prayer, repentance, confession, and the abandonment of sin. He taught them honesty, forbearance, mercy, and compassion, enjoining upon them to love not only those who loved them, but those who hated them and treated them despitefully. In all this He was revealing to them the character of the Father, who is long-suffering, merciful, and gracious, slow to anger, and full of goodness and truth.

When Moses asked the Lord to show him His glory, the Lord said, "I will make all My goodness pass before thee." "And the Lord passed by before him, and proclaimed, The Lord, The Lord God, merciful and gracious, long-suffering, and abundant in goodness and truth, keeping mercy for thousands, forgiving iniquity and transgression and sin, and that will by no means clear the guilty. . . . And Moses made haste, and bowed his head toward the earth, and worshiped." Exodus 33:19; 34:6-8. When we are able to comprehend the character of God, as did Moses, we, too, shall make haste to bow in adoration and praise.

The wisdom of God alone can unfold the mysteries of the plan of salvation. The wisdom of men may or may not be valuable, as experience shall prove; but the wisdom of God is indispensable. Miss what you may in the line of worldly attainments, but you must have faith in the pardon brought to you at infinite cost, or all the wisdom attained on earth will perish with you.

Shall we bring into our schools the sower of tares? Shall we permit men who have been taught by the enemy of all truth, to have the education of our youth? Or shall we take the word of God as our guide? Why take the unstable words of men as exalted wisdom, when a greater and certain wisdom is at your command? Why present inferior authors to the attention of students, when He whose words are spirit and life invites, "Come, . . . and learn of Me"? Matthew 11:28, 29.

"Labor not for the meat which perisheth," Christ admonished, "but for that meat which endureth unto everlasting life, which the Son of man shall give unto you: for Him hath God the Father sealed." John 6:27. When we obey these words, we shall rightly understand the teachings of the Scriptures, and esteem the truth as the most valuable treasure with which to store the mind. We shall have within us a wellspring of the water of life. We shall pray, as did the psalmist, "Open Thou mine eyes, that I may behold wondrous things out of Thy law;" and we shall find, as he did, that "the judgments of the Lord are true and righteous altogether. More to be desired are they than gold, yea, than much fine gold: sweeter also than honey and the honeycomb. Moreover by them is Thy servant warned: and in keeping of them there is great reward." Psalms 119:18; 19:9-11.

It is only life that can beget life. He alone has life who is connected with the Source of life, and only such can be a channel of life. In order that the teacher may accomplish the object of his work, he should be a living embodiment of truth, a living channel through which wisdom and life may flow. A pure life, the result of sound principles and right habits, should therefore be regarded as his most essential qualification.

UNSELFISH SERVICE THE LAW OF HEAVEN

Love, the basis of creation and of redemption, is the basis of true education. This is made plain in the law that God has given as the guide of life. The first and great commandment is, "Thou shalt love the Lord thy God with all thy heart, and with all thy soul, and with all thy mind, and with all thy strength." Mark 12:30. To love Him, the Infinite, the Omniscient One, with the whole strength and mind and heart, means the highest development of every power. It means that in the whole being—the body, the mind, as well as the soul—the image of God is to be restored.

Like the first is the second commandment, "Thou shalt love thy neighbor as thyself." Mark 12:31. The law of love calls for the devotion of body, mind, and soul to the service of God and our fellow men. And this service, while making us a blessing to others, brings the greatest blessing to ourselves. Unselfishness underlies all true development. Through unselfish service we receive the highest culture of every faculty.

The Result of Self-Seeking

Lucifer in heaven desired to be first in power and authority; he wanted to be God, to have the rulership of heaven; and to this end he won many of the angels to his side. When with his rebel host he was cast out from the courts of God, the work of rebellion and self-seeking was continued on earth. Through the temptation to self-indulgence and ambition Satan accomplished the fall of our first parents; and from that time to the present the gratification of human ambition and the indulgence of selfish hopes and desires have proved the ruin of mankind.

Under God, Adam was to stand at the head of the earthly family, to maintain the principles of the heavenly family. This would have brought peace and happiness. But the law that none "liveth to himself" (Romans 14:7), Satan was determined to oppose. He desired to live for self. He sought to make himself a center of influence. It was this that had incited rebellion in heaven, and it was man's acceptance of this principle that brought sin on earth. When Adam sinned, man broke away from the heaven-ordained center. A demon became the central power in the world. Where God's throne should have been, Satan placed his throne. The world laid its homage, as a willing offering, at the feet of the enemy.

The transgression of God's law brought woe and death in its train. Through disobedience man's powers were perverted, and selfishness took the place of love. His nature became so weakened that it was impossible for him to resist the power of evil; and the tempter saw being fulfilled his purpose to thwart the divine plan of man's creation and fill the earth with misery and desolation. Men had chosen a ruler who chained them to his car as captives.

The Remedy

Looking upon man, God saw his desperate rebellion, and He devised a remedy. Christ was His gift to the world for man's reconcilement. The Son of God was appointed to come to this earth to take humanity and by His own example to be a great educating power among men. His experience in man's behalf was to enable men to resist Satan's power. He came to mold character and to give mental power, to shed abroad the beams of true education, that the true aim of life might not be lost sight of. The sons of men had had a practical knowledge of evil; Christ came to the world to show them that He had planted for them the tree of life, the leaves of which are for the healing of the nations.

Christ's life on earth teaches that to obtain the higher education does not mean to gain popularity, to secure worldly advantage, to have all the temporal wants abundantly supplied, and to be honored by the titled and wealthy of earth. The Prince of life suffered the inconveniences of poverty, that He might discern the needs of the poor—He who by His divine power could supply the needs of a hungry multitude. Not to wear the gorgeous robes of the high priest, not to possess the riches of the Gentiles, did He come to this earth, but to minister to the suffering and the needy. His life rebukes all self-seeking. As He went about doing good He made plain the character of God's law and the nature of His service.

Christ might have opened to men the deepest truths of science. He might have unlocked mysteries which have required many centuries of toil and study to penetrate. He might have made suggestions in scientific lines that till the close of time would have afforded food for thought and stimulus for invention. But He did not do this. He said nothing to gratify curiosity or to stimulate selfish ambition. He did not deal in abstract theories, but in that which is essential to the development of character, that which will enlarge man's capacity for knowing God, and increase his power to do good. Instead of directing the people to study men's theories about God, His word, or His works, Christ taught them to behold Him as manifested in His works, in His word, and by His providences. He brought their minds in contact with the mind of the Infinite. He unfolded principles that struck at the root of selfishness.

Those who are ignorant of education as it was taught and exemplified in the life of Christ are ignorant of what constitutes the higher education. His life of humiliation and death of shame paid the redemption price for every soul. He gave Himself for the uplifting of the fallen and the sinful. Can we imagine an education higher than that to be gained in co-operation with Him?

To everyone Christ gives the command, "Go work today in My vineyard for the glory of My name. Represent before a world laden with corruption the blessedness of true education. The weary, the heavy-laden, the brokenhearted, the perplexed—point them to Christ, the source of all strength, all life, all hope." To teachers the word is spoken, "Be faithful minutemen. Seek for the higher education, for entire conformity to the will of God. You will surely reap the reward that comes from its reception. As you place yourselves where you can be recipients of the blessing of God, the name of the Lord will be magnified through you."

Not lip service, not profession, but humble, devoted lives, is that for which God is seeking. Teachers and students are to know by experience what it means to live consecrated lives, which reveal the sacred principles that are the basis of Christian character. Those who give themselves to learn the way and will of God are receiving the highest education that it is possible for mortals to receive. They are building their experience, not on the sophistries of the world, but upon principles that are eternal.

It is the privilege of every student to take the life and teachings of Christ as his daily study. Christian education means the acceptance, in sentiment and principle, of the teachings of the Saviour. It includes a daily, conscientious walking in the footsteps of Christ, who consented to come to the world in the form of humanity, that He might give to the human race a power that they could gain by no other means. What was that power? The power to take the teachings of Christ and follow them to the letter.

In His resistance of evil and His labor for others, Christ gave to men an example of the highest education. He revealed God to His disciples in a way that wrought in their hearts a special work, such as He has long been urging us to allow Him to do in our hearts. There are many who in dwelling so largely on theory have lost sight of the living power of the Saviour's example. They have lost sight of Him as the self-denying, humble worker. What they need is to behold Jesus. Daily they need the fresh revealing of His presence. They need to follow more closely His example of self-renunciation and sacrifice.

We need the experience that Paul had when he wrote, "I am crucified with Christ: nevertheless I live; yet not I, but Christ liveth in me: and the life which I now live in the flesh I live by the faith of the Son of God, who loved me, and gave Himself for me." Galatians 2:20.

The knowledge of God and of Jesus Christ expressed in character is the very highest education. It is the key that opens the portals of the heavenly city. This knowledge it is God's purpose that all who put on Christ shall possess.

_____

He whose mind is enlightened by the opening of God's word to his understanding will realize his responsibility to God and to the world, and he will feel that his talents must be developed in a way that will produce the very best results; for he is to "show forth the praises" of Him who has called him "out of darkness into His marvelous light." 1 Peter 2:9. While growing in grace and in a knowledge of the Lord Jesus Christ, he will realize his own imperfections, he will feel his real ignorance, and he will seek constantly to preserve and put to the stretch his powers of mind, that he may become an intelligent Christian. Students who are imbued with the Spirit of Christ will grasp knowledge with all their faculties. Without this experience, education is disrobed of its true brightness and glory.

The entrance of God's word is the application of divine truth to the heart, purifying and refining the soul through the agency of the Holy Spirit. The faculties devoted unreservedly to God, under the guidance of the divine Spirit, develop steadily and harmoniously. Devotion and piety establish so close a relation between Jesus and His disciples that the Christian becomes like Him. Through the power of God, his weak, vacillating character becomes changed to one of strength and steadfastness. He becomes a person of sound principle, clear perception, and reliable, well-balanced judgment. Having a connection with God, the source of light and understanding, his views, unbiased by his own preconceived opinions, become broader, his discernment more penetrative and farseeing. The knowledge of God, the understanding of His revealed will, as far as human minds can grasp it, will, when received into the character, make efficient men.

Knowledge is power, but it is a power for good only when united with true piety. It must be vitalized by the Spirit of God in order to serve the noblest purposes. The closer our connection with God, the more fully can we comprehend the value of true science; for the attributes of God, as seen in His created works, can be best appreciated by him who has a knowledge of the Creator of all things, the Author of all truth. Such can make the highest use of knowledge; for when brought under the full control of the Spirit of God, their talents are rendered useful to the fullest extent.

FOR FURTHER STUDY

THE ESSENTIAL KNOWLEDGE

Christ's Object Lessons, pp. 106-114.
Education, pp. 13-30.
Fundamentals of Christian Education, pp. 368-372, 392-396, 512-515.
Ministry of Healing, The, pp. 409-426.
Messages to Young People, pp. 36-40, 169-172.

THE FIRST OF SCIENCES

Christ's Object Lessons, p. 134.
Fundamentals of Christian Education, pp. 186-190.
Messages to Young People, pp. 189-191.

UNSELFISH SERVICE THE LAW OF HEAVEN

Adventist Home, The, pp. 484-490.
Desire of Ages, The, p. 21.
Education, pp. 301-309.
Ministry of Healing, The, p. 457.
Testimonies, vol. 8, p. 328.

THE AIM OF OUR SCHOOLS

"That our sons may be as plants grown up in their youth; that our daughters may be as cornerstones, polished after the similitude of a palace."

OUR CHILDREN AND YOUTH DEMAND OUR CARE

There has been altogether too little attention paid to our children and youth, and they have failed to develop as they should in the Christian life, because the church members have not looked upon them with tenderness and sympathy, desiring that they might be advanced in the divine life.

In our large churches very much might be done for the youth. Shall they have less special labor; shall fewer inducements be held out to them to become full-grown Christians—men and women in Christ Jesus—than were afforded them in the denominations which they have left for the truth's sake? Shall they be left to drift hither and thither, to become discouraged, and to fall into the temptations that are lurking everywhere to catch their unwary feet? If they err, and fall from the steadfastness of their integrity, do the members of the church who have neglected to care for the lambs, censure and blame them, and magnify their failures? Are their shortcomings talked of and exposed to others, and are they left in discouragement and despair?

The work that lies next to our church members is to become interested in our youth; for they need kindness, patience, tenderness, line upon line, precept upon precept. Oh, where are the fathers and mothers in Israel? There ought to be a large number who would be stewards of the grace of Christ, who would feel not merely a casual but a special interest in the young. There ought to be those whose hearts are touched by the pitiable situation in which our youth are placed, and who realize that Satan is working by every conceivable device to draw them into his net.

God requires that the church arouse from her lethargy and see what is the manner of service demanded of her at this time of peril. The lambs of the flock must be fed. The Lord of heaven is looking on to see who is doing the work He would have done for the children and youth. The eyes of our brethren and sisters should be anointed with heavenly eyesalve, that they may discern the necessities of the time. We must be aroused to see what needs to be done in Christ's spiritual vineyard, and go to work.

A Liberal Education to Be Provided

As a people who claim to have advanced light, we are to devise ways and means by which to bring forth a corps of educated workmen for the various departments of the work of God. We need a well-disciplined, cultivated class of young men and women in our sanitariums, in the medical missionary work, in the offices of publication, in the conferences of different states, and in the field at large. We need young men and women who have a high intellectual culture, in order that they may do the best work for the Lord. We have done something toward reaching this standard, but still we are far behind where we should be.

As a church, as individuals, if we would stand clear in the judgment, we must make more liberal efforts for the training of our young people, that they may be better fitted for the various branches of the great work committed to our hands. We should lay wise plans, in order that the ingenious minds of those who have talent may be strengthened and disciplined, and polished after the highest order, that the work of Christ may not be hindered for lack of skillful laborers, who will do their work with earnestness and fidelity.

All to Be Trained

The church is asleep, and does not realize the magnitude of this matter of educating the children and youth. "Why," one says, "what is the need of being so particular to educate our youth thoroughly? It seems to me that if you take a few who have decided to follow a literary calling or some other calling that requires a certain discipline, and give due attention to them, that is all that is necessary. It is not required that the whole mass of our youth be so well trained. Will not this answer every essential requirement?"

I answer, No, most decidedly not. What selection should we be able to make out of the numbers of our youth? How could we tell who would be the most promising, who would render the best service to God? In our judgment we might look upon the outward appearance, as Samuel did when he was sent to find the anointed of the Lord. When the noble sons of Jesse passed before him, and his eye rested upon the handsome countenance and fine stature of the eldest son, to Samuel it seemed that the anointed of the Lord was before him. But the Lord said to him, "Look not on his countenance, or on the height of his stature; because I have refused him: for the Lord seeth not as man seeth; for man looketh on the outward appearance, but the Lord looketh on the heart." Not one of these noble-looking sons of Jesse would the Lord accept. But when David, the youngest son, a mere youth, was called from the field, and passed before Samuel, the Lord said, "Arise, anoint him: for this is he." 1 Samuel 16:7, 12.

Who can determine which one of a family will prove to be efficient in the work of God? There should be general education of all its members, and all our youth should be permitted to have the blessings and privileges of an education at our schools, that they may be inspired to become laborers together with God. They all need an education, that they may be fitted for usefulness, qualified for places of responsibility in both private and public life. There is a great necessity of making plans that there may be a large number of competent workers, and many should fit themselves as teachers, that others may be trained and disciplined for the great work of the future.

A Fund for Schoolwork

The church should take in the situation, and by their influence and means seek to bring about this much-desired end. Let a fund be created by generous contributions for the establishment of schools for the advancement of educational work. We need men well trained, well educated, to work in the interests of the churches. They should present the fact that we cannot trust our youth to go to seminaries and colleges established by other denominations; that we must gather them into schools where their religious training shall not be neglected.

High Aims

God would not have us in any sense behind in educational work. Our colleges should be far in advance in the highest kind of education. . . . If we do not have schools for our youth, they will attend other seminaries and colleges, and will be exposed to infidel sentiments, to cavilings and questionings concerning the inspiration of the Bible. There is a great deal of talk concerning higher education, and many suppose that higher education consists wholly in an education in science and literature; but this is not all. The highest education includes the knowledge of the word of God, and is comprehended in the words, "That they might know Thee the only true God, and Jesus Christ, whom Thou has sent." John 17:3.

The highest class of education is that which will give such knowledge and discipline as will lead to the best development of character, and will fit the soul for that life which measures with the life of God. Eternity is not to be lost out of our reckoning. The highest education is that which will teach our children and youth the science of Christianity, which will give them an experimental knowledge of God's ways, and will impart to them the lessons that Christ gave to His disciples, of the paternal character of God.

"Thus saith the Lord, Let not the wise man glory in his wisdom, neither let the mighty man glory in his might, let not the rich man glory in his riches: but let him that glorieth glory in this, that he understandeth and knoweth Me." Jeremiah 9:23, 24. . . . Let us seek to follow the counsel of God in all things; for He is infinite in wisdom. Though we have come short of doing what we might have done for our youth and children in the past, let us now repent, and redeem the time.—*Special Testimonies on Education,* pages 197-202; written April 28, 1896.

The Responsibility of Church Members

There is no work more important than the education of our youth. I am glad that we have institutions where they can be separated from the corrupting influences so prevalent in the schools of the present day. Our brethren and sisters should be thankful that in the providence of God our colleges have been established, and should stand ready to sustain them by their means. Every influence should be brought to bear to educate the youth and to elevate their morals. They should be trained to have courage to resist the tide of moral pollution in this degenerate age. With a firm hold upon divine power, they may stand in society to mold and fashion, rather than to be fashioned after the world's model.

When the youth come to our colleges, they should not be made to feel that they have come among strangers who do not care for their souls. We must guard them, fighting back Satan, that he shall not take them out of our arms. There should be fathers and mothers in Israel who will watch for their souls as they that must give an account. Brethren and sisters, do not hold yourselves aloof from the youth, as if you had no particular concern or responsibility for them. You who have long professed to be Christians have a work to do, patiently and kindly to lead them in the right way. You should show them that you love them because they are younger members of the Lord's family, the purchase of His blood.

The future of society will be determined by the youth of today. Satan is making earnest, persevering efforts to corrupt the mind and debase the character of every youth; and shall we who have more experience stand as mere spectators, and see him accomplish his purpose without hindrance? Let us stand at our post as minutemen, to work for these youth, and through the help of God to hold them back from the pit of destruction. In the parable, while men slept the enemy sowed tares; and while you, my brethren and sisters, are unconscious of his work, Satan is gathering an army of youth under his banner; and he exults, for through them he carries on his warfare against God.

The Teacher's Privilege

The teachers in our schools have a heavy responsibility to bear. They must be in words and character what they wish their students to become—men and women that fear God and work righteousness. If they are acquainted with the way themselves, they can train the youth to walk in it. They will not only educate them in the sciences, but will train them to have moral independence, to work for Jesus, and to take up burdens in His cause.

Teachers, what opportunities are yours! What a privilege is within your reach of molding the minds and characters of the youth under your charge! What a joy it will be to you to meet them round the great white throne, and to know that you have done what you could to fit them for immortality! If your work stands the test of the great day, like sweetest music will fall upon your ears the benediction of the Master, "Well done, thou good and faithful servant: . . . enter thou into the joy of thy Lord." Matthew 25:21.

In the great harvest field there is abundance of work for all, and those who neglect to do what they can will be found guilty before God. Let us work for time and for eternity. Let us work with all the powers that God has bestowed upon us, and He will bless our well-directed efforts.

The Saviour longs to save the young. He would rejoice to see them around His throne, clothed in the spotless robes of His righteousness. He is waiting to place upon their heads the crown of life, and to hear their happy voices join in ascribing honor and glory and majesty to God and the Lamb in the song of victory that shall echo and re-echo through the courts of heaven.

THE PRIMAL OBJECT OF EDUCATION

By a misconception of the true nature and object of education, many have been led into serious and even fatal errors. Such a mistake is made when the regulation of the heart or the establishment of principles is neglected in the effort to secure intellectual culture, or when eternal interests are overlooked in the eager desire for temporal advantage.

To make the possession of worldly honor or riches our ruling motive is unworthy of one who has been redeemed by the blood of Christ. It should rather be our aim to gain knowledge and wisdom that we may become better Christians, and be prepared for greater usefulness, rendering more faithful service to our Creator, and by our example and influence leading others also to glorify God. Here is something real, something tangible—not only words, but deeds. Not only the affections of the heart, but the service of the life, must be devoted to our Maker.

The One Perfect Pattern

To bring man back into harmony with God, so to elevate and ennoble his moral nature that he may again reflect the image of the Creator, is the great purpose of all the education and discipline of life. So important was this work that the Saviour left the courts of heaven and came in person to this earth, that He might teach men how to obtain a fitness for the higher life. For thirty years He dwelt as a man among men, passed through the experiences of human life as a child, a youth, a man; He endured the severest trials that He might present a living illustration of the truths He taught. For three years as a teacher sent from God He instructed the children of men; then, leaving the work to chosen colaborers, He ascended to heaven. But His interest in it has not abated. From the courts above He watches with the deepest solicitude the progress of the cause for which He gave His life.

The character of Christ is the one perfect pattern which we are to copy. Repentance and faith, the surrender of the will, and the consecration of the affections to God are the means appointed for the accomplishment of this work. To obtain a knowledge of this divinely ordained plan should be our first study; to comply with its requirements, our first effort.

Solomon declares that "the fear of the Lord is the beginning of wisdom." Proverbs 9:10. Concerning the value and importance of this wisdom, he writes: "Wisdom is the principal thing; therefore get wisdom: and with all thy getting get understanding." Proverbs 4:7. "For the merchandise of it is better than the merchandise of silver, and the gain thereof than fine gold. She is more precious than rubies: and all the things thou canst desire are not to be compared unto her." Proverbs 3:14, 15.

The School of Christ

He who is seeking with diligence to acquire the wisdom of human schools should remember that another school also claims him as a student. Christ was the greatest teacher the world ever saw. He brought to man knowledge direct from heaven. The lessons which He

has given us are what we need for both the present and
the future state. He sets before us the true aims of life,
and how we may secure them.

In the school of Christ, students are never graduated.
Among the pupils are both old and young. Those who
give heed to the instructions of the divine Teacher constantly advance in wisdom, refinement, and nobility of
soul, and thus they are prepared to enter that higher
school where advancement will continue throughout eternity.

Infinite Wisdom sets before us the great lessons of life
—lessons of duty and happiness. These are often hard to
learn, but without them we can make no real progress.
They may cost us effort and tears, and even agony, but we
must not falter or grow weary. We shall at last hear the
Master's call, "Child, come up higher."

It is in this world, amid its trials and temptations, that
we are to gain a fitness for the society of the pure and
holy. Those who become so absorbed in less important
studies that they cease to learn in the school of Christ are
meeting with infinite loss. They insult the divine Teacher
by the rejection of the provisions of His grace. The
longer they continue in their course, the more hardened
they are in sin. Their retribution will be proportioned to
the infinite value of the blessings they have spurned.

In the religion of Christ there is a regenerating influence that transforms the entire being, lifting man
above every debasing, groveling vice, and raising the
thoughts and desires toward God and heaven. Linked
to the Infinite One, man is made partaker of the divine

nature. Upon him the shafts of evil have no effect; for he is clothed with the panoply of Christ's righteousness.

Every faculty, every attribute, with which the Creator has endowed the children of men is to be employed for His glory; and in this employment is found its purest, holiest, happiest exercise. While religious principle is held paramount, every advance step taken in the acquirement of knowledge or in the culture of the intellect is a step toward the assimilation of the human with the Divine, the finite with the Infinite.

The Bible as an Educator

As an educator, the Holy Scriptures are without a rival. The Bible is the most ancient and the most comprehensive history that men possess. It came fresh from the Fountain of eternal truth, and throughout the ages a divine hand has preserved its purity. It lights up the far-distant past, where human research seeks in vain to penetrate. In God's word only do we behold the power that laid the foundations of the earth and that stretched out the heavens. Here only do we find an authentic account of the origin of nations. Here only is given a history of our race unsullied by human pride or prejudice.

In the word of God the mind finds subjects for the deepest thought, the loftiest aspirations. Here we may hold communion with patriarchs and prophets, and listen to the voice of the Eternal as He speaks with men. Here we behold the Majesty of heaven as He humbled Himself to become our substitute and surety, to cope singlehanded with the powers of darkness and to gain the victory in our behalf. A reverent contemplation of such themes as these cannot fail to soften, purify, and ennoble the heart, and at the same time to inspire the mind with new strength and vigor.

Those who regard it as brave and manly to treat the claims of God with indifference and contempt are thereby betraying their own folly and ignorance. While they boast their freedom and independence, they are really in bondage to sin and Satan.

A clear conception of what God is and what He requires us to be will lead to wholesome humility. He who studies aright the Sacred Word will learn that human intellect is not omnipotent. He will learn that without the help which none but God can give, human strength and wisdom are but weakness and ignorance.

He who is following the divine guidance has found the only true source of saving grace and real happiness, and has gained the power of imparting happiness to all around him. No man can really enjoy life without religion. Love to God purifies and ennobles every taste and desire, intensifies every affection, and brightens every worthy pleasure. It enables men to appreciate and enjoy all that is true, and good, and beautiful.

But that which above all other considerations should lead us to prize the Bible is that in it is revealed to men the will of God. Here we learn the object of our creation and the means by which that object may be attained. We learn how to improve wisely the present life and how to secure the future life. No other book can satisfy the questionings of the mind or the cravings of the heart. By obtaining a knowledge of God's word and giving heed thereto, men may rise from the lowest depths of degradation to become the sons of God, the associates of sinless angels.

Lessons From Nature

In the varied scenes of nature also are lessons of divine wisdom for all who have learned to commune with God. The pages that opened in undimmed brightness to the gaze of the first pair in Eden bear now a shadow. A blight has fallen upon the fair creation. And yet, wherever we turn, we see traces of the primal loveliness; wherever we turn, we hear the voice of God and behold His handiwork.

From the solemn roll of the deep-toned thunder and old ocean's ceaseless roar, to the glad songs that make the forests vocal with melody, nature's ten thousand voices speak His praise. In earth and sea and sky, with their marvelous tint and color, varying in gorgeous contrast or blended in harmony, we behold His glory. The everlasting hills tell of His power. The trees that wave their green banners in the sunlight and the flowers in their delicate beauty point to their Creator. The living green that carpets the brown earth tells of God's care for the humblest of His creatures. The caves of the sea and the depths of the earth reveal His treasures. He who placed the pearls in the ocean and the amethyst and chrysolite among the rocks is a lover of the beautiful. The sun rising in the heavens is a representative of Him who is the life and light of all that He has made. All the brightness and beauty that adorn the earth and light up the heavens speak of God.

Shall we, then, in the enjoyment of His gifts, forget the Giver? Let them rather lead us to contemplate His goodness and His love. Let all that is beautiful in our earthly home remind us of the crystal river and green fields, the waving trees and living fountains, the shining city and the white-robed singers, of our heavenly home— that world of beauty which no artist can picture, no mortal tongue describe. "Eye hath not seen, nor ear heard, neither have entered into the heart of man, the things which God hath prepared for them that love Him." 1 Corinthians 2:9.

To dwell forever in this home of the blest, to bear in soul, body, and spirit, not the dark traces of sin and the curse, but the perfect likeness of our Creator, and through ceaseless ages to advance in wisdom, in knowledge, and in holiness, ever exploring new fields of thought, ever finding new wonders and new glories, ever increasing in capacity to know and to enjoy and to love, and knowing that there is still beyond us joy and love and wisdom infinite—such is the object to which the Christian's hope is pointing, for which Christian education is preparing. To secure this education, and to aid others to secure it, should be the object of the Christian's life.

———————

Let us never lose sight of the fact that Jesus is a wellspring of joy. He does not delight in the misery of human beings, but loves to see them happy.

THE HEAVENLY PATTERN

We are rapidly nearing the final crisis in this world's history, and it is important that we understand that the educational advantages offered by our schools are to be different from those offered by the schools of the world. Neither are we to follow the routine of worldly schools. The instruction given in Seventh-day Adventist schools is to be such as to lead to the practice of true humility. In speech, in dress, in diet, and in the influence exerted, is to be seen the simplicity of true godliness.

Our teachers need to understand the work that is to be done in these last days. The education given in our schools, in our churches, in our sanitariums, should present clearly the great work to be accomplished. The need of weeding from the life every worldly practice that is opposed to the teachings of the word of God, and of supplying its place with deeds that bear the mark of the divine nature, should be made clear to the students of all grades. Our work of education is ever to bear the impress of the heavenly, and thus reveal how far divine instruction excels the learning of the world.

To some this work of entire transformation may seem impossible. But if this were so, why go to the expense of attempting to carry on a work of Christian education at all? Our knowledge of what true education means is to lead us ever to seek for strict purity of character. In all our association together we are to bear in mind that we are fitting for transfer to another world; the principles of heaven are to be learned and practiced; the superiority of the future life to this life is to be impressed upon the mind of every learner. Teachers who fail to bring this into their work of education fail of having a part in the great work of developing character that can meet the approval of God.

As the world in this age comes more and more under the influence of Satan, the true children of God will desire more and more to be taught of Him. Teachers should be employed who will give a heavenly mold to the characters of the youth. Under the influence of such teachers, foolish and unessential practices will be exchanged for habits and practices befitting the sons and daughters of God.

As wickedness in the world becomes more pronounced, and the teachings of evil are more fully developed and widely accepted, the teachings of Christ are to stand forth exemplified in the lives of converted men and women. Angels are waiting to co-operate in every department of the work. This has been presented to me again and again. At this time the people of God, men and women who are truly converted, are to learn, under the training of faithful teachers, the lessons that the God of heaven values.

The most important work of our educational institutions at this time is to set before the world an example that will honor God. Holy angels are to supervise the work through human agencies, and every department is to bear the mark of divine excellence.

All our health institutions, all our publishing houses, all our institutions of learning, are to be conducted more and more in accordance with the instruction that has been given. When Christ is recognized as the head of all our working forces, more and more thoroughly will our institutions be cleansed from every common, worldly practice. The show and the pretense, and many of the exhibitions that in the past have had a place in our schools, will find no place there when teachers and students seek to carry out God's will on earth as it is done in heaven. Christ, as the chief working agency, will mold and fashion characters after the divine order; and students and teachers, realizing that they are preparing for the higher school in the courts above, will put away many things that are now thought to be necessary, and will magnify and follow the methods of Christ.

The thought of the eternal life should be woven into all to which the Christian sets his hand. If the work performed is agricultural or mechanical in its nature, it may still be after the pattern of the heavenly. It is the privilege of the preceptors and teachers of our schools to reveal in all their work the leading of the Spirit of God. Through the grace of Christ every provision has been made for the perfecting of Christlike characters; and God is honored when His people, in all their social and business dealings, reveal the principles of heaven.

The Lord demands uprightness in the smallest as well as in the largest matters. Those who are accepted at last as members of the heavenly court, will be men and women who here on earth sought to carry out the Lord's will in every particular, who sought to put the impress of heaven upon their earthly labors.

The Lord gave an important lesson to His people in all ages when to Moses on the mount He gave instruction regarding the building of the tabernacle. In that work He required perfection in every detail. Moses was proficient in all the learning of the Egyptians; he had a knowledge of God, and God's purposes had been revealed to him in visions; but he did not know how to engrave and embroider.

Israel had been held all their days in the bondage of Egypt, and although there were ingenious men among them, they had not been instructed in the curious arts which were called for in the building of the tabernacle. They knew how to make bricks, but they did not understand how to work in gold or silver. How was the work to be done? Who was sufficient for these things? These were questions that troubled the mind of Moses.

Then God Himself explained how the work was to be accomplished. He signified by name the persons He desired to do a certain work. Bezaleel was to be the architect. This man belonged to the tribe of Judah—a tribe that God delighted to honor.

"And the Lord spake unto Moses, saying, See, I have called by name Bezaleel the son of Uri, the son of Hur, of the tribe of Judah: and I have filled him with the Spirit of God, in wisdom, and in understanding, and in knowledge, and in all manner of workmanship, to devise cunning works, to work in gold, and in silver, and in brass, and in cutting of stones, to set them, and in carving of timber, to work in all manner of workmanship.

"And I, behold, I have given with him Aholiab, the

son of Ahisamach, of the tribe of Dan: and in the hearts of all that are wisehearted I have put wisdom, that they may make all that I have commanded thee." Exodus 31:1-6.

In order that the earthly tabernacle might represent the heavenly, it must be perfect in all its parts, and it must be, in every smallest detail, like the pattern in the heavens. So it is with the characters of those who are finally accepted in the sight of heaven.

The Son of God came down to this earth that in Him men and women might have a representation of the perfect characters which alone God could accept. Through the grace of Christ every provision has been made for the salvation of the human family. It is possible for every transaction entered into by those who claim to be Christians to be as pure as the deeds of Christ. And the soul who accepts the virtues of Christ's character and appropriates the merits of His life is as precious in the sight of God as is His own beloved Son. Sincere and uncorrupted faith is to Him as gold and frankincense and myrrh—the gifts of the Wise Men to the Child of Bethlehem, and the evidence of their faith in Him as the promised Messiah.

———

Let the child and the youth be taught that every mistake, every fault, every difficulty, conquered, becomes a steppingstone to better and higher things. It is through such experiences that all who have ever made life worth the living have achieved success.—*Education,* page 296.

CHARACTER BUILDING

"Whosoever heareth these sayings of Mine," Christ said, "and doeth them, I will liken him unto a wise man, which built his house upon a rock: and the rain descended, and the floods came, and the winds blew, and beat upon that house; and it fell not: for it was founded upon a rock. And everyone that heareth these sayings of Mine, and doeth them not, shall be likened unto a foolish man, which built his house upon the sand: and the rain descended, and the floods came, and the winds blew, and beat upon that house; and it fell: and great was the fall of it." Matthew 7:24-27.

The great work of parents and teachers is character building—seeking to restore the image of Christ in those placed under their care. A knowledge of the sciences sinks into insignificance beside this great aim; but all true education may be made to help in the development of a righteous character. The formation of character is the work of a lifetime, and it is for eternity. If all could realize this, and would awake to the fact that we are individually deciding our own destiny and the destinies of our children for eternal life or eternal ruin, what a change would take place! How differently would our probationary time be occupied, and with what noble characters would our world be filled!

The question that should come home to each of us is, Upon what foundation am I building? We have the privilege of striving for immortal life; and it is of the greatest importance that we dig deep, removing all the rubbish, and build on the solid rock, Christ Jesus. He is the sure foundation. "Other foundation can no man lay than that is laid, which is Jesus Christ." 1 Corinthians 3:11. In Him alone is our salvation. "There is none other name under heaven given among men, whereby we must be saved." Acts 4:12.

The foundation firmly laid, we need wisdom that we may know how to build. When Moses was about to erect the sanctuary in the wilderness, he was cautioned, "See . . . that thou make all things according to the pattern showed to thee in the mount." Hebrews 8:5. In His law, God has given us the pattern. Our character building is to be after "the pattern showed to thee in the mount." The law is the great standard of righteousness. It represents the character of God, and is the test of our loyalty to His government. And it is revealed to us, in all its beauty and excellence, in the life of Christ. . . .

Thoroughness is necessary to success in the work of character building. There must be an earnest purpose to carry out the plan of the Master Builder. The timbers must be solid. No careless, unreliable work can be accepted, for this would ruin the building. The powers of the whole being are to be put into the work. It demands the strength and energy of manhood; there is no reserve to be wasted in unimportant matters. . . . There must be earnest, careful, persevering effort to break away from the customs, maxims, and associations of the world. Deep thought, earnest purpose, steadfast integrity, are essential.

There must be no idleness. Life is an important thing, a sacred trust; and every moment should be wisely improved, for its results will be seen in eternity. God requires each one to do all the good possible. The talents which He has entrusted to our keeping are to be made the most of. He has placed them in our hands to be used to His name's honor and glory, and for the good of our fellow men. . . .

The Lord has precious promises in this life for those who keep His law. He says, "My son, forget not My law; but let thine heart keep My commandments: for length of days, and long life, and peace, shall they add to thee. Let not mercy and truth forsake thee: bind them about thy neck; write them upon the table of thine heart: so shalt thou find favor and good understanding in the sight of God and man." Proverbs 3:1-4.

But a better than earthly reward awaits those who, basing their work on the solid Rock, build up symmetrical characters, in accordance with the living word. For them is prepared "a city which hath foundations, whose builder and maker is God." Hebrews 11:10. Its streets are paved with gold. In it is the Paradise of God, watered by the river of life, which proceeds from the throne. In the midst of the street, and on either side of the river, is the tree of life, which yields its fruit every month; "and the leaves of the tree were for the healing of the nations."

Parents, teachers, students, remember that you are building for eternity. See that your foundation is sure; then build firmly, and with persistent effort, but in gentleness, meekness, love. So shall your house stand unshaken, not only when the storms of temptation come, but when the overwhelming flood of God's wrath shall sweep over the world.—*Special Testimonies on Education*, pages 72-77.

TEACHERS AND TEACHING

True education means more than taking a certain course of study. It is broad. It includes the harmonious development of all the physical powers and the mental faculties. It teaches the love and fear of God, and is a preparation for the faithful discharge of life's duties.

There is an education which is essentially worldly. Its aim is success in the world, the gratification of selfish ambition. To secure this education many students spend time and money in crowding their minds with unnecessary knowledge. The world accounts them learned; but God is not in their thoughts. They eat of the tree of worldly knowledge, which nourishes and strengthens pride. In their hearts they become disobedient and estranged from God; and their entrusted gifts are placed on the enemy's side. Much of the education at the present time is of this character. The world may regard it as highly desirable; but it increases the peril of the student.

There is another kind of education that is very different. Its fundamental principle, as stated by the greatest Teacher the world has ever known, is, "Seek ye first the kingdom of God, and His righteousness." Matthew 6:33. Its aim is not selfish; its purpose is to honor God and to serve Him in the world. Both the studies pursued and the industrial training sought have this object in view. The word of God is studied; a vital connection with God is maintained, and the better feelings and traits of character are brought into exercise. This kind of education produces results as lasting as eternity. "The fear of the Lord is the beginning of wisdom" (Proverbs 9:10), and better than all knowledge is an understanding of His word.

What shall be the character of the education given in our schools? Shall it be according to the wisdom of this world, or according to the wisdom which is from above? . . . Teachers are to do more for their students than to impart a knowledge of books. Their position as guide and instructor of the youth is most responsible, for to them is given the work of molding mind and character. Those who undertake this work should possess well-balanced, symmetrical characters. They should be refined in manner, neat in dress, careful in all their habits; and they should have that true Christian courtesy that wins confidence and respect. The teacher should be himself what he wishes his students to become.

Teachers are to watch over their students as the shepherd watches over the flock entrusted to his charge. They should care for souls as they that must give an account.

The teacher may understand many things in regard to the physical universe; he may know about the structure of animal life, the discoveries of natural science, the inventions of mechanical art; but he cannot be called educated, he is not fitted for his work as an instructor of the youth, unless he has in his own soul a knowledge of God and of Christ. He cannot be a true educator until he is himself a learner in the school of Christ, receiving an education from the divine Instructor.

God Our Dependence

God is the source of all wisdom. He is infinitely wise and just and good. Apart from Christ, the wisest men that ever lived cannot comprehend Him. They may profess to be wise; they may glory in their attainments; but mere intellectual knowledge, aside from the great truths that center in Christ, is as nothingness. "Let not the wise man glory in his wisdom: . . . but let him that glorieth glory in this, that he understandeth and knoweth Me, that I am the Lord which exercise loving-kindness, judgment, and righteousness, in the earth." Jeremiah 9:23, 24.

If men could see for a moment beyond the range of finite vision, if they could catch a glimpse of the Eternal, every mouth would be stopped in its boasting. Men living in this little atom of a world are finite; God has unnumbered worlds that are obedient to His laws and are conducted with reference to His glory. When men have gone as far in scientific research as their limited powers will permit, there is still an infinity beyond what they can apprehend.

Before men can be truly wise, they must realize their dependence upon God, and be filled with His wisdom. God is the source of intellectual as well as spiritual power. The greatest men who have reached what the world regards as wonderful heights in science are not to be compared with the beloved John or the apostle Paul. It is when intellectual and spiritual power are combined that the highest standard of manhood is attained. Those who do this, God will accept as workers together with Him in the training of minds.

To know oneself is a great knowledge. The teacher who rightly estimates himself will let God mold and discipline his mind. And he will acknowledge the source of his power. . . . Self-knowledge leads to humility and to trust in God, but it does not take the place of efforts for self-improvement. He who realizes his own deficiencies will spare no pains to reach the highest possible standard of physical, mental, and moral excellence. No one should have a part in the training of youth who is satisfied with a lower standard.

An Effective Helper

The true teacher will try by precept and example to win souls to Christ. He must receive the truth in the love of it and let it cleanse his heart and mold his life. Every teacher should be under the full control of the Holy Spirit. Then Christ can speak to the heart, and His voice is the voice of love. And the love of God, received into the heart, is an active power for good, quickening and enlarging the mind and soul. With his own heart warm with divine love, the teacher will lift up the Man of Calvary, not to give the students a casual glimpse, but to fasten their attention until Jesus shall seem to them the "chiefest among ten thousand," and the One "altogether lovely." Song of Solomon 5:10, 16.

The Holy Spirit is an effective helper in restoring the image of God in the human soul, but Its efficiency and power have not been appreciated in our schools. It came into the schools of the prophets, bringing even the thoughts into harmony with the will of God. There was a living connection between heaven and these schools;

and the joy and thanksgiving of loving hearts found expression in songs of praise in which angels joined.

The Holy Spirit comes to the world as Christ's representative. It not only speaks the truth, but It is the truth—the faithful and true Witness. It is the great Searcher of hearts and is acquainted with the characters of all.

The Holy Spirit has often come to our schools and has not been recognized, but has been treated as a stranger, perhaps even as an intruder. Every teacher should know and welcome this heavenly Guest. If the teachers will open their own hearts to receive the Spirit, they will be prepared to co-operate with It in working for their students. And when It is given free course, It will effect wonderful transformations. It will work in each heart, correcting selfishness, molding and refining the character, and bringing even the thoughts into captivity to Christ.

The great aim of the teacher should be the perfecting of Christian character in himself and in his students. Teachers, let your lamps be trimmed and burning, and they will not only be lights to your students, but will send out clear and distinct rays to the homes and neighborhoods where your students live, and far beyond into the moral darkness of the world.—*Special Testimonies on Education,* pages 47-52; written May 15, 1896.

———

Our brethren say the plea comes from ministers and parents that there are scores of young people in our ranks who need the advantages of our training schools, but they cannot attend unless tuitions are lower.

Those who plead for low tuition should carefully weigh matters on all sides. If students cannot of themselves command sufficient means to pay the actual expense of good and faithful work in their education, is it not better that their parents, their friends, or the churches to which they belong, or largehearted, benevolent brethren in their conference, should assist them, than that a burden of debt should be brought upon the school? It would be far better to let the many patrons of the institution share the expense, than for the school to run in debt.

The churches in different localities should feel that a solemn responsibility rests upon them to train youth and educate talent to engage in missionary work. When they see those in the church who give promise of making useful workers, but who are not able to support themselves in the school, they should assume the responsibility of sending them to one of our training schools. There is excellent ability in the churches that needs to be brought into service. There are persons who would do good service in the Lord's vineyard, but many are too poor to obtain without assistance the education that they require. The churches should feel it a privilege to take a part in defraying the expenses of such.

Those who have the truth in their hearts are always openhearted, helping where it is necessary. They lead out, and others imitate their example. If there are some who should have the benefit of the school, but who cannot pay full price for their tuition, let the churches show their liberality by helping them.

Besides this, in each conference a fund should be raised

to lend to worthy poor students who desire to give themselves to the missionary work; in some cases such students should even receive donations. When the Battle Creek College was first opened, there was a fund placed in the Review and Herald office for the benefit of those who wished to obtain an education, but had not the means. This was used by several students until they could get a good start; then from their earnings they would replace what they had drawn, so that others might be benefited by the fund.

Some provision should now be made for the maintenance of such a fund to lend to poor but worthy students who desire to prepare themselves for missionary work. The youth should have it plainly set before them that they must work their own way as far as possible, and thus partly defray their expenses. That which costs little will be appreciated little, but that which costs a price somewhere near its real value will be estimated accordingly.

————

A teacher's advantages may have been limited, so that he does not possess as high literary qualifications as he might desire; yet if he has true insight into human nature, if he has an appreciation of the magnitude of his work, and a genuine love for it; if he has a willingness to labor earnestly and humbly and perseveringly, he will comprehend the needs of his pupils, and by his sympathetic spirit will win their hearts and leads them onward and upward. His efforts will be so well directed that the school will become a living, growing power for good, full of the spirit of real advancement.

FOR FURTHER STUDY

Our Children and Youth Demand Our Care
Adventist Home, The, pp. 187-189, 279-281.
Testimonies, vol. 5, p. 11.
vol. 6, pp. 126-131, 136-138, 213-218.

The Primal Object of Education
Education, pp. 13-19.
Fundamentals of Christian Education, pp. 83-91, 231-235, 541-545.

Character Building
Child Guidance, pp. 161-190, 193-220.
Education, pp. 225-229.
Messages to Young People, pp. 15-18, 78-80, 163-165, 345-350.

Teachers and Teaching
Child Guidance, pp. 31-39, 63-76.
Education, pp. 275-287.
Fundamentals of Christian Education, pp. 212-219, 260-276, 516-519, 525-527.
Testimonies, vol. 5, pp. 84-94.
vol. 7, pp. 267-276.

GENERAL PRINCIPLES

THE RIGHT EDUCATION

It is the nicest work ever assumed by men and women
to deal with youthful minds. The greatest care should be
taken in the education of youth, to vary the manner of
instruction so as to call forth the high and noble powers
of the mind. Parents and schoolteachers are certainly
disqualified to educate children properly if they have not
first learned the lessons of self-control, patience, forbearance, gentleness, and love. What an important position
for parents, guardians, and teachers! There are very
few who realize the most essential wants of the mind,
and how to direct the developing intellect, the growing
thoughts and feelings of youth. . . .

Individuality in Children

The education of children, at home or at school, should
not be like the training of dumb animals; for children
have an intelligent will, which should be directed to control all their powers. Dumb animals need to be trained;
for they have not reason and intellect. But the human
mind must be taught self-control. It must be educated to
rule the human being, while animals are controlled by a
master and are trained to be submissive to him. The
master is mind, judgment, and will for his beast.

A child may be so trained as to have, like the beast, no will of his own. Even his individuality may be merged in the one who superintends his training; his will, to all intents and purposes, is subject to the will of the teacher. Children who are thus educated will ever be deficient in moral energy and individual responsibility. They have not been taught to move from reason and principle; their wills have been controlled by another, and the mind has not been called out, that it might expand and strengthen by exercise. They have not been directed and disciplined with respect to their peculiar constitutions and capabilities of mind, to put forth their strongest powers when required.

Teachers should not stop here, but should give special attention to the cultivation of the weaker faculties, that all the powers may be brought into exercise and carried forward from one degree of strength to another, that the mind may attain due proportions.

Cause of Instability in Youth

There are many families of children who appear to be well trained while under the training discipline; but when the system which has held them to set rules is broken up, they seem to be incapable of thinking, acting, or deciding for themselves. These children have been so long under iron rule, not allowed to think and act for themselves in those things in which it was highly proper that they should, that they have no confidence in themselves to move out upon their own judgment, having an opinion of their own. And when they go out from their parents to act for themselves, they are easily led by others' judgment in the wrong direction. They have not stability of character. They have not been thrown upon their own judgment as fast and as far as practicable, and therefore their minds have not been properly developed and strengthened. They have been so long absolutely controlled by their parents that they rely wholly upon them; their parents are mind and judgment for them.

On the other hand, the young should not be left to think and act independently of the judgment of their parents and teachers. Children should be taught to respect experienced judgment. They should be so educated that their minds will be united with the minds of their parents and teachers, and so instructed that they can see the propriety of heeding their counsel. Then when they go forth from the guiding hand, their characters will not be like the reed trembling in the wind. . . .

Those parents and teachers who boast of having complete control of the minds and wills of the children under their care would cease their boastings could they trace out the future lives of the children who are thus brought into subjection by force or through fear. These are almost wholly unprepared to share in the stern responsibilities of life. When these youth are no longer under their parents and teachers, and are compelled to think and act for themselves, they are almost sure to take a wrong course and yield to the power of temptation. They do not make this life a success, and the same deficiencies are seen in their religious life.

Could the instructors of children and youth have the result of their mistaken discipline mapped out before them, they would change their plan of education. . . . God never designed that one human mind should be under the complete control of another. And those who make efforts to have the individuality of their pupils merged in themselves, to be mind, will, and conscience for them, assume fearful responsibilities. These scholars may, upon certain occasions, appear like well-drilled soldiers; but when the restraint is removed, there will be seen in them a want of independent action from firm principle.

Those who make it their object so to educate their pupils that they may see and feel that the power lies in themselves to make men and women of firm principle, qualified for any position in life, are the most useful and permanently successful teachers. Their work may not show to the very best advantage to careless observers, and their labors may not be valued as highly as are those of the teacher who holds the minds and wills of his scholars by absolute authority; but the future lives of the pupils will show the fruits of the better plan of education.

There is danger that both parents and teachers will command and dictate too much, while they fail to come sufficiently into social relation with their children or scholars. They often hold themselves too much reserved, and exercise their authority in a cold, unsympathizing manner, which cannot win the hearts of their children and pupils. If they would gather the children close to them and show that they love them, and would manifest an interest in all their efforts and even in their sports, sometimes even being a child among them, they would make the children very happy and would gain their love and win their confidence. And the children would more quickly learn to respect and love the authority of their parents and teachers.

Personal Qualifications of the Teacher

The habits and principles of the teacher should be considered of even greater importance than his literary qualifications. If he is a sincere Christian, he will feel the necessity of having an equal interest in the physical, mental, moral, and spiritual education of his pupils. In order to exert the right influence, he should have perfect control over himself, and his own heart should be richly imbued with love for his pupils, which will be seen in his looks, words, and acts. He should have firmness of character, and then he can mold the minds of his pupils, as well as instruct them in the sciences.

The early education of the youth generally shapes their characters for life. Those who deal with the young should be very careful to call out the qualities of the mind, that they may better know how to direct its powers so that they may be exercised to the very best account.

Close Confinement at School

The system of education carried out for generations back has been destructive to health, and even to life itself. Many young children have passed five hours each day in schoolrooms not properly ventilated, nor sufficiently large for the healthful accommodation of the scholars. The air of such rooms soon becomes poison to the lungs that inhale it. Little children, whose limbs and muscles are not strong and whose brains are undeveloped, have been kept confined indoors to their injury. Many have but a slight hold on life to begin with, and the confinement in school from day to day makes them nervous and diseased. Their bodies are dwarfed because of the exhausted condition of their nerves.

And if the lamp of life goes out, the parents and teachers do not consider that they had any direct influence in quenching the vital spark. When standing by the graves of their children, the afflicted parents look upon their bereavement as a special dispensation of Providence, when, by inexcusable ignorance, it was their own course that destroyed the lives of their children. To charge their death to Providence is blasphemy. God wanted the little ones to live and be disciplined, that they might have beautiful characters, and glorify Him in this world and praise Him in the better world. . . .

To become acquainted with the wonderful human organism, the bones, muscles, stomach, liver, bowels, heart, and pores of the skin, and to understand the dependence of one organ upon another for the healthful action of all, is a study in which most mothers take no interest. They know nothing of the influence of the body upon the mind, or of the mind upon the body. The mind, which allies the finite to the Infinite, they do not seem to understand. Every organ of the body was made to be servant to the mind. The mind is the capital of the body.

Children are allowed to eat flesh meats, spices, butter, cheese, pork, rich pastry, and condiments generally. They are also allowed to eat of unhealthful food at irregular hours and between meals. These things do their work of deranging the stomach, exciting the nerves to unnatural action, and enfeebling the intellect. Parents do not realize that they are sowing the seed that will bring forth disease and death.

Many children have been ruined for life by urging the intellect and neglecting to strengthen the physical powers. Many have died in childhood because of the course pursued by injudicious parents and schoolteachers in forcing their young intellects, by flattery or fear, when they were too young to see the inside of a schoolroom. Their minds have been taxed with lessons when they should not have been called out, but kept back until the physical constitution was strong enough to endure mental effort. Small children should be left as free as lambs to run out of doors, to be free and happy, and should be allowed the most favorable opportunities to lay the foundation for sound constitutions.

The Ideal Plan

Parents should be the only teachers of their children until they have reached eight or ten years of age. As fast as their minds can comprehend it, the parents should open before them God's great book of nature. The mother should have less love for the artificial in her house and in the preparation of her dress for display, and should take time to cultivate, in herself and in her children, a love for the beautiful buds and opening flowers. By calling the attention of her children to the different colors and variety of forms, she can make them acquainted with God, who made all the beautiful things which attract and delight them. She can lead their minds up to their Creator, and awaken in their young hearts a love for their heavenly Father, who has manifested so great love for them. Parents can associate God with all His created works.

The only schoolroom for children until eight or ten years of age should be in the open air, amid the opening flowers and nature's beautiful scenery, and their most familiar textbook the treasures of nature. These lessons, imprinted upon the minds of young children amid the pleasant, attractive scenes of nature, will not be soon forgotten. . . .

In the early education of children, many parents and teachers fail to understand that the greatest attention needs to be given to the physical constitution, that a healthy condition of body and mind may be secured. It has been the custom to encourage children to attend school when they were mere babes needing a mother's care. When of a delicate age, they are frequently crowded into ill-ventilated schoolrooms, where they sit in wrong positions upon poorly constructed benches, and as a result the young and tender frames of some have become deformed.

The disposition and habits of youth will be very likely to be manifested in mature manhood. You may bend a young tree into almost any shape that you choose, and if it remains and grows as you have bent it, it will be a deformed tree, and will ever tell of the injury and abuse received at your hands. You may, after it has had years of growth, try to straighten the tree, but all efforts will prove unavailing. It will ever be a crooked tree.

This is the case with the minds of youth. They should be carefully and tenderly trained in childhood. They may be trained in the right direction or in the wrong, and in their future lives they will pursue the course in which they were directed in youth. The habits formed in youth will grow with the growth and strengthen with the strength. . . .

Physical Degeneracy

Man came from the hand of his Creator perfect and beautiful in form, and so filled with vital force that it was more than a thousand years before his corrupt appetites and passions and general violations of physical law were sensibly felt upon the race. More recent generations have felt the pressure of infirmity and disease more rapidly and heavily with every generation. The vital forces have been greatly weakened by the indulgence of appetite and lustful passion. . . . The violation of physical law, and the consequence,—human suffering,—have so long prevailed that men and women look upon the present state of sickness, suffering, debility, and premature death as the appointed lot of humanity. . . .

The strange absence of principle which characterizes this generation, and which is shown in their disregard of the laws of life and health, is astonishing. . . . With the majority the principal anxiety is, What shall I eat? what shall I drink? and wherewithal shall I be clothed? . . . The moral powers are weakened because men and women will not live in obedience to the laws of health and make this great subject a personal duty. . . . The majority . . . remain in ignorance of the laws of their being, and indulge appetite and passion at the expense of intellect and morals; and they seem willing to remain in ignorance of the result of their violation of nature's laws. They indulge the depraved appetite in the use of slow poisons, which corrupt the blood and undermine the nervous force, and in consequence bring upon themselves sickness and death. . . .

Importance of Home Training

One great cause of the existing deplorable state of things is that parents do not feel under obligation to bring up their children to conform to physical law. Mothers love their children with an idolatrous love and indulge their appetite when they know that it will injure their health and thereby bring upon them disease and unhappiness. This cruel kindness is manifested to a great extent in the present generation. The desires of children are gratified at the expense of health and happy tempers, because it is easier for the mother, for the time being, to gratify them than to withhold that for which they clamor. Thus mothers are sowing the seed that will spring up and bear fruit.

The children are not educated to deny their appetites and restrict their desires, and they become selfish, exacting, disobedient, unthankful, unholy. Mothers who are doing this work will reap with bitterness the fruit of the seed they have sown. They have sinned against Heaven and against their children, and God will hold them accountable.

Had education for generations back been conducted upon an altogether different plan, the youth of this generation would not now be so depraved and worthless. The managers and teachers of schools should have been those who understood physiology, and who had an interest, not only to educate the youth in the sciences, but teach them how to preserve health, so that they might use their knowledge to the best account after they had obtained it. . . .

Regulation of Employment and Amusement

In order for children and youth to have health, cheerfulness, vivacity, and well-developed muscles and brains, they should be much in the open air, and have well-regulated employment and amusement. Children and youth who are kept at school and confined to books cannot have sound physical constitutions. The exercise of the brain in study, without corresponding physical exercise, has a tendency to attract the blood to the brain, and the circulation of the blood through the system becomes unbalanced. The brain has too much blood, and the extremities too little. There should be rules regulating the studies of children and youth to certain hours, and then a portion of their time should be spent in physical labor. And if their habits of eating, dressing, and sleeping are in accordance with physical law, they can obtain an education without sacrificing physical and mental health. . . .

There should have been connected with the schools, establishments for carrying on various branches of labor, that the students might have employment and the necessary exercise out of school hours. The students' employment and amusements should have been regulated with reference to physical law, and should have been adapted to preserve to them the healthy tone of all the powers of body and mind. Then a practical knowledge of business could have been obtained while their literary education was being gained.

Students at school should have had their moral sensibilities aroused to see and feel that society has claims upon them, and that they should live in obedience to natural law, so that they can, by their existence and influence, by precept and example, be an advantage and blessing to society. It should be impressed upon the youth that all have an influence that is constantly telling upon society, to improve and elevate, or to lower and debase. The first study of the young should be to know themselves and how to keep their bodies in health.

Result of Continued Application

Many parents keep their children at school nearly the year round. These children go through the routine of study mechanically, but do not retain that which they learn. Many of these constant students seem almost destitute of intellectual life. The monotony of continual study wearies the mind, and they take but little interest in their lessons; and to many the application to books becomes painful. They have not an inward love of thought and an ambition to acquire knowledge. They do not encourage in themselves habits of reflection and investigation.

Children are in great need of proper education in order that they may be of use in the world. But any effort that exalts intellectual culture above moral training is misdirected. Instructing, cultivating, polishing, and refining the youth and children should be the main burden of both parents and teachers. Close reasoners and logical thinkers are few, for the reason that false influences have checked the development of the intellect. The supposition of parents and teachers that continued study would strengthen the intellect has proved erroneous; for in many cases it has had the opposite effect. . . .

We are living in an age when almost everything is superficial. There is but little stability and firmness of character, because the training and education of children from their cradle is superficial. Their characters are built upon sliding sand. Self-denial and self-control have not been molded into their characters. They have been petted and indulged until they are spoiled for practical life. . . .

Children should be so trained and educated that they will expect temptations, and calculate to meet difficulties and dangers. They should be taught to have control over themselves, and nobly to overcome difficulties; and if they do not willfully rush into danger, and needlessly place themselves in the way of temptation, if they shun evil influences and vicious society, and then are unavoidably compelled to be in dangerous company, they will have strength of character to stand for the right and to preserve principle, and come forth in the strength of God with their morals untainted. If youth who have been properly educated make God their trust, their moral powers will stand the most powerful test.—*Testimonies for the Church,* vol. 3, pp. 131-144.

OUR COLLEGE

There is danger that our college will be turned away from its original design. God's purpose has been made known—that our people should have an opportunity to study the sciences, and at the same time to learn the requirements of His word. Biblical lectures should be given; the study of the Scriptures should have the first place in our system of education.

Students are sent from great distances to attend the college at Battle Creek, for the very purpose of receiving instruction from the lectures on Bible subjects. But for one or two years past, there has been an effort to mold our school after other colleges. When this is done, we can give no encouragement to parents to send their children to Battle Creek College.

The moral and religious influences should not be put in the background. In times past, God has worked with the efforts of the teachers, and many souls have seen the truth and embraced it, and have gone to their homes to live henceforth for God, as the result of their connection with the college. As they saw that Bible study was made a part of their education they were led to regard it as a matter of greater interest and importance.

Education of Young Men for the Ministry

Too little attention has been given to the education of young men for the ministry. This was the primary object to be secured in the establishment of the college. In no case should this be ignored or regarded as a matter of secondary importance. For several years, however, but few have gone forth from that institution prepared to teach the truth to others.

Some who came at great expense, with the ministry in view, have been encouraged by the teachers to take a thorough course of study, which would occupy a number of years and, in order to obtain means to carry out these plans, have entered the canvassing field and given up all thought of preaching. This is entirely wrong. We have not many years in which to work, and teachers and principal should be imbued with the Spirit of God, and work in harmony with His revealed will, instead of carrying out their own plans. We are losing much every year because we do not heed what God has said upon these points.

Our college is designed of God to meet the advancing wants for this time of peril and demoralization. The study of books only cannot give students the discipline they need. A broader foundation must be laid. The college was not brought into existence to bear the stamp of any one man's mind. Teachers and principal should work together as brethren. They should consult together, and also counsel with ministers and responsible men, and, above all else, seek wisdom from above, that all their decisions in reference to the school may be such as will be approved of God. . . .

A more comprehensive education is needed—an education which will demand from teachers and principal such thought and effort as mere instruction in the sciences does not require. The character must receive proper discipline for its fullest and noblest development. The students should receive at college such training as will enable them to maintain a respectable, honest, virtuous standing in society, against the demoralizing influences which are corrupting the youth.

It would be well could there be connected with our college, land for cultivation, and also workshops, under the charge of men competent to instruct the students in the various departments of physical labor. Much is lost by a neglect to unite physical with mental taxation. The leisure hours of the students are often occupied with frivolous pleasures, which weaken physical, mental, and moral powers. Under the debasing power of sensual indulgence, or the untimely excitement of courtship and marriage, many students fail to reach that height of mental development which they might otherwise have attained. . . .

Bible Study

If morality and religion are to live in a school, it must be through a knowledge of God's word. Some may urge that if religious teaching is to be made prominent, our school will become unpopular; that those who are not of our faith will not patronize the college. Very well, then let them go to other colleges, where they will find a system of education that suits their taste. Our school was established, not merely to teach the sciences, but for the purpose of giving instruction in the great principles of God's word and in the practical duties of everyday life. This is the education so much needed at the present time.

If a worldly influence is to bear sway in our school, then sell it out to worldlings, and let them take the entire control; and those who have invested their means in that institution will establish another school, to be conducted, not upon the plan of popular schools nor according to the desires of principal and teachers, but upon the plan which God has specified.

In the name of my Master I entreat all who stand in responsible positions in that school to be men of God. When the Lord requires us to be distinct and peculiar, how can we crave popularity or seek to imitate the customs and practices of the world? God has declared His purpose to have one college in the land where the Bible shall have its proper place in the education of the youth. Will we do our part to carry out that purpose? . . .

Through the medium of the press, knowledge of every kind is placed within the reach of all; and yet how large a share of every community are depraved in morals and superficial in mental attainments! If the people would but become Bible readers, Bible students, we should see a different state of things.

In an age like ours, in which iniquity abounds, and God's character and His law are alike regarded with contempt, special care must be taken to teach the youth to study, to reverence and obey the divine will as revealed to man. The fear of the Lord is fading from the minds of our youth because of their neglect of Bible study.

Principal and teachers should have a living connection with God and should stand firmly and fearlessly as witnesses for Him. Never from cowardice or worldly policy let the word of God be placed in the background. Students will be profited intellectually, as well as morally and spiritually, by its study. . . .

The Teacher's Responsibility

There is a work to be done for every teacher in our college. Not one is free from selfishness. If the moral and religious character of the teachers were what it should be, a better influence would be exerted upon the students. The teachers do not seek individually to perform their own work with an eye single to the glory of God. Instead of looking to Jesus and copying His life and character, they look to self, and aim too much to meet a human standard.

I wish I could impress upon every teacher a full sense of his responsibility for the influence which he exerts upon the young. Satan is untiring in his efforts to secure the service of our youth. With great care he is laying his snare for the inexperienced feet. The people of God should jealously guard against his devices.

God is the embodiment of benevolence, mercy, and love. Those who are truly connected with Him cannot be at variance with one another. His Spirit ruling in the heart will create harmony, love, and unity. The opposite of this is seen among the children of Satan. It is his work to stir up envy, strife, and jealousy. In the name of my Master I ask the professed followers of Christ, What fruit do you bear?

In the system of instruction used in the common schools, the most essential part of education is neglected —the religion of the Bible. Education not only affects to a great degree the life of the student in this world, but its influence extends to eternity. How important, then, that the teachers be persons capable of exerting a right influence! They should be men and women of religious experience, daily receiving divine light to impart to their pupils.

The Parents' Part

But the teacher should not be expected to do the parents' work. There has been, with many parents, a fearful neglect of duty. Like Eli, they fail to exercise proper restraint; and then they send their undisciplined children to college, to receive the training which the parents should have given them at home.

The teachers have a task which few appreciate. If they succeed in reforming these wayward youth, they receive but little credit. If the youth choose the society of the evil-disposed, and go on from bad to worse, then the teachers are censured and the school is denounced. In many cases the censure justly belongs to the parents. They had the first and most favorable opportunity to control and train their children when the spirit was teachable and the mind and heart were easily impressed. But through the slothfulness of the parents the children are permitted to follow their own will until they become hardened in an evil course.

Let parents study less of the world and more of Christ; let them put forth less effort to imitate the customs and fashions of the world, and devote more time and effort to molding the minds and characters of their children according to the divine model. Then they could send forth their sons and daughters fortified by pure morals and a noble purpose, to receive an education for positions of usefulness and trust. Teachers who are controlled by the love and fear of God could lead such youth still onward and upward, training them to be a blessing to the world and an honor to their Creator.

Connected with God, every instructor will exert an influence to lead his pupils to study God's word and obey His law. He will direct their minds to the contemplation of eternal interests, opening before them vast fields for thought, grand and ennobling themes, which the most vigorous intellect may put forth all its powers to grasp, and yet feel that there is an infinity beyond.

The Need of Counseling Together

The evils of self-esteem and an unsanctified independence, which most impair our usefulness, and which will prove our ruin if not overcome, spring from selfishness. "Counsel together" is the message which has been again and again repeated to me by the angel of God. By influencing one man's judgment, Satan may endeavor to control matters to suit himself. He may succeed in misleading the minds of two persons; but when several consult together, there is more safety. Every plan will be more closely criticized, every advance move more carefully studied. Hence there will be less danger of precipitate, ill-advised moves, which would bring confusion and perplexity. In union there is strength; in division there is weakness and defeat.

God is leading out a people and preparing them for translation. Are we who are acting a part in this work standing as sentinels for God? Are we seeking to work unitedly? Are we willing to become servants of all? Are we following our Great Exemplar?

Fellow laborers, we are each sowing seed in the fields of life. As is the seed, so will be the harvest. If we sow distrust, envy, jealousy, self-love, bitterness of thought and feeling, we shall reap bitterness to our own souls. If we manifest kindness, love, tender thought for the feelings of others, we shall receive the same in return.

Christian Courtesy

The teacher who is severe, critical, overbearing, heedless of others' feelings, must expect the same spirit to be manifested toward himself. He who wishes to preserve his own dignity and self-respect must be careful not to wound needlessly the self-respect of others. This rule should be sacredly observed toward the dullest, the youngest, the most blundering students. What God intends to do with these apparently uninteresting youth, you do not know. He has, in the past, accepted persons no more promising or attractive, to do a great work for Him. His Spirit, moving upon the heart, has aroused every faculty to vigorous action. The Lord saw in those rough, unhewn stones, precious material, that would stand the test of storm and heat and pressure. God sees not as man sees. He judges not from appearance, but he searches the heart and judges righteously.

The teacher should ever conduct himself as a Christian gentleman. He should stand in the attitude of a friend and counselor to his pupils. If all our people—teachers, ministers, and lay members—would cultivate the spirit of Christian courtesy, they would far more readily find access to the hearts of the people; many more would be led to examine and receive the truth. When every teacher shall forget self, and feel a deep interest in the success and prosperity of his pupils, realizing that they are God's property, and that he must render an account for his influence upon their minds and characters, then we shall have a school in which angels will love to linger. Jesus will look approvingly upon the work of the teachers and will send His grace into the hearts of the students. . . .

The True Test of Prosperity

If you lower the standard in order to secure popularity and an increase of numbers, and then make this increase a cause of rejoicing, you show great blindness. If numbers were an evidence of success, Satan might claim the preeminence; for, in this world, his followers are largely in the majority. It is the degree of moral power pervading the college, that is a test of its prosperity. It is the virtue, intelligence, and piety of the people composing our churches, not their numbers, that should be a source of joy and thankfulness.

Without the influence of divine grace, education will prove no real advantage; the learner becomes proud, vain, and bigoted. But that education which is received under the ennobling, refining influence of the Great Teacher will elevate man in the scale of moral value with God. It will enable him to subdue pride and passion, and to walk humbly before God, as dependent upon Him for every capability, every opportunity, and every privilege.

I speak to the workers in our college: You must not only profess to be Christians, but you must exemplify the character of Christ. Let the wisdom from above pervade all your instruction. In a world of moral darkness and corruption let it be seen that the spirit by which you are moved to action is from above, not from beneath. While you rely wholly upon your own strength and wisdom, your best efforts will accomplish little. If you are prompted by love to God, His law being your foundation, your work will be enduring. While the hay, wood, and stubble are consumed, your work will stand the test.

The youth placed under your care you must meet again around the great white throne. If you permit your uncultivated manners or uncontrolled tempers to bear sway, and thus fail to influence these youth for their eternal good, you must, at that day, meet the grave consequences of your work. By a knowledge of the divine law and obedience to its precepts, men may become the sons of God. By a violation of that law, they become servants of Satan. On the one hand, they may rise to any height of moral excellence; or on the other hand, they may descend to any depth of iniquity and degradation. The workers in our college should manifest a zeal and earnestness proportionate to the value of the prize at stake—the souls of their students, the approval of God, eternal life, and the joys of the redeemed.

As colaborers with Christ, with so favorable opportunities to impart the knowledge of God, our teachers should labor as if inspired from above. The hearts of the youth are not hardened, nor their ideas and opinions stereotyped, as are those of older persons. They may be won to Christ by your holy demeanor, your devotion, your

Christlike walk. It would be much better to crowd them less in the study of the sciences, and give them more time for religious privileges. Here a grave mistake has been made. . . .

God's Purpose for the College

No limit can be set to our influence. One thoughtless act may prove the ruin of many souls. The course of every worker in our college is making impressions upon the minds of the young, and these are borne away to be reproduced in others. It should be the teacher's aim to prepare every youth under his care to be a blessing to the world. This object should never be lost sight of. There are some who profess to be working for Christ, yet who occasionally go over to the side of Satan and do his work. Can the Saviour pronounce these good and faithful servants? Are they, as watchmen, giving the trumpet a certain sound? . . .

Our Saviour bids us, "Watch ye and pray, lest ye enter into temptation." Mark 14:38. If we encounter difficulties, and in Christ's strength overcome them; if we meet enemies, and in Christ's strength put them to flight; if we accept responsibilities, and in Christ's strength discharge them faithfully, we are gaining a precious experience. We learn, as we could not otherwise have learned, that our Saviour is a present help in every time of need.

There is a great work to be done in our college, a work which demands the co-operation of every teacher; and it is displeasing to God for one to discourage another. But nearly all seem to forget that Satan is an accuser of the brethren, and they unite with the enemy in his work. While professed Christians are contending, Satan is laying his snares for the inexperienced feet of children and youth. Those who have had a religious experience should seek to shield the young from his devices. They should never forget that they themselves were once enchanted with the pleasures of sin. We need the mercy and forbearance of God every hour, and how unbecoming for us to be impatient with the errors of the inexperienced youth! So long as God bears with them, dare we, fellow sinners, cast them off?

We should ever look upon the youth as the purchase of the blood of Christ. As such they have demands upon our love, our patience, our sympathy. If we would follow Jesus we cannot restrict our interest and affection to ourselves and our own families; we cannot give our time and attention to temporal matters and forget the eternal interests of those around us. . . . "Love one another, as I have loved you" (John 15:12), is the command of Jesus. Look at His self-denial; behold the manner of love He has bestowed upon us; and then seek to imitate the Pattern.—*Testimonies for the Church,* vol. 5, pp. 21-35; read in College Hall, December, 1881.

If we ever know the truth, it will be because we practice it. We must have a living experience in the things of God before we are able to understand His word. This experimental knowledge is what strengthens the intellect and builds us up into Christ our living Head.

DEPORTMENT OF STUDENTS

Those students who profess to love God and obey the truth should possess that degree of self-control and strength of religious principle that will enable them to remain unmoved amid temptations and to stand up for Jesus in the college, at their boarding houses, or wherever they may be. Religion is not to be worn merely as a cloak in the house of God; religious principles should characterize the entire life. Those who are drinking at the fountain of life will not, like the worldling, manifest a longing desire for change and pleasure. In their deportment and character will be seen the rest and peace and happiness that they have found in Jesus by daily laying their perplexities and burdens at His feet. They will show that in the path of obedience and duty there is contentment and even joy. Such ones will exert an influence over their fellow students which will tell upon the entire school.

Those who compose this faithful army will refresh and strengthen the teachers by discouraging every species of unfaithfulness, of discord, and of neglect to comply with the rules and regulations. Their influence will be saving, and their works will not perish in the great day of God, but will follow them into the future world; and the influence of their life here will tell throughout the ceaseless ages of eternity.

One earnest, conscientious, faithful young man in a school is an inestimable treasure. Angels of heaven look lovingly upon him, and in the ledger of heaven is recorded every work of righteousness, every temptation resisted, every evil overcome. He is laying up a good foundation against the time to come, that he may lay hold on eternal life.

Upon Christian youth depend in a great measure the preservation and perpetuity of the institutions which God has devised as a means by which to advance His work. Never was there a period when results so important depended upon a generation of men. Then how important that the young should be qualified for this great work, that God may use them as His instruments! Their Maker has claims upon them which are paramount to all others.

It is God who has given life and every physical and mental endowment that the youth possess. He has bestowed upon them capabilities for wise improvement, that they may do a work which will be as enduring as eternity. In return for His great gifts He claims a due cultivation and exercise of the intellectual and moral faculties. He did not give them these faculties merely for their amusement, or to be abused in working against His will and His providence, but to advance the knowledge of truth and holiness in the world. In return for His continued kindness and infinite mercies He claims their goodness, their veneration, their love. He justly requires obedience to His laws and to all wise regulations which will restrain and guard the youth from Satan's devices and lead them in paths of peace.

The wild, reckless character of many of the youth in this age of the world is heartsickening. If the youth could see that in complying with the laws and regulations of our institutions, they are only doing that which will improve their standing in society, elevate the character, ennoble the mind, and increase their happiness, they would not rebel against just rules and wholesome requirements, nor engage in creating suspicion and prejudice against these institutions.

With energy and fidelity our youth should meet the demands upon them, and this will be a guarantee of success. Young men who have never made a success in the temporal duties of life will be equally unprepared to engage in the higher duties. A religious experience is gained only through conflict, through disappointment, through severe discipline of self, through earnest prayer. The steps to heaven must be taken one at a time, and every advance step gives strength for the next.

Association With Others

While at school, students should not allow their minds to become confused by thoughts of courtship. They are there to gain a fitness to work for God, and this thought is ever to be uppermost. Let all students take as broad a view as possible of their obligations to God. Let them study earnestly how they can do practical work for the Master during their student life. Let them refuse to burden the souls of their teachers by showing a spirit of levity and a careless disregard of rules.

Students can do much to make the school a success by working with their teachers to help other students, and by zealously endeavoring to lift themselves above cheap, low standards. Those who co-operate with Christ will become refined in speech and in temper. They will not be unruly and self-caring, studying their own selfish pleasure and gratification. They will bend all their efforts to work with Christ as messengers of His mercy and love. They are one with Him in spirit and in action. They seek to store the mind with the precious treasures of God's word, that each may do his appointed work.

In all our dealings with students, age and character must be taken into account. We cannot treat the young and the old just alike. There are circumstances under which men and women of sound experience and good standing may be granted some privileges not given to the younger students. The age, the conditions, and the turn of mind must be taken into consideration. We must be wisely considerate in all our work. But we must not lessen our firmness and vigilance in dealing with students of all ages, nor our strictness in forbidding the unprofitable and unwise association of young and immature students.

In our schools in Battle Creek, Healdsburg, and Cooranbong I have borne a straight testimony concerning these matters. There were those who thought the restraint too severe; but we told them plainly what could be and what could not be, showing them that our schools are established at great expense for a definite purpose, and that all which would hinder the accomplishment of this purpose must be put away.

Again and again I stood before the students in the Avondale school with messages from the Lord regarding the deleterious influence of free and easy association between young men and young women. I told them that if they did not keep themselves to themselves, and endeavor to make the most of their time, the school would not benefit them, and those who were paying their expenses would be disappointed. I told them that if they were determined to have their own will and their own way, it would be better for them to return to their homes and to the guardianship of their parents. This they could do at any time if they decided not to stand under the yoke of obedience, for we did not design to have a few leading spirits in wrongdoing demoralizing the other students.

I told the principal and teachers that God had laid upon them the responsibility of watching for souls as they that must give account. I showed them that the wrong course pursued by some of the students would mislead other students, if it were continued, and for this God would hold the teachers responsible. Some students would attend school who had not been disciplined at home, and whose ideas of proper education and its value were perverted. If these were allowed to carry things in their way, the object for which the school was established would be defeated, and the sin would be charged against the guardians of the schools, as if they had committed it themselves.

God holds everyone responsible for the influence that surrounds his soul, on his own account and on the account of others. He calls upon young men and women to be strictly temperate, and conscientious in the use of their faculties of mind and body. Their capabilities can be properly developed only by the most diligent use of their opportunities and the wise appropriation of their powers to the glory of God and the benefit of their fellow men.

To know what constitutes purity of mind, soul, and body is an important part of education. Paul summed up the attainments possible for Timothy by saying, "Keep thyself pure." 1 Timothy 5:22. Impurity of thought, word, or action will not be indulged by the child of God. Every encouragement and the richest blessings are held up before the overcomers of evil practices, but the most fearful penalties are laid upon those who profane the body and defile the soul.

Teachers, blessed are the pure in heart—*now;* not, Blessed will be the pure in heart. "Blessed are the pure in heart: for they shall see God." Matthew 5:8. Yes, as did Moses, they shall endure the seeing of Him who is invisible. They have the assurance of the richest blessings, both in this life and in the life that is to come.

Students, if you will watch and pray, and make earnest efforts in the right direction, you will be thoroughly imbued with the spirit of Christ. "Put ye on the Lord Jesus Christ, and make not provision for the flesh, to fulfill the lusts thereof." Romans 13:14. Be determined that you will make the school a success. If you will heed the instruction given in the word of God you may go forth with a development of intellectual and moral power that will cause even angels to rejoice, and God will joy over you with singing. Under such discipline you will secure the fullest development of your faculties. Let not the buoyancy and the lust of youth through manifold temptations make your day of opportunity and privilege a failure. Day by day put on Christ, and in the brief season of your test and trial here below maintain your dignity in the strength of God, as co-workers with the highest agencies of heaven.

It is the privilege of the faithful teacher to reap day by day the visible results of his patient, persevering labor of love. It is his to watch the growth of the tender plants as they bud, and blossom, and bear the fruit of order, punctuality, faithfulness, thoroughness, and true nobility of character. It is his to see a love for truth and right growing and strengthening in these children and youth for whom he is held responsible. What can give him greater returns than to see his pupils developing characters that will make them noble and useful men and women, fitted to occupy positions of responsibility and trust—men and women who in the future will wield a power to hold in check evil influences and help in dispelling the moral darkness of the world?

As the teacher awakens in the minds of his pupils a realization of the possibilities before them, as he causes them to grasp the truth that they may become useful, noble, trustworthy men and women, he sets in motion waves of influence that, even after he himself has gone to rest, will reach onward and ever onward, giving joy to the sorrowing and inspiring hope in the discouraged. As he lights in their minds and hearts the lamp of earnest endeavor, he is rewarded by seeing its bright rays diverge in every direction, illuminating not only the lives of the few who daily sit before him for instruction, but through them the lives of many others.

FOR FURTHER STUDY

THE RIGHT EDUCATION

Child Guidance, pp. 293-299.
Fundamentals of Christian Education, pp. 15-46, 113-122, 328-330, 405-415, 429-437.
Messages to Young People, pp. 169, 170.
Testimonies, vol. 3, pp. 131-135.

OUR COLLEGE

Child Guidance, pp. 328-336.
Fundamentals of Christian Education, pp. 488-491.
Testimonies, vol. 4, pp. 418-449.
vol. 5, pp. 11-15, 21-36, 59-61.
vol. 6, pp. 141-151.

DEPORTMENT OF STUDENTS

Fundamentals of Christian Education, pp. 191-195.

THE HOME SCHOOL

"They shall live with their children."

THE CHILD'S FIRST SCHOOL

In His wisdom the Lord has decreed that the family shall be the greatest of all educational agencies. It is in the home that the education of the child is to begin. Here is his first school. Here, with his parents as instructors, he is to learn the lessons that are to guide him throughout life—lessons of respect, obedience, reverence, self-control. The educational influences of the home are a decided power for good or for evil. They are in many respects silent and gradual, but if exerted on the right side, they become a far-reaching power for truth and righteousness. If the child is not instructed aright here, Satan will educate him through agencies of his choosing. How important, then, is the school in the home!

In the home school—the first grade—the very best talent should be utilized. Upon all parents there rests the obligation of giving physical, mental, and spiritual instruction. It should be the object of every parent to secure to his child a well-balanced, symmetrical character. This is a work of no small magnitude and importance—a work requiring earnest thought and prayer no less than patient, persevering effort. A right foundation must be laid, a framework, strong and firm, erected, and then day by day the work of building, polishing, perfecting, must go forward.

Children may be trained for the service of sin or for the service of righteousness. Solomon says, "Train up a child in the way he should go: and when he is old, he will not depart from it." Proverbs 22:6. This language is positive. The training that Solomon enjoins is to direct, educate, develop. But in order for parents to do this work, they must themselves understand the "way" the child should go. It is impossible for parents to give their children proper training unless they first give themselves to God, learning of the Great Teacher lessons of obedience to His will.

Physical training, the development of the body, is far more easily given than spiritual training. The nursery, the playground, the workshop; the sowing of the seed, and the gathering of the harvest—all these give physical training. Under ordinarily favorable circumstances a child naturally gains healthful vigor and a proper development of the bodily organs. Yet even in physical lines the child should be carefully trained.

Soul culture, which gives purity and elevation to the thoughts and fragrance to word and act, requires more painstaking effort. It takes patience to keep every evil motive weeded from the garden of the heart. The spiritual training should in no case be neglected; for "the fear of the Lord is the beginning of wisdom." Psalm 111:10. By some, education is placed next to religion, but true education is religion. The Bible should be the child's first textbook. From this book, parents are to give wise instruction. The word of God is to be made the rule of the life. From it the children are to learn that God is their Father; and from the beautiful lessons of His word they are to gain a knowledge of His character. Through the inculcation of its principles they are to learn to do justice and judgment.

For some reason many parents dislike to give their children religious instruction, and they leave them to pick up in Sabbath school the knowledge which it is their privilege and duty to impart. Such parents fail to fulfill the responsibility laid upon them, to give their children an all-round education. God commands His people to bring up their children in the nurture and admonition of the Lord. What does this mean—the nurture and admonition of the Lord? It means to teach them to order the life by the requirements and lessons of the word; to help them to gain a clear understanding of the terms of entrance into the city of God. Not to all who would enter will the gates of that city be opened, but to those only who have studied to know God's will, and have yielded their lives to His control.

Parents, let the instruction you give your children be simple, and be sure that it is clearly understood. The lessons that you learn from the word you are to present to their young minds so plainly that they cannot fail to understand. By simple lessons drawn from the word of God and their own experience, you may teach them how to conform their lives to the highest standard. Even in childhood and youth they may learn to live thoughtful, earnest lives that will yield a rich harvest of good.

The Family Altar

In every Christian home God should be honored by the morning and evening sacrifices of prayer and praise. Children should be taught to respect and reverence the hour of prayer. It is the duty of Christian parents, morning and evening, by earnest prayer and persevering faith, to make a hedge about their children.

In the church at home the children are to learn to pray and to trust in God. Teach them to repeat God's law. Concerning the commandments the Israelites were instructed: "Thou shalt teach them diligently unto thy children, and shalt talk of them when thou sittest in thine house, and when thou walkest by the way, and when thou liest down, and when thou risest up." Deuteronomy 6:7. Come in humility, with a heart full of tenderness, and with a sense of the temptations and dangers before yourselves and your children; by faith bind them to the altar, entreating for them the care of the Lord. Train the children to offer their simple words of prayer. Tell them that God delights to have them call upon Him.

Will the Lord of heaven pass by such homes and leave no blessing there? Nay, verily. Ministering angels will guard the children who are thus dedicated to God. They hear the offering of praise and the prayer of faith, and they bear the petitions to Him who ministers in the sanctuary for His people and offers His merits in their behalf.

Home Discipline

The children are to be taught that their capabilities were given them for the honor and glory of God. To this end they must learn the lesson of obedience, for only by lives of willing obedience can they render to God the service He requires. Before the child is old enough to reason, he must be taught to obey. By gentle, persistent effort the habit should be established. Thus to a great degree may be prevented those later conflicts between will and authority that do so much to arouse in the minds of the youth alienation and bitterness toward parents and teachers, and too often resistance of all authority, human and divine.

Let children be shown that true reverence is revealed by obedience. God has commanded nothing that is un-essential, and there is no other way of manifesting reverence so pleasing to Him as by obedience to that which He has spoken.

The mother is the queen of the home, and the children are her subjects. She is to rule her household wisely, in the dignity of her motherhood. Her influence in the home is to be paramount; her word, law. If she is a Christian, under God's control, she will command the respect of her children. Tell your children exactly what you require of them. Then let them understand that your word must be obeyed. Thus you are training them to respect the commandments of God, which plainly declare, "Thou shalt," and "Thou shalt not."

Few parents begin early enough to teach their children to obey. The child is usually allowed to get two or three years the start of its parents, who forbear to discipline it, thinking it too young to learn to obey. But all this time self is growing strong in the little being, and every day makes harder the parent's task of gaining control. At a

very early age children can comprehend what is plainly
and simply told them, and by kind and judicious management can be taught to obey. Never should they be allowed to show their parents disrespect. Self-will should
never be permitted to go unrebuked. The future well-
being of the child requires kindly, loving, but firm discipline.

There is a blind affection that gives the children the
privilege of doing as they please. But to allow a child to
follow his natural impulses is to allow him to deteriorate
and to become proficient in evil. Wise parents will not
say to their children, "Follow your own choice; go where
you will, and do what you will;" but, "Listen to the instruction of the Lord." Wise rules and regulations must
be made and enforced, that the beauty of the home life
may not be spoiled.

It is impossible to depict the evil that results from
leaving a child to its own will. Some who go astray
because of neglect in childhood will later, through the
inculcation of practical lessons, come to their senses; but
many are lost forever because in childhood and youth
they received only a partial, one-sided culture. The child
who is spoiled has a heavy burden to carry throughout
his life. In trial, in disappointment, in temptation, he will
follow his undisciplined, misdirected will. Children who
have never learned to obey will have weak, impulsive
characters. They seek to rule, but have not learned to
submit. They are without moral strength to restrain their
wayward tempers, to correct their wrong habits, or to
subdue their uncontrolled wills. The blunders of untrained, undisciplined childhood become the inheritance

of manhood and womanhood. The perverted intellect can scarcely discern between the true and the false.

Parents who truly love Christ will bear witness to this in a love for their children that will not indulge, but will work wisely for their highest good. They will lend every sanctified energy and ability to the work of saving their children. Instead of treating them as playthings, they will regard them as the purchase of Christ, and will teach them that they are to become the children of God. Instead of allowing them to indulge evil temper and selfish desires, they will teach them lessons of self-restraint. And the children will be happier, far happier, under proper discipline than if left to do as their unrestrained impulses suggest. A child's truest graces consist in modesty and obedience—in attentive ears to hear the words of direction, in willing feet and hands to walk and work in the path of duty.

Making Home Attractive

While many parents err on the side of indulgence, others go to the opposite extreme, and rule their children with a rod of iron. They seem to forget that they themselves were once children. They are dignified, cold, unsympathetic. Childish mirth and waywardness, the restless activity of the young life, find no excuse in their eyes. Trifling misdemeanors are treated as grave sins. Such discipline is not Christlike. Children thus trained fear their parents, but do not love them; they do not confide in them their childish experiences. Some of the most valuable qualities of mind and heart are chilled to death as a tender plant before the wintry blast.

While we are not to indulge blind affection, neither are we to manifest undue severity. Children cannot be brought to the Lord by force. They can be led, but not driven. "My sheep hear My voice, and I know them, and they follow Me," Christ declares. John 10:27. He does not say, My sheep hear My voice and are forced into the path of obedience. Never should parents cause their children pain by harshness or unreasonable exactions. Harshness drives souls into Satan's net.

Administer the rules of the home in wisdom and love, not with a rod of iron. Children will respond with willing obedience to the rule of love. Commend your children whenever you can. Make their lives as happy as possible. Provide them with innocent amusements. Make the home a Bethel, a holy, consecrated place. Keep the soil of the heart mellow by the manifestation of love and affection, thus preparing it for the seed of truth. Remember that the Lord gives the earth not only clouds and rain, but the beautiful, smiling sunshine, causing the seed to germinate and the blossom to appear. Remember that children need not only reproof and correction, but encouragement and commendation, the pleasant sunshine of kind words.

The home should be to the children the most attractive place in the world, and the mother's presence should be its greatest charm. Children have sensitive, loving natures. They are easily pleased and easily made unhappy. By gentle discipline, in loving words and acts, mothers may bind their children to their hearts.

Above all things, parents should surround their children with an atmosphere of cheerfulness, courtesy, and love. A home where love dwells and where it finds expression in looks, in words, in acts, is a place where angels delight to dwell. Parents, let the sunshine of love, cheer, and happy content enter your own hearts, and let its sweet influence pervade the home. Manifest a kindly, forbearing spirit, and encourage the same in your children, cultivating all those graces that will brighten the home life. The atmosphere thus created will be to the children what air and sunshine are to the vegetable world, promoting health and vigor of mind and body.

Instead of sending her children from her that she may not be annoyed by their noise or troubled by their little wants, let the mother plan amusement or light work to employ the active hands and minds. By entering into their feelings and directing their amusements and employments, the mother will gain the confidence of her children; thus she can the more effectually correct wrong habits or check the manifestation of selfishness or passion. A word of caution or reproof spoken at the right time will be of great value. By patient, watchful love she can turn the minds of the children in the right direction, cultivating in them beautiful and attractive traits of character.

Unpromising Children

There are some children who need more patient discipline and kindly training than others. They have received as a legacy unpromising traits of character, and because of this they need the more of sympathy and love.

By persevering labor these wayward ones may be prepared for a place in the work of the Master. They may possess undeveloped powers, which, when aroused, will enable them to fill places far in advance of those from whom more has been expected.

If you have children with peculiar temperaments, do not, because of this, let the blight of discouragement rest upon their lives. There should be no loud-voiced commands, no unkind, exasperating words, no harsh, severe, or gloomy expressions. Help them by the manifestation of forbearance and sympathy. Strengthen them by loving words and kindly deeds to overcome their defects of character.

The work of "breaking the will" is contrary to the principles of Christ. The will of the child must be directed and guided. Save all the strength of the will, for the human being needs it all; but give it proper direction. Treat it wisely and tenderly, as a sacred treasure. Do not hammer it in pieces; but by precept and true example wisely fashion and mold it until the child comes to years of responsibility.

When and How to Punish

The mother may ask, "Shall I never punish my child?" Whipping may be necessary when other resorts fail; yet she should not use the rod if it is possible to avoid doing so. But if milder measures prove insufficient, punishment that will bring the child to its senses should in love be administered. Frequently one such correction will be enough for a lifetime, to show the child that he does not hold the lines of control.

And when this step becomes necessary, the child should be seriously impressed with the thought that this is not done for the gratification of the parent, or to indulge arbitrary authority, but for the child's own good. He should be taught that every fault uncorrected will bring unhappiness to himself, and will displease God. Under such discipline children will find their greatest happiness in submitting their wills to the will of their heavenly Father.

Often we do more to provoke than to win. I have seen a mother snatch from the hand of her child something that was giving it special pleasure. The child did not know the reason of this, and naturally felt abused. Then followed a quarrel between parent and child, and a sharp chastisement ended the scene as far as outward appearance was concerned; but that battle left an impression on the tender mind that would not be easily effaced. This mother acted unwisely. She did not reason from cause to effect. Her harsh, injudicious action stirred the worst passions in the heart of her child, and on every similar occasion these passions would be aroused and strengthened.

Think you that God takes no cognizance of the way such children are corrected? He knows, and He also knows what might be the blessed results if the work of correction were done in a way to win rather than to repel.

Never correct your child in anger. An exhibition of passion on your part will not cure your child's evil temper. That is the time of all times when you should act with humility and patience and prayer. Then is the time to kneel down with the children and ask the Lord for pardon. Before you cause your child physical pain, you will, if you are a Christian father or mother, reveal the love you have for your erring little one. As you bow before God with your child you will present before the sympathizing Redeemer His own words, "Suffer the little children to come unto Me, and forbid them not: for of such is the kingdom of God." Mark 10:14. That prayer will bring angels to your side. Your child will not forget these experiences, and the blessing of God will rest upon such instruction, leading him to Christ.

When children realize that their parents are trying to help them, they will bend their energies in the right direction. And to the children who have right instruction in the home, the advantages of our schools will be greater than to those who are allowed to grow up without spiritual help at home.

Children who have not experienced the cleansing power of Jesus are the lawful prey of the enemy, and the evil angels have easy access to them. Some parents are careless and suffer their children to grow up with but little restraint. Parents have a great work to do in the matter of correcting and training their children, and in bringing them to God and claiming His blessing upon them. By the faithful and untiring efforts of the parents, and the blessing and grace bestowed upon the children in response to the prayers of the parents, the power of the evil angels may be broken and a sanctifying influence shed upon the children. Thus the powers of darkness will be driven back.

SAFEGUARDING THE YOUNG

From their infancy the youth need to have a firm barrier built up between them and the world, that its corrupting influence may not affect them. Parents must exercise unceasing watchfulness, that their children be not lost to God. The vows of David, recorded in the 101st psalm, should be the vows of all upon whom rest the responsibilities of guarding the influences of the home. The psalmist declares: "I will set no wicked thing before mine eyes: I hate the work of them that turn aside; it shall not cleave to me. A froward heart shall depart from me: I will not know a wicked person. Whoso privily slandereth his neighbor, him will I cut off: him that hath an high look and a proud heart will not I suffer. Mine eyes shall be upon the faithful of the land, that they may dwell with me: he that walketh in a perfect way, he shall serve me. He that worketh deceit shall not dwell within my house: he that telleth lies shall not tarry in my sight." Psalm 101:3-7.

The youth should not be left to learn good and evil indiscriminately, the parents thinking that at some future time the good will predominate and the evil lose its influence. The evil will increase faster than the good. It is possible that the evil which children learn may be eradicated after many years, but who would trust to this? Whatever else they neglect, parents should never leave their children free to wander in the paths of sin.

Choosing Associates

Parents should remember that association with those of lax morals and coarseness of character will have a detrimental influence upon the youth. If they fail to choose proper society for their children, if they allow them to associate with youth of questionable morals, they place them, or permit them to place themselves, in a school where lessons of depravity are taught and practiced. They may feel that their children are strong enough to withstand temptation; but how can they be sure of this? It is far easier to yield to evil influences than to resist them. Ere they are aware of it, their children may become imbued with the spirit of their associates and may be degraded or ruined.

Parents, guard the principles and habits of your children as the apple of the eye. Allow them to associate with no one with whose character you are not well acquainted. Permit them to form no intimacy until you are assured that it will do them no harm. Accustom your children to trust your judgment and experience. Teach them that you have clearer perception of character than they in their inexperience can have, and that your decisions must not be disregarded.

The Choice of Reading

Parents should endeavor to keep out of the home every influence that is not productive of good. In this matter some parents have much to learn. To those who feel free to read story magazines and novels I would say:

You are sowing seed the harvest of which you will not care to garner. From such reading there is no spiritual strength to be gained. Rather it destroys love for the pure truth of the word. Through the agency of novels and story magazines, Satan is working to fill with unreal and trivial thoughts, minds that should be diligently studying the word of God. Thus he is robbing thousands upon thousands of the time and energy and self-discipline demanded by the stern problems of life.

The susceptible, expanding mind of the child longs for knowledge. Parents should keep themselves well informed, that they may give the minds of their children proper food. Like the body, the mind derives its strength from the food it receives. It is broadened and elevated by pure, strengthening thoughts; but it is narrowed and debased by thoughts that are of the earth earthy.

Parents, you are the ones to decide whether the minds of your children shall be filled with ennobling thoughts or with vicious sentiments. You cannot keep their active minds unoccupied, neither can you frown away evil. Only by the inculcation of right principles can you exclude wrong thoughts. Unless parents plant the seeds of truth in the hearts of their children, the enemy will sow tares. Good, sound instruction is the only preventive of the evil communications that corrupt good manners. Truth will protect the soul from the endless temptations that must be encountered.

Let the youth be taught to give close study to the word of God. Received into the soul, it will prove a mighty barricade against temptation. "Thy word," the psalmist declares, "have I hid in mine heart, that I might not sin against Thee." "By the word of Thy lips I have kept me from the paths of the destroyer." Psalms 119:11; 17:4.

Teaching Children to Be Useful

One of the surest safeguards of the young is useful occupation. Children who are trained to industrious habits, so that all their hours are usefully and pleasantly employed, have no inclination to repine at their lot and no time for idle daydreaming. They are in little danger of forming vicious habits or associations.

In the home school the children should be taught how to perform the practical duties of everyday life. While they are still young, the mother should give them some simple task to do each day. It will take longer for her to teach them how than it would to do it herself; but let her remember that she is to lay for their character building the foundation of helpfulness. Let her remember that the home is a school in which she is the head teacher. It is hers to teach her children how to perform the duties of the household quickly and skillfully. As early in life as possible they should be trained to share the burdens of the home. From childhood, boys and girls should be taught to bear heavier and still heavier burdens, intelligently helping in the work of the family firm.

When children reach a suitable age, they should be provided with tools. They will be found to be apt pupils. If the father is a carpenter, he should give his boys lessons in carpentry.

From the mother the children are to learn habits of

neatness, thoroughness, and dispatch. To allow a child to take an hour or two in doing a piece of work that could easily be done in half an hour is to allow it to form dilatory habits. Habits of industry and thoroughness will be an untold blessing to the youth in the larger school of life, upon which they must enter as they grow older.

Children are not to be allowed to think that everything in the house is their plaything, to do with as they please. Instruction in this line should be given even to the smallest children. By correcting this habit, you will destroy it. God designs that the perversities natural to childhood shall be rooted out before they become habits. Do not give the children playthings that are easily broken. To do this is to teach lessons in destructiveness. Let them have a few playthings, and let these be strong and durable. Such suggestions, small though they may seem, mean much in the education of the child.

Mothers should guard against training their children to be dependent and self-absorbed. Never give them cause to think that they are the center and that everything must revolve around them. Some parents give much time and attention to amusing their children; but children should be trained to amuse themselves, to exercise their own ingenuity and skill. Thus they will learn to be content with simple pleasures. They should be taught to bear bravely their little disappointments and trials. Instead of calling attention to every trifling pain or hurt, divert their minds; teach them to pass lightly over little annoyances and discomforts.

Study how to teach the children to be thoughtful of

others. The youth should be early accustomed to submission, self-denial, and regard for others' happiness.

They should be taught to subdue the hasty temper, to withhold the passionate word, to manifest unvarying kindness, courtesy, and self-control.

Burdened with many cares, the mother may sometimes feel that she cannot take time patiently to instruct her little ones and to give them love and sympathy. But she should remember that if the children do not find in their parents and in their homes that which will satisfy their desire for sympathy and companionship, they will look to other sources, where both mind and character may be endangered.

Give some of your leisure hours to your children; associate with them in their work and in their sports, and win their confidence. Cultivate their friendship. Give them responsibilities to bear, small at first, and larger as they grow older. Let them see that you think they help you. Never, never let them hear you say, "They hinder me more than they help me."

If possible, the home should be out of the city, where the children can have ground to cultivate. Let them each have a piece of ground of their own; and as you teach them how to make a garden, how to prepare the soil for seed, and the importance of keeping all the weeds pulled out, teach them also how important it is to keep unsightly, injurious practices out of the life. Teach them to keep down wrong habits as they keep down the weeds in their gardens. It will take time to teach these lessons, but it will pay, greatly pay.

Tell your children about the miracle-working power

of God. As they study the great lesson book of nature, God will impress their minds. The farmer plows his land and sows his seed, but he cannot make the seed grow. He must depend on God to do that which no human power can do. The Lord puts His vital power into the seed, causing it to spring forth into life. Under His care the germ of life breaks through the hard crust encasing it, and springs up to bear fruit. First appears the blade, then the ear, then the full corn in the ear. As the children are told of the work that God does for the seed, they learn the secret of growth in grace.

There is untold value in industry. Let the children be taught to do something useful. More than human wisdom is needed that parents may understand how best to educate their children for a useful, happy life here, and for higher service and greater joy hereafter.

The Physical Well-Being

Parents should seek to awaken in their children an interest in the study of physiology. From the first dawn of reason the human mind should become intelligent in regard to the physical structure. We may behold and admire the work of God in the natural world, but the human habitation is the most wonderful. It is therefore of the highest importance that among the studies selected for children, physiology occupy an important place. All children should study it. And then parents should see to it that practical hygiene is added.

Children are to be trained to understand that every organ of the body and every faculty of the mind is the gift of a good and wise God, and that each is to be used to His glory. Right habits in eating and drinking and dressing must be insisted upon. Wrong habits render the youth less susceptible to Bible instruction. The children are to be guarded against the indulgence of appetite, and especially against the use of stimulants and narcotics. The tables of Christian parents should not be loaded down with food containing condiments and spices.

There are but few among the young who have any definite knowledge of the mysteries of life. The study of the wonderful human organism, the relation and dependence of all its complicated parts, is one in which most mothers take little if any interest. They do not understand the influence of the body upon the mind or of the mind upon the body. They occupy themselves with needless trifles and then plead that they have no time to obtain the information which they need in order to care properly for the health of their children. It is less trouble to trust them to the doctors. Thousands of children die through the ignorance of their parents regarding the laws of hygiene.

If parents themselves would obtain knowledge upon this subject and feel the importance of putting it to a practical use, we should see a better condition of things. Teach your children to reason from cause to effect. Show them that if they violate the laws of their being they must pay the penalty in suffering. If you cannot see as rapid improvement as you desire, do not be discouraged, but instruct them patiently and press on until victory is gained. Recklessness in regard to bodily health tends to recklessness in morals.

Do not neglect to teach your children how to prepare wholesome food. In giving them these lessons in physiology and in good cooking, you are teaching them the first steps in some of the most useful branches of education and inculcating principles which are needful elements in their religious life.

Teach your children from the cradle to practice self-denial and self-control. Teach them to enjoy the beauties of nature, and in useful employment to exercise all the powers of mind and body. Bring them up to have sound constitutions and good morals, to have sunny dispositions and sweet tempers. Teach them that to yield to temptation is weak and wicked; to resist is noble and manly.

Let all, both old and young, give diligent heed to the words penned by the wise man three thousand years ago: "My son, forget not my law; but let thine heart keep my commandments: for length of days, and long life, and peace, shall they add to thee. Let not mercy and truth forsake thee: bind them about thy neck; write them upon the table of thine heart: so shalt thou find favor and good understanding in the sight of God and man." Proverbs 3:1-4.

Unity in Government

Unitedly and prayerfully the father and mother should bear the grave responsibility of guiding their children aright. It is chiefly upon the mother that the work of child training devolves, but the father should not become so absorbed in business life or in the study of books that he cannot take time to study the natures and necessities of his children. He should help in devising ways by which they may be kept busy in useful labor agreeable to their varying dispositions.

The father of boys should come into close contact with his sons, giving them the benefit of his larger experience and talking with them in such simplicity and tenderness that he binds them to his heart. He should let them see that he has their best interests, their happiness, in view all the time. As the priest of the household, he is accountable to God for the influence that he exerts over every member of the family.

The mother should feel her need of the Holy Spirit's guidance, that she herself may have a genuine experience in submission to the way and will of God. Then, through the grace of Christ, she can be a wise, gentle, loving teacher. To do her work as it should be done requires talent and skill and patient, thoughtful care. It calls for self-distrust and earnest prayer. Let every mother strive by persevering effort to fulfill her obligations. Let her bring her little ones to Jesus in the arms of faith, telling Him her great need, and asking for wisdom and grace. Earnestly, patiently, courageously, she should seek to improve her own abilities, that she may use aright the highest powers of the mind in the training of her children.

As united rulers of the home kingdom, let father and mother show kindness and courtesy to each other. Never should their deportment militate against the precepts they seek to inculcate. They must maintain purity of heart and life if they would have their children pure. They must train and discipline self if they would have their children subject to discipline. They must set before their children an example worthy of imitation. Should they be remiss in this respect, what will they answer if the children entrusted to them stand before the bar of heaven as witnesses to their neglect? How terrible will be their realization of loss and failure as they face the Judge of all the earth!

One great reason why there is so much evil in the world today is that parents occupy their minds with other things to the exclusion of the work that is all-important— the task of patiently and kindly teaching their children the way of the Lord. Parents should allow nothing to prevent them from giving to their children all the time that is necessary to make them understand what it means to obey and trust the Lord fully.

Before visitors, before every other consideration, your children should come first. The time spent in needless sewing, God would have you spend in educating them in essential things. That unnecessary garment you are making, that extra dish you think you will prepare—let it be neglected rather than the education of your children. The labor due your child during its early years will admit of no neglect. There is no time in its life when the rule should be forgotten, Line upon line, precept upon precept, here a little, and there a little. Deny your children anything rather than the instruction which, if faithfully followed, will make them good and useful members of society, and will prepare them for citizenship in the kingdom of heaven.

A Missionary Training

Upon parents rests the responsibility of developing in their children those capabilities which will enable them to do good service for God. God sees all the possibilities in that mite of humanity. He sees that with proper training the child will become a power for good in the world. He watches with anxious interest to see whether the parents will carry out His plan, or whether by mistaken kindness they will thwart His purpose, indulging the child to his present and eternal ruin. To transform this helpless and apparently insignificant being into a blessing to the world and an honor to God is a great and grand work.

Parents, help your children to fulfill God's purpose for them. In the home they are to be trained to do missionary work that will prepare them for wider spheres of usefulness. Train them to be an honor to the One who died to gain for them eternal life in the kingdom of glory. Teach them that God has a part for them to act in His great work. The Lord will bless them as they work for Him. They can be His helping hand.

Your home is the first field in which you are called to labor. The precious plants in the home garden demand your first care. Consider carefully your work, its nature, its bearings, its results, ever remembering that your looks, your words, your actions, have a direct bearing on the future of your dear ones. Your work is not to fashion beauty on canvas, or to chisel it from marble, but to impress upon a human soul the image of the divine.

Give your children intellectual culture and moral training. Fortify their young minds with firm, pure principles. While you have opportunity, lay the foundation for a noble manhood and womanhood. Your labor will be rewarded a thousandfold.

This is your day of trust, your day of responsibility and opportunity. Soon will come your day of reckoning. Take up your work with earnest prayer and faithful endeavor. Teach your children that it is their privilege to receive every day the baptism of the Holy Spirit. Let Christ find you His helping hand to carry out His purposes. By prayer you may gain an experience that will make your ministry for your children a perfect success.

Seventh-day Adventist parents should more fully realize their responsibilities as character builders. God places before them the privilege of strengthening His cause through the consecration and labors of their children. He desires to see gathered out from the homes of our people a large company of youth who, because of the godly influences of their homes, have surrendered their hearts to Him, and go forth to give Him the highest service of their lives. Directed and trained by the godly instruction of the home, the influence of the morning and evening worship, the consistent example of parents who love and fear God, they have learned to submit to God as their teacher and are prepared to render Him acceptable service as loyal sons and daughters. Such youth are prepared to represent to the world the power and grace of Christ.

WHAT SHALL OUR CHILDREN READ?

What shall our children read? This is a serious question and one that demands a serious answer. It troubles me to see in Sabbathkeeping families periodicals and newspapers containing continued stories which leave no impressions for good on the minds of children and youth. I have watched those whose taste for fiction was thus cultivated. They have had the privilege of listening to the truth, of becoming acquainted with the reasons of our faith; but they have grown to maturer years destitute of true piety and practical godliness. They manifest no devotion and reflect no heavenly light upon their associates to lead them to the fount of all true knowledge.

It is during the first years of a child's life that his mind is most susceptible to impressions either good or evil. During these years decided progress is made in either a right direction or a wrong one. On one hand, much worthless information may be gained; on the other, much solid, valuable knowledge. The strength of intellect, the substantial knowledge, are possessions which the gold of Ophir could not buy. Their price is above gold or silver.

The kind of education that fits the youth for practical life, they naturally do not choose. They urge their desires, their likes and dislikes, their preferences and inclinations; but if parents have correct views of God, of the truth, and of the influences and associations that should surround their children, they will feel that upon them rests the God-given responsibility of carefully guiding the inexperienced youth.

Many youth are eager for books. They read anything that they can obtain. I appeal to the parents of such children to control their desire for reading. Do not permit upon your tables the magazines and newspapers in which are found love stories. Supply their place with books that will help the youth to put into their character building the very best material—the love and fear of God, the knowledge of Christ. Encourage your children to store the mind with valuable knowledge, to let that which is good occupy the soul and control its powers, leaving no place for low, debasing thoughts. Restrict the desire for reading matter that does not furnish good food for the mind. The money expended for story magazines may not seem much, but it is too much to spend for that which gives so much that is misleading, and so little that is good in return. Those who are in God's service should spend neither time nor money in unprofitable reading.

Worthless Reading

The world is deluged with books that might better be consumed than circulated. Books on sensational topics, published and circulated as a money-making scheme, might better never be read by the youth. There is a satanic fascination in such books. The heartsickening recital of crimes and atrocities has a bewitching power upon many, exciting them to see what they can do to bring themselves into notice, even by the wickedest deeds. The enormities, the cruelties, the licentious practices, portrayed in some of the strictly historical writings, have acted as leaven on many minds, leading to the commission of similar acts.

Books that delineate the satanic practices of human beings are giving publicity to evil. These horrible particulars need not be lived over, and no one who believes the truth for this time should act a part in perpetuating the memory of them. When the intellect is fed and stimulated by this depraved food, the thoughts become impure and sensual.

There is another class of books—love stories and frivolous, exciting tales—which are a curse to everyone who reads them, even though the author may attach a good moral. Often religious statements are woven all through these books, but in most cases Satan is but clothed in angel robes to deceive and allure the unsuspicious. The practice of story reading is one of the means employed by Satan to destroy souls. It produces a false, unhealthy excitement, fevers the imagination, unfits the mind for usefulness, and disqualifies it for any spiritual exercise. It weans the soul from prayer and from the love of spiritual things.

Readers of frivolous, exciting tales become unfitted for the duties of practical life. They live in an unreal world. I have watched children who have been allowed to make a practice of reading such stories. Whether at home or abroad, they were restless, dreamy, unable to converse except upon the most commonplace subjects. Religious thought and conversation was entirely foreign to their minds. With the cultivation of an appetite for sensational stories, the mental taste is perverted, and the mind is not satisfied unless fed upon this unwholesome food. I can think of no more fitting name for those who indulge in such reading than mental inebriates. Intemperate habits of reading have an effect upon the brain similar to that which intemperate habits of eating and drinking have upon the body.

Those who indulge the habit of racing through an exciting story are simply crippling their mental strength and disqualifying their minds for vigorous thought and research. Some youth, and even some of mature age, have been afflicted with paralysis from no other cause than excess in reading. The nerve power of the brain was kept constantly excited, until the delicate machinery became worn and refused to act. Some of its fine mechanism gave way, and paralysis was the result.

There are men and women now in the decline of life who have never recovered from the effects of intemperance in reading. The habit formed in early years grew with their growth and strengthened with their strength. Their determined efforts to overcome the sin of abusing the intellect were partially successful, but they have never recovered the full vigor of mind that God bestowed upon them.

Infidel Authors

Another source of danger against which we should be constantly on guard is the reading of infidel authors. Such works are inspired by the enemy of truth, and no one can read them without imperiling the soul. It is true that some who are affected by them may finally recover; but all who tamper with their evil influence place themselves on Satan's ground, and he makes the most of his advantage. As they invite his temptations they have not wisdom to discern or strength to resist them. With a fascinating, bewitching power, unbelief and infidelity fasten themselves upon the mind.

We are constantly surrounded by unbelief. The very atmosphere seems charged with it. Only by constant effort can we resist its power. Those who value their salvation should shun infidel writings as they would shun the leprosy.

Preoccupy the Soil

The best way to prevent the growth of evil is to preoccupy the soil. Instead of recommending your children to read *Robinson Crusoe,* or fascinating stories of real life, such as *Uncle Tom's Cabin,* open the Scriptures to them, and spend some time each day in reading and studying God's word. The mental tastes must be disciplined and educated with the greatest care. Parents must begin early to unfold the Scriptures to the expanding minds of their children, that proper habits of thought may be formed.

No effort should be spared to establish right habits of study. If the mind wanders, bring it back. If the intellectual and moral tastes have been perverted by overwrought and exciting tales of fiction, so that there is a disinclination to apply the mind, there is a battle to be fought to overcome this habit. A love for fictitious reading should be overcome at once. Rigid rules should be enforced to hold the mind in the proper channel.

Between an uncultivated field and an untrained mind there is a striking similarity. In the minds of children and youth the enemy sows tares, and unless parents keep watchful guard, these will spring up to bear their evil fruit. Unceasing care is needed in cultivating the soil of the mind and sowing it with the precious seed of Bible truth. Children should be taught to reject trashy, exciting tales, and to turn to sensible reading, which will lead the mind to take an interest in Bible story, history, and argument. Reading that will throw light upon the Sacred Volume and quicken the desire to study it is not dangerous, but beneficial.

The Sabbath School Lesson

The Sabbath school affords to parents and children an opportunity for the study of God's word. But in order for them to gain that benefit which they should gain in the Sabbath school, both parents and children should devote time to the study of the lesson, seeking to obtain a thorough knowledge of the facts presented and also of the spiritual truths which these facts are designed to teach. We should especially impress upon the minds of the youth the importance of seeking the full significance of the scripture under consideration.

Parents, set apart a little time each day for the study of the Sabbath school lesson with your children. Give up the social visit if need be, rather than sacrifice the hour devoted to the lessons of sacred history. Parents as well as children will receive benefit from this study. Let the more important passages of Scripture connected with the lesson be committed to memory, not as a task, but as a privilege. Though at first the memory be defective, it will gain strength by exercise, so that after a time you will delight thus to treasure up the words of truth. And the habit will prove a most valuable aid to spiritual growth.

The Home Reading Circle

Let our people show that they have a live interest in medical missionary work. Let them prepare themselves for usefulness by studying the literature that has been prepared for our instruction on these subjects. Those who study and practice the principles of right living will be greatly blessed, both physically and spiritually. An understanding of the philosophy of health is a safeguard against many of the evils that are continually increasing.

Fathers and mothers, obtain all the help you can from the study of our books and publications. Take time to read to your children from the health books, as well as from the books treating more particularly on religious subjects. Teach them the importance of caring for the body, the house they live in. Form a home reading circle, in which every member of the family shall lay aside the busy cares of the day and unite in study. Especially will the youth who have been accustomed to reading novels and cheap storybooks, receive benefit from joining in the evening family study.

The Bible

Above all, take time to read the Bible—the Book of books. A daily study of the Scriptures has a sanctifying, uplifting influence upon the mind. Bind the Holy Volume to your hearts. It will prove to you a friend and guide in perplexity.

Both old and young neglect the Bible. They do not

make it their study, the rule of their life. Especially are the young guilty of this neglect. Most of them find time to read other books, but the Book that points out the way to eternal life is not daily studied. Idle stories are attentively read, while the Bible is neglected. This Book is our guide to a higher, holier life. The youth would pronounce it the most interesting book they ever read had not their imagination been perverted by the reading of fictitious stories.

Youthful minds fail to reach their noblest development when they neglect the highest source of wisdom—the word of God. That we are in God's world, in the presence of the Creator; that we are made in His likeness; that He watches over us and loves us and cares for us—these are wonderful themes for thought, and lead the mind into broad, exalted fields of meditation. He who opens mind and heart to the contemplation of such themes as these will never be satisfied with trivial, sensational subjects.

The importance of seeking a thorough knowledge of the Scriptures can hardly be estimated. "Given by inspiration of God," able to make us "wise unto salvation," rendering the man of God "perfect, throughly furnished unto all good works" (2 Timothy 3:15-17), the Bible has the highest claim to our reverent attention. We should not be satisfied with a superficial knowledge, but should seek to learn the full meaning of the words of truth, to drink deep of the spirit of the Holy Oracles.

THE PARABLE OF THE GROWING SEED

Jesus taught by illustrations and parables drawn from nature and from the familiar events of everyday life. . . . In this way He associated natural things with spiritual, linking the things of nature and the life experience of His hearers with the sublime truths of the written word. And whenever afterward their eyes rested on the objects with which He has associated eternal truth, His lessons were repeated.

One of Christ's most beautiful and impressive parables is that of the sower and the seed. "So is the kingdom of God," He said, "as if a man should cast seed into the ground; and should sleep, and rise night and day, and the seed should spring and grow up, he knoweth not how. For the earth bringeth forth fruit of herself; first the blade, then the ear, after that the full corn in the ear." Mark 4:26-28. . . . He who gave this parable, Himself created the tiny seed, gave it its vital properties, and ordained the laws that should govern its growth; and He made it a living illustration of truth in both the natural and the spiritual world.

The truths which this parable teaches were made a living reality in Christ's own life. In both His physical and His spiritual nature He followed the divine order of growth, illustrated by the plant, as He wishes all youth to do. Although He was the Majesty of heaven, the King of glory, He became a babe in Bethlehem, and for a time represented the helpless infant in its mother's care.

In childhood, Jesus did the works of an obedient child. He spoke and acted with the wisdom of a child, and not of a man, honoring His parents, and carrying out their wishes in helpful ways, according to the ability of a child. But at each stage of His development He was perfect, with the simple, natural grace of a sinless life. The Sacred Record says of His childhood, "The Child grew, and waxed strong in spirit, filled with wisdom: and the grace of God was upon Him." And of His youth it is recorded, "Jesus increased in wisdom and stature, and in favor with God and man." Luke 2:40, 52.

The work of parents and teachers is here suggested. . . . They should aim so to cultivate the tendencies of the youth that at each stage of their life they may represent the natural beauty appropriate to the period, unfolding naturally, as do the plants in the garden.

The Beauty of Simplicity

Those children are most attractive who are natural and unaffected. It is not wise to give children special notice and repeat their clever sayings before them. Vanity should not be encouraged by praising their looks, their words, or their actions. Nor should they be dressed in an expensive or showy manner. This encourages pride in them and awakens envy in the hearts of their companions. Teach the children that the true adorning is not outward. "Whose adorning let it not be that outward adorning of plaiting the hair, and of wearing of gold, or of putting on of apparel; but let it be the hidden man of the heart, in that which is not corruptible, even the ornament of a meek and quiet spirit, which is in the sight of God of great price." 1 Peter 3:3, 4. . . .

The little ones should be educated in childlike simplicity. They should be trained to be content with the small, helpful duties and the pleasures and experiences natural to their years. Childhood answers to the blade in the parable, and the blade has a beauty peculiarly its own. The children should not be forced into a precocious maturity, but should retain as long as possible the freshness and grace of their early years.

The Garden of the Heart

The parable of the sower and the seed conveys a deep spiritual lesson. The seed represents the principles sown in the heart, and its growth the development of character. Make the teaching on this point practical. The children can prepare the soil and sow the seed; and as they work, the parent or teacher can explain to them the garden of the heart, with the good or bad seed sown there; and that as the garden must be prepared for the natural seed, so the heart must be prepared for the seed of truth. As the plant grows, the correspondence between the natural and the spiritual sowing can be continued.

The little children may be Christians, having an experience in accordance with their years. This is all that God expects of them. They need to be educated in spiritual things; and parents should give them every advantage, that they may form characters after the similitude of the character of Christ.

The mind will never cease to be active. It is open to influences, good or bad. As the human countenance is stamped by the sunbeam on the polished plate of the artist, so are thoughts and impressions stamped on the mind of the child; and whether these impressions are of the earth earthy, or moral and religious, they are well-nigh ineffaceable. When reason is awakening, the mind is most susceptible; and so the very first lessons are of great importance. These lessons have a powerful influence in the formation of character. If they are of the right stamp, and if, as the child advances in years, they are followed up with patient perseverance, the earthly and the eternal destiny will be shaped for good. This is the word of the Lord: "Train up a child in the way he should go: and when he is old, he will not depart from it." Proverbs 22:6.

Parents, give your children to the Lord, and ever keep before their minds that they belong to Him, that they are the lambs of Christ's flock, watched over by the True Shepherd. Hannah dedicated Samuel to the Lord; and it is said of him, "Samuel grew, and the Lord was with him, and did let none of his words [the Lord's words through Samuel] fall to the ground." 1 Samuel 3:19. In the case of this prophet and judge in Israel are presented the possibilities that are placed before the child whose parents co-operate with God, doing their appointed work.

Children are a heritage from the Lord, and they are to be trained for His service. This is the work that rests upon parents and teachers with solemn, sacred force, which they cannot evade or ignore. To neglect this work marks them as unfaithful servants; but there is a reward when the seed of truth is early sown in the heart and carefully tended.

Christ concludes the parable: "But when the fruit is brought forth, immediately he putteth in the sickle, because the harvest is come." Mark 4:29. When the harvest of the earth is reaped, we shall see the result of our toil; for we shall see those for whom we have labored and prayed gathered into the heavenly garner. So shall we enter into the joy of our Lord, when "He shall see of the travail of His soul, and shall be satisfied." Isaiah 53:11.—*Special Testimonies on Education,* pages 67-72.

The mother's work often seems to her an unimportant service. It is a work that is rarely appreciated. Others know little of her many cares and burdens. Her days are occupied with a round of little duties, all calling for patient effort, for self-control, for tact, wisdom, and self-sacrificing love; yet she cannot boast of what she has done as any great achievement. She has only kept things in the home running smoothly. Often weary and perplexed, she has tried to speak kindly to the children, to keep them busy and happy, and to guide their little feet in the right path. She feels that she has accomplished nothing. But it is not so. Heavenly angels watch the careworn mother, noting the burdens she carries day by day. Her name may not have been heard in the world, but it is written in the Lamb's book of life.

TEACHING LESSONS OF HELPFULNESS

Life is not given to be spent in idleness and self-pleasing. Great possibilities have been placed before everyone who will develop his God-given capabilities. For this reason the training of the young is a matter of highest importance. Every child born into the home is a sacred trust. God says to the parents, "Take this child, and bring it up for Me, that it may be an honor to My name, and a channel through which My blessings shall flow to the world." To fit the child for such a life, something more is called for than a partial, one-sided education which shall develop the mental at the expense of the physical powers. All the faculties of mind and body need to be developed; and this is the work which parents, aided by the teacher, are to do for the children and youth placed under their care.

The first lessons are of great importance. It is customary to send very young children to school. They are required to study from books things that tax their young minds, and often they are taught music. Frequently the parents have but limited means, and an expense is incurred which they can ill afford, but everything must be made to bend to this artificial line of education. This course is not wise. A nervous child should not be overtaxed in any direction and should not learn music until he is physically well developed.

The mother should be the teacher, and home the school where every child receives his first lessons; and these lessons should include habits of industry. Mothers, let the little ones play in the open air; let them listen to the songs of the birds, and learn the love of God as expressed in His beautiful works. Teach them simple lessons from the book of nature and the things about them; and as their minds expand, lessons from books may be added and firmly fixed in their memory. But let them also learn, even in their earliest years, to be useful. Train them to think that, as members of the household, they are to act a disinterested, helpful part in sharing the domestic burdens and to seek healthful exercise in the performance of necessary home duties.

It is essential for parents to find useful employment for their children, which will involve the bearing of responsibilities as their age and strength will permit. The children should be given something to do that will not only keep them busy, but will interest them. The active hands and brains must be employed from the earliest years. If parents neglect to turn their children's energies into useful channels, they do them great injury, for Satan is ready to find them something to do. . . .

The Co-operation of Teacher and Parent

When the child is old enough to be sent to school, the teacher should co-operate with the parents, and manual training should be continued as part of the school studies. There are many students who object to this kind of work in the schools. They think useful employment, like learning a trade, degrading; but such have an incorrect idea of what constitutes true dignity. . . .

Christ's Example

In his earth life Christ was an example to all the human family, and He was obedient and helpful in the home. He learned the carpenter's trade, and worked with His own hands in the little shop at Nazareth. . . . The Bible says of Jesus, "The Child grew, and waxed strong in spirit, filled with wisdom: and the grace of God was upon Him." Luke 2:40. As He worked in childhood and youth, mind and body were developed. He did not use His physical powers recklessly, but in such a way as to keep them in health, that He might do the best work in every line. . . .

In the children and youth an ambition should be awakened to take their exercise in doing something that will be beneficial to themselves and helpful to others. The exercise that develops mind and character, that teaches the hands to be useful, that trains the young to bear their share of life's burdens, is that which gives physical strength and quickens every faculty. And there is a reward in virtuous industry, in the cultivation of the habit of living to do good.

The children of the wealthy should not be deprived of the great blessing of having something to do to increase the strength of brain and muscle. Work is not a curse, but a blessing. God gave sinless Adam and Eve a beautiful garden to tend. This was pleasant work, and none but pleasant work would have entered our world had not the first pair transgressed God's commandments. . . . The wealthy are not to be deprived of the privilege and bless-

ing of a place among the world's workers. They should
realize that they are responsible for the use they make of
their entrusted possessions; that their strength, their time,
and their money are to be used wisely, and not for selfish
purposes. . . .

The approval of God rests with loving assurance upon
the children who cheerfully take their part in the duties
of domestic life, sharing the burdens of father and mother.
They will be rewarded with health of body and peace of
mind; and they will enjoy the pleasure of seeing their
parents take their share of social enjoyment and healthful
recreation, thus prolonging their lives. Children trained
to the practical duties of life will go out from the home
to be useful members of society, with an education far
superior to that gained by close confinement in the schoolroom at an early age, when neither the mind nor the body
is strong enough to endure the strain.

At home and in the school, by precept and example,
the children and youth should be taught to be truthful,
unselfish, industrious. They should not be allowed to
spend their time in idleness; their hands should not be
folded in inaction. Parents and teachers should work for
the accomplishment of this object—the development of all
the powers, and the formation of right character. But
when parents realize their responsibilities, there will be
far less left for the teachers to do.

Heaven is interested in this work in behalf of the
young. The parents and teachers who by wise instruction, in a calm, decided manner, accustom children to
think of and care for others, will help them to overcome
their selfishness and will close the door against many

temptations. Angels of God will co-operate with these faithful instructors. Angels are not commissioned to do this work themselves; but they will give strength and efficiency to those who, in the fear of God, seek to train the young to a life of usefulness.

―――――――

Our schools are the Lord's special instrumentality to fit the children and youth for missionary work. Parents should understand their responsibility and help their children to appreciate the great privileges and blessings that God has provided for them in educational advantages.

But their domestic education should keep pace with their education in missionary lines. In childhood and youth practical and literary training should be combined. Children should be taught to have a part in domestic duties. They should be instructed how to help father and mother in the little things that they can do. Their minds should be trained to think, their memories taxed to remember their appointed work; and in the training to habits of usefulness in the home they are being educated in doing practical duties appropriate to their age.

If children have proper home training, they will not be found upon the streets, receiving the haphazard education that so many receive. Parents who love their children in a sensible way will not permit them to grow up with lazy habits and ignorant of how to do home duties. Ignorance is not acceptable to God and is unfavorable for the doing of His work.

CO-OPERATION BETWEEN THE HOME
AND THE SCHOOL

It is in the home school that our boys and girls are to be prepared to attend the church school. Parents should constantly keep this in mind, and as teachers in the home should consecrate every power of the being to God, that they may fulfill their high and holy mission. Diligent, faithful instruction in the home is the best preparation that children can receive for school life. Wise parents will help their children to understand that in the school life, as in the home, they are to strive to please God, to be an honor to Him.

To shield their children from contaminating influences, parents should instruct them in the principles of purity. Those children who in the home form habits of obedience and self-control will have little difficulty in their school life, and will escape many of the temptations that beset the youth. Parents should train their children to be true to God under all circumstances and in all places. They should surround them with influences that tend to strengthen character. With such a training, children, when sent away to school, will not be a cause of disturbance or anxiety. They will be a support to their teachers and an example and encouragement to their fellow pupils.

What the Teacher Should Be

In the choice of a teacher for the children, great care should be shown. Church-school teachers should be men and women who have a humble estimate of themselves, who are not filled with vain conceit. They should be faithful workers, filled with the true missionary spirit, workers who have learned to put their trust in God and to labor in His name. They should possess the attributes of Christ's character—patience, kindness, mercy, and love; and into the daily experience they should bring the Saviour's righteousness and peace. Then, working with fragrant influence, they will give evidence of what grace can do through human agents who make God their trust.

Let every church school established be conducted with such order that Christ can honor the schoolroom with His presence. The Master will accept no cheap, shoddy service. Let teachers be learners, putting the whole mind to the task of learning how to do efficient service. They should ever carry a burden for souls—not that they themselves can save souls, but as God's helping hand they have the privilege of winning their pupils to Christ.

Teachers, let there be no folly in your conversation. In the schools you undertake to conduct, set a proper example before the children by each morning presenting them to God in prayer. Then look to Him for strength every hour and believe that He is helping you. As you do this you will gain the affection of the children. It is not such hard work to manage children, thank God. We have a Helper, one infinitely stronger than we are. Oh, I am so thankful that we do not have to depend upon ourselves, but upon strength from above!

If your life is hid with Christ in God, a divine Helper will stand beside you, and you will be one with the Saviour and one with those you are teaching. Never exalt self; exalt Christ, glorify Him, honor Him before the world. Say, I stand under the bloodstained banner of Prince Immanuel. I am wholly on the Lord's side. Show sympathy and tenderness in dealing with your pupils. Reveal the love of God. Let the words you speak be kind and encouraging. Then as you work for your students, what a transformation will be wrought in the characters of those who have not been properly trained in the home! The Lord can make even youthful teachers channels for the revealing of His grace, if they will consecrate themselves to Him.

Requiring Obedience

The teacher should bring true self-respect into all that he does. He should not allow himself to be quick-tempered. He should not punish harshly children that are in need of reform. Let him understand that self must be kept in subjection. He should never forget that over him is a divine Teacher, whose pupil he is, and under whose control he is ever to be. As the teacher humbles the heart before God, it will be softened and subdued by the thought of his own shortcomings. He will realize something of the meaning of the words, "You, that were sometime alienated and enemies in your mind by wicked works, yet now hath He reconciled in the body of His flesh through death, to present you holy and unblamable and unreprovable in His sight." Colossians 1:21, 22.

Sometimes there is in the school a disorderly element that makes the work very hard. Children who have not received a right education make much trouble, and by their perversity make the heart of the teacher sad. But let him not become discouraged. Test and trial bring experience. If the children are disobedient and unruly, there is all the more need of strenuous effort. The fact that there are children with such characters is one of the reasons why church schools should be established. The children whom parents have neglected to educate and discipline must be saved if possible.

In the school as well as in the home there should be wise discipline. The teacher must make rules to guide the conduct of his pupils. These rules should be few and well considered, and once made they should be enforced. Every principle involved in them should be so placed before the student that he will be convinced of its justice. Thus he will feel a responsibility to see that the rules which he himself has helped to frame are obeyed.

Parents to Strengthen the Teacher's Hands

The teacher should not be left to carry the burden of his work alone. He needs the sympathy, the kindness, the co-operation, and the love of every church member. The parents should encourage the teacher by showing that they appreciate his efforts. Never should they say or do anything that will encourage insubordination in their children. But I know that many parents do not co-operate with the teacher. They do not foster in the home the good influence exerted in the school. Instead of carrying out in the home the principles of obedience taught in the school, they allow their children to do as they please, to go hither and thither without restraint. And if the teacher exercises authority in requiring obedience, the children carry to their parents an exaggerated, distorted account of the way in which they have been dealt with. The teacher may have done only that which it was his painful duty to do; but the parents sympathize with their children, even though they are in the wrong. And often those parents who themselves rule in anger are the most unreasonable when their children are restrained and disciplined in school.

There are church members who have been quick to catch up unkind suppositions and to speak disparagingly of the teacher before other church members and even in the presence of the children. Some have talked freely and bitterly concerning a teacher without clearly understanding the difficulty of which they were speaking. This should not be. The one who thinks that a teacher has done wrong should follow the directions given in the word: "If thy brother shall trespass against thee, go and tell him his fault between thee and him alone." Matthew 18:15. Until this has been done, no one is justified in telling others of a brother's mistakes.

Parents, when the church-school teacher tries so to train and discipline your children that they may gain eternal life, do not in their presence criticize his actions, even though you may think him too severe. If you desire them to give their hearts to the Saviour, co-operate with the teacher's efforts for their salvation. How much better it is for children, instead of hearing criticism, to hear from the lips of their mother words of commendation regarding the work of the teacher. Such words make lasting impressions and influence the children to respect the teacher.

We are not to concern ourselves so much about the course that others are following, as about the course that we ourselves are following. If the children attending a church school do not improve in manners, the parents should not unduly blame the teacher. Rather they should closely examine themselves to see if they are such teachers as God can approve. In many cases children are greatly neglected in the home and are more disorderly there than they are in the school. If children who for years have been left to follow their own inclinations and desires are not led by the efforts of the teacher to live Christlike lives, shall the parents, because of this, set in circulation unkind criticisms concerning the teacher?

God's method of government is an example of how children are to be trained. There is no oppression in the Lord's service, and there is to be no oppression in the home or in the school. Yet neither parents nor teachers should allow disregard of their word to pass unnoticed. Should they neglect to correct the children for doing wrong, God will hold them accountable for their neglect. But let them be sparing of censure. Let kindness be the law of the home and of the school. Let the children be taught to keep the law of the Lord, and let a firm, loving influence restrain them from evil.

Parents should remember that much more will be

accomplished by the work of the church school if they themselves realize the advantage that their children will obtain in such a school, and unite wholeheartedly with the teacher. By prayer, by patience, by forbearance, parents can undo much of the wrong caused by impatience and unwise indulgence. Let parents and teacher take hold of the work together, the parents remembering that they themselves will be helped by the presence in the community of an earnest, God-fearing teacher.

Parents, make every effort in your power to place your children in the most favorable situation for forming the character that God wants them to form. Use every spiritual sinew and muscle in the effort to save your little flock. The powers of hell will unite for its destruction, but God will lift up for you a standard against the enemy. Pray much more than you do. Lovingly, tenderly, teach your children to come to God as their heavenly Father. By your example teach them self-control and helpfulness. Tell them that Christ lived not to please Himself.

Gather up the rays of divine light that are shining upon your pathway. Walk in the light as Christ is in the light. As you take hold of the work of helping your children to serve God, the most provoking trials will come; but do not lose your hold; cling to Jesus. He says, "Let him take hold of My strength, that he may make peace with Me; and he shall make peace with Me." Isaiah 27:5. Difficulties will arise; you will meet with obstacles; but look constantly to Jesus. When an emergency arises, ask, Lord, what shall I do now? If you refuse to fret or scold, the Lord will show you the way. He will help you to use the talent of speech in so Christlike a way that peace and love will reign in the home. By following a consistent course of action, you may be evangelists in the home, ministers of grace to your children.

A Sympathetic Understanding

The school work in a place where a church school has been established should never be given up unless God plainly directs that this should be done. Adverse influences may seem to conspire against the school, but with God's help the teacher can do a grand, saving work in changing the order of things. If he labors patiently, earnestly, perseveringly, in Christ's lines, the reformatory work done in the school may extend to the homes of the children, bringing into them a purer, more heavenly atmosphere. This is indeed missionary work of the highest order.

If parents faithfully act their part, the work of the teacher will be greatly lightened. His hope and courage will be increased. Parents whose hearts are filled with the love of Christ will refrain from finding fault and will do all in their power to encourage and help the one whom they have chosen as teacher for their children. They will be willing to believe that he is just as conscientious in his work as they are in theirs.

The teachers in the home and the teachers in the school should have a sympathetic understanding of one another's work. They should labor together harmoniously, imbued with the same missionary spirit, striving together to benefit the children physically, mentally, and spiritually, and to develop characters that will stand the test of temptation.

HOME SCHOOLS

As we go forward in establishing church schools we shall find a work to be done for the children in places where it has been thought a school could not be maintained. As far as possible, all our children should have the privilege of a Christian education. To provide this we must sometimes establish home church schools. It would be well if several families in a neighborhood would unite to employ a humble, God-fearing teacher to give to the parents that help that is needed in educating their children. This will be a great blessing to many isolated groups of Sabbathkeepers, and a plan more pleasing to the Lord than that which has been sometimes followed, of sending young children away from their homes to attend one of our larger schools.

Our small companies of Sabbathkeepers are needed to hold up the light before their neighbors; and the children are needed in their homes, where they may be a help to their parents when the hours of study are ended. The well-ordered Christian home, where young children can have parental discipline that is after the Lord's order, is the best place for them.

The tender years of childhood are years of heavy responsibility for fathers and mothers. Parents have a sacred duty to perform in teaching their children to help bear the burdens of the home, to be content with plain, simple food, and neat, inexpensive dress. The requirements of the parents should always be reasonable; kindness should be expressed, not by foolish indulgence, but by wise direction. Parents are to teach their children pleasantly, without scolding or faultfinding, seeking to bind the hearts of the little ones to them by silken cords of love. Let all, fathers and mothers, teachers, elder brothers and sisters, become an educating force to strengthen every spiritual interest and to bring into the home and the school life a wholesome atmosphere, which will help the younger children to grow up in the nurture and admonition of the Lord.

Bible Study in the Home

Our children are the Lord's property; they have been bought with a price. This thought should be the mainspring of our labors for them. The most successful method of securing their salvation and of keeping them out of the way of temptation is to instruct them constantly in the word of God. And as parents become learners with their children, they will find their own growth in grace and in a knowledge of the truth more rapid. Unbelief will disappear; faith and activity will increase; assurance and confidence will deepen as they thus follow on to know the Lord. Their prayers will undergo a transformation, becoming more earnest and sincere. Christ is the head of His church, the unfailing dependence of His people; He will give the needed grace to those who seek Him for wisdom and instruction.

God would have us consider these things in their sacred importance. It is the privilege of brothers and sisters and parents to co-operate in teaching the children how to drink the gladness of Christ's life by learning to follow His example. To the older children in these isolated families I will say: It is not necessary that all should drop the home responsibilities to attend our boarding schools, in order to obtain a fitting for service. Remember that right in the home there is a work to do for the Master. In the home there are younger children to be instructed, and thus relieve the mother's burdens.

Let the elder members of the family bear in mind that this part of the Lord's vineyard needs to be faithfully cultivated, and resolve that they will put forth their best capabilities to make home attractive and to deal patiently and wisely with the younger children. There are young persons in our homes whom the Lord has qualified to give to others the knowledge they have gained. Let these strive to keep spiritual lessons fresh in mind. And while they are teaching they can also be studying. Thus they may be learners while teaching. New ideas will come to them, and the hours of study will be a decided pleasure as well as profit.

Missionary Agencies

I speak to fathers and mothers: You can be educators in your homes; you can be spiritual missionary agencies. Let fathers and mothers feel their need of being home missionaries, the need of keeping the atmosphere of the home free from the influence of unkind and hasty speech, the need of making the home a place where angels of God can come in and bless and give success to the efforts put forth.

Let parents unite in providing a place for the daily instruction of their children, choosing as teacher one who is apt to teach, and who, as a consecrated servant of

Christ, will increase in knowledge while imparting instruction. The teacher who has consecrated herself to the service of God will be able to do a definite work in missionary service and will instruct the children in the same lines.

Let fathers and mothers co-operate with the teacher, laboring earnestly for the salvation of their children. If parents will realize the importance of these small educating centers, co-operating to do the work that the Lord desires to have done at this time, the plans of the enemy for our children will be largely frustrated.

"Train up a child in the way he should go: and when he is old, he will not depart from it." Proverbs 22:6. Children are sometimes tempted to chafe under restraint; but in afterlife they will bless their parents for the faithful care and strict watchfulness that guarded and guided them in their years of inexperience.

By hasty, unfounded criticism the influence of the faithful, self-sacrificing teacher is often well-nigh destroyed. Many parents whose children have been spoiled by indulgence leave to the teacher the unpleasant task of repairing their neglect; and then by their own course they make his task almost hopeless. Their criticism and censure of the school management encourage insubordination in the children and confirm them in wrong habits.

If criticism or suggestion in regard to the teacher's work becomes necessary, it should be made to him in private. If this proves ineffective, let the matter be referred to those who are responsible for the management of the school. Nothing should be said or done to weaken the children's respect for the one upon whom their well-being in so great degree depends.—*Education,* page 284.

Parents should keep ever before their minds the object to be gained—the perfection of the characters of their children. Those parents who educate their children aright, weeding from their lives every unruly trait, are fitting them to become missionaries for Christ in truth, in righteousness, in holiness. He who in his childhood does service for God, adding to his "faith virtue; and to virtue knowledge; and to knowledge temperance; and to temperance patience; and to patience godliness; and to godliness brotherly kindness; and to brotherly kindness charity" (2 Peter 1:5-7), is fitting himself to hear and to respond to the call, "Child, come up higher; enter the higher school."

Do you think we shall not learn anything there? We have not the slightest idea of what will then be opened before us. With Christ we shall walk beside the living waters. He will unfold to us the beauty and glory of nature. He will reveal what He is to us, and what we are to Him. Truth we cannot know now, because of finite limitations, we shall know hereafter.

Neither the church school nor the college affords the opportunities for establishing a child's character building upon the right foundation that are afforded in the home.

FOR FURTHER STUDY

THE CHILD'S FIRST SCHOOL

Acts of the Apostles, The, pp. 203-205.
Adventist Home, The, pp. 15-28, 177-186, 190-199.
Child Guidance, pp. 17-28.
Desire of Ages, The, pp. 511-517.
Ministry of Healing, The, pp. 349-394.
Messages to Young People, pp. 329-334.
Patriarchs and Prophets, pp. 140-144, 260, 560-562, 574-580.
Testimonies, vol. 1, pp. 384-405.
    vol. 3, pp. 532, 533.
    vol. 4, pp. 197-213.
    vol. 5, pp. 36-45, 319-331, 423, 424.
    vol. 6, pp. 93, 94.
    vol. 7, pp. 47, 48.

SAFEGUARDING THE YOUNG

Adventist Home, The, pp. 401-409.
Patriarchs and Prophets, pp. 168, 169.
Testimonies, vol. 1, pp. 156, 157, 216-220, 390-405, 546, 547.
    vol. 3, pp. 560-570.
    vol. 4, pp. 134-143.
    vol. 7, pp. 17, 27, 63.

WHAT SHALL OUR CHILDREN READ?

Adventist Home, The, pp. 410-418.
Education, p. 227
Fundamentals of Christian Education, pp. 92-94, 167-173, 381-389.
Messages to Young People, pp. 271-282, 290.
Patriarchs and Prophets, p. 504.
Testimonies, vol. 1, pp. 125, 126, 134, 135, 504.
    vol. 2, pp. 236, 410.
    vol. 4, pp. 497-499.
    vol. 5, pp. 516-520.
    vol. 7, pp. 164-166.

THE PARABLE OF THE GROWING SEED

Adventist Home, The, pp. 200-203.

TEACHING LESSONS OF HELPFULNESS

Adventist Home, The, pp. 282-290.
Child Guidance, pp. 119-121.
Testimonies, vol. 1, pp. 393-395.
    vol. 2, pp. 182, 369-371.
    vol. 4, pp. 96-98.

CO-OPERATION BETWEEN THE HOME AND THE SCHOOL

Child Guidance, pp. 300-302, 318, 327.
Education, pp. 283-286.
Fundamentals of Christian Education, pp. 64-70.

HOME SCHOOLS

Fundamentals of Christian Education, pp. 149-161.

THE CHURCH SCHOOL

"Where is the flock that was given thee, thy beautiful flock?"

OUR RESPONSIBILITY

Nothing is of greater importance than the education of our children and young people. The church should arouse and manifest a deep interest in this work; for now as never before, Satan and his host are determined to enlist the youth under the black banner that leads to ruin and death.

God has appointed the church as a watchman, to have a jealous care over the youth and children, and as a sentinel to see the approach of the enemy and give warning of danger. But the church does not realize the situation. She is sleeping on guard. In this time of peril, fathers and mothers must arouse and work as for life, or many of the youth will be forever lost.

While we should put forth earnest efforts for the masses of the people around us, and push the work into foreign fields, no amount of labor in this line can excuse us for neglecting the education of our children and youth. They are to be trained to become workers for God. Both parents and teachers, by precept and example, are so to instill the principles of truth and honesty into the minds and hearts of the young that they will become men and women who are as true as steel to God and His cause.

Parents and teachers do not estimate the magnitude of the work given them in training the young. The experience of the children of Israel was written for us "upon whom the ends of the world are come." 1 Corinthians 10:11. As in their day, so now the Lord would have the children gathered out from those schools where worldly influences prevail, and placed in our own schools, where the word of God is made the foundation of education.

If ever we are to work in earnest, it is now. The enemy is pressing in on all sides, like a flood. Only the power of God can save our children from being swept away by the tide of evil. The responsibility resting upon parents, teachers, and church members, to do their part in co-operation with God, is greater than words can express.

To train the young to become true soldiers of the Lord Jesus Christ is the most noble work ever given to man. Only devout and consecrated men and women, who love children and can see in them souls to be saved for the Master, should be chosen as church-school teachers. Teachers who study the word of God as it should be studied will know something of the value of the souls under their care, and from them the children will receive a true Christian education.

In the closing scenes of this earth's history many of these children and youth will astonish people by their witness to the truth, which will be borne in simplicity, yet with spirit and power. They have been taught the fear of the Lord, and their hearts have been softened by a careful and prayerful study of the Bible. In the near future many children will be endued with the Spirit of God, and will do a work in proclaiming the truth to the world, that at that time cannot well be done by the older members of the church.

The Lord would use the church school as an aid to the parents in educating and preparing their children for this time before us. Then let the church take hold of the school work in earnest and make it what the Lord desires it to be.

We cannot afford to separate spiritual from intellectual training. Well may parents dread intellectual greatness for their children, unless it is balanced by a knowledge of God and His ways. This lies at the foundation of all true knowledge. In the place of unsanctified rivalry for earthly honor, let it be the highest ambition of our students to go forth from their school life as missionaries for God, educators who will teach what they have learned. Students who leave school with this purpose will draw to Christ not only men and women, but children and youth. They will do a work in the world that not all the powers of evil can counteract.

Teachers, awake to your responsibilities, your privileges. Well may you inquire, Who is sufficient for these things? "My grace is sufficient for thee" (2 Corinthians 12:9) is the assurance of the Great Teacher. If you leave Him out of the question, seeking not His aid, hopeless indeed is your task. But in His wisdom and strength you may nobly succeed.

THE WORK TO BE DONE FOR OUR CHILDREN

I have been pointed to the churches that are scattered in different localities, and have been shown that the strength of these churches depends upon their growth in usefulness and efficiency. . . . In all our churches there should be schools, and teachers in these schools who are missionaries. It is essential that teachers be trained to act well their part in the important work of educating the children of Sabbathkeepers, not only in the sciences, but in the Scriptures. These schools, established in different localities, and conducted by God-fearing men or women, as the case demands, should be built on the same principles as were the schools of the prophets.

Special care should be given to the education of the youth. The children are to be trained to become missionaries; they must be helped to understand distinctly what they must do to be saved. Few have the instruction in religious lines that is essential. If the instructors have a religious experience themselves, they will be able to communicate to their students the knowledge of the love of God that they have received. These lessons can be given only by those who are themselves truly converted. This is the noblest missionary work that any man or woman can undertake.

When very young, children should be educated to read, to write, to understand figures, to keep their own accounts. They may go forward, advancing step by step in this knowledge. But before everything else, they should be taught that the fear of the Lord is the beginning of wisdom. They should be educated line upon line, precept upon precept, here a little and there a little; but the one aim before the teacher should be to educate the children to know God, and Jesus Christ whom He has sent.

Teach the youth that sin in any line is defined in the Scriptures as "transgression of the law." 1 John 3:4. . . . Teach them in simple language that they must be obedient to their parents and give their hearts to God. Jesus Christ is waiting to accept and bless them if they will only come to Him and ask Him to pardon all their transgressions and take away their sins. And when they ask Him to pardon all their transgressions they must believe that He does it.

God wants every child of tender age to be His child, to be adopted into His family. Young though they may be, the youth may be members of the household of faith and have a most precious experience. They may have hearts that are tender and ready to receive impressions that will be lasting. They may have their hearts drawn out in confidence and love for Jesus, and live for the Saviour. Christ will make them little missionaries. The whole current of their thought may be changed, so that sin will not appear a thing to be enjoyed, but to be shunned and hated.

Small children, as well as those who are older, will be benefited by this instruction; and in thus simplifying the plan of salvation, the teachers will receive as great blessings as those who are taught. The Holy Spirit of God will impress the lessons upon the receptive minds of the children, that they may grasp the ideas of Bible truth in their simplicity. And the Lord will give an experience to these children in missionary lines; He will suggest to them lines of thought that even the teachers did not have. The children who are properly instructed will be witnesses to the truth.

Teachers who are nervous and easily irritated should not be placed over the youth. They must love the children because they are the younger members of the Lord's family. The Lord will inquire of them, as of the parents, "Where is the flock that was given thee, thy beautiful flock?" Jeremiah 13:20. . . .

In educating the children and youth, teachers should not allow one passionate word or gesture to mar their work, for in so doing they imbue the students with the same spirit which they themselves possess. The Lord would have our primary schools, as well as those for older students, of that character that angels of God can walk through the room, and behold, in the order and principle of government, the order and government of heaven. This is thought by many to be impossible; but every school should begin with this, and work most earnestly to preserve the spirit of Christ in temper, in communications, in instruction, the teachers placing themselves in the channel of light where the Lord can use them as His agents to reflect His own likeness of character. The teachers may know that, as God-fearing instructors, they have helpers every hour to impress upon the hearts of the children the valuable lessons given.

The Lord works with every consecrated teacher; and it is for the teacher's own interest for him to realize this. Instructors who are under the discipline of God receive grace and truth and light through the Holy Spirit to communicate to the children. They are under the greatest Teacher the world has ever known, and how unbecoming it would be for them to have an unkind spirit, a sharp voice, full of irritation! In this they would perpetuate their own defects in the children.

Oh, for a clear perception of what we might accomplish if we would learn of Jesus! The springs of heavenly peace and joy, unsealed in the soul of the teacher by the magic words of Inspiration, will become a mighty river of influence, to bless all who connect with him.

Do not think that the Bible will become a tiresome book to the children. Under a wise instructor the word will become more and more desirable. It will be to them as the bread of life, it will never grow old. There is in it a freshness and beauty that attract and charm the children and youth. It is like the sun shining upon the earth, giving its brightness and warmth, yet never exhausted. By lessons from Bible history and doctrine, the children and youth can learn that all other books are inferior to this. They can find here a fountain of mercy and love.

God's holy, educating Spirit is in His word. A light, a new and precious light, shines forth from every page. Truth is there revealed, and words and sentences are made bright and appropriate for the occasion, as the voice of God speaking to them.

We need to recognize the Holy Spirit as our enlightener. That Spirit loves to address the children and discover to them the treasures and beauties of the word. The promises spoken by the Great Teacher will captivate the senses and animate the soul of the child with a spiritual power that is divine. There will grow in the receptive mind a familiarity with divine things which will be as a barricade against the temptations of the enemy.

The work of teachers is an important one. They should make the word of God their meditation. God will communicate by His own Spirit with the soul. Pray as you study, "Open Thou mine eyes, that I may behold wondrous things out of Thy law." Psalm 119:18. When the teacher will rely upon God in prayer, the Spirit of Christ will come upon him, and God will work through him by the Holy Spirit upon the mind of the student. The Holy Spirit fills mind and heart with hope and courage and Bible imagery, which will be communicated to the student. The words of truth will grow in importance, and will assume a breadth and fullness of meaning of which he has never dreamed. The beauty and virtue of the word of God have a transforming influence upon mind and character; the sparks of heavenly love will fall upon the hearts of the children as an inspiration. We may bring hundreds and thousands of children to Christ if we will work for them.—*Special Testimony to the Battle Creek Church;* written at Cooranbong, N.S.W., Australia, Dec. 15, 1897.

THE WORK OF THE CHURCH SCHOOL

The church has a special work to do in educating and training its children that they may not, in attending school or in any other association, be influenced by those of corrupt habits. The world is full of iniquity and disregard of the requirements of God. The cities have become as Sodom, and our children are daily exposed to many evils. Those who attend the public schools often associate with others more neglected than they, those who, aside from the time spent in the schoolroom, are left to obtain a street education. The hearts of the young are easily impressed; and unless their surroundings are of the right character, Satan will use these neglected children to influence those who are more carefully trained. Thus, before Sabbathkeeping parents know what is being done, the lessons of depravity are learned, and the souls of their little ones are corrupted. . . .

Church Schools Needed

Many families, who, for the purpose of educating their children, move to places where our large schools are established, would do better service for the Master by remaining where they are. They should encourage the church of which they are members to establish a church school where the children within their borders could receive an all-round, practical Christian education. It would be vastly better for their children, for themselves, and for the cause of God, if they would remain in the smaller churches, where their help is needed, instead of going to the larger churches, where, because they are not needed, there is a constant temptation to fall into spiritual inactivity.

Wherever there are a few Sabbathkeepers, the parents should unite in providing a place for a day school where their children and youth can be instructed. They should employ a Christian teacher, who, as a consecrated missionary, shall educate the children in such a way as to lead them to become missionaries. . . .

The Character of Church Schools and of Their Teachers

The character of the work done in our church schools should be of the very highest order. Jesus Christ, the Restorer, is the only remedy for a wrong education, and the lessons taught in His word should ever be kept before the youth in the most attractive form. The school discipline should supplement the home training, and both at home and at school simplicity and godliness should be maintained. Men and women will be found who have talent to work in these small schools, but who cannot work to advantage in the larger ones. As they practice the Bible lessons, they will themselves receive an education of the highest value.

In selecting teachers, we should use every precaution, knowing that this is as solemn a matter as the selecting of persons for the ministry. Wise men who can discern character should make the selection; for the very best talent that can be secured is needed to educate and mold the minds of the young, and to carry on successfully the many lines of work that will need to be done by the teachers in our church schools. No person of an inferior or narrow cast of mind should be placed in charge of one of these schools. Do not place over the children young, inexperienced teachers who have no managing ability; for their efforts will tend to disorganization. Order is heaven's first law, and every school should in this respect be a model of heaven.

To place over young children, teachers who are proud and unloving is wicked. A teacher of this stamp will do great harm to those who are rapidly developing character. If teachers are not submissive to God, if they have no love for the children over whom they preside, or if they show partiality for those who please their fancy, and manifest indifference to those who are less attractive, or to those who are restless and nervous, they should not be employed; for the result of their work will be a loss of souls for Christ.

Teachers are needed, especially for the children, who are calm and kind, manifesting forbearance and love for the very ones who most need it. Jesus loved the children. . . . He always treated them with kindness and respect, and teachers are to follow His example. They should have the true missionary spirit; for the children are to be trained to become missionaries.

Our church schools need teachers who have high moral qualities; those who can be trusted; those who are sound in the faith and who have tact and patience; those who walk with God and abstain from the very appearance of evil. . . .

Results of Church-School Work

When properly conducted, church schools will be the means of lifting the standard of truth in the places where they are established; for children who are receiving a Christian education will be witnesses for Christ. As Jesus in the temple solved mysteries which priests and rulers had not discerned, so in the closing work of this earth, children who have been rightly educated will in their simplicity speak words which will be an astonishment to men who now talk of "higher education."

As the children sang in the temple courts, "Hosanna; Blessed is He that cometh in the name of the Lord" (Mark 11:9), so in these last days children's voices will be raised to give the last message of warning to a perishing world. When heavenly intelligences see that men are no longer permitted to present the truth, the Spirit of God will come upon the children, and they will do a work in the proclamation of the truth which the older workers cannot do because their way will be hedged up.

Our church schools are ordained by God to prepare the children for this great work. Here children are to be instructed in the special truths for this time, and in practical missionary work. They are to enlist in the army of workers to help the sick and the suffering. Children can take part in the medical missionary work and by their jots and tittles can help to carry it forward. Their investments may be small, but every little helps, and by their efforts many souls will be won to the truth. By them God's message will be made known and His saving health to all nations. Then let the church carry a burden for the lambs of the flock. Let the children be educated and trained to do service for God, for they are the Lord's heritage.—*Testimonies for the Church,* vol. 6, pp. 193-203.

The system of grading is sometimes a hindrance to the pupil's real progress. Some pupils are slow at first, and the teacher of these youth needs to exercise great patience. But these pupils may after a short time learn so rapidly as to astonish him. Others may appear to be very brilliant, but time may show that they have blossomed too suddenly. The system of confining children rigidly to grades is not wise.

The importance of the teacher's physical qualifications can hardly be overestimated; for the more perfect his health, the more perfect will be his labor. The mind cannot be clear to think and strong to act when the physical powers are suffering the results of feebleness or disease. The heart is impressed through the mind; but if, because of physical inability, the mind loses its vigor, the channel to the higher feelings and motives is to that extent obstructed, and the teacher is less able to discriminate between right and wrong. When suffering the results of ill health, it is not an easy matter to be patient and cheerful, or to act with integrity and justice.

CHRIST AS THE EXAMPLE AND TEACHER
OF YOUTH

The example of Jesus is a light to the young, as well as to those of more mature years, for His was a representative childhood and youth. From His earliest years His example was perfect. As a little child He was obedient to His parents and to the laws of nature, "and the grace of God was upon Him." Luke 2:40.

Jesus did not, like many youth, devote His time to amusement. He studied the word until He became familiar with its sayings. Even in His childhood His life and all His habits were in harmony with the Scriptures, and He was skillful in their use. . . . Besides the written word, Jesus studied the book of nature, finding delight in the beautiful things of His own creation. He was in sympathy with humanity in all its varied joys and sorrows. He identified Himself with all—with the weak and helpless, the lowly, the needy, and the afflicted.

In His teaching, Christ drew His illustrations from the great treasury of household ties and affections, and from nature. The unknown was illustrated by the known; sacred and divine truths, by natural, earthly things, with which the people were most familiar. These were the things that would speak to their hearts, and make the deepest impression on their minds.

The words of Christ placed the teachings of nature in a new aspect and made them a new revelation. He could speak of the things which His own hands had made, for they had qualities and properties that were peculiarly His own. In nature, as in the sacred pages of the Old Testament Scriptures, divine, momentous truths are revealed; and in His teaching, Jesus laid these open before the people, bound up with the beauty of natural things. . . .

As interpreted by Jesus, flower and shrub, the seed sown and the seed harvested, contained lessons of truth, as did also the plant that springs out of the earth. He plucked the beautiful lily and placed it in the hands of children and youth, and as they looked into His own youthful face, fresh with the sunlight of His Father's countenance, He gave the lesson, "consider the lilies of the field, how they grow [in the simplicity of natural beauty and loveliness]; they toil not, neither do they spin: and yet I say unto you, That even Solomon in all his glory was not arrayed like one of these." Then followed the assurance, "Wherefore, if God so clothe the grass of the field, which today is, and tomorrow is cast into the oven, shall He not much more clothe you, O ye of little faith?" Matthew 6:28-30. . . .

In His work as a public teacher, Christ never lost sight of the children. When wearied with the bustle and confusion of the crowded city, tired of contact with crafty and hypocritical men, His spirit found rest and peace in the society of innocent little children. His presence never repelled them. His large heart of love could comprehend their trials and necessities, and find happiness in their simple joys; and He took them in His arms and blessed them.

In these children who were brought in contact with Him, Jesus saw the future men and women who should be heirs of His grace and subjects of His kingdom, and some of whom would become martyrs for His sake. He knew that these children would listen to Him and accept Him as their Redeemer far more readily than would the grown people, many of whom were worldly-wise and hardhearted. In His teaching He came down to their level. He, the Majesty of heaven, did not disdain to answer their questions and simplify His important lessons to meet their childish understanding. He planted in their expanding minds the seeds of truth, which in after years would spring up and bear fruit unto eternal life.

Parents and teachers, Jesus is still saying, "Suffer little children, and forbid them not, to come unto Me." Matthew 19:14. They are the most susceptible to the teachings of Christianity; their hearts are open to influences of piety and virtue, and strong to retain the impressions received. —*Special Testimonies on Education,* pages 62-66; written May 17, 1896.

To develop the minds and hearts of the youth, and not hinder their growth by an unwarranted control of one mind over another, requires tact and understanding. Teachers are needed who are able to deal wisely with the different phases of character; who are quick to see and to make the most of opportunities to do good; who possess enthusiasm, who are "apt to teach;" and who can inspire thought, quicken energy, and impart courage.

THE BIBLE LESSON

In all that men have written, where can be found anything that has such a hold upon the heart, anything so well adapted to awaken the interest of the little ones, as the stories of the Bible? In these simple stories may be made plain the great principles of the law of God. Thus by illustrations best suited to the child's comprehension, parents and teachers may begin very early to fulfill the Lord's injunction concerning His precepts: "Thou shalt teach them diligently unto thy children, and shalt talk of them when thou sittest in thine house, and when thou walkest by the way, and when thou liest down, and when thou risest up." Deuteronomy 6:7.

The use of object lessons, blackboards, and maps will be an aid in explaining these lessons and fixing them in the memory. Parents and teachers should constantly seek for improved methods. The teaching of the Bible should have our freshest thought, our best methods, and our most earnest effort.

In order to do effective study, the interest of the child must be enlisted. Especially by the one who has to do with children and youth differing widely in disposition, training, and habits of thought, this is a matter not to be lost sight of. In teaching children the Bible, we may gain much by observing the bent of their minds, the things in which they are interested, and by arousing their interest to see what the Bible says about these things. He who created us with our various aptitudes has in His word given something for everyone. As the pupils see that the lessons of the Bible apply to their own lives, teach them to look to it as a counselor.

Help them also to appreciate its wonderful beauty. Many books of no value, books that are exciting and unhealthful, are recommended, or at least permitted to be used, because of their supposed literary value. Why should we direct our children to drink of these polluted streams, when they may have free access to the pure fountains of the word of God? The Bible has a fullness, a strength, a depth of meaning, that is inexhaustible. Encourage the children and youth to seek out its treasures, both of thought and of expression.

As the beauty of these precious things attracts their minds, a softening, subduing power will touch their hearts. They will be drawn to Him who has thus revealed Himself to them. And there are few who will not desire to know more of His works and ways.

The Victory of Faith

There is much to be learned by the children and youth in regard to early piety. "This is the victory that overcometh the world, even our faith." 1 John 5:4. That faith must not be led to embrace superstitious, fictitious sentiments. Leave out such ideas from your teaching, and give the children and youth the same kind of instruction that Christ gave—lessons of faith in a plain "Thus saith the Lord."

The work of conquering evil is to be done through faith. Those who go into the battlefield will find that they must put on the whole armor of God. The shield of faith will be their defense and will enable them to be more than conquerors. Nothing else will avail but this—faith in the Lord of hosts, and obedience to His orders. Vast armies furnished with every other facility will avail nothing in the last great conflict. Without faith, an angel host could not help. Living faith alone will make them invincible and enable them to stand in the evil day, steadfast, unmovable, holding the beginning of their confidence firm unto the end.

Young men and women who do not give evidence that the truth has begun its sanctifying work upon their hearts will make a failure in attempting to teach any church school. None are to choose the easiest place and seek to understand only that which pleases of the word of God, obeying those things which harmonize with their desires, and excusing themselves from accepting that which cuts across inclination and calls for self-denial and cross-bearing. Especially should teachers of the children and youth be learners of the way of obedience. True faith asks the Lord, "What wilt Thou have me to do?" and when the way is marked out by the Master, faith is ready to do His will, at whatever hardship or sacrifice.

Teachers, study the simplicity of the Scriptures, so that you may learn to make their truths plain to youthful minds. Your earnest desire for the present and eternal good of the children under your care should bring you often to your knees to seek counsel of Him who is too wise to err, too good to leave you in the helplessness of your own wisdom.

Bible instruction is to be made forcible by the holy life of the teacher. God-fearing teachers will practice every principle they seek to imprint on the minds of the children. Such teachers do not see their heavenly Father except by the eye of faith; but they have learned of Him; they read His love in the most trying dispensations. They do not judge their Creator by dispensations; they are partakers of His divine nature. They can trust Him who withheld not His only-begotten Son, knowing that with Him He will give all things for their spiritual and eternal good.

If the teacher has learned his lessons from Jesus Christ, and has learned for the purpose of bringing these lessons fully into his own life, he can teach successfully. Those who are daily learners of the Great Teacher will have a most precious treasure house from which to draw things new and old.

To church-school teachers I would say: Know that you are controlled by the Holy Spirit. Reveal in your lives the transforming influence of the truth. Do your utmost to improve your own capabilities, that you may teach your students how to make improvement.

As soon as your minds harmonize with the mind of God, you will be brought into touch with an intelligence that will communicate to you lessons that will be of invaluable help in your work of teaching. As you tell the children the story of the cross, your own souls will be lifted above gloom and despondencey. In considering the Redeemer's infinite sacrifice, you will lose all desire for the things of this world.

TEACHING FROM NATURE

While the Bible should hold the first place in the education of children and youth, the book of nature is next in importance. God's created works testify to His love and power. He has called the world into being, with all that it contains. God is a lover of the beautiful; and in the world which He has fitted up for us He has not only given us everything necessary for our comfort, but He has filled the heavens and the earth with beauty. We see His love and care in the rich fields of autumn, and His smile in the glad sunshine. His hand has made the castle-like rocks and the towering mountains. The lofty trees grow at His command; He has spread earth's green velvet carpet and dotted it with shrubs and flowers.

Why has He clothed the earth and trees with living green, instead of with dark, somber brown? Is it not that they may be more pleasing to the eye? And shall not our hearts be filled with gratitude as we read the evidences of His wisdom and love in the wonders of His creation?

The same creative energy that brought the world into existence is still exerted in upholding the universe and continuing the operations of nature. The hand of God guides the planets in their orderly march through the heavens. It is not because of inherent power that year by year the earth continues her motion round the sun and produces her bounties. The word of God controls the elements. He covers the heavens with clouds and prepares rain for the earth. He makes the valleys fruitful and "grass to grow upon the mountains." Psalm 147:8.

It is through His power that vegetation flourishes, that the leaves appear and the flowers bloom.

The whole natural world is designed to be an interpreter of the things of God. To Adam and Eve in their Eden home, nature was full of the knowledge of God, teeming with divine instruction. To their attentive ears it was vocal with the voice of wisdom. Wisdom spoke to the eye and was received into the heart, for they communed with God in His created works. As soon as the holy pair transgressed the law of the Most High, the brightness from the face of God departed from the face of nature. Nature is now marred and defiled by sin. But God's object lessons are not obliterated; even now, rightly studied and interpreted, she speaks of her Creator. . . .

The most effective way to teach the heathen who know not God is through His works. In this way, far more readily than by any other method, they can be made to realize the difference between their idols, the works of their own hands, and the true God, the Maker of heaven and earth. . . . There is a simplicity and purity in these lessons direct from nature that makes them of the highest value to others besides the heathen. The children and youth, all classes of students, need the lessons to be derived from this source. In itself the beauty of nature leads the soul away from sin and worldly attractions, and toward purity, peace, and God.

For this reason the cultivation of the soil is good work for children and youth. It brings them into direct contact with nature and nature's God. And that they may have this advantage, there should be, as far as possible, in connection with our schools, large flower gardens and extensive lands for cultivation.

An education amid such surroundings is in accordance with the directions which God has given for the instruction of youth; but it is in direct contrast with the methods employed in the majority of schools. . . . The minds of the young have been occupied with books of science and philosophy, where the thorns of skepticism have been only partially concealed; with vague, fanciful fairy stories; or with the works of authors who, although they may write on Scripture subjects, weave in their own fanciful interpretations. The teaching of such books is as seed sown in the heart. It grows and bears fruit, and a plentiful harvest of infidelity is reaped. The result is seen in the depravity of the human family.

A return to simpler methods will be appreciated by the children and youth. Work in the garden and field will be an agreeable change from the wearisome routine of abstract lessons to which the young minds should never be confined. To the nervous child or youth, who finds lessons from books exhausting and hard to remember, it will be especially valuable. There is health and happiness for him in the study of nature; and the impressions made will not fade out of his mind, for they will be associated with objects that are continually before his eyes.

In the natural world, God has placed in the hands of the children of men the key to unlock the treasure house of His word. The unseen is illustrated by the seen; divine wisdom, eternal truth, infinite grace, are understood by the things that God has made. Then let the children and youth become acquainted with nature and nature's laws. Let the mind be developed to its utmost capacity and the physical powers trained for the practical duties of life. But teach them also that God has made this world fair because He delights in our happiness; and that a more beautiful home is preparing for us in that world where there will be no more sin. The word of God declares: "Eye hath not seen, nor ear heard, neither have entered into the heart of man, the things which God hath prepared for them that love Him." 1 Corinthians 2:9.

The little children should come especially close to nature. Instead of putting fashion's shackles upon them, let them be free like the lambs to play in the sweet, fresh sunlight. Point them to shrubs and flowers, the lowly grass and the lofty trees, and let them become familiar with their beautiful, varied, and delicate forms. Teach them to see the wisdom and love of God in His created works; and as their hearts swell with joy and grateful love, let them join the birds in their songs of praise.

Educate the children and youth to consider the works of the great Master Artist, and to imitate the attractive graces of nature in their character building. As the love of God wins their hearts, let them bring into their lives the beauty of holiness. So shall they use their capabilities to bless others and to honor God.—*Special Testimonies on Education,* pages 58-62; written May 20, 1896.

Nature is full of lessons of the love of God. Rightly understood, these lessons lead to the Creator. They point from nature to nature's God, teaching those simple, holy truths that cleanse the mind and bring it into close touch with God.

The Great Teacher calls on nature to reflect the light that floods the threshold of heaven, that men and women may be led to obey His word. And nature does the bidding of the Creator. To the heart softened by the grace of God, the sun, the moon, the stars, the lofty trees, the flowers of the field, utter their words of counsel and advice. The sowing of the seed carries the mind to spiritual seed sowing. The tree stands forth declaring that a good tree cannot bear evil fruit, neither can an evil tree bear good fruit. "Ye shall know them by their fruits." Matthew 7:16. Even the tares have a lesson to teach. They are of Satan's sowing, and if left unchecked, will spoil the wheat by their rank growth.

When man is reconciled to God, the things of nature speak to him in words of heavenly wisdom, bearing testimony to the eternal truth of God's word. As Christ tells us the meaning of the things in nature, the science of true religion flashes forth, explaining the relation of the law of God to the natural and the spiritual world.

The swallow and the crane observe the changes of the seasons. They migrate from one country to another to find a climate suitable to their convenience and happiness, as the Lord designed they should. They are obedient to the laws which govern their life. But the beings formed in the image of God fail to honor Him by obeying the laws of nature. By disregarding the laws that govern the human organism, they disqualify themselves for serving

God. He sends them warnings to beware how they break His law in breaking the laws of life; but habit is strong, and they will not heed. The days are filled with pain of body and disquietude of mind because they are determined to follow wrong habits and practices. They will not reason from cause to effect, and they sacrifice health, peace, and happiness to their ignorance and selfishness.

The wise man addresses the indolent in the words: "Go to the ant, thou sluggard; consider her ways, and be wise: which having no guide, overseer, or ruler, provideth her meat in the summer, and gathereth her food in the harvest." Proverbs 6:6-8. The habitations that the ants build for themselves show skill and perseverance. Only one little grain at a time can they handle, but by diligence and perseverance they accomplish wonders.

Solomon points to the industry of the ant as a reproach to those who waste their hours in idleness or in practices that corrupt soul and body. The ant prepares for future seasons; but many gifted with reasoning powers fail to prepare for the future immortal life.

———

The sun, the moon, the stars, the solid rocks, the flowing stream, the broad, restless ocean, teach lessons that all would do well to heed.

UNDER DISCIPLINE TO CHRIST

Every teacher who has to do with the education of young students should remember that children are affected by the atmosphere that surrounds the teacher, whether it be pleasant or unpleasant. If the teacher is connected with God, if Christ abides in his heart, the spirit that is cherished by him will be felt by the children. If teachers enter the schoolroom with a provoked, irritated spirit, the atmosphere surrounding their souls will also leave its impression.

The teachers who work in this part of the Lord's vineyard need to be self-possessed, to keep their temper and feelings under control, and in subjection to the Holy Spirit. They should give evidence of having, not a one-sided experience, but a well-balanced mind, a symmetrical character. Learning daily in the school of Christ, such teachers can wisely educate the children and youth. Self-cultured, self-controlled, under discipline to Christ, having a living connection with the Great Teacher, they will have an intelligent knowledge of practical religion; and keeping their own souls in the love of God, they will know how to exercise the grace of patience and Christlike forbearance. They will discern that they have a most important field in the Lord's vineyard to cultivate. They will lift the heart to God in the sincere prayer, "Lord, be Thou my pattern;" and then, beholding Christ, they will do the work of Christ.

Well-balanced minds and symmetrical characters are

required of teachers in every line. The work of teaching should not be given into the hands of young men and women who do not know how to deal with human minds, who have never learned to keep themselves under discipline to Jesus Christ, to bring even the thoughts into captivity to Him. They know so little about the controlling power of grace upon their own hearts and characters that they have much to unlearn, and must learn entirely new lessons in Christian experience.

There are all kinds of characters to deal with in the children and youth, and their minds are impressionable. Many of the children who attend our schools have not had proper training at home. Some have been left to do as they pleased; others have been found fault with and discouraged. Very little pleasantness and cheerfulness have been shown them; few words of approval have been spoken to them. They have inherited the defective characters of their parents, and the discipline of the home has been no help in the formation of right character. To place as teachers of these children and youth, young men and women who have not developed a deep, earnest love for God and for the souls for whom Christ has died, is to make a mistake that may result in the loss of many souls. Those who easily become impatient and irritated should not be educators.

Teachers should remember that they are not dealing with men and women, but with children who have everything to learn. And it is much more difficult for some to learn than for others. The dull pupil needs much more encouragement than he receives. If there are placed over these varied minds teachers who love to order and dictate and to magnify their authority, teachers who deal with partiality, having favorites to whom they show preference, while others are treated with exactitude and severity, confusion and insubordination will result. Teachers who are not blessed with a pleasant, well-balanced disposition may be placed in charge of children, but a great wrong is done to those whom they educate.

A teacher may have sufficient education and knowledge in the sciences to instruct, but has it been ascertained that he has tact and wisdom to deal with human minds? If instructors have not the love of Christ abiding in their hearts, they are not fit to bear the grave responsibilities placed upon those who educate the youth. Lacking the higher education themselves, they know not how to deal with human minds. Their own insubordinate hearts are striving for control; and to subject the plastic minds and characters of the children to such discipline is to leave upon the mind scars and bruises that will never be removed.

Inquire, teachers, you who are doing your work not only for time but for eternity, Does the love of Christ constrain me as I deal with the souls for whom He has given His life? Under His discipline do old traits of character, not in conformity with the will of God, pass away and qualities the opposite take their place? or am I, by my unsanctified words and my impatience, my want of that wisdom which is from above, confirming these youth in their perverse spirit?

When a teacher manifests impatience or fretfulness

toward a child, the fault may not be with the child one half so much as with the teacher. Teachers become tired with their work, and something the children say or do does not accord with their feelings. Will they at such times, through a failure to exercise tact and wisdom, let Satan's spirit enter and lead them to arouse in the children feelings that are disagreeable and unpleasant? The teacher who loves Jesus, and who appreciates the saving power of His grace, cannot, dare not, let Satan control his spirit. Everything will be put away that would corrupt his influence, because it opposes the will of God and endangers the souls of the precious sheep and lambs.

When Christ is formed within, the hope of glory, then the truth of God will so act upon the natural temperament that its transforming power will be seen in changed characters. You will not then, by revealing an unsanctified heart and temper, turn the truth of God into a lie before any of your pupils. Nor will you, by manifesting a selfish, un-Christlike spirit, give the impression that the grace of Christ is not sufficient for you at all times and in all places. You will show that the authority of God over you is not in name only, but in reality and truth.

Let every teacher who accepts the responsibility of teaching the children and youth, examine himself. Let him ask himself, Has the truth of God taken possession of my soul? Has the wisdom which comes from Jesus Christ, which is "first pure, then peaceable, gentle, and easy to be entreated, full of mercy and good fruits, without partiality, and without hypocrisy," been brought into my character? Do I cherish the principle that "the fruit of righteousness is sown in peace of them that make peace"? James 3:17, 18.

Teachers, Jesus is in your school every day. His great heart of infinite love is drawn out, not only for the best-behaved children, who have the most favorable surroundings, but for the children who have by inheritance objectionable traits of character. Even parents have not understood how much they are responsible for the qualities developed in their children, and they have not had the tenderness and wisdom to deal with them, whom they have made what they are. They have failed to trace back to the cause of the discouraging developments that are a trial to them. But Jesus looks upon these children with pity and love. He understands; for He reasons from cause to effect.

Sharp words and continual censure bewilder the child, but do not reform him. Keep back the pettish word; keep your own spirit under discipline to Christ. Then you will learn to pity and to sympathize with those who are brought under your influence. Do not show impatience or harshness. If these children did not need educating, they would not be in school. They are to be patiently, kindly helped up the ladder of progress, climbing step by step in obtaining knowledge. Take your stand by the side of Jesus. Possessing His attributes, you will be the possessor of keen, tender sensibilities and will make the cause of the erring your own.

The religious life of a large number of teachers who profess to be Christians is such as to show that they are not Christians. They are constantly misrepresenting Christ. They have a religion that is subject to and controlled by circumstances. If everything happens to move in a way that pleases them, if there are no irritating circumstances to call out their unsubdued, un-Christlike natures, they are condescending and pleasant and very attractive. But the truth is not to be practiced only when we feel like it, but at all times and in all places. The Lord is not served by a man's hasty impulse, his fitful performances. If, when things occur in the family or in association with others, which ruffle their peace and provoke the temper, teachers would lay everything before God, asking for His grace before they engage in their daily work; if they would know for themselves that the love and power and grace of God are in their own hearts, angels of God would go with them into the schoolroom.

It means much to bring children under the direct influence of the Spirit of God, to train and discipline them, to bring them up in the nurture and admonition of the Lord. The formation of right habits, the inculcation of a right spirit, will call for earnest efforts in the name and strength of Jesus.

"Every high priest . . . can have compassion on the ignorant, and on them that are out of the way; for that he himself also is compassed with infirmity." Hebrews 5:1, 2. This truth can in the highest sense be exemplified before the children. Let teachers bear it in mind when they are tempted to be impatient and angry with the children because of misbehavior. Let them remember that angels of God are looking sorrowfully upon them. If the children err and misbehave, then it is all the more essential that those who are placed over them should be able to teach them, by precept and example, how to act.

In no case are teachers to lose self-control, to manifest impatience and harshness, and a want of sympathy and love. Those who are naturally fretful, easily provoked, and who have cherished the habit of criticism and evil thinking, should find some other kind of work, where their unlovely traits of character will not be reproduced in the children and youth. In the place of being fitted to instruct the children, such teachers need one to teach them the lessons of Jesus Christ.

If the teacher has the love of Christ abiding in the heart as a sweet fragrance, a savor of life unto life, he may bind the children under his care to himself. Through the grace of Christ he may be an instrument in God's hands to enlighten, lift up, encourage, and help to purify the soul temple from its defilement, until the character shall be transformed by the grace of Christ, and the image of God be revealed in the soul.

Said Christ, "I sanctify Myself, that they also might be sanctified." John 17:19. This is the work that devolves on every Christian teacher. There must be no haphazard work in this matter; for the education of the children requires very much of the grace of Christ and the subduing of self. Heaven sees in the child the undeveloped man or woman, with capabilities and powers that, if correctly guided and developed, will make him or her one with whom the divine agencies can co-operate—a laborer together with God.

An Object Lesson

The parable of the good shepherd represents the responsibility of every minister and of every Christian who has accepted a position as teacher of the children and youth. The one that has strayed from the fold is not followed with harsh words and a whip but with winning invitations to return. The ninety and nine that had not strayed do not call for the sympathy and tender, pitying love of the shepherd. But the shepherd follows the sheep and lambs that have caused him the greatest anxiety and have engrossed his sympathies most deeply. He leaves the rest of the sheep, and his whole energies are taxed to find the one that is lost.

And then the picture—praise God!—the shepherd returns with the sheep, carrying it in his arms, and rejoicing at every step. "Rejoice with me," he says, "for I have found my sheep which was lost." Luke 15:6. I am so thankful that we have the picture of the sheep found. There is no picture presented before our imagination of a sorrowful shepherd returning without the sheep. This is the lesson that the undershepherds are to learn—success in bringing the sheep and lambs back to the fold.

The wisdom of God, His power, and His love are without parallel. They are the divine guarantee that not one, even, of the straying sheep and lambs is overlooked, not one left unsuccored. A golden chain—the mercy and compassion of divine power—is passed around every one of these imperiled souls.

A Wide Field

To those who are accepted as teachers in our schools

is opened a wide field for labor and cultivation, for the sowing of the seed, and the harvesting of the ripened grain. What should give greater satisfaction than to educate the children and youth to love God and keep His commandments? What should give greater joy than to see these children and youth following Christ, the Great Shepherd? What should shed more sunshine through the soul of the devoted worker than to know that his patient, persevering labor in the Lord is not in vain, to see his pupils experiencing joy in their souls for sins forgiven, to see them receiving the impressions of the Spirit of God in true nobility of character and in the restoration of the moral image of God, seeking for that peace which comes from the Prince of Peace? The truth a bondage? Yes, in one sense; for it binds the soul in willing captivity to the Saviour, bowing the heart to the gentleness of Christ.

While right principles and correct habits are of first importance among the qualifications of the teacher, it is indispensable that he should have a thorough knowledge of the sciences. With uprightness of character, high literary acquirements should be combined.

If you are called to be a teacher, you are called to be a learner also. If you take upon yourself the sacred responsibility of teaching others, you take upon yourself the duty of becoming master of every subject you seek to teach. Be not content with dull thoughts, an indolent mind, or a loose memory. It is a noble thing to teach; it is a blessed thing to learn. True knowledge is a precious possession, and the more the teacher has of it, the better will be his work.

In sending children to the public schools, parents are placing them under demoralizing influences—influences that injure the morals and habits. In such surroundings, children often receive instruction that trains them to be enemies of Christ. They lose sight of piety and virtue.

Many public schools are permeated by the baneful influence of boys and girls who are experts in sin. And the children who are allowed to play on the street are also obtaining a training that thoughtless parents will sometime learn leads to recklessness and lawlessness.

God has given inquiring minds to youth and children. Their reasoning powers are entrusted to them as precious talents. It is the duty of parents to keep the matter of their education before them in its true meaning; for it comprehends many lines. They should be taught to improve every talent, expecting that all will be used in the service of Christ for the uplifting of fallen humanity.

Much of the success of a church school depends upon the teacher chosen. The one placed in charge of a school should be of suitable age; and where the number of students is large enough, assistants should be chosen from among the older ones. Thus the students will gain an experience of great value.

FOR FURTHER STUDY

Our Responsibility
: *Child Guidance,* pp. 312-317.

The Work of the Church School
: *Child Guidance,* pp. 303-311.
Testimonies, vol. 6, pp. 193-205.

Christ as the Example and Teacher of Youth
: *Desire of Ages, The,* p. 74.

The Bible Lesson
: *Child Guidance,* pp. 41-44.
Fundamentals of Christian Education, pp. 123-128.

Teaching From Nature
: *Acts of the Apostles, The,* pp. 571, 572.
Child Guidance, pp. 45-60.
Christ's Object Lessons, pp. 17-89.
Desire of Ages, The, pp. 70, 71, 291.
Education, pp. 99-120.
Patriarchs and Prophets, pp. 599, 600.
Testimonies, vol. 4, p. 581.
    vol. 8, pp. 326-328.
Thoughts From the Mount of Blessing, pp. 95-98.

Under Discipline to Christ
: *Education,* pp. 275-282.
Testimonies, vol. 5, pp. 653, 654.

THE INTERMEDIATE SCHOOL

"Understanding is a wellspring of life unto him that hath it."

INTERMEDIATE SCHOOLS

Intermediate schools are highly essential. In these schools thorough work is to be done; for many students will go forth from them directly into the great harvest field. They will go forth to use what they have learned, as canvassers and as helpers in various lines of evangelistic work. Many workers, after laboring for a time in the field, will feel the need of further study, and with the experience gained in the field will be prepared to value school privileges and to make rapid advancement. Some will desire an education in the higher branches of study. For these our colleges have been established.

The word of God is to lie at the foundation of all the work done in our intermediate schools. And the students are to be shown the true dignity of labor. They are to be taught that God is a constant worker. Let every teacher take hold heartily with a group of students, working with them, and teaching them how to work. As the teachers do this, they will gain a valuable experience. Their hearts will be bound up with the hearts of the students, and this will open the way for successful teaching.

It would be a sad mistake for us to fail to consider thoroughly the purpose for which each of our schools is established. This is a matter that should be faithfully studied by our responsible men in each union conference, in order that the youth may be surrounded by circumstances the most favorable for the formation of characters strong enough to withstand the evils of this world.

We have a great work before us, and there is need of many educated laborers who have fitted themselves for positions of trust. As our youth are trained for service in the cause of God, the Bible must lie at the foundation of their education. The principles of truth contained in the word of God will be a safeguard against the evil influences of the world.

Efforts to educate our children and youth in the fear of the Lord without making a study of the word prominent, are sadly misdirected. Unless there is such a training as will lead to a recognition and an abhorrence of sin, moral deformity will result. Our children should be removed from the evil influences of the public school and placed where thoroughly converted teachers may educate them in the Holy Scriptures. Thus students will be taught to make the word of God the grand rule of their lives.

———

Some may ask, "How are such schools to be established?" We are not a rich people, but if we pray in faith, and let the Lord work in our behalf, He will open ways before us to establish small schools in retired places for the education of our youth, not only in the Scriptures and in book learning, but in many lines of manual labor.

The necessity of establishing such schools is urged

upon me very strongly because of the cruel neglect of many parents properly to educate their children in the home. Many fathers and mothers have seemed to think that if the lines of control were put into the hands of their children they would develop into useful young men and women. But the Lord has instructed me in regard to this matter. In the visions of the night I saw standing by the side of these neglected children the one who was cast out of the heavenly courts because he originated sin. He, the enemy of souls, was watching for opportunities to gain control of the mind of every child whose parents had not given faithful instruction in regard to Satan's snares.

———

In planning for the education of their children outside the home, parents should realize that it is no longer safe to send them to the public school, and should endeavor to send them to schools where they will obtain an education based on a Scriptural foundation. Upon every Christian parent there rests the solemn obligation of giving to his children an education that will lead them to gain a knowledge of the Lord and to become partakers of the divine nature through obedience to God's will and way.

The Work of the Fernando School

The question has been asked, "What shall we teach in the Fernando school?"

Teach fundamentals. Teach that which is practical. You should not make a great parade before the world, telling what you expect to do, as if you were planning something wonderful. No, indeed. Boast neither of the branches of study you expect to teach nor of the industrial work you hope to do; but tell everyone who inquires, that you intend to do the best you can to give your students a physical, mental, and spiritual training that will fit them for usefulness in this life and prepare them for the future immortal life.

What influence do you think it would have to publish in your announcement of the school that you will endeavor to give the students a training that will prepare them for the future, immortal life because you desire to see them live throughout the ceaseless ages of eternity? I believe such a statement would have a far greater influence upon the brethren and sisters of this conference, and upon the community in the midst of which the school is established, than would the display of a number of courses of study in ancient and modern languages and other higher branches of study.

Let the school prove itself. Then the patrons will not be disappointed, and the students will not claim that they were promised instruction in certain studies which, after entering the school, they were not permitted to take up.

Let it be understood at the beginning that the Bible lies at the foundation of all education. An earnest study of God's word, resulting in transformation of character and in a fitness for service, will make the Fernando school a power for good. My brethren who are connected with this school, your strength lies not in the number of languages you may teach, or in telling how large a "college" you have. Keep silent on these points. Silence in regard to the great things you plan to do will help you more than all the positive assertions and all the promises that you might publish in your announcements. By faithfulness in the school you should demonstrate that you are working on foundation principles, principles that will prepare the students for entrance through the pearly gates into the heavenly city. The saving of souls is worth far more than mere intellectual training. A pretentious display of human learning, the manifestation of pride of personal appearance, is worthless. The Lord values obedience to His will; for only by walking humbly and obediently before Him, can man glorify God.

In giving us the privilege of studying His word, the Lord has set before us a rich banquet. Many are the benefits derived from feasting on His word, which is represented by Him as His flesh and blood, His spirit and life. By partaking of this word our spiritual strength is increased; we grow in grace and in a knowledge of the truth. Habits of self-control are formed and strengthened. The infirmities of childhood—fretfulness, willfulness, selfishness, hasty words, passionate acts—disappear, and in their place are developed the graces of Christian manhood and womanhood.

If your students, besides studying God's word, learn no more than how to use correctly the English language in reading, writing, and speaking, a great work will have been accomplished. Those who are trained for service in the Lord's cause should be taught how to talk properly in ordinary conversation and before congregations. Many a laborer's usefulness is marred by his ignorance in regard to correct breathing and clear, forcible speaking. Many have not learned to give the right emphasis to the words they read and speak. Often the enunciation is indistinct. A thorough training in the use of the English language is of far more value to a youth than a superficial study of foreign languages, to the neglect of his mother tongue.

Let the school be conducted along the lines of the ancient schools of the prophets, the word of God lying at the foundation of all the education given. Let not the students attempt to grasp the higher rounds of the ladder first. There are those who have attended other schools, thinking that they could obtain an advanced education; but they have been so intent on reaching the higher rounds of the ladder that they have not been humble enough to learn of Christ. Had they placed their feet on the lower rounds first, they would have made progress, learning more and still more of the Great Teacher.

The instructors will find it greatly to their advantage to take hold disinterestedly with the students in manual labor, showing them how to work. By co-operating with the youth in this practical way, the teachers can bind the hearts of the students to themselves by the cords of sympathy and brotherly love. Christian kindness and sociability are powerful factors in winning the affections of the youth.

Teachers, take hold of the schoolwork with diligence and patience. Realize that yours is not a common work. You are laboring for time and for eternity, molding the minds of your students for entrance into the higher school. Every right principle, every truth learned in an earthly school, will advance us just that much in the heavenly school. As Christ walked and talked with His disciples during His ministry on this earth, so will He teach us in the school above, leading us beside the river of living waters and revealing to us truths that in this life must remain hidden mysteries because of the limitations of the human mind, so marred by sin. In the heavenly school we shall have opportunity to attain, step by step, to the greatest heights of learning. There, as children of the heavenly King, we shall ever dwell with the members of the royal family; there we shall see the King in His beauty and behold His matchless charms.

The Training of Missionaries

It is important that we should have intermediate schools and academies. To us has been committed a great work—the work of proclaiming the third angel's message to every nation, kindred, tongue, and people. We have but few missionaries. From home and abroad are coming many urgent calls for workers. Young men and women, the middle-aged, and in fact all who are able to engage in the Master's service, should be putting their minds to the stretch in an effort to prepare to meet these calls. From the light God has given me, I know that we do not use the faculties of the mind half as diligently as we should in an effort to fit ourselves for greater usefulness. If we consecrate mind and body to God's service, obeying His law, He will give us sanctified moral power for every undertaking.

Every man and woman in our ranks, whether a parent or not, ought to be intensely interested in the Lord's vineyard. We cannot afford to allow our children to drift away into the world and to fall under the control of the enemy. Let us come up to the help of the Lord, to the help of the Lord against the mighty. Let us do all in our power to make our schools a blessing to our youth. Teachers and students, you can do much to bring this about by wearing the yoke of Christ, daily learning of Him His meekness and lowliness. Those who are not directly connected with the school can help to make it a blessing by giving it their hearty support. Thus we shall all be "laborers together with God," and receive the reward of the faithful, even an entrance into the school above.

Sept. 17, 1902.

Further Instruction

It is not wise for a new school to lift its banner and promise to do a high grade of work before proving that it is fully able to do preparatory work. It should be the great aim in every intermediate school to do most thorough work in the common branches.

In every school that is established among us, the teachers should begin humbly, not grasping the higher rounds of the ladder before they have climbed the lower ones. They are to climb round after round, beginning at the bottom. They are to be learners even as they teach the common branches. When they have learned the meaning of the simplicity of true education they will better understand how to prepare students for advanced studies. Teachers are to learn as they teach. Advancement is to be made, and by advancement experience is to be gained.

Our teachers should not think that their work ends with giving instruction from books. Several hours each day should be devoted to working with the students in some line of manual training. In no case should this be neglected.

In every school there should be those who have a store of patience and disciplinary talent, who will see to it that every line of work is kept up to the highest standard. Lessons in neatness, order, and thoroughness are to be given. Students should be taught how to keep in perfect order everything in the school and about the grounds.

Before he attempts to guide the youth, a teacher should learn to control himself. If he is not a constant learner in the school of Christ; if he has not the discernment and discrimination that would enable him to employ wise methods in his work; if he cannot govern those in his charge with firmness, yet pleasantly and kindly, how can he be successful in his teaching? The teacher who is not under the control of God needs to heed the invitation, "Take My yoke upon you, and learn of Me; for I am meek and lowly in heart: and ye shall find rest unto your souls. For My yoke is easy, and My burden is light." Matthew 11:29, 30.

Every teacher should learn daily of Jesus, wearing His yoke of restraint, sitting in His school as a student, obeying the rules of Christian principle. The teacher who is not under the guidance of the Master Teacher will not be able to meet successfully the different developments that arise as the result of the natural perversity of childhood and youth.

Let the teacher bring peace and love and cheerfulness into his work. Let him not allow himself to become angry or provoked. The Lord is looking upon him with intense interest, to see if he is being molded by the divine Teacher. The child who loses his self-control is far more excusable than the teacher who allows himself to become angry and impatient. When a stern reproof is to be given, it may still be given in kindness. Let the teacher beware of making the child stubborn by speaking to him harshly. Let him follow every correction with drops of the oil of kindness. He should never forget that he is dealing with Christ in the person of one of Christ's little ones.

Let it be a settled maxim that in all school discipline, faithfulness and love are to reign. When a student is corrected in such a way that he is not made to feel that the teacher desires to humiliate him, love for the teacher springs up in his heart.

Saint Helena, California, May 17, 1903.

In the night season I was speaking earnestly to the brethren in Southern California in reference to the school at Fernando. Perplexing questions had arisen in reference to the school. One in authority was in the assembly, and He gave counsel in regard to the way in which the school should be conducted. Our Counselor said: "If you follow on to know the Lord, you will know that His going forth is prepared as the morning. The teachers in the school should be learners with the students in all the instruction given. They are constantly to receive grace and wisdom from the Source of all wisdom.

"You are just beginning your work. Not all your ideas are positively correct. Not all your methods are wise. It is not possible that your work at its beginning will be perfect. But as you advance, you will learn how to use to better advantage the knowledge that you are gaining. In order to do their work in harmony with the Lord's will, teachers must keep their minds open to receive instruction from the Great Teacher."

Los Angeles, California, Sept. 18, 1902.

You will certainly make a serious mistake if you undertake, with a few students and a few teachers, to do the advanced work that is carried forward with so much difficulty and expense in our larger schools. It will be better for your students and for the school, for those who require the advanced studies, to go to the college, and thus leave your faculty free to devote their best energies to doing thorough work in teaching the common branches.

What is it that will make our schools a power? It is not the size of the buildings; it is not the number of advanced studies taught. It is the faithful work done by teachers and students, as they begin at the lower rounds of the ladder of progress and climb diligently round by round.

Secure a strong man to stand as principal of your school, a man whose physical strength will support him in doing thorough work as a disciplinarian; a man who is qualified to train the students in habits of order, neatness, and industry. Do thorough work in whatever you undertake. If you are faithful in teaching the common branches, many of your students could go directly into the work as canvassers, colporteurs, and evangelists. We need not feel that all workers must have an advanced education.

———

The youth in all our institutions are to be molded and fashioned and disciplined for God; and in this work the Lord's mercy and love and tenderness are ever to be revealed. This is not to degenerate into weakness and sentimentality. We are to be kind, yet firm. And let teachers remember that while decision is needful, they are never to be harsh or condemnatory, never to manifest an overbearing spirit. Let them keep calm, revealing the better way by refusing to be provoked to anger.

God wants us to demonstrate His love by showing a living interest in the youth under our care. Hold them up before the Lord, and ask Him to do for them what you cannot do. Let them see that you realize your need of divine help.

———

The teacher should constantly aim at simplicity and effectiveness. He should teach largely by illustration, and even in dealing with older pupils should be careful to make every explanation plain and clear. Many pupils well advanced in years are but children in understanding. —*Education,* page 233.

VALUE OF THE COMMON BRANCHES

In education the work of climbing must begin at the lowest round of the ladder. The common branches should be fully and prayerfully taught. Many who feel that they have finished their education are faulty in spelling and in writing, and can neither read nor speak correctly. Not a few who study the classics and other higher branches of learning, and who reach certain standards, finally fail because they have neglected to do thorough work in the common branches. They have never obtained a good knowledge of the English language. They need to go back and begin to climb from the first round of the ladder.

It is a mistake to allow students in our preparatory schools to choose their own studies. This mistake has been made in the past, and as a result students who had not mastered the common branches have sought to climb higher than they were prepared to go. Some who could not speak the English language correctly have desired to take up the study of foreign languages.

Students who, on coming to school, ask to be allowed to take the higher studies, should first be examined in the elementary branches. I was talking with a teacher in one of our conference schools, and he told me that some had come to his school with diplomas showing that they had taken some of the higher studies in other schools.

"Did you examine every such student," I inquired, "to find out whether he had received proper instruction in those branches?"

"Why," said the teacher, "in all these cases we could not give the students full credit for the work done in the past, as represented by the diplomas. Their training even in the common branches had been very defective." And thus it is in many instances.

Teachers should be careful to give the students what they most need, instead of allowing them to take what studies they choose. They should test the accuracy and knowledge of the students; then they can tell whether they have reached the heights to which they think they have attained.

One of the fundamental branches of learning is language study. In all our schools special care should be taken to teach the students to use the English language correctly in speaking, reading, and writing. Too much cannot be said in regard to the importance of thoroughness in these lines. One of the most essential qualifications of a teacher is the ability to speak and read distinctly and forcibly. He who knows how to use the English language fluently and correctly can exert a far greater influence than one who is unable to express his thoughts readily and clearly.

Voice culture should be taught in the reading class; and in other classes the teacher should insist that the students speak distinctly and use words which express their thoughts clearly and forcibly. Students should be taught to use their abdominal muscles in breathing and speaking. This will make the tones more full and clear.

Let the students be made to understand that God has given to everyone a wonderful mechanism—the human body—which we are to use to glorify Him. The powers of the body are constantly working in our behalf, and if we choose we may bring them under control.

We may have knowledge, but unless the habit is acquired of using the voice correctly, our work will be a failure. Unless we can clothe our ideas in appropriate language, of what avail is our education? Knowledge will be of little value to us unless we cultivate the talent of speech; but it is a wonderful power when combined with the ability to speak wise, helpful words, and to speak them in a way that will command attention.

Let all guard against becoming annoyed in spirit because they have to be drilled in these common branches. It should be impressed upon students that they will themselves be educators of others, and for this reason they should strive earnestly to improve.

To learn to tell convincingly and impressively that which one knows is of especial value to those who desire to be workers in the cause of God. The more expression we can put into the words of truth, the more effective these words will be on those who hear. A proper presentation of the Lord's truth is worthy of our highest effort.

Unless students who are preparing for work in the cause of God are trained to speak in a clear, straightforward manner, they will be shorn of half their influence for good. Whatever his calling is to be, the student should learn to control the voice. The ability to speak plainly and distinctly, in full, round tones, is invaluable in any line of work, and it is indispensable to those who desire to become ministers, evangelists, Bible workers, or canvassers.

When voice culture, reading, writing, and spelling take their rightful place in our schools, there will be seen a great change for the better. These subjects have been neglected because teachers have not recognized their value. But they are more important than Latin and Greek. I do not say that it is wrong to study Latin and Greek, but I do say that it is wrong to neglect the subjects that lie at the foundation of education in order to tax the mind with the study of these higher branches.

It is a matter of great importance that students obtain an education that will fit them for successful business life. We must not be satisfied with the one-sided education given in many schools. The common branches must be thoroughly mastered, and a knowledge of bookkeeping should be considered as important as a knowledge of grammar. All who expect to engage in the work of the Lord should learn how to keep accounts. In the world there are many who have made a failure of business and are looked upon as dishonest, who are true at heart, but who have failed to succeed because they did not know how to keep accounts.

To spell correctly, to write a clear, fair hand, and to keep accounts, are necessary accomplishments. Bookkeeping has strangely dropped out of school work in many places, but this should be regarded as a study of primary importance. A thorough preparation in these studies will fit students to stand in positions of trust.

———

To every student I would say, Never rest satisfied with a low standard. In attending school, be sure that you have in view a noble, holy object. Go because you desire to fit yourselves for service in some part of the Lord's vineyard. Do all that you can to attain this object. You can do more for yourselves than anyone can do for you. And if you do all that you can for yourselves, what a burden you will lift from the principal and the teachers!

Before attempting to study the higher branches of literary knowledge, be sure that you thoroughly understand the simple rules of English grammar and have learned to read and write and spell correctly. Climb the lower rounds of the ladder before reaching for the higher rounds.

Do not spend time in learning that which will be of little use to you in your afterlife. Instead of reaching out for a knowledge of the classics, learn first to speak the English language correctly. Learn how to keep accounts. Gain a knowledge of those lines of study that will help you to be useful wherever you are.

The instruction which the Lord has sent us, warning students and teachers against spending years of study in school, does not apply to young boys and girls. These need to go through the proper period of thorough discipline and study of the common branches and the Bible until they have reached an age of more mature and reliable judgment.

THE INFLUENCE OF ASSOCIATION

God's word places great stress upon the influence of association, even on men and women. How much greater is its power on the developing mind and character of children and youth! The company they keep, the principles they adopt, the habits they form, will decide the question of their usefulness here and of their future destiny.

It is a terrible fact, and one that should make the hearts of parents tremble, that in so many schools and colleges to which the youth are sent for mental discipline and culture, influences prevail which misshape the character, divert the mind from life's true aims, and debase the morals. Through contact with the irreligious, the pleasure loving, and the corrupt, many youth lose the simplicity and purity, the faith in God, and the spirit of self-sacrifice that Christian fathers and mothers have cherished and guarded by careful instruction and earnest prayer.

It is inevitable that the youth will have associates, and they will necessarily feel their influence. There are mysterious links that bind souls together so that the heart of one answers to the heart of another. One catches the ideas, the sentiments, the spirit, of another. This association may be a blessing or a curse. The youth may help and strengthen one another, improving in deportment, in disposition, in knowledge; or, by permitting themselves to become careless and unfaithful, they may exert an influence that is demoralizing.

The matter of choosing associates is one which students should learn to consider seriously. Among the youth who attend our schools there will always be found two classes, those who seek to please God and to obey their teachers, and those who are filled with a spirit of lawlessness. If the youth go with the multitude to do evil, their influence will be cast on the side of the adversary of souls; they will mislead those who have not cherished principles of unswerving fidelity.

It has been truly said, "Show me your company, and I will show you your character." The youth fail to realize how sensibly both their character and their reputation are affected by their choice of associates. One seeks the company of those whose tastes and habits and practices are congenial. He who prefers the society of the ignorant and vicious to that of the wise and good shows that his own character is defective. His tastes and habits may at first be altogether dissimilar to the tastes and habits of those whose company he seeks; but as he mingles with this class, his thoughts and feelings change; he sacrifices right principles and insensibly yet unavoidably sinks to the level of his companions. As a stream always partakes of the property of the soil through which it runs, so the principles and habits of youth invariably become tinctured with the character of the company in which they mingle.

Students should be taught to resist firmly the allurements to evil which come through association with other youth. Compassed as they are by temptation, an indwelling Christ is their only safeguard against evil. They must learn to look to Jesus continually, to study His virtues, to make Him their daily pattern. Then truth, brought into the inner sanctuary of the soul, will sanctify the life.

They must be trained to weigh their actions, to reason from cause to effect, to measure the eternal loss or gain to the life given to serve the purposes of the enemy or devoted to the service of righteousness. They should be taught to choose as their companions those who give evidence of uprightness of character, those who practice Bible truth. By association with those who walk according to principle, even the careless will learn to love righteousness. And by the practice of right doing there will be created in the heart a distaste for that which is cheap and common and at variance with the principles of God's word.

Strength of character consists of two things—power of will and power of self-control. Many youth mistake strong, uncontrolled passion for strength of character; but the truth is that he who is mastered by his passions is a weak man. The real greatness and nobility of the man is measured by his power to subdue his feelings, not by the power of his feelings to subdue him. The strongest man is he who, while sensitive to abuse, will yet restrain passion and forgive his enemies.

God has given us intellectual and moral power, but to a great extent everyone is the architect of his own character. Every day the structure more nearly approaches completion. The word of God warns us to take heed how we build, to see that our building is founded upon the eternal rock. The time is coming when our work will stand revealed just as it is. Now is the time for all to cultivate the powers that God has given them, that they may form characters for usefulness here and for a higher life hereafter.

Faith in Christ as a personal Saviour will give strength and solidity to the character. Those who have genuine faith in Christ will be sober-minded, remembering that God's eye is upon them, that the Judge of all men is weighing moral worth, that heavenly intelligences are watching to see what manner of character is being developed.

The reason that so grave mistakes are made by the youth is that they do not learn from the experience of those who have lived longer than they have. Students cannot afford to pass off with jest or ridicule the cautions and instruction of parents and teachers. They should cherish every lesson, realizing at the same time their need of deeper teaching than any human being can give. When Christ abides in the heart by faith, His Spirit becomes a power to purify and vivify the soul. Truth in the heart cannot fail of having a correcting influence upon the life. Let both teachers and students hold the truth of God as a treasure of the highest value, which must not be dimmed or tarnished by practices that are out of harmony with its holy character.

Let those students who are away from their homes, no longer under the direct influence of their parents, remember that the eye of their heavenly Father is upon them. He loves the youth. He knows their necessities, He understands their temptations. He sees in them great possibilities, and is ready to help them to reach the highest standard, if they will realize their need and seek Him for help.

Students, night and day the prayers of your parents are rising to God in your behalf; day by day their loving

interest follows you. Listen to their entreaties and warnings, and determine that by every means in your power
you will lift yourselves above the evil that surrounds you.
You cannot discern how insidiously the enemy will work
to corrupt your minds and habits, and develop in you
unsound principles.

You may see no real danger in taking the first step in
frivolity and pleasure seeking, and think that when you
desire to change your course you will be able to do right
as easily as before you yielded yourselves to do wrong.
But this is a mistake. By the choice of evil companions
many have been led step by step from the path of virtue
into depths of disobedience and dissipation to which at
one time they would have thought it impossible for them
to sink.

The student who yields to temptation weakens his
influence for good, and he who by a wrong course of
action becomes the agent of the adversary of souls must
render to God an account for the part he has acted
in laying stumbling blocks in the way of others. Why
should students link themselves with the great apostate?
Why should they become his agents to tempt others?
Rather, why should they not study to help and encourage
their fellow students and their teachers? It is their privilege to help their teachers bear the burdens and meet
the perplexities that Satan would make discouragingly
heavy and trying. They may create an atmosphere that
will be helpful, exhilarating. Every student may enjoy the consciousness that he has stood on Christ's
side, showing respect for order, diligence, and obedience,
and refusing to lend one jot of his ability or influence

to the great enemy of all that is good and uplifting.

The student who has a conscientious regard for truth and a true conception of duty can do much to influence his fellow students for Christ. The youth who are yoked up with the Saviour will not be unruly; they will not study their own selfish pleasure and gratification. Because they are one with Christ in spirit, they will be one with Christ in action. The older students in our schools should remember that it is in their power to mold the habits and practices of the younger students; and they should seek to make the best of every opportunity. Let these students determine that they will not through their influence betray their companions into the hands of the enemy.

Jesus will be the helper of all who put their trust in Him. Those who are connected with Christ have happiness at their command. They follow the path where their Saviour leads, for His sake crucifying the flesh, with its affections and lusts. They have built their hopes on Christ, and the storms of earth are powerless to sweep them from the sure foundation.

It rests with you, young men and women, to decide whether you will become trustworthy and faithful, ready and resolute to take your stand for the right under all circumstances. Do you desire to form correct habits? Then seek the company of those who are sound in morals, and whose aim tends to that which is good. The precious hours of probation are granted that you may remove every defect from the character, and this you should seek to do, not only that you may obtain the future life, but that you may be useful in this life. A good character is a capital of more value than gold or silver. It is unaffected by panics or failures, and in that day when earthly possessions shall be swept away, it will bring rich returns. Integrity, firmness, and perseverance are qualities that all should seek earnestly to cultivate; for they clothe the possessor with a power which is irresistible— a power which makes him strong to do good, strong to resist evil, strong to bear adversity.

The love of truth, and a sense of the responsibility to glorify God, are the most powerful of all incentives to the improvement of the intellect. With this impulse to action the student cannot be a trifler. He will be always in earnest. He will study as under the eye of God, knowing that all heaven is enlisted in the work of his education. He will become noble-minded, generous, kind, courteous, Christlike, efficient. Heart and mind will work in harmony with the will of God.

The youth who are in harmony with Christ will choose companions who will help them in right doing, and will shun society that gives no aid in the development of right principles and noble purposes. In every place are to be found youth whose minds are cast in an inferior mold. When brought into association with this class, those who have placed themselves without reserve on the side of Christ will stand firmly by that which reason and conscience tell them is right.

FOR FURTHER STUDY

INTERMEDIATE SCHOOLS
>   *Child Guidance,* pp. 328-336.
>   *Fundamentals of Christian Education,* pp. 488-491.

VALUE OF THE COMMON BRANCHES
>   *Education,* pp. 234-239.

INFLUENCE OF ASSOCIATION
>   *Adventist Home, The,* pp. 455-471.
>   *Messages to Young People,* pp. 419, 423, 424, 432.
>   *Testimonies,* vol. 1, pp. 400-405, 512, 513.
>   vol. 2, pp. 222, 407, 408.
>   vol. 3, pp. 41-47 (courtship), 362-367.
>   vol. 4, pp. 209, 435, 436, 587-591, 622-624.
>   vol. 5, pp. 111-113 (courtship), 222, 223, 542-546.

THE TEACHER AND THE WORK

"The Lord God hath given me the tongue of the learned, that I should know how to speak a word in season to him that is weary."

SOME OF THE CHRISTIAN TEACHER'S NEEDS

To the teacher is committed a most important work—a work upon which he should not enter without careful and thorough preparation. He should feel the sacredness of his calling and give himself to it with zeal and devotion. The more of true knowledge a teacher has, the better will be his work. The schoolroom is no place for surface work. No teacher who is satisfied with superficial knowledge will attain a high degree of efficiency.

But it is not enough that the teacher possess natural ability and intellectual culture. These are indispensable, but without a spiritual fitness for the work he is not prepared to engage in it. He should see in every pupil the handiwork of God—a candidate for immortal honors. He should seek so to educate, train, and discipline the youth that each may reach the high standard of excellence to which God calls him.

The purpose of education is to glorify God; to enable men and women to answer the prayer, "Thy kingdom come. Thy will be done in earth, as it is in heaven." Matthew 6:10. God invites teachers to be His helping hand in carrying out this purpose. He asks them to bring into their work the principles of heaven, the A B C of true education. The teacher who has not yet learned these principles should begin now to study them. And as he learns, he will develop a fitness to teach others.

A Personal Knowledge of Christ

Every Christian teacher should have an intelligent understanding of what Christ is to him individually. He should know how to make the Lord his strength and efficiency, how to commit the keeping of his soul to God as unto a faithful Creator. From Christ proceeds all the knowledge essential to enable teachers to be workers together with God—knowledge which opens to them the widest fields of usefulness.

Many do not appreciate this knowledge, but in obtaining an education they seek for that which will be regarded by their fellow men as wonderful knowledge. Teachers, let your boasting be in God, not in science, not in foreign languages or in anything else that is merely human. Let it be your highest ambition to practice Christianity in your lives.

"Then shall we know, if we follow on to know the Lord: His going forth is prepared as the morning." Hosea 6:3. As the light of the sun shines with increasing power from morning till noonday, so, as you advance in the opening light of God's word, you will receive more light.

Those who accept the responsibility that rests upon all teachers should be constantly advancing. They should not be content to dwell on the lowlands of Christian experience, but should be ever climbing higher. With the word of the Lord in their hands, and the love of souls pointing them to constant diligence, they should advance step by step in efficiency.

The Teacher's Need of Prayer

Every teacher should daily receive instruction from Christ and should labor constantly under His guidance. It is impossible for him rightly to understand or to perform his work unless he is much with God in prayer. Only by divine aid, combined with earnest, self-denying effort, can he hope to do his work wisely and well.

Unless the teacher realizes the need of prayer and humbles his heart before God, he will lose the very essence of education. He should know how to pray and what language to use in prayer. "I am the vine," Jesus said, "ye are the branches: he that abideth in Me, and I in him, the same bringeth forth much fruit: for without Me ye can do nothing." John 15:5. The teacher should let the fruit of faith be manifest in his prayers. He should learn how to come to the Lord and plead with Him until he receives the assurance that his petitions are heard.

Dealing With Students as Individuals

The teacher should carefully study the disposition and character of his pupils, that he may adapt his teaching to their peculiar needs. He has a garden to tend, in which are plants differing widely in nature, form, and development. A few may appear beautiful and symmetrical, but many have become dwarfed and misshapen by neglect.

Those to whom was committed the care of these plants left them to the mercy of circumstances, and now the difficulties of correct cultivation are increased tenfold.

Harmonious Development

No one branch of study should receive special attention to the neglect of others equally important. Some teachers devote much time to a favorite branch, drilling students upon every point, and praising them for their progress, while in other essential studies these students may be deficient. Such instructors are doing their pupils a great wrong. They are depriving them of that harmonious development of the mental powers which they should have, as well as of knowledge which they sorely need.

In these matters, teachers are too often controlled by ambitious and selfish motives. While they labor with no higher object, they cannot inspire their pupils with noble desires or purposes. The keen, active minds of the youth are quick to detect every defect of character, and they will copy defects far more readily than they will the graces of the Holy Spirit.

The Power of a Happy Disposition

Continual association with inferiors in age and mental training tends to make the teacher tenacious of his rights and opinions, and leads him to guard jealously his position and dignity. Such a spirit is opposed to the meekness and humility of Christ. A neglect to cherish these graces hinders advancement in the divine life. Many thus build barriers between themselves and Jesus, so that His love cannot flow into their hearts, and then they complain that they do not see the Sun of Righteousness. Let them forget self and live for Jesus, and the light of heaven will bring gladness to their souls.

No man or woman is fitted for the work of teaching who is fretful, impatient, arbitrary, or dictatorial. These traits of character work great harm in the schoolroom. Let not the teacher excuse his wrong course by the plea that he has naturally a hasty temper or that he has erred ignorantly. In his position he stands where ignorance or lack of self-control is sin. He is writing upon souls lessons that will be carried all through life, and he should train himself never to speak a hasty word, never to lose his self-control.

Above all others, he who has the training of the youth should beware of indulging a morose or gloomy disposition; for this will cut him off from sympathy with his students, and without sympathy he cannot hope to benefit them. We should not darken our own path or the path of others with the shadow of our trials. We have a Saviour to whom to go, into whose pitying ear we may pour every complaint. We may leave all our cares and burdens with Him, and then our labor will not seem hard or our trials severe.

"Rejoice in the Lord alway," the apostle Paul exhorts, "and again I say, Rejoice." Philippians 4:4. Whatever your disposition may be, God is able so to mold it that it will be sweet and Christlike. By the exercise of living faith you can separate from everything that is not in accordance with the mind of God, and thus bring heaven into your life here below. Doing this, you will have sunshine at every step. When the enemy seeks to enshroud the soul with darkness, sing faith and talk faith, and you will find that you have sung and talked yourself into the light.

We open to ourselves the floodgates of woe or joy. If we permit our thoughts to be engrossed with the troubles and trifles of earth, our hearts will be filled with unbelief, gloom, and foreboding If we set our affections on things above, the voice of Jesus will speak to our hearts, murmuring will cease, and vexing thoughts will be lost in praise to our Redeemer. Those who dwell upon God's great mercies and are not unmindful of His lesser gifts, will put on the girdle of gladness and make melody in their hearts to the Lord. Then they will enjoy their work. They will stand firm at their post of duty. They will have a placid temper, a trustful spirit.

Increase by Use

The teacher should not think that all his time is to be spent in the study of books. By putting into practice what he learns, he will obtain more than he will by mere study. As he uses his knowledge he will receive more. Some who have but one talent feel that they can do nothing. They hide their talent in the earth, as it were; and because they receive no increase they murmur against God. But if they would use the ability given them, their talent would double. It is by a faithful use of talents that they are multiplied. As we use aright the advantages God gives us, He increases our capabilities for service.

Because you are teachers, do not think that it is unnecessary to obtain a training in the simplest duties of life. Because you are studying books, do not neglect the everyday duties around you. Wherever you are, weave into your life all the usefulness possible, and you will find your minds more capable of expansion, more vigorous in grasping the lessons you endeavor to learn. By performing with faithfulness every practical duty that falls to you, you are becoming better qualified to educate those who need to learn how to do these things.

An Appeal

There are some who love the society of the world, who regard the companionship of the worldling as something to be desired above the companionship of those who love God and keep His commandments. Teachers, know enough to obey God. Know enough to follow the footsteps of Jesus, to wear the yoke of Christ. Do you desire the wisdom of God? Then humble yourselves before Him; walk in the way of His commandments; determine that you will make the most of every opportunity granted you. Gather every ray of light that falls across your pathway. Follow the light. Bring the teachings of truth into your life practice. As you humble yourselves under the mighty hand of God, He will lift you up. Commit your work to Him; labor in faithfulness, in sincerity, in truth, and you will find that each day's labor brings its reward.

Teachers must have a living faith or they will be separate from Christ. The Saviour does not ask how much favor you have with the world, how much praise you are receiving from human lips; but He does ask you to live so that He can put His seal upon you. Satan is seeking to cast his shadow across your pathway, that he may hinder the success of your work. You must have within you a power from above, that in the name of Jesus of Nazareth you may resist the power which is working from beneath. To have in the heart the Spirit of Christ is of infinitely more consequence than the possession of worldly recognition.

To the teacher is committed a great work—a work for which, in his own strength, he is wholly insufficient. Yet if, realizing his own weakness, he clings to Jesus, he will become strong in the strength of the Mighty One. He must bring to his difficult task the patience, forbearance, and gentleness of Christ. His heart must glow with the same love that led the Lord of life and glory to die for a lost world. Patience and perseverance will not fail of a reward. The best efforts of the faithful teacher will sometimes prove unavailing, yet he will see fruit for his labor. Noble characters and useful lives will richly repay his toil and care.

Human nature is worth working upon. It is to be elevated, refined, sanctified, and fitted with the inward adorning. Through the grace of God in Jesus Christ, which reveals salvation and immortality and life, His heritage are to be educated, not in the minutia of etiquette, the world's fashions and forms, but in the science of godliness.

THE NECESSITY OF DOING OUR BEST

The Lord has made provision that the nobler powers of the mind should be trained for high pursuits. But instead of this, men pervert the faculties of the mind and press them into the service of temporal interests, as if the attainment of the things of this earth were of supreme importance. In this way the higher powers are dwarfed and men remain unqualified for the duties of life that devolve upon them. If the nobler powers of the mind are not cultivated, they fail to act with integrity, even in the obligations relating to this life. It is Satan's design that the faculties of the mind shall become belittled and sensualized, but it is not God's will that any should yield the mind to the control of the evil one. In intellectual and in spiritual pursuits, He would have His children make progress. . . .

The lifework given us is that of preparation for the life eternal. If we accomplish this work as God designs we shall, every temptation may work for our advancement; for as we resist its allurements we make progress in the divine life. In the heat of the conflict, unseen agencies will be by our side, commanded of heaven to aid us in our wrestlings; and in the crisis, strength and firmness and energy will be imparted to us, and we shall have more than mortal power.

But unless the human agent brings his will into harmony with the will of God, unless he forsakes every idol and overcomes every wrong practice, he will not succeed in the warfare, but will be finally overcome. Those who would be conquerors must engage in conflict with unseen agencies; inward corruption must be overcome, and every thought must be brought into subjection to Christ.

The Holy Spirit is ever at work, seeking to purify, refine, and discipline the souls of men, in order that they may become fitted for the society of saints and angels. . . . As children of God, we should make earnest efforts to be overcomers; and as students who seek to honor and glorify God, we should study to show ourselves approved of Him, workmen that need not to be ashamed.

The Right Use of the Gift of Speech

The workman for God should make earnest efforts to become a representative of Christ, discarding all uncomely gestures and uncouth speech. He should endeavor to use correct language. There is a large class who are careless in the way they speak, yet by careful, painstaking attention these may become representatives of the truth. Every day they should make advancement. They should not detract from their usefulness and influence by cherishing defects of manner, tone, or language. Common, cheap expressions should be replaced by sound, pure words. By constant watchfulness and earnest discipline the Christian youth may keep his tongue from evil and his lips from speaking guile.

We should be careful not to give an incorrect pronunciation of our words. There are men among us who in theory know better than to use incorrect language, yet who in practice make frequent mistakes. The Lord would have us careful to do our best, making wise use of our faculties and opportunities. He has endowed men with gifts with which to bless and edify others; it is our duty so to educate ourselves that we may be fitted for the great work committed to us. . . .

In reading or in recitation the pronunciation should be clear. A nasal tone or an ungainly attitude should be at once corrected. Any lack of distinctness should be marked as defective. Many have allowed themselves to form the habit of speaking in a thick, indistinct way, as if their tongue were too large for their mouth. This habit has greatly hindered their usefulness.

If those who have defects in their manner of utterance will submit to criticism and correction, they may overcome these defects. They should perseveringly practice speaking in a low, distinct tone, exercising the abdominal muscles in deep breathing, and making the throat the channel of communication. Many speak in a rapid way and in a high, unnatural key. Such a practice will injure the throat and lungs. As a result of continual abuse, the weak, inflamed organs will become diseased, and consumption may result.

Christ's Method

Ministers and teachers should give special attention to the cultivation of the voice. They should learn to speak, not in a nervous, hurried manner, but with a slow, distinct, clear utterance, preserving the music of the voice.

The Saviour's voice was as music to the ears of those who had been accustomed to the monotonous, spiritless preaching of the scribes and Pharisees. He spoke slowly and impressively, emphasizing those words to which He wished His hearers to give special heed. Old and young, ignorant and learned, could catch the full meaning of His words. This would have been impossible had He spoken in a hurried way and rushed sentence upon sentence without a pause. The people were very attentive to Him, and it was said of Him that He spoke not as the scribes and Pharisees, for His word was as of one who had authority. . . .

Christ's manner of teaching was beautiful and attractive, and it was ever characterized by simplicity. He unfolded the mysteries of the kingdom of heaven through the use of figures and symbols with which His hearers were familiar; and the common people heard Him gladly, for they could comprehend His words. There were no high-sounding words used, to understand which it was necessary to consult a dictionary.

Jesus illustrated the glories of the kingdom of God by the use of the experiences and occurrences of earth. In compassionate love and tenderness He cheered and comforted and instructed all who heard Him; for grace was poured upon His lips that He might convey to men in the most attractive way the treasures of truth.

This is the way in which He would have us present His truth to others. The power of speech is of great value, and the voice should be cultivated for the blessing of those with whom we come in contact.

In Prayer

I am pained as I see how little the gift of speech is appreciated. In reading the Bible, in engaging in prayer, in bearing testimony in meeting, how necessary is clear, distinct utterance! And how much is lost in family worship when the one offering prayer bows the face down and speaks in a low, feeble voice! But as soon as family worship is over, those who could not speak loud enough to be heard in prayer, can usually speak in clear, distinct tones, and there is no difficulty in hearing what they say. Prayer that is thus uttered is appropriate for the closet, but not edifying in family or public worship; for unless those assembled can hear what is said, they cannot say Amen. Nearly all can speak loud enough to be heard in ordinary conversation, and why should they not speak thus when called upon to bear testimony or to offer prayer?

When speaking of divine things, why not speak in distinct tones and in a manner that will make it manifest that you know whereof you speak, and are not ashamed to show your colors? Why not pray as if you had a conscience void of offense, and could come to the throne of grace in humility, yet with holy boldness, lifting up holy hands without wrath and doubting? Do not bow down and cover up your faces as if there were something that you desired to conceal; but lift up your eyes toward the heavenly sanctuary, where Christ your Mediator stands before the Father to present your prayers, mingled with His own merit and spotless righteousness, as fragrant incense.

You are invited to come, to ask, to seek, to knock; and you are assured that you will not come in vain. Jesus says, "Ask, and it shall be given you; seek, and ye shall find; knock, and it shall be opened unto you: for everyone that asketh receiveth; and he that seeketh findeth; and to him that knocketh it shall be opened." Matthew 7:7, 8.

Christ illustrates the willingness of God to bless by the willingness of a father to grant the request of his child. He says, "If a son shall ask bread of any of you that is a father, will he give him a stone? or if he ask a fish, will he for a fish give him a serpent? or if he shall ask an egg, will he offer him a scorpion? If ye then, being evil, know how to give good gifts unto your children: how much more shall your heavenly Father give the Holy Spirit to them that ask Him?" Luke 11:11-13.

We come to God in the name of Jesus by special invitation, and He welcomes us to His audience chamber. He imparts to the humble, contrite soul that faith in Christ by which he is justified. Jesus blots out as a thick cloud his transgressions, and the comforted heart exclaims, "O Lord, I will praise Thee: though Thou wast angry with me, Thine anger is turned away, and Thou comfortedst me." Isaiah 12:1. Such a one will understand by his own experience the words of Paul, "With the heart man believeth unto righteousness; and with the mouth confession is made unto salvation." Romans 10:10.

Man then becomes an agent whom God can employ to work out His purposes. He represents Christ, holding forth to the world His mercy and love. He has a testimony that he desires others to hear. In the language of the psalmist he says, "Bless the Lord, O my soul: and all that is within me, bless His holy name. Bless the Lord, O my soul, and forget not all His benefits: who forgiveth all thine iniquities; who healeth all thy diseases; who redeemeth thy life from destruction; who crowneth thee with loving-kindness and tender mercies." Psalm 103:1-4.

In Witnessing for Christ

God has given us the gift of speech that we may recite to others His dealing with us, that His love and compassion may touch other hearts, and that praise may arise from other souls also to Him who has called them out of darkness into His marvelous light. The Lord has said, "Ye are My witnesses." Isaiah 43:10. But all who are called to be witnesses for Christ must learn of Him, that they may be efficient witnesses. As children of the heavenly King, they should educate themselves to bear testimony in a clear, distinct voice and in such a manner that no one may receive the impression that they are reluctant to tell of the mercies of the Lord.

In social meeting, prayer should be offered so that all may be edified; those who take part in this exercise should follow the example given in the Lord's beautiful prayer for the world. This prayer is simple, clear, comprehensive, and yet not long and spiritless, as the prayers offered in public sometimes are. These spiritless prayers might better not be uttered; for they are a mere form, without vital power, and they fail to bless or edify.

The apostle Paul writes: "Even things without life

giving sound, whether pipe or harp, except they give a distinction in the sounds, how shall it be known what is piped or harped? for if the trumpet give an uncertain sound, who shall prepare himself to the battle? So likewise ye, except ye utter by the tongue words easy to be understood, how shall it be known what is spoken? for ye shall speak into the air.

"There are, it may be, so many kinds of voices in the world, and none of them is without signification. Therefore if I know not the meaning of the voice, I shall be unto him that speaketh a barbarian, and he that speaketh shall be a barbarian unto me. Even so ye, forasmuch as ye are zealous of spiritual gifts, seek that ye may excel to the edifying of the church." 1 Corinthians 14:7-12.

In all our religious services we should seek to conduct ourselves in a way that will edify others, working as much as lies in our power for the perfection of the church. "Wherefore let him that speaketh in an unknown tongue pray that he may interpret. For if I pray in an unknown tongue, my spirit prayeth, but my understanding is unfruitful. What is it then? I will pray with the spirit, and I will pray with the understanding also. ... Else when thou shalt bless with the spirit, how shall he that occupieth the room of the unlearned say Amen at thy giving of thanks, seeing he understandeth not what thou sayest? For thou verily givest thanks well, but the other is not edified.

"I thank my God, I speak with tongues more than ye all: yet in the church I had rather speak five words with my understanding, that by my voice I might teach others also, than ten thousand words in an unknown tongue." Verses 13-19.

The principle presented by Paul concerning the gift of tongues is equally applicable to the use of the voice in prayer and social meeting. We would not have anyone who is defective in this respect cease from offering public prayer, or from bearing witness to the power and love of Christ.

I do not write these things to silence you, for there has already been too much silence in our meetings; but I write that you may consecrate your voice to Him who gave you this gift, and may realize the necessity of cultivating it so that you may edify the church by what you say. If you have acquired the habit of speaking in a low, indistinct way, you should regard it as a defect, and put forth earnest efforts to overcome, that you may honor God and edify His children.

In our devotional meetings, our voices should express by prayer and praise our adoration of the heavenly Father, that all may know that we worship God in simplicity and truth, and in the beauty of holiness. Precious indeed in this world of sin and ignorance is the gift of speech, the melody of the human voice, when devoted to the praise of Him who hath loved us and given Himself for us.

Consecration of the Voice

The gift of speech has been greatly abused and widely perverted from its intended purpose; but let those who claim to be children of the heavenly King awake to their responsibility, and make the most of this talent. Let no one say, "It is of no use for me to try to pray; for others do not hear me." Rather let him say, "I will make earnest effort to overcome this God-dishonoring habit of speaking in a low, indistinct tone. I will put myself under discipline until my voice shall be audible even to those who are dull of hearing."

Let the voices of the followers of Christ be so trained that instead of crowding words together in a thick, indistinct way, their utterance may be clear, forcible, and edifying. Do not let the voice fall after each word, but keep it up so that each sentence will be full and complete. Will it be worth disciplining yourself, if by so doing you are able to add interest to the service of God and to edify His children? The voice of thanksgiving, praise, and rejoicing is heard in heaven. The voices of the angels in heaven unite with the voices of the children of God on earth as they ascribe honor and glory and praise to God and to the Lamb for the great salvation provided.

Let everyone seek to do his best. Let those who have enlisted under the banner of Prince Immanuel grow daily in grace and efficiency. Let the teachers in our institutions endeavor so to train their students in all lines of education that they may come forth properly disciplined to bless mankind and to glorify God.

It is essential that students be trained to read in a clear, distinct tone. We have been pained as we have attended conference meetings, tract society meetings, and meetings of various kinds, where reports were read in an almost inaudible voice or in a hesitating manner or a muffled tone. One half the interest in a meeting is killed when the participants do their part in an indifferent, spiritless fashion. They should learn to speak in such a way that they can edify those who listen. Let everyone connected with missionary work qualify himself to speak in a clear, attractive way, enunciating his words perfectly.

The proper use of the vocal organs will bring benefit to the physical health and increase the usefulness and influence. It is through falling into bad habits of speech that people become tedious readers and speakers, but those who are looked upon as intelligent enough to become missionary workers or to transact business ought to have intelligence enough to reform in their manner of speaking. By judicious exercise they may expand the chest and strengthen the muscles. By giving heed to proper instruction, by following health principles in regard to the expansion of the lungs and the culture of the voice, our young men and women may become speakers who can be heard; and the exercise necessary for this accomplishment will prolong life.

Those who gain correct ideas on the subject of voice culture will see the necessity of educating and training themselves so that they may honor God and bless others. They will put themselves under patient, efficient teachers and learn to read in a way that will preserve the melody of the voice. With an eye single to the glory of God they will make the most of their natural abilities. Commanding their own powers, they will not be embarrassed by defects of speech, and their usefulness in the cause of God will be increased.

A DEEPER CONSECRATION

The teachers employed in our schools should be acquainted with God by an experimental knowledge. They should know Him because they obey all the commandments He has given. Jehovah engraved His Ten Commandments on tables of stone, that all the inhabitants of earth might understand His eternal, unchangeable character. Those teachers who desire to advance in learning and proficiency need to lay hold of these wonderful revelations of God. But it is only as heart and mind are brought into harmony with God that they will understand the divine requirements.

None need concern themselves about those things which the Lord has not revealed to us. In these days, speculation will abound, but God declares, "The secret things belong unto the Lord." Deuteronomy 29:29. The voice that spoke to Israel from Sinai is speaking in these last days to men and women, saying, "Thou shalt have no other gods before Me." Exodus 20:3. The law of God was written with His own finger on tables of stone, thus showing that it could never be changed or abrogated. It is to be preserved through the eternal ages, immutable as the principles of His government. Men have set their will against the will of God, but this cannot silence His words of wisdom and command, though they may set their speculative theories in opposition to the teachings of revelation, and exalt human wisdom above a plain "Thus saith the Lord."

It should be the determination of every soul, not so much to seek to understand all about the conditions that will prevail in the future state, as to know what the Lord requires of him in this life. It is the will of God that each professing Christian shall perfect a character after the divine similitude. By studying the character of Christ revealed in the Bible, by practicing His virtues, the believer will be changed into the same likeness of goodness and mercy. Christ's work of self-denial and sacrifice brought into the daily life will develop the faith that works by love and purifies the soul. There are many who wish to evade the cross-bearing part, but the Lord speaks to all when He says, "If any man will come after Me, let him deny himself, and take up his cross, and follow Me." Matthew 16:24.

A great work is to be accomplished by the setting forth of the saving truths of the Bible. This is the means ordained of God to stem the tide of moral corruption in the earth. Christ gave His life to make it possible for man to be restored to the image of God. It is the power of His grace that draws men together in obedience to the truth. Those who would experience more of the sanctification of the truth in their own souls should present this truth to those who are ignorant of it. Never will they find a more elevating, ennobling work.

The Teacher an Evangelist

The work of educating our youth as outlined for us in the instruction given by God, is to be sacredly maintained. We must choose as teachers those who will educate in right lines. Said my Instructor, "Let not teachers be chosen to educate and train the youth who will not maintain the simplicity of Christ's methods. His teachings contain the very essence of sanctified simplicity."

Those who present matters to the students in an uncertain light are not fitted for the work of teaching. No man is qualified for this work unless he is daily learning to speak the words of the Teacher sent from God. Now is the time to sow the gospel seed. The seed we sow must be that which will produce the choicest fruit. We have no time to lose. The work of our schools is to become more and more in character like the work of Christ. Only the power of the grace of God working on human hearts and minds will make and keep the atmosphere of our schools and churches clean.

There have been teachers in our schools who could pass well in a worldly institution of learning, but who were unfitted for the training of our youth because they were ignorant of the truths of the gospel of Christ. They were unable to bring the simplicity of Christ into their labors. It should be the work of every teacher to make prominent those truths that have called us out to stand as a peculiar people before the world, and which are able to keep us in harmony with heaven's laws. In the messages that have been sent us from time to time, we have truths that will accomplish a wonderful work of reform in our characters if we will give them place. They will prepare us for entrance into the city of God. It is our privilege to make continual advancement to a higher grade of Christian living.

Loma Linda

One night I was awakened and instructed to write a straight testimony regarding the work of our school at Loma Linda. By that school a solemn, sacred work is to be done. The teachings of health reform are to stand out clearly and brightly, that all the youth in attendance may learn to practice them. All our educators should be strict health reformers.

The Lord desires that genuine missionaries shall go out as pioneers from our schools. They are to be fully consecrated to the work as laborers together with God daily enlarging their sphere of usefulness. The influence of a consecrated medical missionary teacher in our schools is invaluable.

We need to be converted from our faulty lives to the faith of the Gospel. Christ's followers have no need to try to shine. If they will behold constantly the life of Christ they will be changed in mind and heart into the same image. Then they will shine without any superficial attempt. The Lord asks for no display of goodness. In the gift of His Son He has made provision that our inward lives may be imbued with the principles of heaven. It is the appropriation of this provision that will lead to a manifestation of Christ to the world. When the people of God experience the new birth, their honesty, their uprightness, their fidelity, their steadfast principles, will unfailingly reveal it.

Oh, what words were spoken to me! What gentleness was recommended through the grace abundantly given! The greatest manifestation that men and women can make of the grace and power of Christ is made when the natural man becomes a partaker of the divine nature, and through the power that the grace of Christ imparts, overcomes the corruption that is in the world through lust.

May 17, 1908. _____

There is a fullness of experience for every teacher to gain. The studies you take will either strengthen your faith and confidence in God, and teach you how to work as His helping hand, or they will leave you in a worse condition than you were before. Those who work out the principles that the Lord has given will stand on vantage ground. The mercies and blessings of heaven will come into their lives, enabling them to work out the will of God.

Teach the simple principles of the word of God, making the Bible the foundation of your study. The true higher education is that which is received by sitting at the feet of Jesus and learning of Him. Let your character building be after the pattern revealed to man in the life of Christ.

In all your work you must do as the husbandman does in laboring for the fruits of the earth. Apparently he throws away the seed; but, buried in the soil, the seed germinates. The power of the living God gives it life and vitality, and there is seen "first the blade, then the ear, after that the full corn in the ear." Mark 4:28. Study this wonderful process. Oh, there is so much to learn, so much to understand! If we improve our minds to the utmost of our ability we shall through the eternal ages continue to study the ways and works of God, and to know more and more of Him.

THE IMPORTANCE OF SIMPLICITY

To the Teachers at Berrien Springs:

I have an earnest desire that you shall every day be learning of the Great Teacher. If you will first draw nigh to God and then to your students, you can do a very precious work. If you are diligent and humble, God will daily give you knowledge and an aptitude to teach. Do your very best to impart to others the blessings He has given you.

With a deep, earnest interest to help your students, carry them over the ground of knowledge. Come as close to them as you can. Unless teachers have the love and gentleness of Christ abounding in their hearts, they will manifest too much of the spirit of a harsh, domineering schoolmaster. "Keep yourselves in the love of God, looking for the mercy of our Lord Jesus Christ unto eternal life. And of some have compassion, making a difference: and others save with fear, pulling them out of the fire; hating even the garment spotted by the flesh." Jude 21-23.

The Lord wishes you to learn how to use the gospel net. Many need to learn this art. In order for you to be successful in your work, the meshes of your net—the application of the Scriptures—must be close, and the meaning easily discerned. Then make the most of drawing in the net. Come right to the point. Make your illustrations self-evident. However great a man's knowledge, it is of no avail unless he is able to communicate it to others.

Let the pathos of your voice, its deep feeling, make its impression on hearts. Urge your students to surrender themselves to God.

Teachers, remember that the Lord is your strength. Strive to give the students ideas that will be to them a savor of life unto life. Teach by illustrations. Ask God to give you words to speak that all can understand.

A little girl once asked me, "Are you going to speak this afternoon?" "No, not this afternoon," I replied. "I am very sorry," she said. "I thought you were going to speak, and I asked several of my companions to come. Will you please ask the minister to speak easy words that we can understand? Will you please tell him that we do not understand large words, like 'justification' and 'sanctification'? We do not know what these words mean."

The little girl's complaint contains a lesson worthy of consideration by teachers and ministers. Are there not many who would do well to heed the request, "Speak easy words, that we may know what you mean"?

Make your explanations clear, for I know that there are many who do not understand many of the things said to them. Let the Holy Spirit mold and fashion your speech, cleansing it from all dross. Speak as little children, remembering that there are many well advanced in years who are but little children in understanding.

By earnest prayer and diligent effort we are to obtain a fitness for speaking. This fitness includes uttering every syllable clearly, placing the force and emphasis where it belongs. Speak slowly. Many speak rapidly, hurrying one word after another so fast that the effect of what they say is lost. Into what you say put the spirit and life of Christ.

On a certain occasion, when Betterton, the celebrated actor, was dining with Dr. Sheldon, archbishop of Canterbury, the archbishop said to him, "Pray, Mr. Betterton, tell me why it is that you actors affect your audiences so powerfully by speaking of things imaginary." "My lord," replied Betterton, "with due submission to Your Grace, permit me to say that the reason is plain: It all lies in the power of enthusiasm. We on the stage speak of things imaginary as if they were real, and you in the pulpit speak of things real as if they were imaginary."

"Feed My lambs;" "feed My sheep," was the commission given to Peter. "And when thou art converted, strengthen thy brethren." John 21:15, 16; Luke 22:32. To those who hear, the gospel is made the power of God unto salvation. Present the gospel in its simplicity. Follow Christ's example, and you will have the reward of seeing your students won to Him.

Sanitarium, California, July 6, 1902.

———

Our people are now being tested as to whether they will obtain their wisdom from the greatest Teacher the world ever knew, or seek to the god of Ekron. Let us determine that we will not be tied by so much as a thread to the educational policies of those who do not discern the voice of God and who will not hearken to His commandments.

A CAUTION

"Know ye not that they which run in a race run all, but one receiveth the prize? So run, that ye may obtain. And every man that striveth for the mastery is temperate in all things. Now they do it to obtain a corruptible crown; but we an incorruptible. I therefore so run, not as uncertainly; so fight I, not as one that beateth the air: but I keep under my body, and bring it into subjection: lest that by any means, when I have preached to others, I myself should be a castaway." 1 Corinthians 9:24-27.

I am constantly presenting the need of every man's doing his best as a Christian, of training himself to realize the growth, the expansion of mind, the nobility of character, which it is possible for each to have. In all that we do we are to sustain a Christlike relation to one another. We are to use every spiritual force for the carrying out of wise plans in earnest action. The gifts of God are to be used for the saving of souls. Our relations to one another are not to be governed by human standards, but by divine love, the love expressed in the gift of God to our world.

The man who stands in a position of responsibility in any of our schools cannot be too careful of his words and his acts. Never should he allow the least approach to familiarity in his relations to the students, such as placing his hand on the arm or shoulder of a girl student. He should in no case give the impression that commonness and familiarity are allowable. His lips and his hands are to express nothing that anyone could take advantage of.

In the past not all of our teachers have been clear and true and firm in this respect. They need to see things in an altogether different light regarding the relations that should exist between the teacher and the student. The life and character must be kept from every stain of evil. Every unholy passion must be kept under the control of sanctified reason through the grace abundantly bestowed of God.

We are living in an atmosphere of satanic witchery. The enemy will weave a spell of licentiousness around every soul that is not barricaded by the grace of Christ. Temptations will come; but if we watch against the enemy, and maintain the balance of self-control and purity, the seducing spirits will have no influence over us. Those who do nothing to encourage temptation will have strength to withstand it when it comes; but those who keep themselves in an atmosphere of evil will have only themselves to blame if they are overcome and fall from their steadfastness. In the future, good reasons will be seen for the warnings given regarding seducing spirits. Then will be seen the force of Christ's words, "Be ye therefore perfect, even as your Father which is in heaven is perfect." Matthew 5:48.

We are to be guided by true theology and common sense. Our souls are to be surrounded by the atmosphere of heaven. Men and women are to watch themselves; they are to be constantly on guard, allowing no word or act that would cause their good to be evil spoken of. He who professes to be a follower of Christ is to watch himself, keeping himself pure and undefiled in thought,

word, and deed. His influence upon others is to be uplifting. His life is to reflect the bright beams of the Sun
of Righteousness.

There is need that much time be spent in secret prayer,
in close communion with God. Thus only can victories
be won. Eternal vigilance is the price of safety.

The Lord's covenant is with His saints. Everyone is
to discern his weak points of character and guard against
them with vigor. Those who have been buried with
Christ in baptism, and been raised in the likeness of His
resurrection, have pledged themselves to live in newness
of life. "If ye then be risen with Christ, seek those things
which are above, where Christ sitteth on the right hand
of God. Set your affection on things above, not on things
on the earth. For ye are dead, and your life is hid with
Christ in God. When Christ, who is our life, shall appear, then shall ye also appear with Him in glory." Colossians 3:1-4.

The Christian youth should be trained to bear responsibilities with brave heart and willing hand. He
should learn to encounter the trials of life with patience
and fortitude, to follow maxims of worth, and to confirm
himself in habits that will enable him to win the victor's
crown. There is no time more favorable in which to
acknowledge the power of Christ's saving grace and to be
controlled by the principles of the divine law.

Wherever in His providence God has placed you, He
will keep you. "As thy days, so shall thy strength be."
Deuteronomy 33:25.

THE GREAT TEACHER

Christ was the greatest teacher the world has ever known. He came to this earth to shed abroad the bright beams of truth, that men might gain a fitness for heaven. "For this cause came I into the world," He declared, "that I should bear witness unto the truth." John 18:37. He came to reveal the character of the Father, that men might be led to worship Him in spirit and in truth.

Man's need for a divine teacher was known in heaven. The pity and sympathy of God were aroused in behalf of human beings, fallen and bound to Satan's chariot car; and when the fullness of time was come, He sent forth His Son. The One appointed in the councils of heaven came to this earth as man's instructor. The rich benevolence of God gave Him to our world, and to meet the necessities of human nature He took humanity upon Himself. To the astonishment of the heavenly host the eternal Word came to this world as a helpless babe. Fully prepared, He left the royal courts and mysteriously allied Himself with fallen human beings. "The Word was made flesh, and dwelt among us." John 1:14.

When Christ left His high command, He might have taken upon Him any condition in life that He chose. But greatness and rank were nothing to Him, and He chose the most humble walk of life. No luxury, ease, or self-gratification came into His experience. The truth of heavenly origin was to be His theme; He was to sow the world with truth, and He lived in such a way as to be accessible to all.

That during His childhood Christ should grow in wisdom and in favor with God and man was not a matter of astonishment, for it was according to the laws of His divine appointment that His talents should develop and His faculties strengthen. He did not seek an education in the schools of the rabbis, for God was His instructor. As He grew older He continued to increase in wisdom. He applied Himself diligently to a study of the Scriptures, for He knew them to be full of invaluable instruction. He was faithful in the discharge of His home duties; and the early morning hours, instead of being spent in bed, often found Him in a retired place, searching the Scriptures and praying to His heavenly Father.

All the prophecies concerning His work and mediation were familiar to Him, especially those having reference to His humiliation, atonement, and intercession. The object of His life on earth was ever before Him, and He rejoiced to think that the gracious purpose of the Lord should prosper in His hands.

Of Christ's teaching it is said, "The common people heard Him gladly." Mark 12:37. "Never man spake like this Man" (John 7:46), declared the officers who were sent to take Him. His words comforted, strengthened, and blessed those who were longing for the peace that He alone could give. There was in His words that which lifted His hearers to a high plane of thought and action. If these words, instead of the words of men, were given to the learner today, we should see evidences of higher intelligence, a clearer comprehension of heavenly things, a deeper knowledge of God, a purer, more vigorous Christian life.

Christ's illustrations were taken from the things of daily life, and although they were simple, they had in them a wonderful depth of meaning. The birds of the air, the lilies of the field, the growing seed, the shepherd and the sheep—with these things Christ illustrated immortal truth; and ever afterward, when His hearers chanced to see these objects, they recalled His words. Thus the truth became a living reality; the scenes of nature and the daily affairs of life were ever repeating to them the Saviour's teaching.

Christ always used simple language, yet His words tested the knowledge of deep, unprejudiced thinkers. His manner of teaching should be followed by teachers of today. Spiritual truths should always be presented in simple language, that they may be comprehended and find lodgment in the heart. Thus Christ addressed the crowds that pressed and thronged about Him; and all, learned and unlearned, were able to comprehend His lessons.

In every school the instruction given should be as easy to understand as was that given by Christ. The use of long words confuses the mind and eclipses the beauty of the thought presented. There is need of teachers who will come close to their students and who will give clear, definite instruction, illustrating spiritual things by the things of nature and by the familiar events of everyday experience.

The Bible reveals Christ to us as the Good Shepherd, seeking with unwearied feet for the lost sheep. By

methods peculiarly His own He helped all who were in
need of help. With tender, courteous grace He ministered
to sin-sick souls, bringing healing and strength. The simplicity and earnestness with which He addressed those in
need hallowed every word. He proclaimed His message
from the mountainside, from the fisherman's boat, in the
desert, in the great thoroughfares of travel. Wherever
He found those ready to listen He was ready to open to
them the treasure house of truth. He attended the yearly
festivals of the Jewish nation, and to the multitudes,
absorbed in outward ceremony, He spoke of heavenly
things, bringing eternity within their view.

The Saviour's entire life was characterized by disinterested benevolence and the beauty of holiness. He is
our pattern of goodness. From the beginning of His
ministry, men began to comprehend more clearly the
character of God. He carried out His teachings in His
own life. He showed consistency without obstinacy,
benevolence without weakness, tenderness and sympathy
without sentimentalism. He was highly social, yet He
possessed a reserve that discouraged any familiarity. His
temperance never led to bigotry or austerity. He was
not conformed to the world, yet He was attentive to the
wants of the least among men.

"Who is this that cometh from Edom, with dyed garments from Bozrah? this that is glorious in His apparel,
traveling in the greatness of His strength?" Isaiah 63:1.
With assurance comes the answer: "Without controversy
great is the mystery of godliness: God was manifest in
the flesh, justified in the Spirit, seen of angels, preached
unto the Gentiles, believed on in the world, received up

into glory." 1 Timothy 3:16. "Being in the form of God," He "thought it not robbery to be equal with God: but made Himself of no reputation, and took upon Him the form of a servant, and was made in the likeness of men: and being found in fashion as a man, He humbled Himself, and became obedient unto death, even the death of the cross. Wherefore God also hath highly exalted Him, and given Him a name which is above every name: that at the name of Jesus every knee should bow, of things in heaven, and things in earth, and things under the earth; and that every tongue should confess that Jesus Christ is Lord, to the glory of God the Father." Philippians 2:6-11.

Teachers can gain efficiency and power only by working as Christ worked. When He is the most powerful influence in their lives, they will have success in their efforts. They will rise to heights that they have not yet gained. They will realize the sacredness of the work entrusted to them, and filled with His Spirit they will be animated with the same desire to save sinners that animated Him. And by their lives of consecration and devotion their students will be led to the feet of the Saviour.

Students cannot afford to wait till their education is considered complete, before using for the good of others that which they have received. Without this, however they may study, however much knowledge they may gain, their education will be incomplete.

CHRISTIAN DISCIPLINE

Dealing with human minds is the most delicate work ever entrusted to mortals, and teachers need constantly the help of the Spirit of God, that they may do their work aright. Among the youth attending school will be found great diversity of character and education. The teacher will meet with impulse, impatience, pride, selfishness, undue self-esteem. Some of the youth have lived in an element of arbitrary restraint and harshness, which has developed in them a spirit of obstinacy and defiance. Others have been treated as pets, allowed by overfond parents to follow their own inclinations. Defects have been excused until the character is deformed.

To deal successfully with these different minds, the teacher needs to exercise great tact and delicacy in management, as well as firmness in government. Dislike and even contempt for proper regulations will often be manifested. Some will exercise their ingenuity in evading penalties, while others will display a reckless indifference to the consequences of transgression. All this will call for patience and forbearance and wisdom on the part of those entrusted with the education of these youth.

The Student's Part

Our schools have been established that in them the youth may learn to obey God and His law, and become fitted for service. Rules for the conduct of those who attend are necessary, and the students should act in harmony with these regulations. No student should think that because he has been allowed to rule in the home he can rule in the school. Suppose that this were allowed; how could the youth be trained to be missionaries? Each student entering one of our schools should place himself under discipline. Those who refuse to obey the regulations should return to their homes.

The teachers are to bind the students to their hearts by the cords of love and kindness and strict discipline. Love and kindness are worth nothing unless united with the discipline that God has said should be maintained. Students come to school to be disciplined for service, trained to make the best use of their powers. If on coming they resolve to co-operate with their teachers, their study will be worth much more to them than if they give up to the inclination to be rebellious and lawless. Let them give the teachers their sympathy and co-operation. Let them take firm hold of the arm of divine power, determining not to turn aside from the path of duty. Let them harness their wrong habits and exert all their influence on the right side. Let them remember that the success of the school depends upon their consecration and sanctification, upon the holy influence they feel bound to exert. Let them set their mark high and be determined to reach it. When asked to go contrary to the rules of the school, let them answer with a decided No.

The Teacher's Part

And every teacher has his own wrong traits of character to watch lest the enemy use him as an agent to destroy souls. The teacher's safety lies in learning daily in the school of Christ. He who learns in this school will hide self in Jesus and will remember that as he deals with his students he is dealing with a blood-bought heritage. In this school he will learn to be patient, humble, generous, noble. The molding hand of God will bring out in the character the divine image.

Let Christ's methods be followed in dealing with those who make mistakes. Unwise actions, the manifestation of undue severity on the part of the teacher, may thrust a student upon Satan's battleground. Prodigals have been kept out of the kingdom of God by the un-Christlikeness of those who claimed to be Christians. "Whoso shall offend one of these little ones which believe in Me," Christ said, "it were better for him that a millstone were hanged about his neck, and that he were drowned in the depth of the sea." Matthew 18:6. It were better not to live than to exist day by day devoid of that love which Christ has enjoined upon His children.

A Christlike nature is not selfish, unsympathetic, cold. It enters into the feelings of those who are tempted and helps the one who has fallen to make the trial a stepping-stone to higher things. The Christian teacher will pray for and with an erring student, but he will not get angry with him. He will not speak sharply to the wrongdoer, thus discouraging a soul who is struggling with the powers of darkness. He will let his heart ascend to God for help, and angels will come to his side to help him in lifting up the standard against the enemy; thus instead of cutting off the erring one from help, he will be enabled to gain a soul for Christ.

Public Exposure of Wrongdoing

Great care should be shown in regard to making public the errors of students. To make public exposure of wrong is harmful in every respect to the wrongdoer and has no beneficial influence upon the school. It never helps a student to humiliate him before his fellow students. This heals nothing, cures nothing, but makes a wound that mortifies.

The love that suffers long and is kind will not magnify an indiscretion into an unpardonable offense, neither will it make capital of others' misdoings. The Scriptures plainly teach that the erring are to be treated with forbearance and consideration. If the right course is followed, the apparently obdurate heart may be won to Christ. The love of Jesus covers a multitude of sins. His grace never leads to the exposing of another's wrongs unless it is a positive necessity.

We are living in a hard, unfeeling, uncharitable world. Satan and his angels are using every means in their power to destroy souls. The good that a teacher will do his students will be proportionate to his belief in them. And let the teacher remember that it is the most unfortunate, those who have a disagreeable temperament, who are rough, stubborn, sullen, that most need love, compassion, and help. Those who most try our patience most need our love.

We shall pass through this world but once; any good that we can do, we should do earnestly, untiringly, in the spirit that Christ brought into His work. How can students who are greatly in need of help be encouraged to press on in the right way? Only by treating them with the love that Christ revealed. You may say we should treat them as they deserve. What if Christ treated us thus? He, the Sinless One, was treated as we deserve, that we, fallen and sinful, might be treated as He deserved. Teachers, treat your unpromising students as you think they richly deserve, and you will cut them off from hope and spoil your influence. Will this pay? No, a hundred times, no. Bind the one who needs your help close to a loving, sympathizing heart, and you will save a soul from death and hide a multitude of sins.

Expelling Students

Great care should be exercised in the matter of expelling students. There are times when this must be done. It is a painful task to separate from the school the one who incites others to disobedience and disloyalty, but for the sake of the other students this is sometimes necessary. God saw that if Satan were not expelled from heaven the angelic host would be in constant danger; and when God-fearing teachers see that to retain a student is to expose others to evil influences, they should separate him from the school. But it should be a very grave fault that calls for this discipline.

When, in consequence of transgression, Adam and Eve were cut off from all hope, when justice demanded the death of the sinner, Christ gave Himself as a sacrifice. "Herein is love, not that we loved God, but that He loved

us, and sent His Son to be the propitiation for our sins."
"All we like sheep have gone astray; we have turned
everyone to his own way; and the Lord hath laid on Him
the iniquity of us all." 1 John 4:10; Isaiah 53:6.

In dealing with their students, teachers are to show the
love of Christ. Without this love they will be harsh and
dictatorial, driving souls away from the fold. They must
be minutemen, ever on guard over self and improving
every opportunity to do good to those in their care. Let
them remember that every one of our schools is to be an
asylum for the sorely tried youth, where their follies will
be wisely and patiently dealt with.

Teachers and students are to come close together
in Christian fellowship. The youth will make many
mistakes, and the teacher is never to forget to be compassionate and courteous. Never is he to seek to show his
superiority. The greatest of teachers are those who are
most patient, most kind. By their simplicity and their
willingness to learn they encourage their students to
climb higher and still higher.

Let teachers remember their own faults and mistakes,
and strive earnestly to be what they wish their students
to become. In their treatment of the youth let them be
wise and pitiful. Let them not forget that these youth are
in need of wholesome, encouraging words and helpful
deeds. Teachers, treat your students as Christ's children,
whom He wants you to help in every time of need.
Make friends of them. Give them practical evidence of
your unselfish interest in them. Help them over the

rough places. Patiently, tenderly, strive to win them to Jesus. Eternity alone will reveal the results of such effort.

More harm than good results from the practice of offering prizes and rewards. By it the ambitious pupil is stimulated to greater effort. Those whose mental powers are already too active for their physical strength are urged on to grasp subjects too difficult for the young mind. The examinations also are a trying ordeal for pupils of this class. Many a promising student has suffered severe illness, perhaps death, as the result of the effort and excitement of such occasions. Parents and teachers should be on their guard against these dangers.

Attention to form and ceremony should not occupy time and strength that rightfully belong to things more essential. Everything in this age of corruption is perverted to display and outward appearance, but this spirit should not find place in our schools. We should teach Bible manners, purity of thought, strict integrity. This is valuable instruction. If the teachers have the mind of Christ and are being molded by the Holy Spirit, they will be kind, attentive, and truly courteous. If they work as in the sight of heaven, they will be Christian ladies and gentlemen. Their refined bearing will be a constant object lesson to the students, who, though at first they may be somewhat uncultured, will day by day be molded by its influence.

FOR FURTHER STUDY

STUDY AND LABOR

Those who recognize science in the humblest work will see in it nobility and beauty, and will take pleasure in performing it with faithfulness and efficiency.

THE DIGNITY OF LABOR

Notwithstanding all that has been said and written regarding the dignity of manual labor, the feeling prevails that it is degrading. Popular opinion has, in many minds, changed the order of things, and men have come to think that it is not fitting for a man who works with his hands to take his place among gentlemen. Men work hard to obtain money; and having gained wealth, they suppose that their money will make their sons gentlemen. But many such fail to train their sons as they themselves were trained, to hard, useful labor. Their sons spend the money earned by the labor of others, without understanding its value. Thus they misuse a talent that the Lord designed should accomplish much good.

The Lord's purposes are not the purposes of men. He did not design that men should live in idleness. In the beginning He created man a gentleman; but though rich in all that the Owner of the universe could supply, Adam was not to be idle. No sooner was he created than his work was given him. He was to find employment and happiness in tending the things that God had created, and in response to his labor his wants were to be abundantly supplied from the fruits of the Garden of Eden.

While our first parents obeyed God, their labor in the garden was a pleasure, and the earth yielded of its abundance for their wants. But when man departed from obedience, he was doomed to wrestle with the seeds of Satan's sowing and to earn his bread by the sweat of his brow. Henceforth he must battle in toil and hardship against the power to which he had yielded his will.

It was God's purpose to alleviate by toil the evil brought into the world by man's disobedience. By toil the temptations of Satan might be made ineffectual and the tide of evil stayed. And though attended with anxiety, weariness, and pain, labor is still a source of happiness and development, and a safeguard against temptation. Its discipline places a check on self-indulgence and promotes industry, purity, and firmness. Thus it becomes a part of God's great plan for our recovery from the Fall.

Manual Labor Versus Games

The public feeling is that manual labor is degrading, yet men may exert themselves as much as they choose at cricket, baseball, or in pugilistic contests, without being regarded as degraded. Satan is delighted when he sees human beings using their physical and mental powers in that which does not educate, which is not useful, which does not help them to be a blessing to those who need their help. While the youth are becoming expert in games that are of no real value to themselves or to others,

Satan is playing the game of life for their souls, taking from them the talents that God has given them, and placing in their stead his own evil attributes. It is his effort to lead men to ignore God. He seeks to engross and absorb the mind so completely that God will find no place in the thoughts. He does not wish people to have a knowledge of their Maker, and he is well pleased if he can set in operation games and theatrical performances that will so confuse the senses of the youth that God and heaven will be forgotten.

One of the surest safeguards against evil is useful occupation, while idleness is one of the greatest curses; for vice, crime, and poverty follow in its wake. Those who are always busy, who go cheerfully about their daily tasks, are the useful members of society. In the faithful discharge of the various duties that lie in their pathway, they make their lives a blessing to themselves and to others. Diligent labor keeps them from many of the snares of him who "finds some mischief still for idle hands to do."

A stagnant pool soon becomes offensive, but a flowing brook spreads health and gladness over the land. The one is a symbol of the idle, the other of the industrious.

Manual Training Among the Israelites

In God's plan for Israel every family had a home on the land with sufficient ground for tilling. Thus were provided both the means and the incentive for a useful, industrious, and self-supporting life. And no devising of men has ever improved upon that plan. To the world's departure from it is owing, to a large degree, the poverty and wretchedness that exist today.

By the Israelites, industrial training was regarded as a duty. Every father was required to see that his sons learned some useful trade. The greatest men of Israel were trained to industrial pursuits. A knowledge of the duties pertaining to housewifery was considered essential for every woman; and skill in these duties was regarded as an honor to women of the highest station.

Various industries were taught in the schools of the prophets, and many of the students sustained themselves by manual labor.

Christ's Example

The path of toil appointed to the dwellers on earth may be hard and wearisome; but it is honored by the footprints of the Redeemer, and he is safe who follows in this sacred way. By precept and example, Christ has dignified useful labor. From His earliest years He lived a life of toil. The greater part of His earthly life was spent in patient work in the carpenter's shop at Nazareth. In the garb of a common laborer the Lord of life trod the streets of the little town in which He lived, going to and returning from His humble toil; and ministering angels attended Him as He walked side by side with peasants and laborers, unrecognized and unhonored.

When He went forth to contribute to the support of the family by His daily toil He possessed the same power as when on the shores of Galilee He fed five thousand hungry souls with five loaves and two fishes. But He did not employ His divine power to lessen His burdens or lighten His toil. He had taken upon Himself the form of humanity, with all its attendant ills, and He did not flinch from its severest trials. He lived in a peasant's home; He was clothed with coarse garments; He mingled with the lowly; He toiled daily with patient hands. His example shows us that it is man's duty to be industrious and that labor is honorable.

The Relation Between Christianity and Human Effort

The things of earth are more closely connected with heaven and are more directly under the supervision of Christ than many realize. All right inventions and improvements have their source in Him who is wonderful in counsel and excellent in working. The skillful touch of the physician's hand, his power and nerve and muscle, his knowledge of the delicate mechanism of the body, is the wisdom of divine power, to be used in behalf of the suffering. The skill with which the carpenter uses his tools, the strength with which the blacksmith makes the anvil ring, come from God. Whatever we do, wherever we are placed, He desires to control our minds, that we may do perfect work.

Christianity and business, rightly understood, are not two separate things; they are one. Bible religion is to be brought into all that we do and say. Human and divine agencies are to combine in temporal as well as spiritual achievements. They are to be united in all human pursuits, in mechanical and agricultural labors, in mercantile and scientific enterprises.

There is a remedy for indolence, and that is to throw

off sluggishness as a sin that leads to perdition, and go to work, using with determination and vigor the physical ability that God has given. The only cure for a useless, inefficient life is determined, persevering effort. Life is not given us to be spent in idleness or self-pleasing; before us are placed great possibilities. In the capital of strength a precious talent has been entrusted to men for labor. This is of more value than any bank deposit and should be more highly prized, for through the possibilities that it affords for enabling men to lead a useful, happy life it may be made to yield interest and compound interest. It is a blessing that cannot be purchased with gold or silver, houses or lands; and God requires it to be used wisely. No man has a right to sacrifice this talent to the corroding influence of inaction. All are as accountable for the capital of physical strength as for their capital of means.

The race is not always to the swift, nor the battle to the strong; and those who are diligent in business may not always be prospered. But it is "the hand of the diligent" that "maketh rich." And while indolence and drowsiness grieve the Holy Spirit and destroy true godliness, they also tend to poverty and want. "He becometh poor that dealeth with a slack hand." Proverbs 10:4.

Judicious labor is a healthful tonic for the human race. It makes the feeble strong, the poor rich, the wretched happy. Satan lies in ambush, ready to destroy those whose leisure gives him opportunity to approach them under some attractive disguise. He is never more successful than when he comes to men in their idle hours.

The Lessons of Contented Industry

Among the evils resulting from wealth, one of the greatest is the fashionable idea that work is degrading. The prophet Ezekiel declares: "Behold, this was the iniquity of thy sister Sodom, pride, fullness of bread, and abundance of idleness was in her and in her daughters, neither did she strengthen the hand of the poor and needy." Ezekiel 16:49. Here are presented before us the terrible results of idleness, which enfeebles the mind, debases the soul, and perverts the understanding, making a curse of that which was given as a blessing. It is the working man or woman who sees something great and good in life, and who is willing to bear its responsibilities with faith and hope.

The essential lesson of contented industry in the necessary duties of life is yet to be learned by many of Christ's followers. It requires more grace, more stern discipline of character, to work for God in the capacity of mechanic, merchant, lawyer, or farmer, carrying the precepts of Christianity into the ordinary business of life, than to labor as an acknowledged missionary in the open field. It requires a strong spiritual nerve to bring religion into the workshop and the business office, sanctifying the details of everyday life, and ordering every transaction according to the standard of God's word. But this is what the Lord requires.

The apostle Paul regarded idleness as a sin. He learned the trade of tentmaking in its higher and lower branches, and during his ministry he often worked at this trade to support himself and others. Paul did not regard as lost the time thus spent. As he worked, the apostle had access to a class of people whom he could not otherwise have reached. He showed his associates that skill in the common arts is a gift from God. He taught that even in everyday toil God is to be honored. His toil-hardened hands detracted nothing from the force of his pathetic appeals as a Christian minister.

God designs that all shall be workers. The toiling beast of burden answers the purpose of its creation better than does the indolent man. God is a constant worker. The angels are workers; they are ministers of God to the children of men. Those who look forward to a heaven of inactivity will be disappointed, for the economy of heaven provides no place for the gratification of indolence. But to the weary and heavy-laden rest is promised. It is the faithful servant who will be welcomed from his labors to the joy of his Lord. He will lay off his armor with rejoicing, and will forget the noise of battle in the glorious rest prepared for those who conquer through the cross of Calvary.

On every hand parents are neglecting to instruct and train their children for useful labor. The youth are allowed to grow up in ignorance of the simple and necessary duties. Those who have been thus unfortunate must awake and take the burden of the matter upon themselves; if they ever expect to succeed in life they must find incentives to the useful employment of their God-given powers.

WORDS OF COUNSEL

It is in the order of God that the physical as well as the mental powers shall be trained; but the character of the physical exercise taken should be in complete harmony with the lessons given by Christ to His disciples. Those lessons should be exemplified in the lives of Christians so that in all the education and self-training of teachers and students the heavenly agencies may not record of them that they are "lovers of pleasures." This is the record now being made of a large number, "Lovers of pleasures more than lovers of God." 2 Timothy 3:4. Thus Satan and his angels are laying their snares for souls. They are working upon the minds of teachers and students to induce them to engage in exercises and amusements which become intensely absorbing, and which are of a character to strengthen the lower passions and to create appetites and passions that will counteract the operations of the Spirit of God upon human hearts.

All the teachers in a school need exercise, a change of employment. God has pointed out what this should be—useful, practical work. But many have turned away from God's plan to follow human inventions to the detriment of spiritual life. Amusements are doing more to counteract the working of the Holy Spirit than anything else, and the Lord is grieved.

Those teachers who have not a progressive religious experience, who are not learning daily lessons in the school of Christ, that they may be examples to the flock, but who accept their wages as the main consideration, are not fit for the solemn position they occupy. "Take heed therefore unto yourselves," the word of God declares, "and to all the flock, over the which the Holy Ghost hath made you overseers, to feed the church of God, which He hath purchased with His own blood." "Feed the flock of God which is among you, taking the oversight thereof, not by constraint, but willingly; not for filthy lucre, but of a ready mind." Acts 20:28; 1 Peter 5:2. These words are spoken to the teachers in all our schools, which are established, as God designed they should be, after the example of the schools of the prophets, to impart knowledge of a high order, not mingling dross with the silver. But false ideas and unsound practices are leavening that which should ever be kept pure, institutions in which the love and fear of God should ever be first.

Let the teachers learn daily lessons in the school of Christ. "Take My yoke upon you, and learn of Me," He says; "for I am meek and lowly in heart: and ye shall find rest unto your souls." Matthew 11:29. There is altogether too little of Christ and too much of self. But those who are under the dictation of the Spirit of God, under the rule of Christ, will be ensamples to the flock. When the Chief Shepherd shall appear, these will receive the crown of life that fadeth not away.

"Likewise, ye younger, submit yourselves unto the elder. Yea, all of you be subject one to another, and be clothed with humility: for God resisteth the proud, and giveth grace to the humble. Humble yourselves therefore under the mighty hand of God, that He may exalt you in due time." 1 Peter 5:5, 6.

All self-uplifting works out the natural result—making character of which God cannot approve. Work and teach; work in Christ's lines, and then you will never work in your own weak ability, but will have the cooperation of the divine.

"Be sober, be vigilant; because your adversary the devil, as a roaring lion, walketh about, seeking whom he may devour." Verse 8. He is on the playground, watching your amusements, and catching every soul whom he finds off guard, sowing his seeds in human hearts, and gaining control of human minds. He is present in every exercise in the schoolroom. Those students who allow their minds to be deeply excited over games are not in the best condition to receive the instruction, the counsel, the reproof, most essential for them.

Physical exercise was marked out by the God of wisdom. Some hours each day should be devoted to useful education in lines of work that will help the students in learning the duties of practical life, which are essential for all our youth.

There is need of everyone in every school and in every other institution being, as was Daniel, in such close connection with the Source of all wisdom that he will be enabled to reach the highest standard in every line. The love and fear of God was before Daniel; and conscious of his amenability to God, he trained all his powers to respond as far as possible to the loving care of the Great Teacher. The four Hebrew children would not allow selfish motives and love of amusements to occupy the golden moments of life. They worked with willing heart and ready mind. This is no higher standard than every Christian youth may reach.

———

Our workers—ministers, teachers, physicians, directors—all need to remember that they are pledged to co-operate with Christ, to obey His directions, to follow His guidance. Every hour they are to ask and receive power from on high. They are to cherish a constant sense of the Saviour's love, of His efficiency, His watchfulness, His tenderness. They are to look to Him as the shepherd and bishop of their souls. Then they will have the sympathy and support of the heavenly angels. Christ will be their joy and crown of rejoicing. Their hearts will be controlled by the Holy Spirit, and they will have a knowledge of the truth which merely nominal believers can never gain.

We do not half comprehend the significance of the Saviour's lessons. We do not realize how much they mean to the beings He has created. He loves the human race. Do you ask how much? I point you to Calvary. But earthly cares and earthly interests hide from our view the things of heavenly origin, so that their importance is not understood. If ministers and teachers had a deeper sense of their spiritual need, they would enter upon their work filled with the realization of the sacredness of their trust, and a higher life would circulate through our churches and institutions.

PHYSICAL LABOR FOR STUDENTS

With the present plan of education, a door of temptation is opened to the youth. Although they generally have too many hours of study they have many hours without anything to do. These leisure hours are frequently spent in a reckless manner. . . . Very many young men who have been religiously instructed at home, and who go out to the schools comparatively innocent and virtuous, become corrupt by associating with vicious companions. They lose self-respect and sacrifice noble principles. Then they are prepared to pursue the downward path; for they have so abused conscience that sin does not appear so exceeding sinful. These evils . . . might be remedied in a great degree if study and labor could be combined. . . .

Some students put the whole being into their studies and concentrate their minds upon the object of obtaining an education. They work the brain, but allow the physical powers to remain inactive. Thus the brain is overworked, and the muscles become weak because they are not exercised. When these students are graduated, it is evident that they have obtained their education at the expense of life. They have studied day and night, year after year, keeping their minds continually upon the stretch, while they have failed to exercise their muscles sufficiently. . . .

Young ladies frequently give themselves up to study, to the neglect of other branches of education even more essential for practical life than the study of books. And after having obtained their education, they are often invalids for life. They have neglected their health by remaining too much indoors, deprived of the pure air of heaven and of the God-given sunlight. These young women might have come from school in health had they combined with their studies household labor and exercise in the open air.

Health is a great treasure. It is the richest possession that mortals can have. Wealth, honor, or learning is dearly purchased if it be at the loss of the vigor of health. None of these attainments can secure happiness if health is wanting. . . .

The Curse of Inaction

In many cases parents who are wealthy do not feel the importance of giving their children an education in the practical duties of life as well as in the sciences. They do not see the necessity, for the good of their children's minds and morals, and for their future usefulness, of giving them a thorough understanding of useful labor. This is due their children, that, should misfortune come, they could stand forth in noble independence, knowing how to use their hands. If they have a capital of strength they cannot be poor even if they have not a dollar.

Many who in youth were in affluent circumstances may be robbed of all their riches and be left with parents and brothers and sisters dependent upon them for sustenance. Then how important that every youth be educated to labor, that he may be prepared for any emergency! Riches are indeed a curse when their possessors let them stand in the way of their sons and daughters' obtaining a knowledge of useful labor, that they may be qualified for practical life. . . .

Poverty, in many cases, is a blessing, for it prevents youth and children from being ruined by inaction. The physical as well as the mental powers should be cultivated and properly developed. The first and constant care of parents should be to see that their children have firm constitutions, that they may be sound men and women. It is impossible to attain this object without physical exercise. For their own physical health and moral good, children should be taught to work, even if there is no necessity so far as want is concerned. If they would have pure and virtuous characters they must have the discipline of well-regulated labor, which will bring into exercise all the muscles. The satisfaction that children have in being useful, and in denying themselves to help others, will be the most healthful pleasure they can enjoy. . . .

Parents, inaction is the greatest curse that ever came upon youth. Your daughters should not be allowed to lie in bed late in the morning, sleeping away the precious hours lent them of God to be used for the best purpose, and for which they will have to give an account to Him. That mother does her daughters great injury who bears the burdens that, for their own present and future good, they should share with her. . . .

Advantages of Physical Labor

Exercise in household labor is of the greatest advantage to young girls. Physical labor will not prevent the cultivation of the intellect: far from it. The advantages gained by physical labor will balance a person and prevent the mind from being overworked. The toil will come upon the muscles and relieve the wearied brain. . . . A sound body is required for a sound intellect. Physical soundness and a practical knowledge of all the necessary household duties will never be a hindrance to a well-developed intellect; both are highly important. . . .

Provision should have been made in past generations for education upon a larger scale. In connection with the schools should have been agricultural and manufacturing establishments. There should also have been teachers of household labor. And a portion of the time each day should have been devoted to labor that the physical and mental powers might be equally exercised. If schools had been established on the plan we have mentioned, there would not now be so many unbalanced minds. . . .

A constant strain upon the brain while the muscles are inactive, enfeebles the nerves and gives to students an almost uncontrollable desire for change and exciting amusements. When they are released, after being confined to study several hours each day, they are nearly wild. Many have never been controlled at home. They have been left to follow inclination, and they think that the restraint of the hours of study is a severe tax upon them; and because they have nothing to do after study hours, Satan suggests sport and mischief for a change. Their influence over other students is demoralizing. . . .

Had there been agricultural and manufacturing establishments connected with our schools, and had competent teachers been employed to educate the youth in the different branches of study and labor, devoting a portion of each day to mental improvement and a portion to physical labor, there would now be a more elevated class of youth to come upon the stage of action, to have influence in molding society. Many of the youth graduated from such institutions would come forth with stability of character. They would have perseverance, fortitude, and courage to surmount obstacles, and such principles that they would not be swayed by a wrong influence however popular.

There should have been experienced teachers to give lessons to young ladies in the cooking department. Young girls should have been taught how to cut, make, and mend garments, and thus become educated for the practical duties of life. For young men, there should have been establishments where they could learn different trades, which would bring into exercise their muscles as well as their mental powers.

If the youth can have but a one-sided education, which is of the greater consequence, a knowledge of the sciences, with all the disadvantages to health and life, or a knowledge of labor for practical life? We unhesitatingly answer, The latter. If one must be neglected, let it be the study of books.

The Education of Girls

There are very many girls who are married and have families who have but little practical knowledge of the duties devolving upon a wife and mother. They can read, and play upon an instrument of music; but they cannot cook. They cannot make good bread, which is very

10—C.T.P.

essential to the health of the family. They cannot cut and make garments, for they have never learned how. They regard these things as unessential, and in their married life they are as dependent upon someone to do these things for them as are their own little children. It is this inexcusable ignorance in regard to the most needful duties of life which makes very many unhappy families. . . .

Equalizing Labor

The minds of thinking men labor too hard. They frequently use their mental powers prodigally; while there is another class whose highest aim in life is physical labor. The latter class do not exercise the mind. Their muscles are exercised, while their brains are robbed of intellectual strength; just as the minds of thinking men are worked while their bodies are robbed of strength and vigor by their neglect to exercise their muscles. . . . If the intellectual would to some extent share the burden of the laboring class, and thus strengthen the muscles, the laboring class might do less, and devote a portion of their time to mental and moral culture. Those of sedentary and literary habits should take physical exercise, even if they have no need to labor as far as means are concerned. Health should be a sufficient inducement to lead them to unite physical with mental labor.

Moral, intellectual, and physical culture should be combined in order to have well-developed, well-balanced men and women. Some are qualified to exercise great intellectual strength, while others are inclined to love and enjoy physical labor. Both of these classes should seek to improve where they are deficient, that they may present to God their entire being, a living sacrifice, holy and acceptable to Him, which is their reasonable service. . . .

Those who are content to devote their lives to physical labor, and leave others to do the thinking for them, while they simply carry out what other brains have planned, will have strength of muscle, but feeble intellects. Their influence for good is small in comparison with what it might be if they would use their brains as well as their muscles. This class fall more readily if attacked by disease, because the system is not vitalized by the electrical force of the brain to resist disease. Men who have good physical powers should educate themselves to think as well as to act, and not depend upon others to be brains for them.

Work Not Degrading

It is a popular error with a large class to regard work as degrading; therefore young men are very anxious to educate themselves to become teachers, clerks, merchants, lawyers, and to occupy almost any position that does not require physical labor. Young women regard housework as belittling. And although the physical exercise required to perform household labor, if not too severe, is calculated to promote health, yet they seek for an education that will fit them to become teachers or clerks, or they learn some trade that will confine them indoors to sedentary employment. . . .

True, there is some excuse for young women not choosing housework for an employment because those who hire kitchen girls generally treat them as servants.

Frequently the employers do not respect them, but treat them as if they were unworthy to be members of the family. They do not give them the privileges they give the seamstress, the copyist, and the teacher of music.

But there can be no employment more important than that of housework. To cook well, to place wholesome food upon the table in an inviting manner, requires intelligence and experience. The one who prepares the food that is to be placed in the stomach, to be converted into blood to nourish the system, occupies a most important and elevated position. The position of copyist, dressmaker, or music teacher cannot equal in importance that of the cook.

A Reformatory Work

Time is too short now to accomplish that which might have been done in past generations; but we can do much, even in these last days, to correct the existing evils in the education of youth. . . .

We are reformers. We desire that our children should study to the best advantage. In order that they may do this, employment should be given them which will call the muscles into exercise. Daily systematic labor should constitute a part of the education of the youth, even at this late period. Much can now be gained by connecting labor with our schools. In following this plan the students will realize elasticity of spirit and vigor of thought, and will be able to accomplish more mental labor in a given time than they could by study alone. And they can leave school with their constitutions unimpaired and with strength and courage to persevere in any position in which the providence of God may place them.

Because time is short, we should work with diligence and double energy. Our children may never enter college, but they can obtain an education in those essential branches which they can turn to a practical use, and which will give culture to the mind and call its powers into exercise. Very many youth who have gone through a college course have not obtained that true education that they can put to practical use.—*Testimonies for the Church,* vol. 3, pp. 148-159.

I appeal to our churches where there are schools, to appoint as teachers of the children and youth those who love the Lord Jesus Christ and who will make the word of God the foundation of education. And they should teach the youth to keep themselves in health by obedience to the laws of right living. Teachers and pupils will derive mental and spiritual help from self-denial, by practicing the principles of health reform. They will surely find, as did Daniel and his companions, that blessings come from conforming the life to God's word.

"Watch and pray," is an injunction often repeated in the Scriptures. In the lives of those who obey this injunction there will be an undercurrent of happiness that will bless all with whom they are brought in contact. Those who are sour and cross in disposition will become sweet and gentle; those who are proud will become meek and lowly.

HEALTH AND EFFICIENCY

Health is an inestimable blessing and one more closely related to conscience and religion than many realize. It has a great deal to do with one's capability for service and should be as sacredly guarded as the character, for the more perfect the health the more perfect will be our efforts for the advancement of God's cause and for the blessing of humanity.

There is an important work to be done in our schools in teaching the youth the principles of health reform. The teachers should exert a reformatory influence in the matter of eating, drinking, and dressing, and should encourage their students to practice self-denial and self-control. The youth should be taught that all their powers are from God; that He has a claim upon every faculty; and that by abusing their health in any way they slight one of God's choicest blessings. The Lord gives them health to use in His service, and the greater their physical strength, the stronger their powers of endurance, the more they can do for the Master. Instead of abusing or overtaxing their physical powers, they should jealously guard them for His use.

Youth is the time to lay up knowledge in those lines that can be put into daily practice throughout the life. Youth is the time to establish good habits, to correct wrong ones, to gain and hold the power of self-control, to accustom oneself to ordering all the acts of life with reference to the will of God and the welfare of one's fellow creatures. Youth is the sowing time that determines the harvest of this life and the life beyond the grave. The habits formed in childhood and youth, the tastes acquired, the self-control gained, are almost certain to determine the future of the man or woman.

The importance of caring for the health should be taught as a Bible requirement. Perfect obedience to God's commands calls for conformity to the laws of the being. The science of education includes as full a knowledge of physiology as can be obtained. No one can properly understand his obligations to God unless he understands clearly his obligations to himself as God's property. He who remains in sinful ignorance of the laws of life and health, or who willfully violates these laws, sins against God.

The time spent in physical exercise is not lost. The student who is constantly poring over his books, while he takes but little exercise in the open air, does himself an injury. A proportionate exercise of the various organs and faculties of the body is essential to the best work of each. When the brain is constantly taxed while the other organs are left inactive, there is a loss of physical and mental strength. The physical powers are robbed of their healthy tone, the mind loses its freshness and vigor, and a morbid excitability is the result.

In order for men and women to have well-balanced minds, all the powers of the being should be called into use and developed. There are in this world many who are one-sided because only one set of faculties has been cultivated, while others are dwarfed from inaction. The education of many youth is a failure. They overstudy, while they neglect that which pertains to the practical life. That the balance of the mind may be maintained, a judicious system of physical work should be combined with mental work that there may be a harmonious development of all the powers.

Students should have manual work to do, and it will not hurt them if in doing this work they become weary. Do you not think that Christ became weary? Indeed He did. Weariness injures no one. It only makes rest the sweeter. The lesson cannot be too often repeated that education will be of little value without physical strength with which to use it. When students leave college, they should have better health and a better understanding of the laws of life than when they entered it.

Overstudy

The student who desires to put the work of two years into one should not be permitted to have his own way. To undertake to do double work means, with many, overtaxation of the mind and neglect of physical exercise. It is not reasonable to suppose that the mind can assimilate an oversupply of mental food, and it is as great a sin to overload the mind as it is to overload the digestive organs.

To those who are desirous of becoming efficient laborers in the cause of God I would say, If you are putting an undue amount of labor on the brain, thinking you will lose ground unless you study all the time, you should at once change your views and your course. Unless greater care is exercised in this respect, there are many who will go down to the grave prematurely.

In regulating the hours for sleep, there should be no haphazard work. Students should not form the habit of burning the midnight oil and taking the hours of the day for sleep. If they have been accustomed to doing this at home, they should correct the habit, going to bed at a seasonable hour. They will then rise in the morning refreshed for the duties of the day. In our schools the lights should be put out at half past nine.

Voice Culture

Voice culture is a subject that has much to do with the health of students. The youth should be taught how to breathe properly and how to read in such a way that no unnatural strain shall come on the throat and lungs, but that the work shall be shared by the abdominal muscles. Speaking from the throat, letting the sound come from the upper part of the vocal organs, impairs the health of these organs and decreases their efficiency. The abdominal muscles are to do the heaviest part of the labor, the throat being used as a channel. Many have died who might have lived had they been taught how to use the voice correctly. The right use of the abdominal muscles in reading and speaking will prove a remedy for many voice and chest difficulties, and the means of prolonging life.

Diet

The character of the food and the manner in which it is eaten exert a powerful influence on the health. Many students have never made a determined effort to control the appetite or to observe proper rules in regard to eating. Some eat too much at their meals, and some eat between meals whenever the temptation is presented.

The need of carefulness in habits of diet should be impressed on the minds of all students. I have been instructed that those attending our schools are not to be served with flesh foods or with preparations of food that are known to be unwholesome. Nothing that will serve to encourage a desire for stimulants should be placed on the table. I appeal to all to refuse to eat those things that will injure the health. Thus they can serve the Lord by sacrifice.

Those who obey the laws of health will give time and thought to the needs of the body and to the laws of digestion. And they will be rewarded by clearness of thought and strength of mind. On the other hand, it is possible for one to spoil his Christian experience by abuse of the stomach. Those things that derange the digestion have a benumbing influence on the finer feelings of the heart. That which darkens the skin and makes it dingy also clouds the spirits and destroys cheerfulness and peace of mind. Every habit that injures the health reacts upon the mind. That time is well spent which is directed to the establishment and preservation of sound physical and mental health. Firm, quiet nerves and a healthy circulation help men to follow right principles and to listen to the promptings of conscience.

Ventilation and Sanitation

Special attention should be paid to ventilation and sanitation. The teacher should put into practical use in the schoolroom the knowledge of the principles of physiology and hygiene. He may thus guard his pupils from many dangers to which they would be exposed through ignorance or neglect of sanitary laws. Many lives have been sacrificed because teachers have not given attention to these things.

Sudden changes of temperature should be avoided. Care should be taken to see that the students do not become chilled by sitting in drafts. It is not safe for the teacher to regulate the heat of the schoolroom by his own feelings. His own good, as well as that of the students, demands that a uniform temperature be maintained.

The Reward of Obedience

The brain is the citadel of the being. Wrong physical habits affect the brain and prevent the attainment of that which the students desire—a good mental discipline. Unless the youth are versed in the science of how to care for the body as well as for the mind, they will not be successful students. Study is not the principal cause of breakdown of the mental powers. The main cause is improper diet, irregular meals, a lack of physical exercise, and careless inattention in other respects to the laws of health. When we do all that we can to preserve the health, then we can ask God in faith to bless our efforts.

Before students talk of their attainments in the so-called "higher education," let them learn to eat and drink to the glory of God and to exercise brain, bone, and muscle in such a way as to fit them for the highest service. A student may devote all his powers to acquiring knowledge, but as he disobeys the laws that govern his being he will weaken his efficiency. By cherishing wrong habits, he loses the power of self-appreciation, and he loses self-control. He cannot reason correctly about matters that concern him most deeply, and becomes reckless and irrational in his treatment of mind and body.

The obligation resting upon us to keep the body in health is an individual responsibility. The Lord requires each one to work out his salvation day by day. He bids us reason from cause to effect, to remember that we are His property, and to unite with Him in keeping the body pure and healthy, and the whole being sanctified to Him.

The youth should be taught that they are not at liberty to do as they please with their lives. God will not hold guiltless those who treat lightly His precious gifts. Men should realize that the greater their endowment of strength, of talent, of means, or of opportunities, the more heavily should the burden of God's work rest upon them, and the more they should do for Him. The youth who are trained to believe that life is a sacred trust will hesitate to plunge into the vortex of dissipation and crime that swallows up so many promising young men of this age.

The teacher whose physical powers are already enfeebled by disease or overwork should pay especial attention to the laws of health. He should take time for recreation. When a teacher sees that his health is not sufficient to stand the pressure of heavy study, he should heed the admonition of nature and lighten the load. He should not take upon himself responsibilities outside of his schoolwork which will so tax him physically and mentally that his nervous system will be unbalanced, for by this course he will be unfitted to deal with minds and cannot do justice either to himself or to his students.

Sometimes the teacher carries into the schoolroom the shadow of darkness that has been gathering on his soul. He has been overtaxed and is nervous, or dyspepsia has colored everything a gloomy hue. He enters the schoolroom with quivering nerves and irritated stomach. Nothing seems to be done to please him; he thinks that his pupils are bent on showing him disrespect; and his sharp criticisms and censure are given on the right hand and on the left. Perhaps one or more of the students commits errors or is unruly. The case is exaggerated in his mind, and he is severe and cutting in his reproof of the one whom he thinks at fault. And the same injustice afterward prevents him from admitting that he has taken a wrong course. To maintain the dignity of his position, he has lost a golden opportunity to manifest the spirit of Christ, perhaps to gain a soul for heaven.

It is the duty of each teacher to do all in his power to present his body to Christ a living sacrifice, physically perfect, as well as morally free from defilement, that Christ may make him a co-worker with Himself in the salvation of souls.

SOME PRINCIPLES OF HEALTHFUL DRESSING

The Bible teaches modesty in dress. "In like manner also, that women adorn themselves in modest apparel." 1 Timothy 2:9. This forbids display in dress, gaudy colors, profuse ornamentation. Any device designed to attract attention to the wearer or to excite admiration is excluded from the modest apparel which God's word enjoins.

Our dress is to be inexpensive—not with "gold, or pearls, or costly array." Money is a trust from God. It is not ours to expend for the gratification of pride or ambition. In the hands of God's children it is food for the hungry and clothing for the naked. It is a defense to the oppressed, a means of health to the sick, of preaching the gospel to the poor. You could bring happiness to many hearts by using wisely the money that is now spent for show. Consider the life of Christ. Study His character, and be partakers with Him in His self-denial.

In the professed Christian world enough is expended for jewels and needlessly expensive dress to feed all the hungry and to clothe the naked. Fashion and display absorb the means that might comfort the poor and the suffering. They rob the world of the gospel of the Saviour's love. . . .

But our clothing, while modest and simple, should be of good quality, of becoming colors, and suited for service. It should be chosen for durability rather than display. It should provide warmth and proper protection.

The wise woman described in the Proverbs "is not afraid of the snow for her household: for all her household are clothed with double garments." Proverbs 31:21, margin.

Our dress should be cleanly. Uncleanliness in dress is unhealthful, and thus defiling to the body and to the soul. "Ye are the temple of God. . . . If any man defile the temple of God, him shall God destroy." 1 Corinthians 3:16, 17.

In all respects the dress should be healthful. "Above all things," God desires us to "be in health" (3 John 2)—health of body and of soul. And we are to be workers together with Him for the health of both soul and body. Both are promoted by healthful dress. It should have the grace, the beauty, the appropriateness, of natural simplicity.

Christ has warned us against the pride of life, but not against its grace and natural beauty. He pointed to the flowers of the field, to the lily unfolding in its purity, and said, "Even Solomon in all his glory was not arrayed like one of these." Matthew 6:29. Thus by the things of nature, Christ illustrates the beauty that heaven values, the modest grace, the simplicity, the purity, the appropriateness, that would make our attire pleasing to Him. The most beautiful dress He bids us wear upon the soul. No outward adorning can compare in value or loveliness with that "meek and quiet spirit" which in His sight is "of great price." 1 Peter 3:4. . . .

Physical Effects of Improper Dress

It was the adversary of all good who instigated the invention of the ever-changing fashions. He desires nothing so much as to bring grief and dishonor to God by working the misery and ruin of human beings. One of the means by which he most effectually accomplishes this is the devices of fashion, that weaken the body as well as enfeeble the mind and belittle the soul.

Women are subject to serious maladies, and their sufferings are greatly increased by their manner of dressing. Instead of preserving their health for the trying emergencies that are sure to come, they by their wrong habits too often sacrifice not only health but life, and leave to their children a legacy of woe in a ruined constitution, perverted habits, and false ideas of life.

One of fashion's wasteful and mischievous devices is the skirt that sweeps the ground. Uncleanly, uncomfortable, inconvenient, unhealthful—all this and more is true of the trailing skirt. It is extravagant, both because of the superfluous material required, and because of the needless wear on account of its length. And whoever has seen a woman in a trailing skirt, with hands filled with parcels, attempt to go up or down stairs, to enter a streetcar, to walk through a crowd, to walk in the rain or on a muddy road, needs no other proof of its inconvenience and discomfort.

Another serious evil is the wearing of skirts so that their weight must be sustained by the hips. This heavy weight, pressing upon the internal organs, drags them downward and causes weakness of the stomach and a feeling of lassitude, inclining the wearer to stoop, which further cramps the lungs, making correct breathing more difficult.

Of late years the dangers resulting from compression of the waist have been so fully discussed that few can be ignorant in regard to them; yet so great is the power of fashion that the evil continues. By this practice, women and young girls are doing themselves untold harm. It is essential to health that the chest have room to expand to its fullest extent in order that the lungs may be enabled to take full inspiration. When the lungs are restricted, the quantity of oxygen received into them is lessened. The blood is not properly vitalized, and the waste, poisonous matter which should be thrown off through the lungs is retained. In addition to this the circulation is hindered, and the internal organs are so cramped and crowded out of place that they cannot perform their work properly.

Tight lacing does not improve the form. One of the chief elements in physical beauty is symmetry, the harmonious proportion of parts. And the correct model for physical development is to be found, not in the figures displayed by French modistes, but in the human form as developed according to the laws of God in nature. God is the author of all beauty, and only as we conform to His ideal shall we approach the standard of true beauty.

Another evil which custom fosters is the unequal distribution of the clothing, so that while some parts of the body have more than is required, others are insufficiently clad. The feet and limbs, being remote from the vital organs, should be especially guarded from cold by abundant clothing. It is impossible to have health when the extremities are habitually cold; for if there is too little blood in them, there will be too much in other portions of the body. Perfect health requires a perfect circulation; but this cannot be had while three or four times as much clothing is worn upon the body where the vital organs are situated as upon the feet and limbs.

A multitude of women are nervous and careworn because they deprive themselves of the pure air that would make pure blood, and of the freedom of motion that would send the blood bounding through the veins, giving life, health, and energy. Many women have become confirmed invalids when they might have enjoyed health, and many have died of consumption and other diseases when they might have lived their allotted term of life, had they dressed in accordance with health principles and exercised freely in the open air.

In order to secure the most healthful clothing, the needs of every part of the body must be carefully studied. The character of the climate, the surroundings, the condition of the health, the age and occupation, must all be considered. Every article of dress should fit easily, obstructing neither the circulation of the blood nor a free, full, natural respiration. Everything worn should be so loose that when the arms are raised the clothing will be correspondingly lifted.

Women who are in failing health can do much for themselves by sensible dressing and exercise. When suitably dressed for outdoor enjoyment, let them exercise in the open air, carefully at first, but increasing the amount of exercise as they can endure it. By taking this course, many might regain health and live to take their share in the world's work.—*The Ministry of Healing,* pages 287-294.

A PRACTICAL TRAINING

Useful manual labor is a part of the gospel plan. The Great Teacher, enshrouded in the pillar of cloud, gave directions to Israel that every youth should be taught some line of useful employment. Therefore it was the custom of the Jews, the wealthy as well as the poorer classes, to teach their sons and daughters some useful trade, so that, should adverse circumstances arise, they would not be dependent upon others, but would be able to provide for their own necessities. They might be instructed in literary lines, but they must also be trained to some craft. This was deemed an indispensable part of their education.

Now, as in the days of Israel, every youth should be instructed in the duties of practical life. Each should acquire a knowledge of some branch of manual labor by which, if need be, he may obtain a livelihood. This is essential, not only as a safeguard against the vicissitudes of life, but from its bearing upon physical, mental, and moral development. Even if it were certain that one would never need to resort to manual labor for support, still he should be taught to work. Without physical exercise no one can have a sound constitution and vigorous health; and the discipline of well-regulated labor is no less essential to the securing of a strong, active mind and a noble character.

Students who have gained book knowledge without gaining a knowledge of practical work cannot lay claim to a symmetrical education. The energies that should have been devoted to business of various lines have been neglected. Education does not consist in using the brain alone. Physical employment is a part of the training essential for every youth. An important phase of education is lacking if the student is not taught how to engage in useful labor.

The healthful exercise of the whole being will give an education that is broad and comprehensive. Every student should devote a portion of each day to active labor. Thus habits of industry will be formed and a spirit of self-reliance encouraged, while the youth will be shielded from many evil and degrading practices that are so often the result of idleness. And this is all in keeping with the primary object of education; for in encouraging activity, diligence, and purity, we are coming into harmony with the Creator.

The greatest benefit is not gained from exercise that is taken as play or exercise merely. There is some benefit in being in the fresh air, and also from the exercise of the muscles; but let the same amount of energy be given to the performance of useful work, and the benefit will be greater. A feeling of satisfaction will be realized, for such exercise carries with it a sense of helpfulness and the approval of conscience for duty well done.

Students should go forth from our schools with educated efficiency, so that when thrown upon their own resources they will have knowledge which they can use and which is needful to success in life. Diligent study is essential, so also is diligent hard work. Play is not essential. Devotion of the physical powers to amusement is not most favorable to a well-balanced mind. If the time employed in physical exercise which step by step leads on to excess were used in working in Christ's lines, the blessing of God would rest upon the worker. The discipline for practical life that is gained by physical labor combined with mental taxation is sweetened by the reflection that it is qualifying mind and body better to perform the work that God designs men to do. The more perfectly the youth understand how to perform the duties of practical life, the greater will be their enjoyment day by day in being of use to others. The mind educated to enjoy useful labor becomes enlarged; through training and discipline it is fitted for usefulness, for it has acquired the knowledge essential to make its possessor a blessing to others.

I cannot find an instance in the life of Christ where He devoted time to play and amusement. He was the great educator for the present and the future life, yet I have not been able to find one instance where He taught the disciples to engage in amusement in order to gain physical exercise. The world's Redeemer gives to every man his work and bids him, "Occupy till I come." Luke 19:13. In doing this the heart warms to the enterprise. All the powers of the being are enlisted in the effort to obey. We have a high and holy calling. Teachers and students are to be stewards of the grace of Christ, and they are always to be earnest.

Industrial Work

In establishing our schools out of the cities, we shall give the students an opportunity to train the muscles to work as well as the brain to think. Students should be taught how to plant, how to gather the harvest, how to build, how to become acceptable missionary workers in practical lines. By their knowledge of useful industries they will often be enabled to break down prejudice; often they will be able to make themselves so useful that the truth will be recommended by the knowledge they possess.

In our school in Australia we educated the youth along these lines, showing them that in order to have an education that is complete, they must divide their time between the gaining of book knowledge and the securing of a knowledge of practical work. Part of each day was spent in manual labor. Thus the students learned how to clear the land, to cultivate the soil, and to build houses; and these lines of work were largely carried on in time that would otherwise have been spent in playing games and seeking for amusement. The Lord blessed the students who devoted their hours to learning lessons of usefulness. To the managers and teachers of that school I was instructed to say:

"Various industries should be carried on in our schools. The industrial instruction given should include the keeping of accounts, carpentry, and all that is comprehended in farming. Preparation should be made for the teaching of blacksmithing, painting, shoemaking, and for cooking, baking, washing, mending, typewriting, and printing. Every power at our command is to be brought into this training work, that students may go forth well equipped for the duties of practical life.

"Students should be given a practical education in agriculture. This will be of inestimable value to many in their future work. The training to be obtained in felling trees and in tilling the soil, as well as in literary lines, is the education that our youth should seek to obtain. Agriculture will open resources for self-support. Other lines of work, adapted to different students, may also be carried on. But the cultivation of the land will bring a special blessing to the workers. We should so train the youth that they will love to engage in the cultivation of the soil.

"There should be opened to the youth means whereby many may, while attending school, learn the trade of carpentry. Under the guidance of experienced workmen, carpenters who are apt to teach, patient, and kind, the youth should be taught how to build substantially and economically. Cottages and other buildings essential to the various lines of schoolwork are to be erected by the students themselves. These buildings should not be crowded close together, or built near the school buildings proper. In the management of the schoolwork, small companies should be formed, who should be taught to carry a full sense of their responsibility. All these things cannot be accomplished at once, but we can begin to work in faith."

With a practical training, students will be prepared to fill useful positions in many places. If in the opening providence of God it becomes necessary to erect a meetinghouse in some locality, the Lord is pleased if there are among His own people those to whom He has given wisdom and skill to perform the necessary work.

Let the students who are engaged in building do their tasks with thoroughness, and let them learn from these tasks lessons that will help in their character building. In order to have perfect characters, they must make their work as perfect as possible. Into every line of labor let there be brought that stability which means true economy. If in our schools the land were more faithfully cultivated, the buildings more disinterestedly cared for by the students, the love of sports and amusements, which causes so much perplexity in our schoolwork, would pass away.

For the lady students there are many employments which should be provided, that they may have a comprehensive and practical education. They should be taught dressmaking and gardening. Flowers should be cultivated and strawberries planted. Thus, while being educated in useful labor, they will have healthful outdoor exercise.

Bookbinding and a variety of other trades should be taught, which will not only furnish physical exercise, but will impart valuable knowledge.

In all our schools there should be those who are fitted to teach cooking. Classes for instruction in this subject should be held. Those who are receiving a training for service suffer a great loss when they do not gain a knowledge of how to prepare food so that it is both wholesome and palatable.

The science of cooking is not a small matter. The skillful preparation of food is one of the most essential arts. It should be regarded as among the most valuable of all the arts, because it is so closely connected with the life. Both physical and mental strength depend to a great degree upon the food we eat; therefore the one who prepares the food occupies an important and elevated position.

Both young men and young women should be taught how to cook economically, and to dispense with everything in the line of flesh food. Let no encouragement be given to the preparation of dishes which are composed in any degree of flesh food; for this is pointing to the darkness and ignorance of Egypt, rather than to the purity of health reform.

Women especially should learn how to cook. What part of the education of a girl is so important as this? Whatever may be her circumstances in life, here is knowledge that she may put to practical use. It is a branch of education which has a most direct influence upon health and happiness. There is practical religion in a loaf of good bread.

Culture on all points of practical life will make our youth useful after they leave the school to go to foreign countries. They will not then have to depend upon the people to whom they go to cook and sew for them, or to build their habitations. And they will be much more influential if they show that they can educate the ignorant how to labor with the best methods and to produce the best results. A smaller fund will be required to sustain such missionaries, because they have put to the very best use their physical powers in useful, practical labor combined with their studies. This will be appreciated where means are difficult to obtain. They will reveal that missionaries can become educators in teaching how to labor.

And wherever they go, all that they have gained in this line will give them standing room.

The Common Arts

Skill in the common arts is a gift from God. He provides both the gift and wisdom to use the gift aright. When He desired a work done on the tabernacle He said, "See, I have called by name Bezaleel the son of Uri, the son of Hur, of the tribe of Judah: and I have filled him with the Spirit of God, in wisdom, and in understanding, and in knowledge, and in all manner of workmanship." Exodus 31:2, 3. Through the prophet Isaiah the Lord said, "Give ye ear, and hear My voice; hearken, and hear My speech. Doth the plowman plow all day to sow? doth he open and break the clods of his ground? When he hath made plain the face thereof, doth he not cast abroad the fitches, and scatter the cumin, and cast in the principal wheat and the appointed barley and the rye in their place? For his God doth instruct him to discretion, and doth teach him.

"For the fitches are not threshed with a threshing instrument, neither is a cart wheel turned about upon the cumin; but the fitches are beaten out with a staff, and the cumin with a rod. Bread corn is bruised; because he will not ever be threshing it, nor break it with the wheel of his cart, nor bruise it with his horsemen. This also cometh forth from the Lord of hosts, which is wonderful in counsel, and excellent in working." Isaiah 28:23-29.

God dispenses His gifts as it pleases Him. He bestows one gift upon one, and another gift upon another, but all for the good of the whole body. It is in God's order that some shall be of service in one line of work, and others in other lines—all working under the selfsame Spirit. The recognition of this plan will be a safeguard against emulation, pride, envy, or contempt of one another. It will strengthen unity and mutual love.

A much larger number of young people need to have the advantages of our schools. They need the manual training course, which will teach them how to live an active, energetic life. Under wise, judicious, God-fearing directors, the students are to be taught different kinds of labor. Every branch of the work is to be conducted in the most thorough, systematic way that long experience and wisdom can enable us to plan and execute.

Let the teachers wake up to the importance of this subject, and teach agriculture and the other industries that it is essential for the students to understand. Let them seek in every department of labor to reach the very best results. Let the science of the word of God be brought into the work, that the students may understand correct principles and may reach the highest possible standard.

Does It Pay?

In many minds the question will arise, Can industrial work in our schools be made to pay? and if it cannot, should it be carried forward?

It would be surprising if industries could be made to pay immediately on being started. Sometimes God permits losses to come to teach us lessons that will keep us from making mistakes that would involve much larger losses. Let those who have had financial losses in their industrial work search carefully to find out the cause and endeavor to manage in such a way that in the future there will be no loss.

Let us remember that we are all members of God's family; and let us remember, too, that Satan and all his host are seeking constantly to force us into making mistakes, that our confidence in ourselves and in others may be destroyed. But when perplexities arise, shall we sit down on the stool of ignorance, and do nothing? God forbid.

There will be apparent drawbacks in the work, but this should not discourage us. The account books may show that the school has suffered some financial loss in carrying on industrial work; but if in these lines of work the students have learned lessons that will strengthen their character building, the books of heaven will show a gain far exceeding the financial loss. How many souls this work has helped to save will never be known till the day of judgment. Satan finds mischief for idle hands to do; but when students are kept busy in useful labor, the Lord has opportunity to work for them.

If, after carrying on manual training for one year, the managers of the school find that there has been a loss, let them seek to discover the reason for this, and guard against it in the future. But let not the spirit of censure prevail, for the Spirit of Christ is grieved when words of unkind criticism are spoken to those who have done their best. In the word of God there is encouragement as well as caution. God forbid that the hands of those who are trying to carry forward this line of work should be weakened.

I urge that our schools be given encouragement in their efforts to develop plans for the training of the youth in agricultural and other lines of industrial work. When, in ordinary business, pioneer work is done and preparation is made for future development, there is frequently a financial loss. But let us remember the blessing that physical exercise brings to the students. Many students have died while endeavoring to acquire an education, because they confined themselves too closely to mental effort.

We must not be narrow in our plans. In industrial training there are unseen advantages which cannot be measured or estimated. Let no one begrudge the effort necessary to carry forward successfully the plan that for years has been urged upon us as of primary importance.

———

Teachers will meet with trials. Discouragements will press upon them as they see their work unappreciated. Satan will strive to afflict them with bodily infirmities, hoping to lead them to murmur against God, to close their eyes to His goodness, His mercy, His love, and the exceeding weight of glory that awaits the overcomer. At such times let teachers remember that God is leading them to more perfect confidence in Him. If in their perplexity they will look to Him in faith, He will bring them from the furnace of trial refined and purified as gold tried in the fire.

Let the hard-pressed, sorely tried one say, "Though He slay me, yet will I trust in Him." "Although the fig tree shall not blossom, neither shall fruit be in the vines; the labor of the olive shall fail, and the fields shall yield no meat; the flock shall be cut off from the fold, and there shall be no herd in the stalls: yet I will rejoice in the Lord, I will joy in the God of my salvation." Job 13:15; Habakkuk 3:17, 18.

————————

Let not teachers have favorites among their students, or give to the bright, quick students the most attention. Those who are apparently the most unpromising most need the tact and kindly words that will bind their hearts to the heart of the teacher.

First impressions are not to be trusted. Students who at first seem dull and slow may in the end make greater progress than those who are naturally quicker. If they are thorough and systematic in their work they will gain much that others will fail to gain. Those who form habits of patient, persevering industry will accomplish more than those of quick, vivacious, brilliant mind, who, though grasping the point quickly, lose it just as readily. The patient ones, though slower to learn, will stand ahead of those who learn so quickly that they do not need to study.

————————

Students should not be so pressed with studies as to neglect the culture of the manners; and above all, they should let nothing interfere with their seasons of prayer, which bring them in connection with Christ. In no case should they deprive themselves of religious privileges.

FOR FURTHER STUDY

RECREATION

"Whatsoever ye do in word or deed, do all in the name of the Lord Jesus."

AS LIGHTS IN THE WORLD

It is God's purpose to manifest through His people the principles of His kingdom. That in life and character they may reveal these principles, He desires to separate them from the customs, habits, and practices of the world. He seeks to bring them nearer to Himself, that He may make known to them His will. His purpose for His people today is the same that He had for Israel when He brought them forth from Egypt. By beholding the goodness, the mercy, the justice, and the love of God revealed in His church, the world is to have a representation of His character. And when the law of God is thus exemplified in the life, even the world will recognize the superiority of those who love and fear and serve God above every other people in the world.

Seventh-day Adventists, above all people, should be patterns of piety, holy in heart and in conversation. To them have been entrusted the most solemn truths ever committed to mortals. Every endowment of grace and power and efficiency has been liberally provided. They look for the near return of Christ in the clouds of heaven. For them to give to the world the impression that their

(321)

faith is not a dominating power in their lives is greatly to
dishonor God.

Because of the increasing power of Satan's temptations,
the times in which we live are full of peril for the children
of God, and we need to learn constantly of the Great
Teacher, that we may take every step in surety and righteousness. Wonderful scenes are opening before us; and
at this time a living testimony is to be borne in the lives
of God's professed people, so that the world may see that
in this age, when evil reigns on every side, there is yet a
people who are laying aside their will and are seeking to
do God's will—a people in whose hearts and lives God's
law is written.

Representatives of Christ

God expects those who bear the name of Christ to
represent Him. Their thoughts are to be pure, their
words noble and uplifting. The religion of Christ is to
be interwoven with all that they do and say. They are
to be a sanctified, purified, holy people, communicating
light to all with whom they come in contact. It is His
purpose that by exemplifying the truth in their lives they
shall be a praise in the earth. The grace of Christ is
sufficient to bring this about. But let God's people remember that only as they believe and work out the principles of the gospel can they fulfill His purpose. Only as
they yield their God-given capabilities to His service will
they enjoy the fullness and the power of the promise
whereon the church has been called to stand.

Before Christ went to His final conflict with the powers of darkness, He lifted up His eyes to heaven and

prayed for His disciples. He said, "I pray not that Thou shouldest take them out of the world, but that Thou shouldest keep them from the evil. They are not of the world, even as I am not of the world. Sanctify them through Thy truth: Thy word is truth." John 17:15-17.

The followers of Christ are to be separate from the world in principles and interests, but they are not to isolate themselves from the world. The Saviour mingled constantly with men, not to encourage them in anything that was not in accordance with God's will, but to uplift and ennoble them. "I sanctify Myself," He declared, "that they also might be sanctified." John 17:19. So the Christian is to abide among men, that the savor of divine love may be as salt to preserve the world from corruption.

Strength in Prayer

Daily beset by temptation, constantly opposed by the leaders of the people, Christ knew that He must strengthen His humanity by prayer. In order to be a blessing to men, He must commune with God, pleading for energy, perseverance, and steadfastness. Thus He showed His disciples where His strength lay. Without this daily communion with God, no human being can gain power for service. Christ alone can direct the thoughts aright. He alone can give noble aspirations and fashion the character after the divine similitude. If we draw near to Him in earnest prayer, He will fill our hearts with high and holy purposes, and with deep longings for purity and righteousness. The dangers thickening around us demand from those who have an experience in the things of God, a watchful supervision. Those who walk humbly before God, distrustful of their own wisdom, will realize their danger and will know God's keeping care.

The power of a higher, purer, nobler life is our great need. The world is watching to see what fruit is borne by professed Christians. It has a right to look for self-denial and self-sacrifice from those who believe advanced truth. It is watching, ready to criticize with keenness and severity our words and acts. Everyone who acts a part in the work of God is weighed in the scales of human discernment. Impressions favorable or unfavorable to Bible religion are constantly being made on the minds of all with whom we have to do.

And God and the angels are watching. God desires His people to show by their lives the advantage of Christianity over worldliness, to show that they are working on a high, holy plane. He longs to see them showing that the truth they have received has made them children of the heavenly King. He longs to make them channels through which He can pour His boundless love and mercy.

Christ is waiting with longing desire for the manifestation of Himself in His church. When the character of the Saviour shall be perfectly reproduced in His people, then He will come to claim His own. It is the privilege of every Christian, not only to look for, but to hasten, the coming of our Lord. Were all who profess His name bearing fruit to His glory, how quickly the whole world would be sown with the seed of the gospel! Quickly the last great harvest would be ripened, and Christ would come.

DANGEROUS AMUSEMENTS FOR THE YOUNG

The desire for excitement and pleasing entertainment is a temptation and a snare to God's people, and especially to the young. Satan is constantly preparing inducements to attract minds from the solemn work of preparation for scenes just in the future. Through the agency of worldlings he keeps up a continual excitement to induce the unwary to join in worldly pleasures. There are shows, lectures, and an endless variety of entertainments that are calculated to lead to a love of the world; and through this union with the world, faith is weakened.

Satan is a persevering workman, an artful, deadly foe. Whenever an incautious word is spoken, whether in flattery or to cause the youth to look upon some sin with less abhorrence, he takes advantage of it and nourishes the evil seed, that it may take root and yield a bountiful harvest. He is in every sense of the word a deceiver, a skillful charmer. He has many finely woven nets, which appear innocent, but which are skillfully prepared to entangle the young and unwary. The natural mind leans toward pleasure and self-gratification. It is Satan's policy to fill the mind with a desire for worldly amusement, that there may be no time for the question, How is it with my soul?

An Unfortunate Age

We are living in an unfortunate age for the young. The prevailing influence in society is in favor of allowing the youth to follow the natural turn of their own minds. If their children are very wild, parents flatter themselves that when they are older and reason for themselves they will leave off their wrong habits and become useful men and women. What a mistake! For years they permit an enemy to sow the garden of the heart, and suffer wrong principles to grow and strengthen, seeming not to discern the hidden dangers and the fearful ending of the path that seems to them the way of happiness. In many cases all the labor afterward bestowed upon these youth will avail nothing.

The standard of piety is low among professed Christians generally, and it is hard for the young to resist the worldly influences that are encouraged by many church members. The majority of nominal Christians, while they profess to be living for Christ, are really living for the world. They do not discern the excellence of heavenly things, and therefore cannot truly love them. Many profess to be Christians because Christianity is considered honorable. They do not discern that genuine Christianity means cross-bearing, and their religion has little influence to restrain them from taking part in worldly pleasures.

Some can enter the ballroom and unite in all the amusements which it affords. Others cannot go to such lengths as this, yet they can attend parties of pleasure, picnics, shows and other places of worldly amusement; and the most discerning eye would fail to detect any difference between their appearance and that of unbelievers.

The Training of Children

In the present state of society it is no easy task for parents to restrain their children and instruct them according to the Bible rule of right. Children often become impatient under restraint and wish to have their own way and to go and come as they please. Especially from the age of ten to eighteen they are inclined to feel that there can be no harm in going to worldly gatherings of young associates. But the experienced Christian parents can see danger. They are acquainted with the peculiar temperaments of their children and know the influence of these things upon their minds, and from a desire for their salvation they should keep them back from these exciting amusements.

When the children decide for themselves to leave the pleasures of the world and to become Christ's disciples, what a burden is lifted from the hearts of careful, faithful parents! Yet even then the labors of the parents must not cease. These youth have just commenced in earnest the warfare against sin and against the evils of the natural heart, and they need in a special sense the counsel and watchcare of their parents.

A Time of Trial Before the Young

Young Sabbathkeepers who have yielded to the influence of the world will have to be tested and proved. The perils of the last days are upon us, and a trial is before the young which many have not anticipated. They will be brought into distressing perplexity, and the genuineness of their faith will be proved. They profess to be looking for the Son of man, yet some of them have been a miserable example to unbelievers. They have not been willing to give up the world, but have united with the world in attending picnics and other gatherings for pleasure, flattering themselves that they were engaging in innocent amusement. Yet it is just such indulgences that separate them from God and make them children of the world.

Some are constantly leaning to the world. Their views and feelings harmonize much better with the spirit of the world than with that of Christ's self-denying followers. It is perfectly natural that they should prefer the company of those whose spirit will best agree with their own. And such have quite too much influence among God's people. They take part with them and have a name among them, but they are a text for unbelievers and for the weak and unconsecrated ones in the church. In this refining time these professors will either be wholly converted and sanctified by obedience to the truth, or they will be left with the world to receive their reward with the worldlings.

God does not own the pleasure seeker as His follower. Those only who are self-denying, and who live lives of sobriety, humility, and holiness, are true followers of Jesus. And such cannot enjoy the frivolous, empty conversation of the lover of the world.

Separation From the World

The true followers of Christ will have sacrifices to make. They will shun places of worldly amusement because they find no Jesus there—no influence which will make them heavenly-minded and increase their growth in grace. Obedience to the word of God will lead them to come out from all these things and be separate.

"By their fruits ye shall know them" (Matthew 7:20), the Saviour declared. All the true followers of Christ bear fruit to His glory. Their lives testify that a good work has been wrought in them by the Spirit of God, and their fruit is unto holiness. Their lives are elevated and pure. Right actions are the unmistakable fruit of true godliness, and those who bear no fruit of this kind reveal that they have no experience in the things of God. They are not in the Vine. Said Jesus, "Abide in Me, and I in you. As the branch cannot bear fruit of itself, except it abide in the vine; no more can ye, except ye abide in Me. I am the Vine, ye are the branches: he that abideth in Me, and I in him, the same bringeth forth much fruit: for without Me ye can do nothing." John 15:4, 5.

Those who would be worshipers of the true God must sacrifice every idol. Jesus said to the lawyer, "Thou shalt love the Lord thy God with all thy heart, and with all thy soul, and with all thy mind. This is the first and great commandment." Matthew 22:37, 38. The first four precepts of the Decalogue allow no separation of affections from God. Nor must anything share our supreme delight in Him. We cannot advance in Christian experience until we put away everything that separates us from God.

The great Head of the church, who has chosen His people out of the world, requires them to be separate from the world. He designs that the spirit of His commandments, by drawing His followers to Himself, shall separate them from worldly elements. To love God and keep His commandments is far away from loving the world's pleasures and its friendship. There is no concord between Christ and Belial.

Promises to the Young

The youth who follow Christ have a warfare before them; they have a daily cross to bear in coming out of the world and imitating the life of Christ. But there are many precious promises on record for those who seek the Saviour early. Wisdom calls to the sons of men, "I love them that love Me; and those that seek Me early shall find Me." Proverbs 8:17.

"Wherefore gird up the loins of your mind, be sober, and hope to the end for the grace that is to be brought unto you at the revelation of Jesus Christ; as obedient children, not fashioning yourselves according to the former lusts in your ignorance: but as He which hath called you is holy, so be ye holy in all manner of conversation." 1 Peter 1:13-15. "For the grace of God that bringeth salvation hath appeared to all men, teaching us that, denying ungodliness and worldly lusts, we should live soberly, righteously, and godly, in this present world; looking for that blessed hope, and the glorious appearing of the great God and our Saviour Jesus Christ; who gave Himself for us, that He might redeem us from all iniquity, and purify unto Himself a peculiar people, zealous of good works." Titus 2:11-14.

ESTABLISHING RIGHT PRINCIPLES IN THE YOUTH

Education comprises more than a knowledge of books. Proper education includes not only mental discipline, but that training which will secure sound morals and correct deportment. . . .

Hundreds of youth of various dispositions and of different education are associated in the school, and great care as well as much patience is required to balance in the right direction minds that have been warped by bad management. Some have never been disciplined, and others have been governed too much and have felt, when away from the vigilant hands that held the reigns of control, perhaps too tightly, that they were free to do as they pleased. They despise the very thought of restraint. These varying elements brought together in our college, bring care, burdens, and weighty responsibility, not only upon teachers, but on the entire church.

The Temptations of Youth

The students at our college are exposed to manifold temptations. They will be brought in contact with individuals of almost every stamp of mind and morals. Those who have any religious experience are censurable if they do not place themselves in a position to resist every evil influence. But many choose to follow inclination. They do not consider that they must make or mar their own happiness. It is in their own power so to improve their time and opportunities as to develop a character that will make them happy and useful. . . .

The Duties of Parents

The dangers of the young are greatly increased as they are thrown into the society of a large number of their own age, of varied character and habits of life. Under these circumstances, many parents are inclined to relax rather than redouble their own efforts to guard and control their children. Thus they cast a tremendous burden upon those who feel the responsibility. When these parents see that their children are becoming demoralized, they are inclined to find fault with those who have charge of the work, when the evils have been caused by the course of the parents themselves.

Instead of uniting with those who bear the burdens, to lift up the standard of morals, and working with heart and soul in the fear of God to correct the wrongs in their children, many parents soothe their own consciences by saying, "My children are no worse than others." They seek to conceal the glaring wrongs which God hates, lest their children shall become offended and take some desperate course. If the spirit of rebellion is in their hearts, far better subdue it now than permit it to increase and strengthen by indulgence. If parents would do their duty, we should see a different state of things. Many of these parents have backslidden from God. They do not have wisdom from Him to perceive the devices of Satan and to resist his snares. . . .

Every son and daughter should be called to account if absent from home at night. Parents should know what company their children are in and at whose house they spend their evenings. Some children deceive their parents with falsehoods to avoid exposure of their wrong course. There are those who seek the society of corrupt companions and secretly visit saloons and other forbidden places of resort in the city. There are students who visit the billiard rooms, and who engage in card playing, flattering themselves that there is no danger. Since their object is merely amusement, they feel perfectly safe. It is not the lower grade alone who do this. Some who have been carefully reared, and educated to look upon such things with abhorrence, are venturing upon the forbidden ground.

The young should be controlled by firm principle, that they may rightly improve the powers which God has given them. But youth follow impulse so much and so blindly, without reference to principle, that they are constantly in danger. Since they cannot always have the guidance and protection of parents and guardians, they need to be trained to self-reliance and self-control. They must be taught to think and act from conscientious principle.

Relaxation and Amusement

Those who are engaged in study should have relaxation. The mind must not be constantly confined to close thought, for the delicate mental machinery becomes worn. The body as well as the mind must have exercise. But there is great need of temperance in amusements, as in every other pursuit. And the character of these amusements should be carefully and thoroughly considered.

Every youth should ask himself, What influence will these amusements have on physical, mental, and moral health? Will my mind become so infatuated as to forget God? Shall I cease to have His glory before me?

Card playing should be prohibited. The associations and tendencies are dangerous. . . . There is nothing in such amusements beneficial to soul or body. There is nothing to strengthen the intellect, nothing to store it with valuable ideas for future use. The conversation is often upon trivial and degrading subjects. . . .

Expertness in handling cards often leads to a desire to put this knowledge and tact to some use for personal benefit. A small sum is staked, and then a larger, until a thirst for gaming is acquired, which leads to certain ruin. How many has this pernicious amusement led to every sinful practice, to poverty, to prison, to murder, and to the gallows! And yet many parents do not see the terrible gulf of ruin that is yawning for our youth.

Among the most dangerous resorts for pleasure is the theater. Instead of being a school for morality and virtue, as is so often claimed, it is the very hotbed of immorality. Vicious habits and sinful propensities are strengthened and confirmed by these entertainments. Low songs, lewd gestures, expressions, and attitudes, deprave the imagination and debase the morals. Every youth who habitually attends such exhibitions will be corrupted in principle. There is no influence in our land more powerful to poison the imagination, to destroy religious impressions, and to blunt the relish for the tranquil pleasures and sober realities of life than theatrical amusements. The love for these scenes increases with every indulgence, as the desire for intoxicating drink strengthens with its use. The only safe course is to shun the theater, the circus, and every other questionable place of amusement.

There are modes of recreation which are highly beneficial to both mind and body. An enlightened, discriminating mind will find abundant means for entertainment and diversion, from sources not only innocent, but instructive. Recreation in the open air, the contemplation of the works of God in nature, will be of the highest benefit.—*Testimonies for the Church,* vol. 4, pp. 648-653.

Youth cannot be made as sedate and grave as old age, the child as sober as the sire. While sinful amusements are condemned, as they should be, let parents, teachers, and guardians of youth provide in their stead innocent pleasures, which will not taint or corrupt the morals. Do not bind down the young to rigid rules and restraints that will lead them to feel themselves oppressed and to break over and rush into paths of folly and destruction. With a firm, kind, considerate hand, hold the lines of government, guiding and controlling their minds and purposes, yet so gently, so wisely, so lovingly, that they will still know that you have their best good in view.

CHRISTIAN RECREATION

While we are seeking to refresh our spirits and invigorate our bodies we are required of God to use all our powers at all times to the best purpose. We can, and should, conduct our recreations in such a manner that we shall be better fitted for the more successful discharge of the duties devolving upon us, and our influence will be more beneficial upon those with whom we associate. We can return from such occasions to our homes improved in mind and refreshed in body, and prepared to engage in the work anew with better hope and better courage.

We are of that class who believe that it is our privilege every day of our lives to glorify God upon the earth; that we are not to live in this world merely for our own amusement, merely to please ourselves. We are here to benefit humanity and to be a blessing to society; and if we let our minds run in that low channel that many who are seeking only vanity and folly permit their minds to run in, how can we be a benefit to our race and generation? how can we be a blessing to society around us? We cannot innocently indulge in any amusement which will unfit us for the more faithful discharge of ordinary duties.

Between the associations of the followers of Christ for Christian recreation, and worldly gatherings for pleasure and amusement, will exist a marked contrast. Instead of prayer and the mentioning of Christ and sacred things, will be heard from the lips of worldlings the silly laugh and the trifling conversation. The idea is to have a general high time. Their amusements commence in folly and end in vanity. Our gatherings should be so conducted, and we should so conduct ourselves, that when we return to our homes we can have a conscience void of offense toward God and man; a consciousness that we have not wounded or injured in any manner those with whom we have been associated, or had an injurious influence over them.

The natural mind leans toward pleasure and self-gratification. It is Satan's policy to manufacture an abundance of this. He seeks to fill the minds of men with a desire for worldly amusement, that they may have no time to ask themselves the question, How is it with my soul? The love of pleasure is infectious. Given up to this, the mind hurries from one point to another, ever seeking for some amusement. Obedience to the law of God counteracts this inclination and builds barriers against ungodliness.

Young men should remember that they are accountable for all the privileges they have enjoyed, for the improvement of their time, and for the right use of their abilities. They may inquire, Shall we have no amusement or recreation? Shall we work, work, work, without variation?

Any amusement in which you can engage asking the blessing of God upon it in faith will not be dangerous. But any amusement which disqualifies you for secret prayer, for devotion at the altar of prayer, or for taking part in the prayer meeting, is not safe, but dangerous.

WORLDLY AMUSEMENTS

If there is anything in our world that should inspire enthusiasm, it is the cross of Calvary. "Behold, what manner of love the Father hath bestowed upon us, that we should be called the sons of God: therefore the world knoweth us not, because it knew Him not." 1 John 3:1. "For God so loved the world, that He gave His only-begotten Son, that whosoever believeth in Him should not perish, but have everlasting life." John 3:16. Christ is to be accepted, believed on, and exalted. This is to be the theme of conversation—the preciousness of Christ. . . .

Parties of Pleasure

While there has been so much fear of excitement and enthusiasm in the service of God, there has been manifest an enthusiasm in another line which to many seems wholly congenial. I refer to the parties of pleasure that have been held among our people. These occasions have taken much of the time and attention of people who profess to be servants of Christ; but have these assemblies tended to the glory of His name? Was Jesus invited to preside over them?

Gatherings for social fellowship may be made in the highest degree profitable and instructive when those who meet together have the love of God glowing in their hearts, when they meet to exchange thoughts in regard to the word of God, or to consider methods for advancing

His work and doing good to their fellow men. When nothing is said or done to grieve the Holy Spirit of God, but He is regarded as a welcome guest, then God is honored, and those who meet together will be refreshed and strengthened.

"Then they that feared the Lord spake often one to another: and the Lord hearkened, and heard it, and a book of remembrance was written before Him for them that feared the Lord, and that thought upon His name. And they shall be Mine, saith the Lord of hosts, in that day when I make up My jewels." Malachi 3:16, 17.

But there has been a class of social gatherings in ——— of an entirely different character, parties of pleasure that have been a disgrace to our institutions and to the church. They encourage pride of dress, pride of appearance, self-gratification, hilarity, and trifling. Satan is entertained as an honored guest and takes possession of those who patronize these gatherings.

A view of one such company was presented to me, where were assembled those who profess to believe the truth. One was seated at the instrument of music, and such songs were poured forth as made the watching angels weep. There was mirth, there was coarse laughter, there was abundance of enthusiasm, and a kind of inspiration; but the joy was such as Satan only is able to create. This is an enthusiasm and infatuation of which all who love God will be ashamed. It prepares the participants for unholy thought and action. I have reason to think that some who were engaged in that scene heartily repented of the shameful performance.

Many such gatherings have been presented to me. I have seen the gaiety, the display in dress, the personal adornment. All want to be thought brilliant and give themselves up to hilarity, foolish jesting, cheap, coarse flattery, and uproarious laughter. The eyes sparkle, the cheek is flushed, conscience sleeps. With eating and drinking and merrymaking, they do their best to forget God. The scene of pleasure is their paradise. And Heaven is looking on, seeing and hearing all. . . .

The tenor of the conversation reveals the treasure of the heart. The cheap, common talk, the words of flattery, the foolish witticism, spoken to create a laugh, are the merchandise of Satan, and all who indulge in this talk are trading in his goods. Impressions are made upon those who hear these things, similar to that made upon Herod when the daughter of Herodias danced before him. All these transactions are recorded in the books of heaven, and at the last great day they will appear in their true light before the guilty ones. Then all will discern in them the alluring, deceptive workings of the devil, to lead them into the broad road and the wide gate that opens to their ruin.

Satan has been multiplying his snares in ———; and professed Christians who are superficial in character and religious experience are used by the tempter as his decoys. This class are always ready for the gatherings for pleasure or sport, and their influence attracts others. Young men and women who have tried to be Bible Christians are persuaded to join the party, and they are drawn into the ring. They do not prayerfully consult the divine standard, to learn what Christ has said in regard to the fruit to be borne on the Christian tree. They do not discern that these entertainments are really Satan's banquet, prepared to keep souls from accepting the call to the marriage supper of the Lamb and preventing them from receiving the white robe of character, which is the righteousness of Christ. They become confused as to what it is right for them as Christians to do. They do not want to be thought singular, and naturally incline to follow the example of others. Thus they come under the influence of those who have never had the divine touch on heart or mind. . . .

Right Attitude of the Christian

The Eternal God has drawn the line of distinction between the saints and the sinners, the converted and the unconverted. The two classes do not blend into each other imperceptibly, like the colors of the rainbow. They are as distinct as midday and midnight.

Those who are seeking the righteousness of Christ will be dwelling upon the themes of the great salvation. The Bible is the storehouse that supplies their souls with nourishing food. They meditate upon the incarnation of Christ, they contemplate the great sacrifice made to save them from perdition, to bring in pardon, peace, and everlasting righteousness. The soul is aglow with these grand and elevating themes. Holiness and truth, grace and righteousness, occupy the thoughts. Self dies, and Christ lives in His servants. In contemplation of the word their hearts burn within them as did the hearts of the two disciples while they went to Emmaus and Christ walked with them by the way and opened to them the scriptures concerning Himself.

How few realize that Jesus, unseen, is walking by their side! How ashamed many would be to hear His voice speaking to them and to know that He heard all their foolish, common talk! And how many hearts would burn with holy joy if they only knew that the Saviour was by their side, that the holy atmosphere of His presence was surrounding them, and they were feeding on the bread of life! How pleased the Saviour would be to hear His followers talking of His precious lessons of instruction and to know that they had a relish for holy things!

When the truth abides in the heart, there is no place for criticism of God's servants, or for picking flaws with the message He sends. That which is in the heart will flow from the lips. It cannot be repressed. The things that God has prepared for those that love Him will be the theme of conversation. The love of Christ is in the soul as a well of water, springing up into everlasting life, sending forth living streams that bring life and gladness wherever they flow.—*Special Testimony to the Battle Creek Church,* Nov. 18, 1896.

————

Christians have many sources of happiness at their command, and they may tell with unerring accuracy what pleasures are lawful and right. They may enjoy such recreations as will not dissipate the mind or debase the soul, such as will not disappoint and leave a sad after influence to destroy self-respect or bar the way to usefulness.

HOLIDAYS UNTO GOD

Would it not be well for us to observe holidays unto God, when we could revive in our minds the memory of His dealing with us? Would it not be well to consider His past blessings, to remember the impressive warnings that have come home to our souls, so that we shall not forget God?

The world has many holidays, and men become engrossed with games, with horse races, with gambling, smoking, and drunkenness. They show plainly under what banner they are standing. They make it evident that they do not stand under the banner of the Prince of life, but that the prince of darkness rules and controls them.

Shall not the people of God more frequently have holy convocations in which to thank God for His rich blessings? Shall we not find time in which to praise Christ for His rest, peace, and joy, and make manifest by daily thanksgiving that we appreciate the great sacrifice made in our behalf, that we may be partakers of the divine nature? Shall we not speak of the prospective rest in the Paradise of God, and tell of the honor and glory in store for the servants of Jehovah? "My people shall dwell in a peaceable habitation, and in sure dwellings, and in quiet resting places." Isaiah 32:18. We are homeward bound, seeking a better country, even a heavenly.

The world is full of excitement. Men act as though they had gone mad over low, cheap, unsatisfying things. How excited have I seen them over the result of a cricket match! I have seen the streets in Sydney densely crowded for blocks and, on inquiring what was the occasion of the excitement, was told that some expert player of cricket had won the game. I felt disgusted.

Why are not the chosen of God more enthusiastic? They are striving for an immortal crown, striving for a home where there will be no need of the light of the sun or moon, or of lighted candle; for the Lord God giveth them light, and they shall reign for ever and ever. They will have a life that measures with the life of God; but the candle of the wicked shall be put out in ignominious darkness, and then shall the righteous shine forth as the sun in the kingdom of their Father. . . .

I do not recommend pleasure parties where young people assemble together for mere amusement, to engage in cheap, nonsensical talk, and where loud, boisterous laughter is to be heard. I do not recommend the kind of gathering where there is a letting down of dignity and the scene is one of weakness and folly.

Many times young men for whom heavenly intelligences have been waiting in order to number them as missionaries for God are drawn into the gatherings for amusement, and are carried away with Satan's fascinations. Instead of being afraid to continue their association with girls whose depth of mind is easily measured, whose character is of a cheap order, they become enamored of them and enter into an engagement. Satan knows that if these young men enter into an engagement with cheap-minded, pleasure-loving, worldly-minded, irreligious young women, they will bind themselves to stumbling blocks. Their usefulness will be largely crippled, if not utterly destroyed. Even if the young men themselves succeed in making an unreserved surrender to God, yet they will find that they are greatly crippled by being bound to an untrained, undisciplined, un-Christlike wife who is dead to God, dead to piety, and dead to true holiness. Their lives will prove unsatisfying and unhappy.

Gatherings for amusement confuse faith and make the motive mixed and uncertain. The Lord accepts no divided heart. He wants the whole man. He made all there is of man. He offered a complete sacrifice to redeem the body and soul of man. That which He requires of those whom He has created and redeemed is summed up in these words: "Thou shalt love the Lord thy God with all thy heart, and with all thy soul, and with all thy mind. . . . Thou shalt love thy neighbor as thyself." Matthew 22:37-39. God will accept nothing less than this.—*Special Testimonies on Education,* pages 80-83.

————

"Let him that thinketh he standeth take heed lest he fall." 1 Corinthians 10:12. There can be no presumption more fatal than that which leads men to venture upon a course of self-pleasing. In view of this solemn warning from God, should not fathers and mothers take heed? Should they not faithfully point out to the youth the dangers that are constantly arising to lead them away from God?

HOW TO SPEND HOLIDAYS

Recreation is needful to those who are engaged in physical labor, and is still more essential for those whose labor is principally mental. It is not essential to our salvation nor for the glory of God to keep the mind laboring constantly and exclusively, even upon religious themes. There are amusements, such as dancing, card playing, chess, checkers, etc., which we cannot approve, because Heaven condemns them. These amusements open the door for great evil. They are not beneficial in their tendency, but have an exciting influence, producing in some minds a passion for those plays which lead to gambling and dissipation. All such plays should be condemned by Christians, and something perfectly harmless should be substituted in their place.

I saw that our holidays should not be spent in patterning after the world, yet they should not be passed by unnoticed, for this will bring dissatisfaction to our children. On these days when there is danger that our children will be exposed to evil influences and become corrupted by the pleasures and excitement of the world, let the parents study to get up something to take the place of these dangerous amusements. Give your children to understand that you have their good and happiness in view.

Let several families living in a city or village unite and leave the occupations which have taxed them physically and mentally, and take an excursion into the country, to the side of a fine lake or to a nice grove, where the scenery of nature is beautiful. They should provide themselves with plain, hygienic food, the very best fruits and grains, and spread their table under the shade of some tree or under the canopy of heaven. The ride, the exercise, and the scenery will quicken the appetite, and they can enjoy a repast which kings might envy.

On such occasions parents and children should feel free from care, labor, and perplexity. Parents should become children with their children, making everything as pleasant for them as possible. Let the whole day be given to recreation.

Exercise in the open air for those whose employment has been within doors and sedentary will be beneficial to health. All who can should feel it a duty to pursue this course. Nothing will be lost, but much gained. They can return to their occupations with new life and new courage to engage in their labor with zeal, and they are better prepared to resist disease.—*Testimonies for the Church,* vol. 1, pp. 514, 515.

———

Many allow the youth to attend parties of pleasure, thinking that amusement is essential for health and happiness; but what dangers are in this path! The more the desire for pleasure is gratified, the more it is cultivated and the stronger it becomes. The life experience is largely made up of self-gratification in amusement. God bids us beware. "Let him that thinketh he standeth take heed lest he fall."

THE DANGER IN AMUSEMENTS

Recent experiences in our colleges and sanitariums lead me to present again instruction that the Lord gave me for the teachers and students in our school at Cooranbong, Australia.

In April, 1900, a holiday was appointed at the Avondale school for Christian workers. The program for the day provided for a meeting in the chapel in the morning, at which I and others addressed the students, calling their attention to what God had wrought in the building up of this school, and to their privilege and opportunities as students.

After the meeting, the remainder of the day was spent by the students in various games and sports, some of which were frivolous, rude, and grotesque.

During the following night I seemed to be witnessing the performances of the afternoon. The scene was clearly laid out before me, and I was given a message for the manager and teachers of the school.

I was shown that in the amusements carried on at the school that afternoon the enemy gained a victory, and teachers were weighed in the balances and found wanting. I was greatly distressed and burdened to think that those standing in responsible positions should open the door and, as it were, invite the enemy in; for this they did in permitting the exhibitions that took place. As teachers, they should have stood firm against giving place to the enemy in any such line. By what they permitted they marred their record and grieved the Spirit of God. The students were encouraged in a course the effects of which were not easily effaced. There is no end to the path of vain amusements, and every step taken in it is a step in a path which Christ has not traveled.

This introduction of wrong plans was the very thing that should have been jealously guarded against. The Avondale school was established, not to be like the schools of the world, but, as God revealed, to be a pattern school. And since it was to be a pattern school, those in charge of it should have perfected everything after God's plan, discarding all that was not in harmony with His will. Had their eyes been anointed with the heavenly eyesalve, they would have realized that they could not permit the exhibition that took place that afternoon, without dishonoring God.

On Wednesday morning when I spoke to the students and to the others who had assembled, the words that the Lord gave me to speak, I did not know anything of what was to take place afterward; for no intimation of it had come to me. How could those at the head of the school harmonize with the words spoken the proceedings that followed, which were of a character to make of no effect the instruction that had just come to them from God? If their perceptions had not been greatly beclouded, they would have understood this instruction as rebuking all such proceedings.

I felt deeply the importance of the words that the Lord gave me at this time for teachers and students. This instruction presented before the students duties of the highest order; and to efface by the amusements afterward entered into, the good impressions made, was virtually saying, "We want not Thy way, O God; we want our own way; we want to follow our own wisdom."

In the night season I was a witness to the performance that was carried on on the school grounds. The students who engaged in the grotesque mimicry that was seen, acted out the mind of the enemy, some in a very unbecoming manner. A view of things was presented before me in which the students were playing games of tennis and cricket. Then I was given instruction regarding the character of these amusements. They were presented to me as a species of idolatry, like the idols of the nations.

There were more than visible spectators on the ground. Satan and his angels were there, making impressions on human minds. Angels of God, who minister to those who shall be heirs of salvation, were also present, not to approve, but to disapprove. They were ashamed that such an exhibition should be given by the professed children of God. The forces of the enemy gained a decided victory, and God was dishonored. He who gave His life to refine, ennoble, and sanctify human beings was grieved at the performance.

Hearing a voice, I turned to see who spoke to me. Then with dignity and solemnity One said, "Is this the celebration for the anniversary of the opening of the school? Is this the gratitude offering you present to God for the blessings He has given you? The world could render as acceptable an offering on this memorial occasion. The teachers are making the same mistake that has been made over and over again. They should learn wisdom from the experiences of the past. The careless, godless world can offer an abundance of such offerings as these, in a much more acceptable manner."

Turning to the teachers, He said, "You have made a mistake the effects of which it will be hard to efface. The Lord God of Israel is not glorified in the school. If at this time the Lord should permit your life to end, many would be lost, eternally separated from God and the righteous."

The Consequence of One Departure From Right

These things are a repetition of the course of Aaron, when at the foot of Sinai he allowed the first beginning of wrong by permitting a spirit of reveling and commonness to come into the camp of Israel. Moses was in the mount with God, and Aaron had been left in charge. He showed his weakness by not standing firmly against the propositions of the people. He could have exercised his authority to hold the congregation back from wrongdoing; but just as in his home he failed with his children, so he showed the same defective administration in his management of Israel. His weakness as a general was seen in his desire to please the people, even at the sacrifice of principle. He lost his power of command at the very first permission that he gave which allowed them to go contrary to God's commands in the least particular. And as a result the spirit of idolatry came in, and the current set in motion could not be stayed until stern and decisive measures had been taken.

It took time and a vast amount of labor and sorrow to wipe out the influence of the proceedings at the Avondale school on that Wednesday afternoon. But the experience was a lesson that helped those in charge of the school to realize the tendency of such amusements.

What an exhibition was this to be reported by the students to their distant friends and acquaintances! It was a witness that showed, not what God had accomplished in the school, but what Satan had accomplished. Serious is the consequence of even one such departure from the instruction that God has given concerning our schools. Once the barriers are broken down, the advance of the enemy will be marked, unless the Lord shall humble hearts and convert minds.

The effort to regain that which was lost by the proceedings of that afternoon cost the teachers much labor. They were severely tried. With the students there was seen a desire for further pleasure and less regard for the instruction of God's word. The Lord of heaven was thus dishonored, and the indulgence of the desires of the human heart in sin and love of pleasure was the education received.

Let those who are educating the youth govern themselves according to the high and holy principles that Christ has given in His word. Let them remember that, as far as possible, they are to recover the ground that has been lost, that they may bring into our schools the spirituality that was seen in the schools of the prophets.

The Bible as Our Counselor

Teachers need an intimate acquaintance with the word of God. The Bible, and the Bible alone, should be their counselor. The word of God is as the leaves of the tree of life. Here is met every want of those who love its teachings and bring them into the practical life. Many of the students who come to our schools are unconverted, though they may have been baptized. They do not know what it means to be sanctified through a belief of the truth. They should be taught to search and understand the Bible, to receive its truths into the heart and carry them out in the daily life. Thus they will become strong in the Lord; for spiritual sinew and muscle are nourished by the bread of life.

The Lord desires His stewards to discharge their duties faithfully in His name and in His strength. By believing His word and acting upon its teachings, they may go on conquering and to conquer. But when men depart from the principles of righteousness, they conceive a high opinion of their own goodness and abilities, and unconsciously they exalt themselves. The Lord allows such ones to walk alone, to follow their own way. Thus He gives them opportunity to see themselves as they are and to manifest to others their weakness. He is seeking to teach them that the Lord's way is always to be closely followed, that His word is to be taken as it reads, and that men are not to devise and plan according to their own judgment, irrespective of His counsel.

Our schools are to be as the schools of the prophets. In them the truths of the Bible are to be earnestly studied. If rightly brought before the mind and thoughtfully dwelt upon, these truths will give the students a desire for that which is infinitely higher than worldly amusement. As they draw near to God, becoming partakers of the divine nature, earthborn amusements will sink into nothingness. The minds of the students will take a higher turn, and beholding the character of Jesus, they will strive to be like Him.

Useful Employment Versus Selfish Pleasure

In the place of providing diversions that merely amuse, arrangements should be made for exercises that will be productive of good. Students are sent to our schools to receive an education that will enable them to go forth as workers in God's cause. Satan would lead them to believe that amusements are necessary to physical health; but the Lord has declared that the better way is for them to get physical exercise through manual training and by letting useful employment take the place of selfish pleasure. The desire for amusement, if indulged, soon develops a dislike for useful, healthful exercise of body and mind such as will make students efficient in helping themselves and others.

God bestows talents upon men, not that these talents may lie unused or be employed in self-gratification, but that they may be used to bless others. God grants men the gift of time for the purpose of promoting His glory. When this time is used in selfish pleasure, the hours thus spent are lost for all eternity.

────────

Our young people need to be surrounded with wholesome, uplifting influences. They are to be kept in the love of the truth. The standard set before them should be high.

FOR FURTHER STUDY

As LIGHTS IN THE WORLD
>*Testimonies,* vol. 7, p. 204.

DANGEROUS AMUSEMENTS FOR THE YOUNG
>*Testimonies,* vol. 1, pp. 269, 288, 289, 496-515, 551, 554, 555.
>>vol. 2, pp. 142-145, 235-237.
>>vol. 4, pp. 435, 436, 624, 625.

CHRISTIAN RECREATION
>*Adventist Home, The,* pp. 493-520, 526-530.
>*Messages to Young People,* pp. 363-370.
>*Testimonies,* vol. 2, pp. 585-594.
>>vol. 4, p. 581.
>>vol. 5, p. 218.

WORLDLY AMUSEMENTS
>*Adventist Home, The,* pp. 521-525.
>*Testimonies,* vol. 9, p. 90.

HOLIDAYS UNTO GOD
>*Adventist Home, The,* pp. 472-483.

THE DANGER IN AMUSEMENTS
>*Education,* pp. 207-213, 269.

THE HOLY SPIRIT IN OUR SCHOOLS

*"Thou gavest also Thy good
Spirit to instruct them."*

THE TEACHER'S NEED OF THE HOLY
SPIRIT'S AID

The Holy Spirit has been given us as an aid in the
study of the Bible. Jesus promised, "The Comforter,
which is the Holy Ghost, whom the Father will send
in My name, He shall teach you all things, and bring
all things to your remembrance, whatsoever I have said
unto you." John 14:26. When the Bible is made the
study book, with earnest supplication for the Spirit's
guidance, and with a full surrender of the heart to be
sanctified through the truth, all that Christ has promised
will be accomplished. The result of such Bible study will
be well-balanced minds. The understanding will be
quickened, the sensibilities aroused. The conscience will
become sensitive; the sympathies and sentiments will be
purified; a better moral atmosphere will be created; and
new power to resist temptation will be imparted. Teachers and students will become active and earnest in the
work of God.

There is a disposition on the part of many teachers not
to be thorough in giving religious instruction. They are
satisfied with a halfhearted service themselves, serving
the Lord only to escape the punishment of sin. Their

halfheartedness affects their teaching. The experience
that they do not desire for themselves they are not
anxious to see their pupils gain. That which has been
given them in blessing has been cast aside as a dangerous
element. The offered visits of the Holy Spirit are met
with the words of Felix to Paul, "Go thy way for this
time; when I have a convenient season, I will call for
thee." Acts 24:25. Other blessings they desire; but that
which God is more willing to give than a father is to give
good gifts to his children; that which is offered abundantly, according to the infinite fullness of God, and
which, if received, would bring all other blessings in its
train—what words shall I use sufficiently to express what
has been done with reference to it? The heavenly Messenger has been repulsed by the determined will. Teachers have virtually said, "Thus far shalt Thou go with my
students, but no farther. We need no enthusiasm in our
school, no excitement. We are much better satisfied to
work with the students ourselves." Thus despite has been
done to God's gracious Messenger.

Are not the teachers in our schools in danger of blasphemy, of charging the Holy Spirit with being a deceiv-
ing power and leading into fanaticism? Where are the
educators that choose the snow of Lebanon which comes
from the rock of the field, or the cold, flowing waters that
come from another place, instead of the murky waters of
the valley?

A succession of showers from the living waters has
come to you at Battle Creek. Each shower was a consecrated inflowing of divine influence; but you did not

recognize it as such. Instead of drinking copiously of the streams of salvation so freely offered through the influence of the Holy Spirit, you turned to satisfy your soul thirst with the polluted waters of human science. The result has been parched hearts in the school and in the church. Those who are satisfied with little spirituality have gone far in unfitting themselves to appreciate the deep movings of the Spirit of God. . . .

There is need of heart conversions among the teachers. A genuine change of thought and methods of teaching is required to place them where they will have a personal relation to a living Saviour. It is one thing to assent to the Spirit's work in conversion, and another thing to accept that Spirit's agency as a reprover, calling to repentance. It is necessary that both teachers and students not only assent to truth, but have a deep practical knowledge of the operations of the Spirit. Its cautions are given because of the unbelief of those who profess to be Christians. . . .

You who have long lost the spirit of prayer, pray, pray earnestly, "Pity Thy suffering cause, pity the church, pity the individual believers, Thou Father of mercies. Take from us everything that defiles. Deny us what Thou wilt, but take not from us Thy Holy Spirit."

There are and ever will be those who do not move wisely, who will, if words of doubt or unbelief are spoken, throw off conviction and choose to follow their own will, and because of their deficiencies Christ has been reproached. Poor, finite mortals have judged the rich and precious outpouring of the Spirit and passed sentence upon it as the Jews passed sentence on the work of Christ.

Lest it be understood in every institution in America that it is not commissioned to you to direct the work of the Holy Spirit and to tell how it shall represent itself. You have been guilty in doing this. May the Lord forgive you, is my prayer. Instead of being repressed and driven back, as it has been, the Holy Spirit should be welcomed and its presence encouraged.

When you sanctify yourself through obedience to the word, the Holy Spirit will give you glimpses of heavenly things. When you seek God with humiliation and earnestness, the words which you have spoken in freezing accents will burn in your heart; the truth will not then languish upon your tongues. . . .

Teachers, trust in God and go forward. "My grace is sufficient for thee" (2 Corinthians 12:9), is the assurance of the Great Teacher. Catch the inspiration of the words, and never, never talk doubt and unbelief. Be energetic. There is no half-and-half service in pure and undefiled religion. "Thou shalt love the Lord thy God with all thy heart, and with all thy soul, and with all thy mind, and with all thy strength." Mark 12:30. The very highest sanctified ambition is demanded of those who believe the word of God.

Tell your students that the Lord Jesus has made every provision that they should go onward, conquering and to conquer. Lead them to trust in the divine promise, "If any of you lack wisdom, let him ask of God, that giveth to all men liberally, and upbraideth not; and it shall be given him." James 1:5. . . .

From God, the fountain of wisdom, proceeds all the knowledge that is of value to man, all that the intellect can grasp or retain. The fruit of the tree representing good and evil is not to be eagerly plucked because it is recommended by one who was once a bright angel in glory. He has said that if men eat thereof, they shall know good and evil; but let it alone. The true knowledge comes not from infidels or wicked men. The word of God is light and truth. The true light shines from Jesus Christ, who "lighteth every man that cometh into the world." John 1:9. From the Holy Spirit proceeds divine knowledge. He knows what humanity needs to promote peace, happiness, and restfulness here in this world, and to secure eternal rest in the kingdom of God.—*Special Testimonies on Education,* pages 26-31; written from Cooranbong, N.S.W., Australia, June 12, 1896.

Human Effort Essential

The agency of the Spirit of God does not remove from us the necessity of exercising our faculties and talents, but teaches us how to use every power to the glory of God. The human faculties, when under the special direction of the grace of God, are capable of being used to the best purpose on earth. Ignorance does not increase the humility or spirituality of any professed follower of Christ. The truths of the divine word can be best appreciated by an intellectual Christian. Christ can be best glorified by those who serve Him intelligently. The great object of education is to enable us to use the power which God has given us in such a manner as to represent the religion of the Bible and promote the glory of God.

We are indebted to Him who gave us existence, for the talents that have been entrusted to us, and it is a duty we owe our Creator to cultivate and improve these talents. Education will discipline the mind, develop its powers, and understandingly direct them, that we may be useful in advancing the glory of God.

Everlasting life! Oh, if we can comprehend this in the lessons that Christ gave! The questions that the disciples brought to the Saviour after the crowds had dispersed and the teachings that He then explained more fully to them are essential for the multitudes today to understand and obey. Practical godliness must be learned. Those who study and practice the teachings of Christ will gain an essential education in Bible knowledge. By the standard of the word of God every teacher will one day be measured by the greatest Teacher this world ever knew. Belief in the grand truths He presented will work a reformation in all who truly receive them.

The love of the truth as it is in Jesus means the love of all that is comprised in the truth Christ taught. Let our teachers strive to follow His example, to cherish His spirit of tender sympathy. Let none leave the love of Christ out of their labors, but let each ask himself the questions, Is my life a consistent life? Am I guided by the Holy Spirit? It is the privilege of every teacher to reveal the power of a pure, consistent, Christ-loving workman. The spiritual-minded teacher will never have an uncertain religion. If he truly loves the service of Christ, he will have spiritual discernment and spiritual life.

A FAILURE TO RECOGNIZE GOD'S MESSENGER

I ask you who are living at the very heart of the work to review the experience of years and see if the "Well done" can truthfully be spoken to you. I ask the teachers in the school to consider carefully, prayerfully, Have you individually watched for your own soul as one who is co-operating with God for its purification from all sin and for its entire sanctification unto Him? Can you by precept and example teach the youth sanctification . . . through the truth unto holiness, obedience to God?

Have you not been afraid of the Holy Spirit? At times it has come with all-pervading influence into the school at Battle Creek and into the schools in other localities. Did you recognize it? Did you accord it the honor due to a heavenly Messenger? When the Spirit seemed to be striving with the youth, did you say, "Let us put aside all study; for it is evident that we have among us a heavenly Guest. Let us give praise and honor to God"? Did you, with contrite hearts, bow in prayer with your students, pleading that you might receive the blessing that the Lord was offering you?

The Great Teacher Himself was among you. How did you honor Him? Was He a stranger to some of the educators? Was there need to send for someone of supposed authority to welcome or repel this Messenger from heaven? Though unseen, His presence was among you. But was not the thought expressed that in school the time ought to be given to study, and that there was a time for everything?—as if the hours devoted to common study were too precious to be given up to the working of the heavenly Messenger.

If you have in this way restricted and repulsed the Holy Spirit of God, I entreat you to repent of it as quickly as possible. If any have closed and padlocked the door of your heart to the Spirit of God, I urge you to unlock the door and to pray with earnestness, "Abide with me." When the Holy Spirit reveals His presence in your schoolroom, tell your students, "The Lord signifies that He has for us today a lesson of heavenly import of more value than our lessons in ordinary lines. Let us listen; let us bow before God and seek Him with the whole heart."

Let me tell you what I know of this heavenly Guest. The Holy Spirit was brooding over the youth during the school hours; but some hearts were so cold and dark that they had no desire for the Spirit's presence, and the light of God was withdrawn. The heavenly Visitant would have opened the understanding, would have given wisdom and knowledge in all lines of study that could be employed to the glory of God. He came to convince of sin and to soften the hearts hardened by long estrangement from God. He came to reveal the great love wherewith God has loved these youth. . . .

A principle of divine origin must pervade our conduct and bind us to God. This will not be in any way a hindrance to the study of true science. "The fear of the Lord is the beginning of wisdom" (Proverbs 9:10); and the man who consents to be molded and fashioned after the divine similitude is the noblest work of God. All who

live in communion with the Creator will have an understanding of His design in their creation. They will have
a sense of their own accountability to God to employ
their faculties to the very best purpose. They will seek
neither to glorify nor to depreciate themselves. . . .

God's Ideal for Man

The religion of Christ never degrades the receiver. It
never makes him coarse or rough, discourteous or self-
important, passionate or hardhearted. On the contrary,
it refines the taste, sanctifies the judgment, and purifies
and ennobles the thoughts, bringing them into captivity
to Jesus Christ.

God's ideal for His children is higher than the highest
human thought can reach. The living God has given in
His holy law a transcript of His character. The greatest
Teacher the world has ever known is Jesus Christ; and
what is the standard He has given for all who believe
in Him? "Be ye therefore perfect, even as your Father
which is in heaven is perfect." Matthew 5:48. As God is
perfect in His high sphere of action, so man may be perfect in his human sphere.

The ideal of Christian character is Christlikeness.
There is opened before us a path of continual advancement. We have an object to reach, a standard to gain,
which includes everything good and pure and noble and
elevated. There should be continual striving and constant progress onward and upward toward perfection of
character. . . .

Without the divine working, man can do no good
thing. God calls every man to repentance, yet man

cannot even repent unless the Holy Spirit works upon his heart. But the Lord wants no man to wait until he thinks he has repented before he takes steps toward Jesus. The Saviour is continually drawing men to repentance; they need only to submit to be drawn, and their hearts will be melted in penitence.

To man is allotted a part in this great struggle for everlasting life—he must respond to the working of the Holy Spirit. It will require a struggle to break through the powers of darkness, and the Spirit works in him to accomplish this. But man is no passive being, to be saved in indolence. He is called upon to strain every muscle and exercise every faculty in the struggle for immortality, yet it is God that supplies the efficiency. No human being can be saved in indolence. The Lord bids us, "Strive to enter in at the strait gate: for many, I say unto you, will seek to enter in, and shall not be able." Luke 13:24. "Wide is the gate, and broad is the way, that leadeth to destruction, and many there be which go in thereat: because strait is the gate, and narrow the way, which leadeth unto life, and few there be that find it." Matthew 7:13, 14.

Unholy Influences at Work

I entreat the students in our schools to be soberminded. The frivolity of the young is not pleasing to God. Their sports and games open the door to a flood of temptations. They are in possession of God's heavenly endowment in their intellectual faculties, and they should not allow their thoughts to be cheap and low. A character formed in accordance with the precepts of God's word will reveal steadfast principles, pure, noble aspirations. The Holy Spirit co-operates with the powers of the human mind, and high and holy impulses are the sure result. . . .

My soul is deeply stirred at the things that have been represented before me. I feel an indignation of spirit that in our institutions so little honor has been given to the living God, and so much honor to that which is supposed to be superior talent, but with which the Holy Spirit has no connection. The Spirit of God is not acknowledged and respected; men have passed judgment upon it; its operations have been condemned as fanaticism, enthusiasm, undue excitement.

God sees that which the blind eyes of the educators do not discern—that immorality of every kind and degree is striving for the mastery, working against the manifestations of the power of the Holy Spirit. The commonest of conversation, and low, perverted ideas are woven into the texture of character and defile the soul.

The low, common pleasure parties, gatherings for eating and drinking, singing and playing on instruments of music, are inspired by a spirit that is from beneath. They are an oblation unto Satan. The exhibitions in the bicycle craze are an offense to God. His wrath is kindled against those who do such things. For in these gratifications the mind becomes besotted, even as in liquor drinking. The door is opened to vulgar associations. The thoughts, allowed to run in a low channel, soon pervert all the powers of the being. Like Israel of old, the pleasure lovers eat and drink, and rise up to play. There is mirth and carousing, hilarity and glee. In all this the youth are following the example of the ungodly authors of some of the books that are placed in their hands for study. All these things are having their effect upon the character.

Those who take the lead in these frivolities bring upon the cause a stain not easily effaced. They wound their own souls, and will carry the scars through their lifetime. The evildoer may see his sins and repent, and God may pardon the transgressor; but the power of discernment which ought ever to be kept keen and sensitive to distinguish between the sacred and the common, is in a great measure destroyed. . . .

I urge upon all to whom these words may come: Review your own course of action, and "take heed to yourselves, lest at any time your hearts be overcharged with surfeiting, and drunkenness, and cares of this life, and so that day come upon you unawares. For as a snare shall it come on all them that dwell on the face of the whole earth." Luke 21:34, 35.—*Special Testimonies on Education,* pages 202-212; written to the teachers in Battle Creek College.

It is a continual struggle to be always on the alert to resist evil, but it pays to obtain one victory after another over self and the powers of darkness. And if the youth are proved and tested, as was Daniel, what honor can they reflect to God by their firm adherence to the right!

MANIFEST WORKING OF THE HOLY SPIRIT

"Yet a little while is the light with you," Jesus said. "Walk while ye have the light, lest darkness come upon you: for he that walketh in darkness knoweth not whither he goeth. While ye have light, believe in the light, that ye may be the children of light." John 12:35, 36.

Some men in the Battle Creek College have a false idea as to what constitutes duty. The Lord God of heaven has caused His Holy Spirit from time to time to move upon the students in the school, that they might acknowledge Him in all their ways so that He might direct their paths. At times the manifestation of the Holy Spirit has been so decided that studies were forgotten, and the greatest Teacher the world ever knew made His voice heard, saying, "Come unto Me, all ye that labor and are heavy-laden, and I will give you rest. Take My yoke upon you, and learn of Me; for I am meek and lowly in heart: and ye shall find rest unto your souls. For My yoke is easy, and My burden is light." Matthew 11:28-30.

The Lord knocked at the door of hearts, and I saw that angels of God were present. There seemed to be no special effort on the part of teachers to influence the students to give their attention to the things of God; but God had a Watcher in the school, who, though His presence was unseen, made His influence felt. . . .

The Lord has been waiting long to impart the greatest, truest joys to the heart. All those who look to Him with undivided hearts, He will greatly bless. Those who have thus looked to Him have caught more distinct views of Jesus as their sin bearer, their all-sufficient sacrifice, and have been hid in the cleft of the Rock, to behold the Lamb of God who taketh away the sins of the world. When we have a sense of Christ's sacrifice in our behalf, our lips are tuned to the highest, loftiest themes of praise.

When the students thus beheld Jesus, the suspension of their studies was counted as no loss. They were catching glimpses of Him who is invisible. They earnestly sought the living God, and the live coal of pardon was placed upon their lips. The Holy Spirit wrought not only for those who had lost their first love, but also for souls who had never placed themselves on the Lord's side. . . . Tokens of His grace and favor called forth rejoicing from the hearts of those who were thus blessed, and it was known that the salvation of God was among His people. . . .

Why should we not expect the Holy Watcher to come into our schools? Our youth are there to receive an education, to acquire a knowledge of the only true God. They are there to learn how to present Christ as a sin-pardoning Saviour. They are there to gather up precious rays of light, that they may diffuse light again. They are there to show forth the loving-kindness of the Lord, to speak of His glory, to sound forth the praises of Him who has called us out of darkness into His marvelous light. . . .

Again and again the heavenly Messenger has been sent to the school. When His presence has been acknowledged, the darkness has fled away, the light has shone forth, and hearts have been drawn to God. The last words spoken by Christ to John were: "The Spirit and the bride say, Come. And let him that heareth say, Come. And let him that is athirst come. And whosoever will, let him take the water of life freely." Revelation 22:17. When we respond to God and say, "Lord, we come," then with joy shall we draw water out of the wells of salvation.

Shall we not keep holy festivals unto God? Shall we not show that we have some enthusiasm in His service? With the grand, ennobling theme of salvation before us, shall we be as cold as statues of marble? If men can become so excited over a match game of cricket, or a horse race, or over foolish things that bring no good to anyone, shall we be unmoved when the plan of salvation is unfolded before us? Let the school and the church henceforth have festivals of rejoicing unto the Lord.— *Special Testimonies on Education,* pages 77-82.

Perils of Worldly-Wise Teachers

All the treasures of heaven were committed to Jesus Christ, that He might impart these precious gifts to the diligent, persevering seeker. He "is made unto us wisdom, and righteousness, and sanctification, and redemption." 1 Corinthians 1:30. But even the prayers of many are so formal that they carry with them no influence for good. They are not a savor of life.

If teachers would humble their hearts before God and

realize the responsibilities they have accepted in taking charge of the youth with the object of educating them for the future immortal life, a marked change would soon be seen in their attitude. Their prayers would not be dry and lifeless, but they would pray with the earnestness of souls who feel their peril. They would learn daily of Jesus, taking the word of God as their lesson book, having a living sense that it is the voice of God, and the atmosphere surrounding their souls would change materially. The temptation to be first would be quenched in the lessons daily learned in the school of Christ. They would not lean so confidently to their own understanding. . . .

The teachers in our schools are today in danger of following in the same track as did the Jews in Christ's day. Whatever may be their position, however they may pride themselves upon their ability to teach, unless they open the chambers of the soul temple to receive the bright rays of the Sun of Righteousness, they are written in the books of heaven as unbelievers. By precept and example they intercept the rays of light that would come to the students. Their danger is in being self-centered and too wise to be instructed.

We are living in a world full of corruption, and if we do not receive the living Christ into our hearts, believing and doing His words, we shall be left as blind as were the Jews. All teachers need to grasp every ray of heavenly light shed upon their pathway; for as instructors they need light. Some say, "Yes, I think I am anxious for this;" but they deceive themselves. Where do you get your light? From what fountain have you been drinking? I have the word of the Lord that not a few of the teachers have left the snow waters of Lebanon for the turbid streams of the valley. God alone can guide us safely in paths which lead to the better country. But the teachers who are not earnestly and intelligently seeking that better country are leading those under their influence to be careless and to neglect the great salvation bought for them at an infinite price.

A close connection with God must be maintained by all our teachers. If God should send His Holy Spirit into our schools to mold hearts, elevate the intellect, and give divine wisdom to the students, there are those who, in their present state, would interpose between God and those who need the light. They would not understand the work of the Holy Spirit; they have never understood it; in the past it has been to them as great a mystery as were Christ's lessons to the Jews. The working of the Holy Spirit of God is not to create curiosity. It is not for men to decide whether they shall lay their hands upon the manifestations of the Spirit of God. We must let God work.

When teachers are willing to sit in the school of Christ and learn of the Great Teacher, they will know far less in their own estimation than they do now. When God becomes the teacher, He will be acknowledged, His name will be magnified. The students will be as were the young men in the schools of the prophets, upon whom the Spirit of God came, and they prophesied.

The great adversary of souls is seeking to bring a dead, lifeless spiritual atmosphere into all our institutions.

He works to turn and twist every circumstance to his own advantage, to the exclusion of Jesus Christ. Today, as in the days of Christ, God cannot do many mighty works because of the unbelief of those who stand in responsible positions. The converting power of God is needed before they will understand the word of God, and be willing to humble themselves before Him as learners.

Finishing at Worldly Schools

Prophecy tells us that we are near the close of time. Intellectual power, natural abilities, supposed excellent judgment, will not prepare the youth to become missionaries for God. No one who is seeking an education for the work and service of God will be made more complete in Jesus Christ by receiving the supposed finishing touch at —— in either literary or medical lines. Many have been unfitted to do missionary work by attending such schools. They have dishonored God by leaving Him on one side and accepting man as their helper. "Them that honor Me I will honor," God declares, "and they that despise Me shall be lightly esteemed." 1 Samuel 2:30. . . .

God's word should be received as the foundation and the finisher of our faith. It is to be received with the understanding and with the whole heart; it is life and is to be incorporated into our very existence. Thus received, the word of God will humble man at the footstool of mercy and separate him from every corrupting influence.

"In the year that King Uzziah died," says Isaiah, "I saw also the Lord sitting upon a throne, high and lifted up, and His train filled the temple. Above it stood the seraphims; each one had six wings; with twain he covered his face, and with twain he covered his feet, and with twain he did fly. And one cried unto another, and said, Holy, holy, holy, is the Lord of hosts: the whole earth is full of His glory. And the posts of the door moved at the voice of him that cried, and the house was filled with smoke." Beholding this grand and glorious representation, the prophet discerned his own imperfections, and those of the people with whom he dwelt. "Woe is me!" he cried, "for I am undone; because I am a man of unclean lips, and I dwell in the midst of a people of unclean lips: for mine eyes have seen the King, the Lord of hosts." Isaiah 6:1-5. Oh, how many who are engaged in this work of responsibility need to behold God as did Isaiah; for in the presence of His glory and majesty self will sink into nothingness.—*Special Testimonies on Education,* pages 165-170; written from Melbourne, Australia, Feb. 10, 1894, to the teachers in Battle Creek College.

Only as the higher life is brought to view, as shown in the teachings of Christ, can any learning and instruction rightly be called higher education; and only by the aid of the Holy Spirit can this education be gained. Man's study of the science of nature, unaided by the Holy Spirit, falls short of the precious things Christ desires him to learn from the things of the natural world; for he fails to be instructed in the great and important truths which concern his salvation.

There are great possibilities in the human understanding when connected with the True Teacher, who in His presentation of the things of the natural world revealed truth in its practical bearings. God works all unseen upon the human heart; for without the divine power operating upon the understanding, the mind of man cannot grasp the sentiments of elevating, ennobling truth. It cannot read the book of nature, nor can it understand the simplicity of godliness found therein. When the human mind is freed from perverting influences, it can receive the lessons of Christ. But no man can understand the true science of education, only as God in His wisdom shall through the Holy Spirit sanctify his observation.

If the students who attend our colleges would be firm and maintain integrity, if they would not associate with those who walk in the paths of sin nor be charmed by their society, like Daniel they would enjoy the favor of God. If they would discard unprofitable amusements and indulgence of appetite, their minds would be clear for the pursuit of knowledge. They would thus gain a moral power that would enable them to remain unmoved when assailed by temptation.

Those who are connected with our institutions in positions of responsibility should take upon themselves the burden of caring for the souls of those placed under their charge.

PROFITABLE STUDY

"The excellency of knowledge is that wisdom giveth life to them that have it."

THE FALSE AND THE TRUE IN EDUCATION

The master mind in the confederacy of evil is ever working to keep out of sight the words of God and to bring into view the opinions of men. He means that we shall not hear the voice of God saying, "This is the way, walk ye in it." Isaiah 30:21. Through perverted educational processes he is doing his utmost to obscure heaven's light.

Philosophical speculation and scientific research in which God is not acknowledged are making skeptics of thousands. In the schools of today the conclusions that learned men have reached as the result of their scientific investigations are carefully taught and fully explained; while the impression is distinctly given that if these learned men are correct, the Bible cannot be. Skepticism is attractive to the human mind. The youth see in it an independence that captivates the imagination, and they are deceived. Satan triumphs. He nourishes every seed of doubt that is sown in young hearts. He causes it to grow and bear fruit, and soon a plentiful harvest of infidelity is reaped.

It is because the human heart is inclined to evil that it

is so dangerous to sow the seeds of skepticism in young minds. Whatever weakens faith in God robs the soul of power to resist temptation. It removes the only real safeguard against sin. We are in need of schools where the youth shall be taught that greatness consists in honoring God by revealing His character in daily life. Through His word and His works we need to learn of God, that our lives may fulfill His purpose.

Infidel Authors

In order to obtain an education, many think it essential to study the writings of infidel authors, because these works contain many bright gems of thought. But who was the originator of these gems of thought? It was God, and God only. He is the Source of all light. Why, then, should we wade through the mass of error contained in the works of infidels for the sake of a few intellectual truths, when all truth is at our command?

How is it that men who are at war with the government of God come into possession of the wisdom which they sometimes display? Satan himself was educated in the heavenly courts, and he has a knowledge of good as well as of evil. He mingles the precious with the vile, and this is what gives him power to deceive. But because Satan has robed himself in garments of heavenly brightness, shall we receive him as an angel of light? The tempter has his agents, educated according to his methods, inspired by his spirit, and adapted to his work. Shall we co-operate with them? Shall we receive the works of his agents as essential to the acquirement of an education?

If the time and effort spent in seeking to grasp the bright ideas of infidels were given to studying the precious things of the word of God, thousands who now sit in darkness and in the shadow of death would be rejoicing in the glory of the Light of life.

Historical and Theological Lore

As a preparation for Christian work many think it essential to acquire an extensive knowledge of historical and theological writings. They suppose that this knowledge will be an aid to them in teaching the gospel. But their laborious study of the opinions of men tends to the enfeebling of their ministry rather than to its strengthening. As I see libraries filled with ponderous volumes of historical and theological lore, I think, Why spend money for that which is not bread? The sixth chapter of John tells us more than can be found in such works. Christ says: "I am the bread of life: he that cometh to Me shall never hunger; and he that believeth on Me shall never thirst." "I am the living bread which came down from heaven: if any man eat of this bread, he shall live forever." "He that believeth on Me hath everlasting life." "The words that I speak unto you, they are spirit, and they are life." John 6:35, 51, 47, 63.

There is a study of history that is not to be condemned. Sacred history was one of the studies in the schools of the prophets. In the record of His dealings with the nations were traced the footsteps of Jehovah. So today we are to consider the dealings of God with the nations of the earth. We are to see in history the fulfillment of prophecy, to study the workings of Providence in the great reformatory movements, and to understand the progress of events in the marshaling of the nations for the final conflict of the great controversy.

Such study will give broad, comprehensive views of life. It will help us to understand something of its relations and dependencies, how wonderfully we are bound together in the great brotherhood of society and nations, and to how great an extent the oppression and degradation of one member means loss to all.

But history, as commonly studied, is concerned with man's achievements, his victories in battle, his success in attaining power and greatness. God's agency in the affairs of men is lost sight of. Few study the working out of His purpose in the rise and fall of nations.

And to a large degree theology, as studied and taught, is but a record of human speculation, serving only to darken "counsel by words without knowledge." Job 38:2. Too often the motive in accumulating these many books is not so much a desire to obtain food for mind and soul, as it is an ambition to become acquainted with philosophers and theologians, a desire to present Christianity to the people in learned terms and propositions.

Not all the books written can serve the purpose of a holy life. "Learn of Me," said the Great Teacher, "take My yoke upon you, learn My meekness and lowliness." Your intellectual pride will not aid you in communicating with souls that are perishing for want of the bread of life. In your study of these books you are allowing them to take the place of the practical lessons you should be learning from Christ. With the results of this study the people are not fed. Very little of the research which is so wearying to the mind furnishes that which will help one to be a successful laborer for souls.

The Saviour came "to preach the gospel to the poor." Luke 4:18. In His teaching He used the simplest terms and the plainest symbols. And it is said that "the common people heard Him gladly." Mark 12:37. Those who are seeking to do His work for this time need a deeper insight into the lessons He has given.

The words of the living God are the highest of all education. Those who minister to the people need to eat of the bread of life. This will give them spiritual strength; then they will be prepared to minister to all classes of people.

The Classics

In the colleges and universities, thousands of youth devote a large part of the best years of life to the study of Greek and Latin. And while they are engaged in these studies, mind and character are molded by the evil sentiments of pagan literature, the reading of which is generally regarded as an essential part of the study of these languages.

Those who are conversant with the classics declare that "the Greek tragedies are full of incest, murder, and human sacrifices to lustful and revengeful gods." Far better would it be for the world were the education gained from such sources to be dispensed with. "Can one go upon hot coals, and his feet not be burned?"

Proverbs 6:28. "Who can bring a clean thing out of an unclean? not one." Job 14:4. Can we, then, expect the youth to develop Christian character while their education is molded by the teaching of those who set at defiance the principles of the law of God?

In casting off restraint, and plunging into reckless amusement, dissipation, and vice, students are but imitating that which is kept before their minds by these studies. There are callings in which a knowledge of Greek and Latin is needed. Some must study these languages. But the knowledge of them essential for practical uses might be gained without a study of literature that is corrupt and corrupting.

And a knowledge of Greek and Latin is not needed by many. The study of dead languages should be made secondary to a study of those subjects that teach the right use of all the powers of body and mind. It is folly for students to devote their time to the acquirement of dead languages, or of book knowledge in any line, to the neglect of a training for life's practical duties.

What do students carry with them when they leave school? Where are they going? What are they to do? Have they the knowledge that will enable them to teach others? Have they been educated to be true fathers and mothers? Can they stand at the head of a family as wise instructors? The only education worthy of the name is that which leads young men and women to be Christlike, which fits them to bear life's responsibilities, fits them to stand at the head of their families. Such an education is not to be acquired by a study of heathen classics. . . .

High-Class Fiction

There are works of fiction that were written for the purpose of teaching truth or exposing some great evil. Some of these works have accomplished good. Yet they have also wrought untold harm. They contain statements and highly wrought pen pictures that excite the imagination and give rise to a train of thought which is full of danger, especially to the youth. The scenes described are lived over and over again in their thoughts. Such reading unfits the mind for usefulness and disqualifies it for spiritual exercise. It destroys interest in the Bible. Heavenly things find little place in the thoughts. As the mind dwells upon the scenes of impurity portrayed, passion is aroused, and the end is sin.

Even fiction which contains no suggestion of impurity, and which may be intended to teach excellent principles, is harmful. It encourages the habit of hasty and superficial reading, merely for the story. Thus it tends to destroy the power of connected and vigorous thought; it unfits the soul to contemplate the great problems of duty and destiny.

By fostering a love for mere amusement, the reading of fiction creates a distaste for life's practical duties. Through its exciting, intoxicating power it is not infrequently a cause of both mental and physical disease. Many a miserable, neglected home, many a lifelong invalid, many an inmate of the insane asylum, has become such through the habit of novel reading.

It is often urged that in order to win the youth from

sensational or worthless literature, we should supply them with a better class of fiction. This is like trying to cure a drunkard by giving him, in the place of whisky or brandy, the milder intoxicants, such as wine, beer, or cider. The use of these would continually foster the appetite for stronger stimulants. The only safety for the inebriate, and the only safeguard for the temperate man, is total abstinence. For the lover of fiction the same rule holds true. Total abstinence is his only safety.

Myths and Fairy Tales

In the education of children and youth, fairy tales, myths, and fictitious stories are now given a large place. Books of this character are used in schools, and they are to be found in many homes. How can Christian parents permit their children to use books so filled with falsehood? When the children ask the meaning of stories so contrary to the teaching of their parents, the answer is that the stories are not true; but this does not do away with the evil results of their use. The ideas presented in these books mislead the children. They impart false views of life and beget and foster a desire for the unreal.

The widespread use of such books at this time is one of the cunning devices of Satan. He is seeking to divert the minds of old and young from the great work of character building. He means that our children and youth shall be swept away by the soul-destroying deceptions with which he is filling the world. Therefore he seeks to divert their minds from the word of God and thus prevent them from obtaining a knowledge of those truths that would be their safeguard.

Never should books containing a perversion of truth be placed in the hands of children or youth. Let not our children, in the very process of obtaining an education, receive ideas that will prove to be seeds of sin. If those with mature minds had nothing to do with such books, they would themselves be far safer, and their example and influence on the right side would make it far less difficult to guard the youth from temptation.

A Purer Fountain

"Bow down thine ear, and hear the words of the wise,
And apply thine heart unto My knowledge. . . .
That thy trust may be in the Lord,
I have made known to thee this day, even to thee.

"Have I not written to thee excellent things
In counsels and knowledge,
That I might make thee know the certainty of the words of truth;
That thou mightest answer the words of truth to them that send unto thee?" Proverbs 22:17-21.

"He established a testimony in Jacob,
And appointed a law in Israel,
Which He commanded our fathers,
That they should make them known to their children;"

"Showing to the generation to come the praises of the Lord,
And His strength, and His wonderful works that He hath done."
"That the generation to come might know them,
Even the children which should be born;
Who should arise and declare them to their children:
That they might set their hope in God." Psalm 78:4-7.

"The blessing of the Lord, it maketh rich,
And He addeth no sorrow with it." Proverbs 10:22.

Christ's Teaching

So also Christ presented the principles of truth in the gospel. In His teaching we may drink of the pure streams that flow from the throne of God. Christ could have imparted to men knowledge that would have surpassed any previous disclosures, and put in the background every other discovery. He could have unlocked mystery after mystery and could have concentrated around these wonderful revelations the active, earnest thought of successive generations till the close of time. But He would not spare a moment from teaching the science of salvation. His time, His faculties, and His life were appreciated and used only as a means for working out the salvation of the souls of men. He had come to seek and to save that which was lost, and He would not be turned from His purpose. He allowed nothing to divert Him.

Christ imparted only that knowledge which could be utilized. His instruction of the people was confined to the needs of their own condition in practical life. The curiosity that led them to come to Him with prying questions He did not gratify. All such questionings He made the occasion for solemn, earnest, vital appeals. To those who were so eager to pluck from the tree of knowledge, He offered the fruit of the tree of life. They found every avenue closed except the way that leads to God. Every fountain was sealed save the fountain of eternal life.

Our Saviour did not encourage any to attend the rabbinical schools of His day, for the reason that their minds would be corrupted with the continually repeated, "They say," or "It has been said." Why, then, should we accept the unstable words of men as exalted wisdom, when a greater, a certain wisdom is at our command?

That which I have seen of eternal things, and that which I have seen of the weakness of humanity, has deeply impressed my mind and influenced my lifework. I see nothing wherein man should be praised or glorified. I see no reason why the opinions of worldly-wise men and so-called great men should be trusted in and exalted. How can those who are destitute of divine enlightenment have correct ideas of God's plans and ways? They either deny Him altogether and ignore His existence, or they circumscribe His power by their own finite conceptions.

Let us choose to be taught by Him who created the heavens and the earth, by Him who set the stars in their order in the firmament and appointed the sun and the moon to do their work.

Knowledge That Can Be Utilized

It is right for the youth to feel that they must reach the highest development of their mental powers. We would not restrict the education to which God has set no limit. But our attainments avail nothing if not put to use for the honor of God and the good of humanity.

It is not well to crowd the mind with studies that require intense application, but that are not brought into use in practical life. Such education will be a loss to the student, for these studies lessen his desire and inclination for the studies that would fit him for usefulness and enable him to fulfill his responsibilities. A practical training is worth far more than any amount of mere theorizing. It is not enough even to have knowledge; we must have ability to use the knowledge aright.

The time, means, and study that so many expend for a comparatively useless education should be devoted to gaining an education that would make them practical men and women, fitted to bear life's responsibilities. Such an education would be of the highest value.

Heart Education

What we need is knowledge that will strengthen mind and soul, that will make us better men and women. Heart education is of far more importance than mere book learning. It is well, even essential, to have a knowledge of the world in which we live; but if we leave eternity out of our reckoning we shall make a failure from which we can never recover. . . .

If the youth understood their own weakness, they would find in God their strength. If they seek to be taught by Him they will become wise in His wisdom, and their lives will be fruitful in blessing to the world. But if they give up their minds to mere worldly and speculative study, and thus separate from God, they will lose all that enriches life.—*The Ministry of Healing*, pages 439-450.

To gain the higher education means to become a partaker of the divine nature. It means to copy the life and character of Christ so that we shall stand on vantage ground as we fight the battles of life. It means to gain daily victories over sin. As we seek for this education, angels of God are our companions; when the enemy comes in like a flood, the Spirit of the Lord lifts up a standard for us against him.

THE KNOWLEDGE THAT ENDURES

I am given words of caution for the teachers in our schools. The work of our schools should bear a different stamp from that borne by some of the most popular of our institutions of learning. Many of the textbooks used in these schools are unnecessary for the work of preparing students for the school above. As a result the youth are not receiving the most perfect Christian education. Those points of study are neglected that are most needed to fit them for missionary work in home and foreign fields, and to prepare them to stand in the last great examination. The education needed is that which will qualify students for practical service, by teaching them to bring every faculty under the control of the Spirit of God. The study book of the highest value is that which contains the instruction of Christ, the Teacher of teachers.

The Lord requires our teachers to put away from our schools those books teaching sentiments which are not in accordance with His word, and to give place to those books that are of the highest value. He will be honored when they show to the world that a wisdom more than human is theirs, because the Master Teacher is standing as their instructor.

There is need of separating from our educational work an erroneous, polluted literature, so that ideas which are the seeds of sin will not be received and cherished as the truth. Let not any suppose that a study of books which will lead to the reception of false ideas, is valuable education. Those ideas which, gaining entrance to the mind,

(389)

separate the youth from the Source of all wisdom, all efficiency, all power, leave them the sport of Satan's temptations. A pure education for the youth in our schools, unmixed with heathen philosophy, is a positive necessity.

We need to guard continually against those books which contain sophistry in regard to geology and other branches of science. Before the theories of men of science are presented to immature students, they need to be carefully sifted from every trace of infidel suggestions. One tiny seed of infidelity sown by a teacher in the heart of a student may spring up and bring forth a harvest of unbelief. The sophistries regarding God and nature that are flooding the world with skepticism are the inspiration of the fallen foe. Satan is a Bible student. He knows the truths that are essential for salvation, and it is his study to divert minds from these truths. Let our teachers beware lest they echo the falsehoods of the enemy of God and man.

It is a mistake to put into the hands of the youth books that perplex and confuse them. The reason sometimes given for this study is that the teacher has passed over this ground, and the student must follow. But if teachers were receiving light and wisdom from the divine Teacher, they would look at this matter in a very different way. They would measure the relative importance of the things to be learned in school. The common, essential branches of education would be more thoroughly taught, and the word of God would be esteemed as the bread sent down from heaven, which sustains all spiritual life.

We are slow to realize how much we need to understand the teachings of Christ and His methods of labor. If these were better understood, much of the instruction given in our schools would be counted as of no value. It would be seen that much that is now taught does not develop the simplicity of true godliness in the life of the student. Finite wisdom would receive less esteem, and the word of God would have a more honored place.

If the teachers in our schools would search the Scriptures for the purpose of securing a better understanding for themselves, opening their hearts to the light given in the word, they would be taught of God. They would love and practice the truth, and would labor to bring in less of the theories and sentiments of men who have never had a connection with God, and more of the knowledge that endures. They would feel a deep soul hunger for the wisdom that comes from above.

Studying to Useless Ends

Often students spend many years in study that is conducted on wrong lines and to useless ends. The mind is trained to think in a wrong channel, taught to grasp those things that are not only utterly worthless, but an injury to the physical and mental health. The student obtains a slender store of information upon many subjects that are of little value to him, a limited knowledge along many lines that he will never use, when he might obtain knowledge that would be of the highest service in practical life, and which would be a storehouse of wisdom from which to draw in time of need.

It is difficult to depart from old customs and established ideas. But few realize the loss that is sustained by many in long courses of study. Much that is crowded into the brain is of no value, yet students suppose this education to be all-sufficient, and after years of study they leave school with their diplomas, believing that they are men and women properly educated and ready for service. In many cases this preparation for service is nothing more than a farce, yet it will continue until teachers receive the wisdom of heaven through the influence of the Holy Spirit.

Many a student has so long taxed the mind to learn that which his reason tells him will never be of any use, that his mental powers have become weakened and incapable of vigorous exertion and persevering effort to comprehend those things which are of vital importance. The money expended in his education, which perhaps was provided as the result of great sacrifice on the part of his parents, is well-nigh wasted; and a misapprehension as to what is of importance leads to a mistake in his lifework.

What a fraud is that education obtained in literary or scientific lines, if it must be stripped from the learner before he is counted worthy to enter upon that life which measures with the life of God, himself saved as by fire. God has given us a probation in which to prepare for the school above. For this the youth are here to be educated, disciplined, and trained. In the lower school of earth they are to form characters that God can approve. They are to receive a training, not in the customs and amusements of worldly society, but in Christ's lines, a training that will fit them to be colaborers with heavenly intelligences. The studies given the youth should be of a character to make them more successful in the service of God, to enable them to follow in the footsteps of Christ and to maintain the great principles that He maintained. Our standard is to be the character of Him who is pure, holy, undefiled. . . .

The knowledge of God is the real essence of education. The education that would supersede this knowledge, or dismiss it from the mind, as Felix dismissed Paul when he spoke to him of temperance, righteousness, and judgment to come, is not of God. Paul's words made Felix tremble; but the governor dismissed the apostle with the words, "Go thy way for this time; when I have a convenient season, I will call for thee." Acts 24:25. And today multitudes are saying the same. Their minds are called to the deep subjects of truth, problems as high as heaven and as broad as eternity; but they say, "I cannot bring these subjects into my daily studies; for they would so stir up my mind as to unfit me for the daily routine of study. I have never mastered Bible problems. I cannot take up this study now. Go thy way for this time; when I have a convenient season, I will call for thee." Thus God's great lesson book is set aside because it is not regarded as the one thing needful.

The Highest Possible Development

I do not wish anyone to receive from the words I have written the impression that the standard of education in our schools is to be in any way lowered. Every student should remember that the Lord requires him to make of himself all that is possible, that he may wisely teach others also. Our students should tax the mental powers; every faculty should reach the highest possible development.

Many students come to college with intellectual habits that are a hindrance to them. One of the most difficult to manage is the habit of performing mental work as a matter of routine, instead of bringing to bear upon each study thoughtful, determined effort to master difficulties and to grasp the principles at the foundation of the subject under consideration. Indolence, apathy, irregularity, are to be dreaded, and the binding of oneself to routine is just as much to be dreaded. Through the grace of Christ it is in the power of students to change this habit of routine, and it is for their best interests and future usefulness rightly to direct the mental faculties, training them to do service under the guidance of the wisest of all teachers, whose power they may claim by faith. This will give them success in their intellectual efforts, in accordance with God's promise.

A thorough education, which will fit young men and women for service, is to be given in our schools. In order to secure such an education the wisdom that comes from God must be made first and most important. All who engage in the acquisition of knowledge should strive to reach the highest round of the ladder. Let students advance as fast and as far as they can; let the field of their study be as broad as their powers can compass; but let them make God their wisdom, clinging to Him who is infinite in knowledge, who can reveal secrets hidden for ages, and who can solve the most difficult problems for minds that believe in Him.

We commend to every student the Book of books as the grandest study for human intelligence, the book that contains the knowledge essential for this life and for the life to come. But I do not encourage a letting down of the educational standard in the study of the sciences. The light that has been given on this subject is clear and should in no case be disregarded.

Putting the Bible First

In the instruction given in our schools, the natural and the spiritual are to be combined. The laws obeyed by the earth reveal the fact that it is under the masterly power of an infinite God. The same principles run through the spiritual and the natural world. Divorce God from the acquisition of knowledge, and you have a lame, one-sided education, dead to all the saving qualities that give true power to man. The Author of nature is the Author of the Bible. Creation and Christianity have one God. God is revealed in nature, and God is revealed in His word. In clear rays the light shines from the sacred page, showing us the living God, as represented in the laws of His government, in the creation of the world, in the heavens that He has garnished. His power is to be recognized as the only means of redeeming the world from the degrading superstitions that are so dishonoring to God and man.

The student who in his school life becomes familiar with the truths of God's word and feels their transforming power upon his heart will represent the character of Christ to the world in a well-ordered life and a godly conversation. God will do great things for those who will open the heart to His word and let it take possession of the soul temple. The departure from the simplicity of true godliness on the part of students has had an influence to weaken character and lessen mental vigor. Their advancement in the sciences has been retarded, while if they had been like Daniel, hearers and doers of the word of God, they would have advanced as he did in all branches of learning upon which they entered. Being pure-minded, they would have become strong-minded. Every intellectual faculty would have been sharpened.

When the Bible is made the guide and counselor, it exerts an ennobling influence upon the mind. Its study more than any other will refine and elevate. It will enlarge the mind of the candid student, endowing it with new impulses and fresh vigor. It will give greater efficiency to the faculties by bringing them in contact with grand, far-reaching truths. If the mind becomes dwarfed and inefficient, it is because it is left to deal with commonplace subjects only. Let the Bible be received as the food of the soul, the best and most effectual means of purifying and strengthening the intellect.

———————

Out of the heart are the issues of life; and the heart of the community, of the church, and of the nation is the household. The well-being of society, the success of the church, the prosperity of the nation, depend upon home influences.

IN CO-OPERATION WITH CHRIST

I am instructed to say to teachers, ministers, and physicians, who hold responsible positions in the work of the third angel's message, You have a solemn work to do, a holy work. Those who hold positions of trust in the cause of God are to perfect the life after the divine similitude. In the home, in the church, before the world, they are to reveal the power of Christian principle to transform the life. Let them work honestly; let them seek to reveal the spirit of Christ in their work; let them ever strive to reach higher ground. As I realize the perilous times before us and the great responsibilities resting upon teachers, ministers, and physicians, a heavy burden comes upon me lest they be unfaithful in the discharge of duty.

"Ye that love the Lord, hate evil," the psalmist exhorts. "He preserveth the souls of His saints; He delivereth them out of the hand of the wicked. Light is sown for the righteous, and gladness for the upright in heart. Rejoice in the Lord, ye righteous; and give thanks at the remembrance of His holiness." Psalm 97: 10-12. Teachers, ministers, and physicians are talking of higher ground to be gained in educational lines; but these words of the psalmist show that it is by serving God that this higher ground will be gained. We should now be putting away evilspeaking, selfish plans, everything that would hurt the influence or confuse the judgment. The heart must be emptied of all self-seeking; the conduct must be such that it will lead no soul into false paths.

The Lord calls upon His people to put away indolence and indifference, and to act like converted men and women. Diligent work is to be done in the circulation of our literature. Faithful work, marked by Christian politeness, is to be done in many missionary lines. The truth is to go forth as a lamp that burneth, that the real meaning of higher education may be clearly understood.

In our towns and cities are souls living in ignorance of the truths of God's word; many are perishing in sin. Some out of curiosity come to our houses of worship. Let every discourse preached be a revelation of the great truths applicable to this time. Unveil the mysteries of redemption before the students in the school and before the congregations who assemble to hear the word. This is knowledge needed by the educated and the unlearned. The highest education will be found in studying the mystery of godliness. The great truths of God's word, if believed and received and carried into the life practice, will result in education of the highest order.

The Saviour in His teachings ever showed the relation between cause and effect. To His followers in every age He speaks, saying, "Let your light so shine before men, that they may see your good works, and glorify your Father which is in heaven." Matthew 5:16. The man or woman who has a knowledge of the truth, but whose life does not express its principles, is hiding his light. My brethren, let the light be brought from under the bushel, that it may make known the truths of the gospel.

Invisible agencies will work through the visible; the supernatural will co-operate with the natural, the heavenly with the earthly; unknown things will be revealed through the known. Let the grace of Christ be revealed to teach that man may be renewed in the likeness of God.

The Saviour's promise, "Whosoever hath, to him shall be given" (Matthew 13:12), applies also to the reception of truth. To him who seeks to understand its teachings will be given increased understanding. To him who reveals that he possesses the spirit of truth will be given a larger measure of the Spirit, that he may work out his own salvation. The work of reflecting Christ to the world will not be done boastingly, but in fear and trembling, yet in the power of the Spirit.

The most desirable education is a knowledge of the mysteries of the kingdom of heaven. He who serves the world sees not the great things of eternal interest prepared for the one who opens his heart to the light of heaven. But he who enters this path of knowledge and perseveres in his search after the hidden wisdom, to him heavenly agencies teach the great lessons which through faith in Christ enable him to be an overcomer. Through this knowledge spiritual perfection is reached; the life becomes holy and Christlike.

Christ's teachings were not impressed upon His hearers by any outward gestures, but by the words and acts of His daily life, by the spirit He revealed. In the higher life that He led as He worked the works of God, He gave to men an example of the outworking of the true higher education. So in the lives of His followers, when a hasty spirit is overcome, when the heart is melted to tenderness for others, when the life is devoted to working the works of Christ, the fruit of the higher education is seen.

Higher education is not gained by the study of a certain class of books that worldly teachers deem essential, but by the study of the word of God. This study will lead to obedience to His requirements and to a constant walking in the footsteps of Christ. There is no education higher than that to be found in the lessons that Christ gave. When these are discarded for the teachings of men, it is time that God's people became converted anew and learned from Christ the simplicity of true godliness.

———

When the converting power of God takes hold of the teachers in our schools, they will recognize that a knowledge of God and of Jesus Christ covers a much broader field than the so-called "advanced methods" of education. But unless they have broader views in regard to what constitutes education, they will experience great hindrance in preparing missionaries to go out to give their knowledge to others.

Teachers, take your position as true educators, and pour into the hearts of the students the living stream of redeeming love. Before their minds are preoccupied with literary work, entreat them to seek Christ and His righteousness. Show them the changes that will surely take place if the heart is given to Christ. Fasten their attention on Him. This will close the door to the foolish aspirations that naturally arise, and will prepare the mind for the reception of divine truth.

TO TEACHERS AND STUDENTS

We have been warned again and again that the character of the education that has been current in the world cannot stand the test of the word of God. The subject of education is one that should interest every Seventh-day Adventist. The Lord says to us, Seventh-day Adventists are not to place themselves under the counsel and instruction of teachers who know not the truth for this time. The molding and fashioning of minds should not be left to men who have not comprehended the importance of a preparation for that life which measures with the life of God.

Some of our teachers have been charmed with the sentiments of infidel authors. In a representation given me, I saw one holding in his hand one of these books and recommending it to our teachers as a book from which real help could be obtained along educational lines. Another was holding in His hand books of an altogether different character. He placed His hand upon the one who had recommended the infidel author, and said, "Advice of the kind you have given is opening the door for Satan with his sophistries to find easy entrance to your school. These books contain sentiments that your students should be instructed to avoid. Human minds are easily charmed with studies that lead to infidelity. These books produce in the minds of the students a distaste for the study of the word of God, which is eternal life to all who follow its instruction. Such books should not find entrance into any school where the youth are being taught to be learners of the greatest of teachers."

With solemn voice the speaker continued, "Do you find in these authors that which you can recommend as essential to true higher education? Would you dare to recommend their study to students who are ignorant of their true character? Wrong habits of thought, when once accepted, become a despotic power that fastens the mind as in a grasp of steel. If many who have received and read these books had never seen them, but had accepted the words of the divine Teacher in their place, they would be far in advance of where they now are in a knowledge of the divine truths of God's word, which make men wise unto salvation. These books have led thousands where Satan led Adam and Eve—to a knowledge that God forbade them to have. Through their teachings, students have been turned away from the word of the Lord to fables."

I am instructed to say to students, In your search for knowledge climb higher than the standard set by the world; follow where Jesus has led the way. And to teachers I would say, Beware how you sow the seeds of unbelief in human hearts and minds. Cleanse yourselves from all filthiness of the flesh and spirit. The crowning glory of Christ's attributes is His holiness. The angels bow before Him in adoration, exclaiming, "Holy, holy, holy, Lord God Almighty." Revelation 4:8. He is declared to be glorious in His holiness. Study the character of God. By beholding Christ, by seeking Him in faith and prayer, you may become like Him.

The standard of education in our schools is lowered as soon as Christ ceases to be the pattern of teachers and students. Teachers are to understand that their work is not confined to the knowledge contained in textbooks; it is to reach higher, far higher than it does. A course of self-discipline is to educate them to conform the character to the divine similitude. Self dies hard; but when teachers have that wisdom which comes from above, they will discern the true object of our educational work, and reforms will be made that will give our youth a training that is according to the Lord's plan of development.

Teacher, weed from your talks all that is not of the highest and best quality. Keep before the students those sentiments only that are essential. Never should the physician, minister, or teacher prolong his talks until the alpha is forgotten in long-drawn-out assertions that are not of the least benefit. When this is done, the mind is swamped with a multitude of words that it cannot retain. Let the talks given be short and right to the point. Let the mind be kept sweet and pure, and open to heaven's first law, "Thou shalt love the Lord thy God with all thy heart, and with all thy soul, and with all thy strength, and with all thy mind; and thy neighbor as thyself." Luke 10:27. If those who act a part in the training of the youth will leave many things unsaid, and present before the students the importance of the principles they must obey in order to have eternal life, there will be seen a work of true reform.

A SPEEDY PREPARATION FOR WORK

The practice of furnishing a few students with every advantage for perfecting their education in so many lines that it would be impossible for them to make use of them all is an injury rather than a benefit to the one who has so many advantages, and it deprives others of the privileges that they need so much. If there were far less of this long-continued preparation, far less exclusive devotion to study, there would be much more opportunity for an increase of the student's faith in God. . . . It has been shown me that some of the students are losing their spirituality, that their faith is becoming weak, and that they do not hold constant communion with God. They spend nearly all their time in the perusal of books; they seem to know but little else. But what advantage will all this preparation be to them? What benefit will they derive for all the time and money spent? I tell you, it will be worse than lost. . . .

There should be most careful consideration as to the best manner of expending money in the education of students. While so much is spent to put a few through an expensive course of study, there are many who are thirsting for the knowledge they should get in a few months; one or two years would be considered a great blessing. If all the means is used in putting a few through several years of study, many young men and women just as worthy cannot be assisted at all. . . .

(404)

Instead of overeducating a few, enlarge the sphere of your charities. Resolve that the means which you use in educating workers for the cause shall not be expended simply upon one, enabling him to get more than he really needs, while others are left without anything at all. Give students a start, but do not feel that it is your duty to carry them year after year. It is their duty to get out into the field to work, and it is your place to extend your charities to others who are in need of assistance. . . .

Too great devotion to study, even of true science, creates an abnormal appetite, which increases as it is fed. This creates a desire to secure more knowledge than is essential to do the work of the Lord. The pursuit of knowledge merely for its own sake diverts the mind from devotion to God, and checks advance along the path of practical holiness. . . . The Lord Jesus imparted only such a measure of instruction as could be utilized. . . . The minds of the disciples were often excited by curiosity; but instead of gratifying their desire to know things which were not necessary for the proper conduct of their work, He opened new channels of thought to their minds. He gave them much needed instruction upon practical godliness. . . .

Intemperance in Study

Intemperance in study is a species of intoxication, and those who indulge in it, like the drunkard, wander from safe paths and stumble and fall in the darkness. The Lord would have every student bear in mind that the eye must be kept single to the glory of God. He is not to exhaust and waste his physical and mental powers in seeking to acquire all possible knowledge of the sciences, but is to preserve the freshness and vigor of all his powers to engage in the work which the Lord has appointed him in helping souls to find the path of righteousness. . . . The command of heaven is to do, to work,—to do something that will reflect glory to God by being a benefit to our fellow men. . . .

The Lord does not choose or accept laborers according to the advantages they have enjoyed, or according to the superior education they have received. The value of the human agent is estimated according to the capacity of the heart to know and understand God. . . . The highest possible good is obtained through a knowledge of God. "This is life eternal, that they might know Thee the only true God, and Jesus Christ, whom Thou hast sent." John 17:3. This knowledge is the secret spring from which flows all power. . . .

The Education of Moses

The education received by Moses, as the king's grandson, was very thorough. Nothing was neglected that would make him a wise man, as the Egyptians understood wisdom. But the most valuable part of Moses' fitting for his lifework was that which he received as a shepherd. As he led his flocks through the wilds of the mountains and into the green pastures of the valleys, the God of nature taught him the highest wisdom. In the school of nature, with Christ as his teacher, he learned lessons of humility, meekness, faith, and trust, all of which bound his soul closer to God. In the solitude of the mountains he learned that which all his instruction in the king's palace was unable to impart to him—simple, unwavering faith and a constant trust in the Lord.

Moses had supposed that his education in the wisdom of Egypt fully qualified him to lead Israel from bondage. Was he not learned in all those things necessary for a general of armies? Had he not had the advantages of the best schools in the land? Yes, he felt that he was able to deliver his people. He set about his work by trying to gain their favor by redressing their wrongs. He killed an Egyptian who was imposing upon one of the Israelites. In this he manifested the spirit of him who was a murderer from the beginning, and proved himself unfit to represent the God of mercy, love, and tenderness.

Moses made a miserable failure of his first attempt; and, like many another, he immediately lost confidence in God and turned his back on his appointed work. He fled from the wrath of Pharaoh. He concluded that because of his great sin in taking the life of the Egyptian, God would not permit him to have any part in the work of delivering his people from their cruel bondage. But the Lord allowed these things that He might teach Moses the gentleness, goodness, and long-suffering that it is necessary for every laborer for the Master to possess in order to be a successful worker in His cause. . . .

Moses had been taught to expect flattery and praise because of his superior abilities; now he was to learn a different lesson. As a shepherd of sheep, Moses learned to care for the afflicted, to nurse the sick, to seek patiently after the straying, to bear long with the unruly, to supply with loving solicitude the wants of the young lambs and the necessities of the old and feeble. In this experience he was drawn nearer to the Chief Shepherd. He became united to, submerged in, the Holy One of Israel. He believed in the great God. He held communion with the Father through humble prayer. He looked to the Highest for an education in spiritual things and for a knowledge of his duty as a faithful shepherd. His life became so closely linked with heaven that God talked with him face to face, "as a man speaketh unto his friend." Exodus 33:11.

Thus educated, Moses was prepared to heed the call of God to exchange his shepherd's crook for the rod of authority; to leave his flock of sheep to take the leadership of an idolatrous, rebellious people. But he was still to depend on the invisible Leader. As the rod was an instrument in his hand, so he was to be a willing instrument in the hand of Christ. He was to be the shepherd of God's people; and through his firm faith and abiding trust in the Lord, many blessings were to come to the children of Israel. . . .

It was implicit faith in God that made Moses what he was. According to all that the Lord commanded him, so he did. All the learning of the wise men could not make Moses a channel through which the Lord could work, until he lost his self-confidence, realized his own helplessness, and put his trust in God; until he was willing to obey God's commands, whether they seemed to his human reason to be right or not. . . .

It was not the teaching of the schools of Egypt that enabled Moses to triumph over his enemies, but an ever-abiding, unflinching faith, a faith that did not fail under the most trying circumstances. At the command of God, Moses advanced, although apparently there was nothing ahead for his feet to tread upon. More than a million people were depending on him, and he led them forward step by step, day by day. God permitted these lonely travels through the wilderness that His people might obtain an experience in enduring hardship, and that when they were in peril they might know that there was relief and deliverance in God alone. Thus they might learn to know and to trust God, and to serve Him with a living faith.

The Most Important Lesson

God is not dependent upon men of perfect education. His work is not to wait while His servants go through such lengthy, elaborate preparations as some of our schools are planning to give. He wants men who appreciate the privilege of being laborers together with Him—men who will honor Him by rendering implicit obedience to His requirements, regardless of previously inculcated theories. There is no limit to the usefulness of those who put self to one side, make room for the working of the Holy Spirit upon their hearts, and live lives wholly consecrated to God, enduring the necessary discipline imposed by the Lord without complaining or fainting by the way. If they will not faint at the rebuke of the Lord, and become hardhearted and stubborn, the Lord will teach both old and young, hour by hour, day by day. He longs to reveal His salvation to the children of men; and if His chosen people will remove the obstructions, He will pour forth the waters of salvation in abundant streams through human channels.

Many who are seeking efficiency for the exalted work of God by perfecting their education in the schools of men will find that they have failed of learning the more important lessons. By neglecting to submit themselves to the impressions of the Holy Spirit, by not living in obedience to all God's requirements, their spiritual efficiency has become weakened; they have lost what ability they had to do successful work for the Lord. Absenting themselves from the school of Christ, they have forgotten the sound of the Teacher's voice, and He cannot direct their course.

Men may acquire all the knowledge possible to be imparted by the human teacher, but God requires of them still greater wisdom. Like Moses, they must learn meekness, lowliness of heart, and distrust of self. Our Saviour Himself, when bearing the test for humanity, acknowledged that of Himself He could do nothing. We also must learn that there is no strength in humanity alone. Man becomes efficient only by becoming partaker of the divine nature.

God's Guidance to Be Sought

From the first opening of a book the student should recognize God as the One who imparts true wisdom. He should seek divine counsel at every step. No arrangement should be made to which God cannot be a party, no union formed of which He cannot approve. From first to last the Author of wisdom should be recognized as the guide. Thus the knowledge obtained from books will be bound off by living faith in the infinite God. The student should not permit himself to be bound down to any particular course of study involving long periods of time, but should be guided in such matters by the Spirit of God. . . .

None should be allowed to pursue a course of study that will weaken their faith in the truth or in the Lord's power, or diminish their respect for a life of holiness. I would warn the students not to advance one step in these lines, not even upon the advice of their instructors or men in positions of authority, unless they have first sought God individually with their hearts thrown open to the influences of the Holy Spirit and have obtained His counsel concerning the contemplated course of study. Let every unholy ambition be blotted out. Let every selfish desire to distinguish yourselves be set aside; let every suggestion from humanity be taken to God, and trust in the guidance of His Spirit. . . .

Do not commit yourselves to the keeping of men, but say, "The Lord is my helper; I will seek His counsel; I will be a doer of His will." All the advantages you may have cannot be a blessing to you, neither can the highest education qualify you to become a channel of light, unless you have the co-operation of the divine Spirit. It is as impossible for us to receive qualifications from men, without the divine enlightenment, as it was for the gods of Egypt to deliver those who trusted in them.

Students must not suppose that every suggestion for them to prolong their studies is in harmony with God's plan. Take every such suggestion to the Lord in prayer, and seek His guidance, not once only, but again and again. Plead with Him until you are convinced whether the counsel is of God or man. . . .

The Lord says, "Watch and pray, that ye enter not into temptation." Matthew 26:41. "Watch" lest your studies accumulate to such proportions and become of such absorbing interest to you that your mind is overburdened and the desire for godliness is crushed out of your soul. With many students the motive and aim which caused them to enter school have gradually been lost sight of, and an unholy ambition to secure a high-class education has led them to sacrifice the truth. Their intense interest to secure a high place among men has caused them to leave the will of their heavenly Father out of their calculations; but true knowledge leads to holiness of life through sanctification of the truth.

Too often, as the studies accumulate, the wisdom from above has been given a secondary place, and the farther the student advances, the less confidence he has in God. He looks upon much learning as the very essence of success in life; but if all would give due consideration to the statement of Christ, "Without Me ye can do nothing" (John 15:5), they would make different plans. Without the vital principles of true religion, without the knowledge of how to serve and glorify the Redeemer, education is more harmful than beneficial. When education in human lines is pushed to such an extent that the love of God wanes in the heart, that prayer is neglected, and that there is a failure to cultivate the spiritual attributes, it is wholly disastrous. It would be far better to cease seeking to obtain an education, and to recover your soul from its languishing condition, than to gain the best of educations and lose sight of eternal advantages. . . .

I would not in any case counsel restriction of the education to which God has set no limit. Our education does not end with the advantages that this world can give. Through all eternity the chosen of God will be learners. But I would advise restriction in following those methods of education which imperil the soul and defeat the purpose for which time and money are spent. Education is a grand lifework; but to obtain true education it is necessary to possess that wisdom which comes from God alone. The Lord God should be represented in every phase of education; but it is a mistake to devote years to the study of one line of book knowledge. After a period of time has been devoted to study, let no one advise students to enter immediately upon another extended line of study, but rather advise them to enter upon the work for which they have been preparing. Let them be encouraged to put into use the education already obtained. . . .

The minds of many need to be renewed, transformed, and molded after God's plan. Many are ruining themselves physically, mentally, and morally by overdevotion to study. They are defrauding themselves for time and for eternity through practicing habits of intemperance in seeking to gain an education. They are losing their desire to learn in the school of Christ lessons of meekness and lowliness of heart. . . .

In View of Christ's Near Return

The thought to be kept before students is that time is short and that they must make speedy preparation for doing the work that is essential for this time. . . . I am bidden to say to you that you know not how soon the crisis will come. It is stealing gradually upon us, as a thief. The sun shines in the heavens, passing over its usual round, and the heavens still declare the glory of God; men are pursuing their usual course of eating and drinking, planting and building, marrying and giving in marriage; merchants are still engaged in buying and selling; publications are still issuing one upon another; men are jostling one against another, seeking to get the highest place; pleasure lovers are still attending theaters, horse races, gambling hells, and the highest excitement prevails; but probation's hour is fast closing, and every case is about to be eternally decided. There are few who believe with heart and soul that we have a heaven to win and a hell to shun; but these show their faith by their works.

The signs of Christ's coming are fast fulfilling. Satan sees that he has but a short time in which to work, and he has set his agencies to work to stir up the elements of the world, that men may be deceived, deluded, and kept occupied and entranced until the day of probation shall be ended and the door of mercy be forever shut.

The kingdoms of this world have not yet become the kingdoms of our Lord and of His Christ. Do not deceive yourselves; be wide awake and move rapidly, for the night cometh in which no man can work. Do not encourage students who come to you burdened with the work of saving their fellow men, to enter upon course after course of study. Do not lengthen out to many years the time for obtaining an education. By so doing you give them the impression that there is time enough, and this very plan proves a snare to their souls.

Many are better prepared, have more spiritual discrimination and knowledge of God, and know more of His requirements, when they enter upon their course of study than when they are graduated. They become inspired with an ambition to become learned men and are encouraged to add to their studies until they become infatuated. They make their books their idol and are willing to sacrifice health and spirituality in order to obtain an education. They limit the time which they should devote to prayer and fail to improve the opportunities which they have to do good. They fail to put to use the knowledge which they have already obtained and do not advance in the science of winning souls. Missionary work becomes less and less desirable, while the passion to excel in book knowledge increases abnormally. In pursuing their studies they separate from the God of wisdom. Some congratulate them on their advancement and encourage them to take degree after degree. . . .

The question was asked, "Do you believe the truth? do you believe the third angel's message? If you do believe, then act your faith." . . . Probationary time will not permit of long-protracted years of drill. God calls; hear His voice as He says, "Go work today in My vineyard." Matthew 21:28. Now, just now, is the time to work. . . .

"The Lord hath His way in the whirlwind and in the storm, and the clouds are the dust of His feet." Nahum 1:3. O that men might understand the patience and long-suffering of God! He is putting under restraint His own attributes. His omnipotent power is under the control of Omnipotence. O that men would understand that God refuses to be wearied out with the world's perversity and still holds out the hope of forgiveness even to the most undeserving! But His forbearance will not always continue. Who is prepared for the sudden change that will take place in God's dealing with sinful men? Who will be prepared to escape the punishment that will certainly fall upon transgressors? . . .

There is a large work to be done, and the vineyard of the Lord needs laborers. Missionaries should enter the field before they are compelled to cease labor. There are now open doors on every side; students cannot afford to wait to complete years of training, for the years before us are not many, and we need to work while the day lasts. . . .

Understand that I say nothing in these words to depreciate education, but I speak to warn those who are in danger of carrying that which is lawful to unlawful extremes, and of making altogether too much of human education. Rather insist upon the development of a Christian experience, for without this the education of the student will be of no avail.

If you see that students are in danger of becoming engrossed in their studies to such an extent as to neglect the study of that Book which gives them information as to how to secure the future welfare of their souls, then do not present the temptation of going deeper, of protracting the time for educational discipline. In this way all that will make the student's education of value to the world will be sunk out of sight. . . .

As long as time shall last, we shall have need of schools. There will always be need of education; but we must be careful lest education absorb every spiritual interest. There is positive peril in advising students to pursue one line of education after another and in leading them to think that by so doing they will attain perfection. The education thus obtained will prove to be deficient in every way. The Lord says: "I will destroy the wisdom of the wise, and will bring to nothing the understanding of the prudent. Where is the wise? where is the scribe? where is the disputer of this world? hath not God made foolish the wisdom of this world? For after that in the wisdom of God the world by wisdom knew not God, it pleased God by the foolishness of preaching to save them that believe." 1 Corinthians 1:19-21.

Moses was learned in all the wisdom of the Egyptians. In the providence of God he received a broad education, but a large part of that education had to be unlearned and accounted as foolishness. Its impression had to be blotted out by forty years of experience in caring for the sheep and the tender lambs. If many who are connected with the work of the Lord could be isolated as was Moses, and could be compelled by circumstances to follow some humble vocation until their hearts became tender, . . . they would not be so prone to magnify their own abilities, or seek to demonstrate that the wisdom of an advanced education could take the place of a sound knowledge of God. . . .

The disciples of Christ are not called upon to magnify men, but to magnify God, the Source of all wisdom. Let educators give the Holy Spirit room to do Its work upon human hearts. The greatest Teacher is represented in the midst of us by the Holy Spirit. However you may study, though you may reach higher and still higher, and occupy every moment of your probationary time in the pursuit of knowledge, you will not become complete. When time is over, you would have to ask yourselves the question, What good have I done to those who are in midnight darkness? To whom have I communicated the knowledge of God or even the knowledge of those things for which I have spent so much time and money?

It will soon be said in heaven, "It is done." "He that is unjust, let him be unjust still: and he which is filthy, let him be filthy still: and he that is righteous, let him be righteous still: and he that is holy, let him be holy still. And, behold, I come quickly; and My reward is with Me, to give every man according as his work shall be." Revelation 22:11, 12. When this fiat goes forth, every case will have been decided.

Far better would it be for laborers to take less work and go about it slowly and humbly, wearing the yoke of Christ and bearing His burdens, than to devote years of preparation for a large work and then fail to bring sons and daughters to God, fail to have any trophies to lay at the feet of Jesus. . . .

How many who know the truth for this time are working in harmony with its principles? It is true that something is being done; but more, far more, should have been done. The work is accumulating, and the time for doing it is diminishing. All should now be burning and shining lights, and yet many are failing to keep their lamps supplied with the oil of grace, trimmed and burning, so that light may gleam out today. Too many are counting on a long stretch of tomorrow, but this is a mistake. Let everyone be educated in such a way as to show the importance of the special work for today. Let everyone labor for God and for souls; let each show wisdom and never be found in idleness, waiting for someone to set him to work. The "someone" who could set you to work is overcrowded with responsibilities, and time is lost in waiting for his directions. God will give you wisdom in reforming at once; for the call is still made, "Son, go work today in My vineyard." "Today if ye will hear His voice, harden not your hearts." Hebrews 3:7, 8. The Lord prefaces the requirement with the endearing word "son." How tender, how compassionate, yet withal, how urgent! His invitation is also a command.—*Special Testimonies on Education,* pages 108-146; written March 21, 1895, to the teachers in the Sanitarium and College at Battle Creek, Michigan.

To know oneself is great knowledge. True self-knowledge leads to a humility that will open the way for the Lord to develop the mind and mold and discipline the character. No teacher can do acceptable work who does not bear in mind his own deficiencies and does not put aside all plans that would weaken spiritual life. When teachers are willing to lay aside that which is unessential for the life eternal, then it can be said that they are working out their own salvation with fear and trembling, and that they are building wisely for eternity.

FOR FURTHER STUDY

THE FALSE AND THE TRUE IN EDUCATION
Fundamentals of Christian Education, pp. 196-200, 331-333.
Ministry of Healing, The, pp. 427-450.
Testimonies, vol. 8, pp. 255-289.

TO TEACHERS AND STUDENTS
Testimonies, vol. 6, pp. 162-167.

A SPEEDY PREPARATION
Fundamentals of Christian Education, pp. 242-244, 334-367.
Ministry of Healing, The, pp. 474, 475.
Testimonies, vol. 3, pp. 223, 224.
vol. 5, p. 22.

THE BIBLE IN EDUCATION

"The words of Jehovah are pure words; as silver tried in a furnace on the earth, purified seven times."

GOD'S WORD A TREASURE HOUSE

The Bible is of the highest value because it is the word of the living God. Of all the books in the world it is the most deserving of study and attention, for it is eternal wisdom. The Bible is a history that tells us of the creation of the world and opens to us past centuries. Without it we should have been left to conjecture and fable in regard to the occurrences of the remote past. It reveals to us the Creator of the heavens and the earth, with the universe that He has brought into being, and it sheds a glorious light over the world to come.

The Bible is a field where are concealed heavenly treasures, and they will remain hidden until, by diligent mining, they are discovered and brought to light. The Bible is a casket containing jewels of inestimable value, which should be so presented as to be seen in their intrinsic luster. But the beauty and excellence of these diamonds of truth are not discerned by the natural eye. The lovely things of the material world are not seen until the sun, dispelling the darkness, floods them with its light. And so with the treasures of God's word; they are not appreciated until they are revealed by the Sun of Righteousness.

(421)

The Bible contains a simple and complete system of theology and philosophy. It is the book that makes us wise unto salvation. It tells us of the love of God as shown in the plan of redemption, imparting the knowledge essential for all students—the knowledge of Christ. . . .

God has not only revealed to us the doctrine of the atonement, holding out the hope of eternal life, but His words are the manna from heaven for the soul to feed upon and receive spiritual strength. The Bible is the great standard of right and wrong, clearly defining sin and holiness. Its living principles, running through our lives like threads of gold, are our only safeguard in trial and temptation.

The Holy Scriptures were the essential study in the schools of the prophets, and they should hold the first place in every educational system, for the foundation of all right education is a knowledge of God. Used as a textbook in our schools, the Bible will do for mind and morals what cannot be done by books of science and philosophy. As a book to discipline and strengthen the intellect, to ennoble, purify, and refine the character, it is without a rival.

God cares for us as intelligent beings, and He has given us His word as a lamp to our feet and a light to our path. Its teachings have a vital bearing upon our prosperity in all the relations of life. Even in our temporal affairs it will be a wiser guide than any other counselor. Its divine instruction points the only way to true success. There is no social position, no phase of human experience, for which the study of the Bible is not an essential preparation.

Finite Wisdom

But the mere reading of the word will not accomplish the result designed of heaven; it must be studied, and cherished in the heart. The Bible has not received the close attention it deserves. It has not been honored above every other book in the education of children and youth. Students devote years to acquiring an education. They study different authors and become acquainted with science and philosophy through books containing the results of human research; but the Book that comes from the divine Teacher has, to a great extent, been neglected. Its value is not discerned; its treasures remain hidden.

An education of this character is defective. Who and what are these men of learning, that the minds and characters of the young should be molded by their ideas? They may publish with pen and voice the best results of their reasoning; but they grasp only an item of the work of God, and in their shortsightedness, calling it science, they exalt it above the God of science.

Man is finite; there is no light in his wisdom. His unaided reason can explain nothing in the deep things of God, nor can he understand the spiritual lessons that God has placed in the material world. But reason is a gift of God, and His Spirit will aid those who are willing to be taught. Man's words, if of any value, echo the words of God. In the education of youth they should never take the place of the divine word.

Cold, philosophical speculations and scientific research in which God is not acknowledged are a positive injury. And the evil is aggravated when, as is often the case, books placed in the hands of the young, accepted as authority and depended upon in their education, are from authors avowedly infidel. Through all the thoughts presented by these men their poisonous sentiments are interwoven. The study of such books is like handling black coals; a student cannot be undefiled in mind who thinks along the line of skepticism.

The authors of these books, which have sown the seeds of doubt and infidelity broadcast over the world, have been under the training of the great enemy of God and man, the acknowledged head of principalities and powers, the ruler of the darkness of this world. The word that God has spoken concerning them is, "They . . . became vain in their imaginations, and their foolish heart was darkened. Professing themselves to be wise, they became fools;" "because that, when they knew God, they glorified Him not as God, neither were thankful." Romans 1:21, 22. They rejected divine truth in its simplicity and purity for the wisdom of this world.

Whenever books by these infidel authors are given the precedence, and the word of God is made secondary, there will be sent out of the schools a class of students no better fitted for the service of God than they were before they received their education.

Cause of Opposition to the Bible

It is not for want of evidence that men doubt divine truth; they are not infidels through ignorance of the character of the word of God. But through sin the whole human organism is deranged, the mind is perverted, the imagination corrupted. Temptations from without find an answering chord within the heart, and the feet slide imperceptibly into sin. And so it is that many hate the Bible. Some would not care if there were not a Bible in the world.

When the Son of God was on trial, the Jews cried out, "Away with Him, crucify Him!" because His pure life and holy teaching convicted them of sin and condemned them; and for the same reason many in their hearts cry out against the word of God. Many, even of the children and youth, have learned to love sin. They hate reflection, and the thought of God is a sting to their conscience. It is because the human heart is inclined to evil that it is so dangerous to sow the seeds of skepticism in young minds.

Science and the Bible

We would not discourage education, nor put a low estimate on mental culture and discipline. God would have us students as long as we remain in the world. Every opportunity for culture should be improved. The faculties need to be strengthened by exercise, the mind is to be trained and expanded by taxing study; but all this may be done while the heart is becoming an easy prey to deception. Wisdom from above must be communicated to the soul. It is the entrance of God's word that "giveth light; it giveth understanding unto the simple." Psalm 119:130. His word is given for our instruction; there is nothing in it that is defective or misleading. The Bible is not to be tested by men's ideas of science, but science is to be brought to the test of the unerring standard.

Yet the study of the sciences is not to be neglected. Books must be used for this purpose; but they should be in harmony with the Bible, for that is the standard. Books of this character should take the place of many of those now in the hands of students.

God is the author of science. Scientific research opens to the mind vast fields of thought and information, enabling us to see God in His created works. Ignorance may try to support skepticism by appealing to science; but instead of upholding skepticism, true science contributes fresh evidences of the wisdom and power of God. Rightly understood, science and the written word agree, and each sheds light on the other. Together they lead us to God by teaching us something of the wise and beneficent laws through which He works.

When the student recognizes God as the source of all knowledge, and honors Him, submitting mind and character to be molded by His word, he may claim the promise, "Them that honor Me I will honor." 1 Samuel 2:30. The more studiously the intellect is cultivated, the more effectively it can be used in the service of God if it is placed under the control of His Spirit. Talents used are talents multiplied. Experience in spiritual things widens the vision of saints and angels, and both increase in capability and knowledge as they work in their respective spheres.

"O the depth of the riches both of the wisdom and knowledge of God! how unsearchable are His judgments, and His ways past finding out!" Romans 11:33.—*Special Testimonies on Education,* pages 52-57; written May 16, 1896.

THE BOOK OF BOOKS

What book can compare with the Bible? An understanding of its teachings is essential for every child and youth, and for those of mature age; for it is the word of God, given to guide the human family to heaven. In the world today there are gods many and doctrines many. Without an understanding of the Scriptures it is impossible for the youth to understand what is truth, or to discern between the sacred and the common.

The word of God should stand as the highest educating book in our world and should be treated with reverential awe. It should be placed in the hands of the children and youth as the great lesson book, that they may know Him whom to know aright is life eternal.

History in the Bible

The grand truths of sacred history possess amazing strength and beauty, and are as far-reaching as eternity. What more important knowledge can be gained than that which outlines the fall of man, and the consequences of that sin which opened the floodgates of woe upon the world; which tells of Christ's first advent? The incarnation of Christ, His divinity, His atonement, His wonderful life in heaven as our advocate, the office of the Holy Spirit—all these vital themes of Christianity are revealed from Genesis to Revelation. Each is a golden link in the perfect chain of truth. Why, then, should not the Scriptures be exalted in every school in our land?

Moses was educated in all the wisdom of the Egyptians, yet he said to Israel, "Behold, I have taught you statutes and judgments, even as the Lord my God commanded me, that ye should do so in the land whither ye go to possess it. Keep therefore and do them; for this is your wisdom and your understanding in the sight of the nations, which shall hear all these statutes, and say, Surely this great nation is a wise and understanding people. For . . . what nation is there so great, that hath statutes and judgments so righteous as all this law, which I set before you this day? Only take heed to thyself, and keep thy soul diligently, lest thou forget the things which thine eyes have seen, and lest they depart from thy heart all the days of thy life: but teach them thy sons, and thy sons' sons." Deuteronomy 4:5-9.

Where shall we find laws more noble, pure, and just than are exhibited on the statute books wherein is recorded the instruction given to Moses for the children of Israel? From what other source can we gather such strength or learn such noble science? What other book will teach men so well how to love, fear, and obey God? What other book presents to students more ennobling science, more wonderful history? It clearly portrays righteousness and foretells the consequence of disloyalty to the law of Jehovah.

The Bible as Literature

As an educating power the Bible is of more value than the writings of all the philosophers of all ages. In its wide range of style and subjects there is something to interest and instruct every mind, to ennoble every interest. The light of revelation shines undimmed into the distant past, where human annals cast not a ray of light. There is poetry which has called forth the wonder and admiration of the world. In glowing beauty, in sublime and solemn majesty, in touching pathos, it is unequaled by the most brilliant productions of human genius. There is sound logic and impassioned eloquence. There are portrayed the noble deeds of noble men, examples of private virtue and public honor, lessons of piety and purity.

A Moral Power

In studying the Scriptures we become acquainted with God and are led to understand our relation to Christ, the Sin Bearer, the surety for the fallen race. No one is left in darkness as to that which God approves or disapproves.

The Bible contains instruction regarding the character God's children must possess. "Blessed are the pure in heart," it declares, "for they shall see God." Matthew 5:8. "Follow peace with all men, and holiness, without which no man shall see the Lord." Hebrews 12:14. "Beloved, now are we the sons of God, and it doth not yet appear what we shall be: but we know that, when He shall appear, we shall be like Him; for we shall see Him as He is. And every man that hath this hope in him purifieth himself, even as He is pure." 1 John 3:2, 3.

This all-important knowledge should be kept before our children and youth, not in an arbitrary, dictatorial manner, but as a divine disclosure, as instruction of the highest value, essential for their present peace in this world of turmoil and strife, and as a preparation for the future eternal life in the kingdom of God. Then place the Holy Word in their hands. Encourage them to search its pages. They will find there treasures of inestimable value. And in receiving Christ as the bread of life they have the pledge of eternal life.

Christ's sayings are pure gold without one particle of dross. When those who have received the false interpretation of the word search the Scriptures with determined effort to know what is truth, the Holy Spirit opens the eyes of their understanding, and the word is to them a new revelation. Their hearts are quickened with a new and living faith, and they behold wondrous things out of His law. The teachings of Christ have a breadth and meaning to them that they have never before understood.

The youth are in need of educators who will keep the principles of the word of God ever before them. If teachers will make Bible precepts their textbook, they will have greater influence over the youth. They will be learners, having a living connection with God. They will endeavor to inculcate ideas and principles that will lead to a fuller knowledge of God, an earnest, growing faith in the blood of Christ, and in the power and efficiency of His grace to keep them from falling. They will constantly seek to build up the strongholds of a healthy, well-balanced Christian experience, that their students may be qualified for usefulness.

THE BIBLE TEACHER

The best ministerial talent should be employed to lead and direct in the teaching of the Bible in our schools. Those chosen for this work need to be thorough Bible students; they should be men who have a deep Christian experience, and their salary should be paid from the tithe.

The Bible teacher should be one who is able to teach the students how to present the truths of the word of God in a clear, winning manner in public and how to do effective evangelistic work from house to house. It is essential that he be skillful in teaching those who have a desire to work for the Master how to use wisely that which they have learned. He should instruct the students to approach the study of the Bible in the spirit of humility, to search its pages, not for proof to sustain human opinions, but with a sincere desire to know what God has said.

Early in their experience our students should be taught to become Bible workers. Those who are consecrated and teachable may have success in active service for Christ while pursuing their courses of study. If they spend much time in prayer, if they humbly take counsel from their instructors, they will grow in a knowledge of how to work for souls. And when they go forth into the great harvest field they may with confidence pray, "Let the beauty of the Lord our God be upon us: and establish Thou the work of our hands upon us; yea, the work of our hands establish Thou it." Psalm 90:17.

In our schools the work of teaching the Scriptures to the youth is not to be left wholly with one teacher for a long series of years. The Bible teacher may be well able to present the truth, and yet it is not the best experience for the students that their study of the word of God should be directed by one man only, term after term and year after year. Different teachers should have a part in the work, even though they may not all have so full an understanding of the Scriptures. If several in our larger schools unite in the work of teaching the Scriptures, the students may thus have the benefit of the talents of several.

Why do we need a Matthew, a Mark, a Luke, a John, a Paul, and all the writers who have borne testimony in regard to the life and ministry of the Saviour? Why could not one of the disciples have written a complete record and thus have given us a connected account of Christ's earthly life? Why does one writer bring in points that another does not mention? Why, if these points are essential, did not all these writers mention them? It is because the minds of men differ. Not all comprehend things in exactly the same way. Certain Scripture truths appeal much more strongly to the minds of some than of others.

The same principle applies to speakers. One dwells at considerable length on points that others would pass by quickly or not mention at all. The whole truth is presented more clearly by several than by one. The Gospels differ, but the records of all blend in one harmonious whole.

So today the Lord does not impress all minds in the

same way. Often through unusual experiences, under special circumstances, He gives to some Bible students views of truth that others do not grasp. It is possible for the most learned teacher to fall far short of teaching all that should be taught.

It would greatly benefit our schools if regular meetings were held frequently in which all the teachers could unite in the study of the word of God. They should search the Scriptures as did the noble Bereans. They should subordinate all preconceived opinions, and taking the Bible as their lesson book, comparing scripture with scripture, they should learn what to teach their students, and how to train them for acceptable service.

The teacher's success will depend largely upon the spirit which is brought into the work. A profession of faith does not make men Christians; but if teachers will open their hearts to the study of the word, they will be able to aid their students to a clearer understanding. Let not the spirit of controversy come in, but let each seek earnestly for the light and knowledge that he needs.

God's word is true philosophy, true science. Human opinions and sensational preaching amount to very little. Those who are imbued with the word of God will teach it in the same simple way that Christ taught it. The world's greatest Teacher used the simplest language and the plainest symbols.

The Lord calls upon His shepherds to feed the flock with pure provender. He would have them present the truth in its simplicity. When this work is faithfully done, many will be convicted and converted by the power of the Holy Spirit. There is need of Bible teachers who will come close to the unconverted, who will search for the lost sheep, who will do personal labor and will give clear, definite instruction.

Never utter sentiments of doubt. Christ's teaching was always positive in its nature. With a tone of assurance bear an affirmative message. Lift up the Man of Calvary higher and still higher; there is power in the exaltation of the cross of Christ.

It is the student's privilege to have clear and accurate ideas of the truth of the word, that he may be prepared to present these truths to other minds. He should be rooted and grounded in the faith. Students should be led to think for themselves, to see the force of truth for themselves, and to speak every word from a heart full of love and tenderness. Urge upon their minds the vital truths of the Bible. Let them repeat these truths in their own language, that you may be sure that they clearly comprehend them. Be sure that every point is fastened upon the mind. This may be a slow process, but it is of ten times more value than rushing over important subjects without giving them due consideration. It is not enough that the student believe the truth for himself. He must be drawn out to state this truth clearly in his own words, that it may be evident that he sees the force of the lesson and makes its application.

In all your teaching never forget that the greatest lesson to be taught and to be learned is the lesson of copartnership with Christ in the work of salvation. The education to be secured by searching the Scriptures is an experimental knowledge of the plan of salvation. Such an education will restore the image of God in the soul. It will strengthen and fortify the mind against temptation and fit the learner to become a worker with Christ in His mission of mercy to the world. It will make him a member of the heavenly family, prepare him to share the inheritance of the saints in light.

The teacher of truth can impart effectively only that which he himself knows by experience. Christ taught the truth because He was the truth. His own thought, His character, His life experience, were embodied in His teaching. So with His servants; those who teach the word must make it their own by personal experience. They must know what it is to have Christ made unto them wisdom and righteousness and sanctification and redemption. Every minister of Christ and every teacher should be able to say with the beloved John, "The life was manifested, and we have seen it, and bear witness, and show unto you that eternal life, which was with the Father, and was manifested unto us." 1 John 1:2.

Often it will seem to the teacher that the word of God has little effect on the minds and hearts of many students; but if his work has been wrought in God, some lessons of divine truth will linger in the memory of the most careless. The Holy Spirit will water the seed sown, and it will spring up after many days and bear fruit to the glory of God.

Simplicity in Teaching

Teachers may learn a lesson from the experience of the farmer who placed the food for his sheep in a crib so high that the young of the flock could not reach it. Some teachers present the truth to their students in a similar manner. They place the crib so high that those whom they teach cannot reach the food. They forget that the students have only a small part of the opportunity that they have had to gain a knowledge of God. They are too high up on the ladder to reach down a helping hand, warm with tenderness and love and deep, earnest interest. Let them step down and by their manner say to the students:

"I will no longer stand so far above you. Let us climb together, and we will see what can be gained by a united study of the Scriptures. Christ is the One who imparts all knowledge. Let us work together in an earnest effort to learn from God how to understand the truths of His word, and how to place these truths before others in their beauty and simplicity.

"Let us study together. I have nothing that you cannot receive if you open your mind to Christ's teachings. The Bible is your guidebook and my guidebook. By asking questions you may suggest ideas that are new to me. Various ways of expressing the truth we are studying will bring light into our class. If any explanation of the word differs from your previous understanding, do not hesitate to state your views of the subject. Light will shine upon us as in the meekness and lowliness of Christ we study together."

This is the way in which the schools of the prophets were conducted. Time was given in the class for a faithful study of the thoughts presented. Hearts were warmed, and the voice of praise and thanksgiving was heard. The sacred gospel was humanized, as in the teachings of Christ. Much was accomplished for both teachers and students. Time was given for each one to partake of the heavenly repast—to study the truths presented and then to add that which he had received from God.

When the right spirit is cherished by teachers and students, they will have special grace from God, enough for each, enough for all, enough continually and forever. As the teacher learns from the divine Teacher, the Bible becomes a lesson book such as God designed it to be, giving clear conceptions to those who strive to grasp its grand and glorious truths. As the students search for truth as for hidden treasure, their minds are enriched with the highest of all knowledge. There is shed into the mind a flood of light on the problem of human life. They see how it is possible for men and women to be sanctified through a belief of the truth as it is in Jesus.

———

The jewels of truth lie scattered over the field of revelation; but they have been buried beneath human traditions, beneath the sayings and commandments of men, and the wisdom from heaven has been practically ignored. Satan has succeeded in making the world believe that the words and achievements of men are of great consequence. There are veins of truth yet to be discovered, but spiritual things are spiritually discerned. One passage of Scripture will prove a key to unlock other passages, and in this way light is shed upon the hidden meaning of the word. By comparing different texts treating on the same subject, viewing their bearing on every side, the true meaning of the Scriptures will be made evident.

A FAILURE TO STUDY GOD'S WORD

That which in the counsels of heaven the Father and the Son deemed essential for man's salvation is clearly presented in the Holy Scriptures. The infinite truths of salvation are stated so plainly that finite beings who desire to know the truth cannot fail to understand. Divine revelations have been made for their instruction in righteousness, that they may glorify God and help their fellow men.

These truths are found in the word of God—the standard by which we are to judge between right and wrong. Obedience to this word is the best shield for the youth against the temptations to which they are exposed while acquiring an education. From this word they learn how to honor God and how to be faithful to humanity, cheerfully performing the duties and meeting the trials that each day brings, and courageously bearing its burdens.

Christ, the Great Teacher, sought to win the minds of men from the contemplation of earthly things, that He might teach them of heavenly things. Had the teachers of His day been willing to be instructed by Him, had they united with Him in sowing the world with the seeds of truth, the world would be far different from what it now is. Had the scribes and Pharisees joined their forces with the Saviour, the knowledge of Christ would have restored the moral image of God in their souls.

But the leaders of Israel turned from the fountain of true knowledge. They studied the Scriptures only to sustain their traditions and enforce their man-made observances. By their interpretation they made them express sentiments that God had never given. Their mystical construction made indistinct that which He had made plain. They disputed over technicalities and practically denied the most essential truths. God's word was robbed of its power, and evil spirits worked their will.

Christ's words contain nothing that is nonessential. The Sermon on the Mount is a wonderful production, yet so simple that a child can study it without misunderstanding. The mount of beatitudes is a symbol of the spiritual elevation on which Christ ever stood. Every word He uttered came from God, and He spoke with the authority of heaven. "The words that I speak unto you," He said, "they are spirit, and they are life." John 6:63. His teaching is full of ennobling, saving truth, to which men's highest ambitions and most profound investigations can bear no comparison. He was alive to the terrible ruin hanging over the race, and He came to save souls by His own righteousness, bringing to the world definite assurance of hope and complete relief.

It is because Christ's words are disregarded, because the word of God is given a second place in education, that infidelity is riot and iniquity is rife. Things of minor consequence occupy the minds of many of the teachers of today. A mass of tradition, containing merely a semblance of truth, is brought into the courses of study given in the schools of the world. The force of much human teaching is found in assertion, not in truth. The teachers of the present day can use only the ability of previous teachers; and yet with all the weighty importance that may be attached to the words of the greatest human authors there is a conscious inability to trace back to the first great principle, the Source of unerring wisdom. There is a painful uncertainty, a constant searching, a reaching for assurance, that can be found only in God. The trumpet of human greatness may be sounded, but it is with an uncertain sound; it is not reliable, and the salvation of souls cannot be assured by it.

In acquiring earthly knowledge, men have thought to gain a treasure; and they have laid the Bible aside, ignorant that it contains a treasure worth everything else. A failure to study and obey God's word has brought confusion into the world. Men have left the guardianship of Christ for the guardianship of the great rebel, the prince of darkness. Strange fire has been mingled with the sacred. The accumulation of things that minister to lust and ambition has brought upon the world the judgment of heaven.

When in difficulty, philosophers and men of science try to satisfy their minds without appealing to God. They ventilate their philosophy in regard to the heavens and the earth, accounting for plagues, pestilences, epidemics, earthquakes, and famines by their supposed science. Questions relating to creation and providence they attempt to solve by saying, This is a law of nature.

Knowledge Through Obedience

Disobedience has closed the door to a vast amount of knowledge that might have been gained from the word of God. Had men been obedient, they would have understood the plan of God's government. The heavenly world would have opened its chambers of grace and glory for exploration. In form, in speech, in song, human beings would have been altogether superior to what they are now. The mystery of redemption, the incarnation of Christ, His atoning sacrifice, would not be vague in our minds. They would be not only better understood, but altogether more highly appreciated.

A failure to study God's word is the great cause of mental weakness and inefficiency. In turning from this word to feed on the writings of uninspired men, the mind becomes dwarfed and cheapened. It is not brought in contact with deep, broad principles of eternal truth. The understanding adapts itself to the comprehension of the things with which it is familiar, and in this devotion to finite things it is weakened, its power is contracted, and after a time it becomes unable to expand.

All this is false education. The work of every teacher should be to fasten the minds of the youth upon the grand truths of the word of Inspiration. This is the education essential for this life and the life to come.

And let it not be thought that this will prevent the study of the sciences or cause a lower standard in education. The knowledge of God is as high as heaven and as broad as the universe. There is nothing so ennobling and invigorating as a study of the great themes which concern our eternal life. Let the youth seek to grasp these God-given truths, and their minds will expand and grow strong in the effort. It will bring every student who is a doer of the word into a broader field of thought and secure for him a wealth of knowledge that is imperishable.

The ignorance that now curses the world in regard to the binding claims of the law of God is the result of neglecting the study of the Scriptures. It is Satan's studied plan so to absorb and engage the mind that God's great Guidebook shall not be regarded as the Book of books and that the sinner shall not be led from the path of transgression into the path of obedience.

Why is it that our youth, and even those of more mature years, are so easily led into temptation and sin? It is because the Bible is not studied and meditated upon as it should be. If it were made the daily study, there would be an inward rectitude, a strength of spirit, that would resist the temptations of the enemy. A firm, decided effort to turn from evil is not seen in the life, because the instruction given by God is disregarded. There is not put forth the effort that there should be to fill the mind with pure, holy thoughts and to rid it of all that is impure and untrue. There is not the choosing of the better part, the sitting at the feet of Jesus, as did Mary, to learn lessons from the divine Teacher.

When God's word is made the man of our counsel, when we search the Scriptures for light, heavenly angels come near to impress the mind and to enlighten the understanding so that it can be truly said, "The entrance of Thy words giveth light; it giveth understanding unto the simple." Psalm 119:130. It is no marvel that there is not more heavenly-mindedness seen among the youth who profess Christianity, when so little attention is given to the word of God. The divine counsels are not heeded;

the divine admonitions are not obeyed. Grace and heavenly wisdom are not sought, that every taint of corruption may be cleansed from the life.

Into Forbidden Paths

If the minds of the youth were directed aright, their conversation would be upon exalted themes. When the mind is pure and the thoughts ennobled by the truth of God, the words will be of the same character, "like apples of gold in baskets of silver." Proverbs 25:11, R.V. But with the present understanding and the present practices, with the low standard that Christians are content to reach, the conversation is cheap and profitless. It is of the earth, earthy, and does not reach even the standard of the more cultured class of worldlings. When Christ and heaven are the theme of contemplation, the conversation will give evidence of the fact. The speech will be seasoned with grace, and the speaker will show that he has been obtaining an education in the school of the divine Teacher.

We are to regard the Bible as God's disclosure to us of eternal things—the things of most consequence for us to know. By the world it is thrown aside as if the perusal of it were finished, but a thousand years of research would not exhaust the hidden treasure it contains. Eternity alone will disclose the wisdom of this Book, for it is the wisdom of an infinite mind. Shall we, then, cultivate a deep hunger for the productions of human authors and disregard the word of God? It is this longing for something they never ought to crave that makes men substitute for true knowledge that which can never make them wise unto salvation. Let not man's assertions be regarded as truth when they are contrary to the word of God.

The Creator of the heavens and the earth, the Source of all wisdom, is second to none. But supposedly great authors, whose works are used as textbooks for study, are received and glorified, though they have no vital connection with God. By such study man has been led into forbidden paths. Minds have been wearied to death through unnecessary work in trying to obtain that which is to them as the knowledge which Adam and Eve disobeyed God in obtaining.

Today young men and women spend years in acquiring an education which is as wood and stubble, to be consumed in the last great conflagration. Upon such an education God places no value. Many students leave school unable to receive the word of God with the reverence and respect which they gave it before they entered. Their faith has been eclipsed in the effort to excel in the various studies. The Bible has not been made a vital matter in their education, but books tainted with infidelity and propagating unsound theories have been placed before them.

All unnecessary matters should be weeded from the courses of study, and only such studies placed before the student as will be of real value to him. With these alone he needs to become familiar, that he may secure the life which measures with the life of God. As the mind is summoned to the consideration of the great themes of salvation, it will rise higher and higher in the comprehension of these subjects, leaving cheap and insignificant matters behind.

An Illustration

What was it that made John the Baptist great? He closed his mind to the mass of tradition presented by the teachers of the Jewish nation, and opened it to the wisdom which comes from above. Before his birth the Holy Spirit testified of John: "He shall be great in the sight of the Lord, and shall drink neither wine nor strong drink; and he shall be filled with the Holy Ghost. . . . And many of the children of Israel shall he turn to the Lord their God. And he shall go before Him in the spirit and power of Elias, to turn the hearts of the fathers to the children, and the disobedient to the wisdom of the just; to make ready a people prepared for the Lord." Luke 1:15-17.

In his prophecy Zacharias said of John, "Thou, child, shalt be called the prophet of the Highest: for thou shalt go before the face of the Lord to prepare His ways; to give knowledge of salvation unto His people by the remission of their sins, through the tender mercy of our God; whereby the Dayspring from on high hath visited us, to give light to them that sit in darkness and in the shadow of death, to guide our feet into the way of peace." And Luke adds, "The child grew, and waxed strong in spirit, and was in the deserts till the day of his showing unto Israel." Luke 1:76-80.

It was John's choice to forgo the enjoyments and luxuries of city life for the stern discipline of the wilderness. Here his surroundings were favorable to habits of simplicity and self-denial. Uninterrupted by the clamor of the world, he could here study the lessons of nature, of revelation, and of providence. The words of the angel to Zacharias had been often repeated by his God-fearing parents. From childhood his mission had been kept before him, and he accepted the holy trust. To him the solitude of the desert was a welcome escape from society in which suspicion, unbelief, and impurity had become well-nigh all-pervading. He distrusted his own power to withstand temptation and shrank from constant contact with sin lest he should lose the sense of its exceeding sinfulness.

But the life of John was not spent in idleness, in ascetic gloom, or in selfish isolation. From time to time he went forth to mingle with men, and he was ever an interested observer of what was passing in the world. From his quiet retreat he watched the unfolding of events. With vision illuminated by the divine Spirit, he studied the characters of men, that he might understand how to reach their hearts with the message of heaven.

Of Christ, Simeon said, "Lord, now lettest Thou Thy servant depart in peace, according to Thy word: for mine eyes have seen Thy salvation, which Thou hast prepared before the face of all people; a light to lighten the Gentiles, and the glory of Thy people Israel." And the record declares, "Jesus increased in wisdom and stature, and in favor with God and man." Luke 2:29-32, 52.

Jesus and John were represented by the educators of that day as ignorant because they had not learned in the schools of the rabbis; but the God of heaven was their Teacher, and all who heard were astonished at their knowledge of the Scriptures.

The first great lesson in all education is to know and understand the will of God. We should bring into every day of life the effort to gain this knowledge. To learn science through human interpretation alone is to obtain a false education, but to learn of God and Christ is to learn the science of heaven. The confusion in education has come because the wisdom and knowledge of God have not been exalted.

The students in our schools are to regard the knowledge of God as above everything else. "The preaching of the cross is to them that perish foolishness; but unto us which are saved it is the power of God. For it is written, I will destroy the wisdom of the wise, and will bring to nothing the understanding of the prudent." "The foolishness of God is wiser than men; and the weakness of God is stronger than men." "But of Him are ye in Christ Jesus, who of God is made unto us wisdom, and righteousness, and sanctification, and redemption: that, according as it is written, He that glorieth, let him glory in the Lord." 1 Corinthians 1:18, 19, 25, 30, 31.

Those who profess to believe the word should daily pray for the light of the Holy Spirit to shine upon the pages of the Sacred Book, that they may be enabled to comprehend the things of the Spirit of God. . . . The words of men, however great, are not able to make us "perfect, throughly furnished unto all good works." 2 Timothy 3:17.

SOME RESULTS OF BIBLE STUDY

The Bible contains all that is needful for the saving of the soul, and at the same time it is adapted to strengthen and discipline the mind. Used as a textbook in our schools, it will be found far more effective than any other book in guiding wisely in the affairs of this life, as well as in aiding the soul to climb the ladder that reaches to heaven. The Bible gives the true seeker an advanced mental drill; he comes from the contemplation of divine things with his faculties enriched. Self is humbled, while God and His truth are exalted. It is because men are unacquainted with the truths of the Bible that there is so much lifting up of man and so little honor given to God.

In searching the pages of God's word, we move through scenes majestic and eternal. We behold Jesus, the Son of God, coming to our world and engaging in the mysterious conflict that discomfited the powers of darkness. How wonderful, how almost incredible, it is that the infinite God would consent to the humiliation of His only-begotten Son! Let students contemplate this great thought. They will not come from such contemplation without being elevated, purified, ennobled.

God's word is the spiritual food by which the Christian must grow strong in spirit and in intellect, that he may do battle for truth and righteousness. The Bible teaches that every besetting sin must be put away, that the warfare against evil must be waged until every wrong is over-come. The human agent must place himself as a willing student in the school of Christ. As he accepts the grace freely offered him, the presence of the Saviour in the thoughts and in the heart will give him decision of pur-pose to lay aside every weight, that the heart may be filled with all the fullness of God.

The simplicity of true godliness must be brought into the education of our young people, if they are to know how to escape the corruption that is in the world. They must be taught that the true followers of Christ will serve God not only when it is in accordance with their inclinations, but also when it involves self-denial and cross-bearing. Besetting sins must be battled with and overcome. Objectionable traits of character, whether hereditary or cultivated, must be compared with the great rule of righteousness, and then conquered in the strength of Christ. Day by day, hour by hour, a vigorous work of self-denial and of sanctification must go on within; then the works will bear witness that Jesus is abiding in the heart by faith. Sanctification does not close the avenues of the soul to knowledge, but expands the mind and inspires it to search for truth as for hidden treasure.

An Unerring Guide

The young man who makes the Bible his guide need not mistake the path of duty and of safety. That Book will teach him to preserve his integrity of character, to be truthful, to practice no deception. It will teach him that he must never transgress God's law in order to accomplish a desired object, even though to obey involves a sacrifice.

It will teach him that the blessing of heaven will not rest upon him if he departs from the path of right doing; that although men may appear to prosper in disobedience, they will surely reap the fruit of their sowing.

Those only who read the Scriptures as the voice of God speaking to them, are true learners. They tremble at the voice of God, for to them it is a living reality. They open their understanding to divine instruction and pray for grace, that they may obtain a preparation for service. As the heavenly torch is placed in his hand, the seeker for truth sees his own frailty, his infirmity, the hopelessness of looking to himself for righteousness. He sees that there is in him nothing that can recommend him to God. He prays for the Holy Spirit, the representative of Christ, to be his constant guide, to lead him into all truth. He repeats the promise, "The Comforter, which is the Holy Ghost, whom the Father will send in My name, He shall teach you all things." John 14:26.

Receiving to Give

The study of the Bible in our schools will give the students special advantages. Those who receive into their hearts the holy principles of truth will work with increasing energy. No circumstances can alter their determination to attain to the highest possible standard. And that which they have received they will impart to others. As they themselves drink from the fountain of living water, from them will flow living streams to bless and refresh others.

The diligent Bible student will constantly increase in

knowledge and discernment. His intellect will grasp elevated subjects and lay hold of the truth of eternal realities. His motives of action will be right. He will use his talent of influence to help others to understand more perfectly their God-given responsibilities. His heart will be a wellspring of joy as he sees success attend his efforts to impart to others the blessings he has received.

The talent of knowledge, sanctified and put to use in the Master's service, is never lost. A self-sacrificing effort to do good will be crowned with success. "We are laborers together with God." 1 Corinthians 3:9. The Lord will co-operate with the human worker. To Him is to be given the praise and the glory for what we are able to accomplish.

The Lord is dishonored by the deterioration or the perversion of the talents He has entrusted to men. It is the duty and the privilege of the Christian to improve his talents. Christ gave His life to purchase for men the privilege of being co-workers with God. Yet thousands who have received much light and many opportunities, do not grasp the blessings that are within their reach.

That education only is wholesome and essential which leads to a knowledge of the value that God has placed upon mankind. The students in our schools are to be taught that they are of value in the sight of God, that they have been bought with an infinite price. They should be made to realize the importance of putting to a right use every faculty of the being. They are to put on Christ; then all their powers will be used in persevering, taxing labor in His service.

The students are to be taught to help those who need encouragement. As they seek to help others they themselves will "grow in grace, and in the knowledge of our Lord and Saviour Jesus Christ" (2 Peter 3:18), and their efficiency will be increased. "Ye are God's husbandry, ye are God's building." 1 Corinthians 3:9. Christians will fulfill the purpose of God for them only as they increase in knowledge and return to Him in earnest service the gifts they have received.

A New Mind

The truths of God's word are not mere sentiments, but the utterances of the Most High. He who makes these truths a part of his life becomes in every sense a new creature. He is not given new mental powers, but the darkness that through ignorance and sin has clouded the understanding is removed.

The words, "A new heart also will I give you" (Ezekiel 36:26), mean, A new mind will I give you. This change of heart is always attended by a clear conception of Christian duty, an understanding of truth. The clearness of our view of truth will be proportionate to our understanding of the word of God. He who gives the Scriptures close, prayerful attention will gain clear comprehension and sound judgment, as if in turning to God he had reached a higher plane of intelligence.

If the mind is set to the task of studying the Bible, the understanding will strengthen and the reasoning faculties will improve. Under the study of the Scriptures the mind expands and becomes more evenly balanced than if occupied in obtaining information from books that have no connection with the Bible.

THE WORD AND WORKS OF GOD

God calls upon teachers to behold the heavens and to study His works in nature. "The heavens declare the glory of God; and the firmament showeth His handiwork. Day unto day uttereth speech, and night unto night showeth knowledge. There is no speech nor language, where their voice is not heard." Psalm 19:1-3. Shall we not strive to understand the wonderful works of God? We should do well to read often the nineteenth psalm, that we may understand how the Lord binds up His law with His created works.

Can we find for our schools any textbook filled with such deep, earnest declarations as is the word of the living God? Then why should this Book be laid aside for the writings of infidel authors? What more valuable book could be placed in the hands of students than that which teaches them how they may inherit eternal life? The lessons of Bible history should be kept before the youth in our schools, that those who have no love for God and no interest in spiritual things may become interested, and learn to love the word.

Christ is the center of all true doctrine. All true religion is found in His word and in nature. He is the One in whom our hopes of eternal life are centered; and the teacher who learns from Him finds a safe anchorage.

All that the mind can grasp is opened before us in the Bible. This is our spiritual food. We are to contemplate the wonderful works of God and repeat to our children the lessons learned, that we may lead them to see His skill, His power, and His grandeur in His created works.

What a God is our God! He rules over His kingdom with diligence and care, and He has built a hedge— the Ten Commandments—about His subjects to preserve them from the results of transgression. In requiring obedience to the laws of His kingdom, God gives His people health and happiness, peace and joy. He teaches them that the perfection of character He requires can be attained only by becoming familar with His word.

It is written in the prophets: "O thou afflicted, tossed with tempest, and not comforted, behold, I will lay thy stones with fair colors, and lay thy foundations with sapphires. And I will make thy windows of agates, and thy gates of carbuncles, and all thy borders of pleasant stones. And all thy children shall be taught of the Lord; and great shall be the peace of thy children. In righteousness shalt thou be established: thou shalt be far from oppression; for thou shalt not fear: and from terror; for it shall not come near thee." Isaiah 54:11-14.

"This shall be the covenant that I will make with the house of Israel; After those days, saith the Lord, I will put My law in their inward parts, and write it in their hearts; and will be their God, and they shall be My people. And they shall teach no more every man his neighbor, and every man his brother, saying, Know the Lord: for they shall all know Me, from the least of them unto the greatest of them, saith the Lord: for I will forgive their iniquity, and I will remember their sin no more." Jeremiah 31:33, 34.

"And many nations shall come, and say, Come, and let us go up to the mountain of the Lord, and to the house of the God of Jacob; and He will teach us of His ways, and we will walk in His paths: for the law shall go forth of Zion, and the word of the Lord from Jerusalem." Micah 4:2.

The Old Testament Scriptures were the lesson book of Israel. . . . There are practical lessons in the word of God, lessons that Christ would have teachers and parents present to the children in the school and in the home. That word teaches living, holy principles, which prompt men to do unto others as they would have others do unto them—principles which they are to bring into the daily life here below, and carry with them into the school above. This is the higher education. No learning of human origin can gain these heights; for they reach into eternity, and are immortalized. We know altogether too little of the greatness of the love and compassion of God.

Let students put to the stretch their mental faculties, that they may comprehend the forty-fifth chapter of Isaiah. Such chapters as this should be brought into our schools as a valuable study. They are better than romance and fables. Why have our schools been so dependent upon books which tell so little of the city we claim to be seeking, whose builder and maker is God? Our lesson books should contain the loftiest themes of thought. Heaven is our home. Our citizenship is above, and our lives must not be devoted to a world that is soon to be destroyed. . . .

Take the Bible as a study book, and see if you are not filled with the love of God. Your heart may be barren, your intellect feeble; but if you will prayerfully study the word of God, light will flash into your mind. God works with every diligent student. Teachers who will learn from the Great Teacher will realize the help of God as did Daniel and his fellows, of whom the record states, "As for these four children, God gave them knowledge and skill in all learning and wisdom: and Daniel had understanding in all visions and dreams." Daniel 1:17. . . .

I could refer to chapter after chapter of the Old Testament Scriptures that contain great encouragement. These Scriptures are a treasure house of precious pearls, and all need them. How much time is spent by intelligent human beings in horse racing, cricket matches, and ball playing! But will indulgence in these sports give men a desire to know truth and righteousness? Will it keep God in their thoughts? Will it lead them to inquire, How is it with my soul?

All the powers of Satan are set in operation to hold the attention to frivolous amusements, and he is gaining his object. He is interposing his devisings between God and the soul. He will manufacture diversions to keep men from thinking about God. The world, filled with sport and pleasure loving, is always thirsting for some new interest; but how little time and thought are given to the Creator of the heavens and the earth!

God calls upon men to see Him in the wonders of the heavens. "Lift up your eyes on high," He says, "and behold who hath created these things, that bringeth out their host by number: He calleth them all by names by the greatness of His might." Isaiah 40:26. God would have us study the works of infinity, and from this study learn to love and reverence and obey Him. The heavens and the earth with their treasures are to teach the lessons of God's love and care and power.

God calls upon His creatures to turn their attention from the confusion and perplexity around them and admire His handiwork. As we study His works, angels from heaven will be by our side to enlighten our minds and guard them from Satan's deceptions. As you look at the wonderful things that God's hand has made, let your proud, foolish heart feel its dependence and inferiority. How terrible it is when the acknowledgment of God is not made when it should be made! How sad to humble oneself when it is too late!

The psalmist declares, "When Thou saidst, Seek ye My face; my heart said unto Thee, Thy face, Lord, will I seek." Psalm 27:8. The whole of this psalm should find a place in the reading and spelling lessons of the school. The twenty-eighth, twenty-ninth, and seventy-eighth psalms tell of the rich blessings bestowed by God upon His people and of their poor returns for all His benefits. The eighty-first psalm explains why Israel was scattered—they forgot God, as the churches in our land are forgetting Him today. Consider also the eighty-ninth, ninetieth, ninety-first, ninety-second, and ninety-third psalms.

These things were written for our admonition, upon whom the ends of the world are come; and should they not be studied in our schools? The word of God contains instructive lessons, given in reproof, in warning, in encouragement, and in rich promises. Would not such food as this be meat in due season to the youth?

An Impressive Representation

In a night vision given me some years ago I was in an assembly where our school problems were being discussed, and the question was asked, "Why has not appropriate matter for reading books and other lesson books been selected and compiled? Why has not the word of God been extolled above every human production? Have you thought that a better knowledge of what the Lord hath said would have a deleterious effect on teachers and students?"

There was a hush in the assembly, and conviction came to students and teachers. Men who had looked upon themselves as wise and strong saw that they were weak and lacking in the knowledge of that Book which concerns the eternal destiny of the human soul.

The Speaker then took from the hands of the teachers books which they had been making their study, some of which had been written by infidel authors and contained infidel sentiments, and laid them on the floor. Then He placed the Bible in their hands, saying, "You have little knowledge of this Book. You know not the Scriptures nor the power of God. When you have taken your students through the course of study you have followed in the past, they will have to unlearn much that they have learned, and this they will find very difficult to do. Objectionable ideas have taken root in their minds, like weeds in a garden, and some will never be able to distinguish between right and wrong. The good and the evil have been intermingled in your work. Doctrines containing a little truth, but with which are woven the opinions and sayings and doings of men, are repeated. The youth will never know the way of life so long as they depend on such instruction."

By every teacher in our schools the only true God is to be uplifted. The prayer of Christ for His disciples was: "I have glorified Thee on the earth: I have finished the work which Thou gavest Me to do. And now, O Father, glorify Thou Me with Thine own self with the glory which I had with Thee before the world was. I have manifested Thy name unto the men which Thou gavest Me out of the world: Thine they were, and Thou gavest them Me; and they have kept Thy word. Now they have known that all things whatsoever Thou hast given Me are of Thee. For I have given unto them the words which Thou gavest Me; and they have received them, and have known surely that I came out from Thee, and they have believed that Thou didst send Me." John 17:4-8.

Who among our teachers are awake and as faithful stewards of the grace of God are giving the trumpet a certain sound? Who are voicing the message of the third angel, calling upon the world to make ready for the great day of God? The message we bear has the seal of the living God.

July 20, 1899.

STUDY THE BIBLE FOR YOURSELVES

There is nothing more calculated to energize the mind and strengthen the intellect than the study of the word of God. No other book is so potent to elevate the thoughts, to give vigor to the faculties, as the broad, ennobling truths of the Bible. If God's word were studied as it should be, men would have a breadth of mind, a nobility of character, and a stability of purpose that are rarely seen in these times. The search for truth will reward the seeker at every turn, and each discovery will open up richer fields for his investigation.

Thousands of men who minister in the pulpit are lacking in essential qualities of mind and character because they do not apply themselves to the study of the Scriptures. They are content with a superficial knowledge of the truths that are full of rich depths of meaning; and they prefer to go on, losing much in every way, rather than to search diligently for the hidden treasure.

Men are changed in accordance with what they contemplate. If commonplace thoughts and affairs take up the attention, the man will be commonplace. If he is too negligent to obtain anything but a superficial understanding of truth, he will not receive the rich blessings that God would be pleased to bestow upon him. It is the law of the mind that it will narrow or expand to the dimensions of the things with which it becomes familiar. The mental powers will surely become contracted and will lose their ability to grasp the deep meanings of the word of God unless they are put vigorously and persistently to the task of searching for truth. The mind will enlarge if it is employed in tracing out the relation of the subjects of the Bible to one another, comparing scripture with scripture, and spiritual things with spiritual. The richest treasures of thought are waiting for the diligent student.

The knowledge of God is not gained without mental effort and prayer for wisdom. Many are convinced that the precious treasures of the kingdom of God and of Christ are contained in the word. They know also that no earthly treasure is gained without painstaking effort. Why should they expect to understand the meaning of the Scriptures without diligent study?

The word of God is light and truth—a lamp to the feet and a light to the path. It is able to guide every step of the way to the city of God. For this reason, Satan has made desperate efforts to obscure the light, that men may not find and keep the path cast up for the ransomed of the Lord to walk in.

As the miner digs for the golden treasure in the earth, so earnestly, persistently, must we seek for the treasure of God's word. In daily study the verse-by-verse method is often most helpful. Let the student take one verse and concentrate his mind on ascertaining the thought that God has put into that verse for him, and then dwell upon the thought until it becomes his own. One passage thus studied until its significance becomes clear is of more value than the perusal of many chapters with no definite purpose in view and no positive instruction gained.

The Bible Its Own Expositor

The Bible is its own expositor. Scripture is to be compared with scripture. The student should learn to view the word as a whole and to see the relation of its parts. He should gain a knowledge of its grand central theme— of God's original purpose for the world, of the rise of the great controversy, and of the work of redemption. He should understand the nature of the two principles that are contending for the supremacy, and should learn to trace their working through the records of history and prophecy to the great consummation. He should see how this controversy enters into every phase of human experience; how in every act of life he himself reveals the one or the other of the two antagonistic motives; and how, whether he will or not, he is even now deciding upon which side of the controversy he will be found.

Every part of the Bible is given by inspiration of God and is profitable. The Old Testament, no less than the New, should receive attention. As we study the Old Testament we shall find living springs bubbling up where the careless reader discerns only a desert.

The Old Testament sheds light upon the New, and the New upon the Old. Each is a revelation of the glory of God in Christ. Christ as manifested to the patriarchs, as symbolized in the sacrificial service, as portrayed in the law, and as revealed by the prophets is the riches of the Old Testament. Christ in His life, His death, and His resurrection; Christ as He is manifested by the Holy

Spirit, is the treasure of the New. Both Old and New present truths that will continually reveal new depths of meaning to the earnest seeker.

When a real love for the Bible is awakened, and the student begins to realize how vast is the field and how precious its treasure, he will desire to seize upon every opportunity for acquainting himself with God's word. Its study will be restricted to no special time or place. And this continuous study is one of the best means of cultivating a love for the Scriptures. Let the student keep his Bible always with him and, as he has opportunity, read a text and meditate upon it. While walking in the streets, waiting at a railway station, waiting to meet an engagement, let him improve the opportunity to gain some precious thought from the treasure house of truth.

The student of the word should not make his opinions a center around which truth is to revolve. He should not search for the purpose of finding texts of Scripture that he can construe to prove his theories, for this is wresting the Scriptures to his own destruction. The Bible student must empty himself of every prejudice, lay his own ideas at the door of investigation, and with humble, subdued heart, with self hid in Christ, with earnest prayer, he should seek wisdom from God. He should seek to know the revealed will of God because it concerns his present and eternal welfare. This word is the directory by which he must learn the way to eternal life.

FOR FURTHER STUDY

MEDICAL STUDIES

*"Not to be ministered unto,
but to minister."*

A CALL FOR GOSPEL MEDICAL
MISSIONARIES

When Jesus sent forth the Twelve on their first mission of mercy, He commissioned them "to preach the kingdom of God, and to heal the sick." Luke 9:2. "As ye go," He said, "preach, saying, The kingdom of heaven is at hand. Heal the sick, cleanse the lepers, raise the dead, cast out devils: freely ye have received, freely give." Matthew 10:7, 8. And as they "went through the towns, preaching the gospel, and healing everywhere" (Luke 9:6), the blessing of heaven accompanied their labors. The fulfillment of the Saviour's commission by the disciples made their message the power of God unto salvation, and through their efforts many were brought to a knowledge of the Messiah.

The Seventy who were sent out a little later were also commissioned to "heal the sick" (Luke 10:9) as well as to announce the advent of the promised Redeemer. In their work of teaching and healing, the disciples followed the example of the Master Teacher, who ministered to both soul and body. The gospel which He taught was a message of spiritual life and physical restoration. Deliverance from sin and the healing of disease were linked together.

And at the close of His earthly ministry, when He charged His disciples with a solemn commission to go "into all the world, and preach the gospel to every creature," He declared that their ministry would receive confirmation through the restoration of the sick to health. Ye "shall lay hands on the sick," He said, "and they shall recover." Mark 16:15, 18. By healing in His name the diseases of the body, they would testify to His power for the healing of the soul.

The Saviour's commission to the disciples includes all believers to the end of time. All to whom the heavenly inspiration has come are put in trust with the gospel. All who receive the life of Christ are ordained to work for the salvation of their fellow men. For this work the church was established, and all who take upon themselves its sacred vows are thereby pledged to be co-workers with Christ.

"They shall lay hands on the sick, and they shall recover." This world is a vast lazar house; but Christ came to heal the sick, to proclaim deliverance to the captives of Satan. He was in Himself health and strength. He imparted His life to the sick, the afflicted, those possessed of demons. He knew that many of those who petitioned Him for help had brought disease upon themselves, yet He did not refuse to heal them. And when virtue from Christ entered into these poor souls, they were convicted of sin, and many were healed of their spiritual disease as well as of their physical maladies.

To many of the afflicted ones who received healing, Christ said, "Sin no more, lest a worse thing come unto thee." John 5:14. Thus He taught that disease is the result of violating God's laws, both natural and spiritual. The great misery in the world would not exist had men from the beginning lived in harmony with the Creator's plan. There are conditions to be observed by all who would preserve health. All should learn what these conditions are. The Lord is not pleased with ignorance in regard to His laws, either natural or spiritual. We are to be workers together with God for the restoration of health to the body as well as to the soul.

And we should teach others how to preserve and to recover health. For the sick we should use the remedies which God has provided in nature, and we should point them to Him who alone can restore. It is our work to present the sick and suffering to Christ in the arms of our faith. We should teach them to believe in the Great Healer. We should lay hold on His promise and pray for the manifestation of His power. The very essence of the gospel is restoration, and the Saviour would have us bid the sick, the hopeless, and the afflicted take hold upon His strength.

Never has the world's need for teaching and healing been greater than it is today. The world is full of those who need to be ministered unto—the weak, the helpless, the ignorant, the degraded. The continual transgression of man for nearly six thousand years has brought sickness, pain, and death as its fruit. Multitudes are perishing for lack of knowledge.

As God's ministers behold the awful results of long-continued sin, their hearts are touched with the world's woe, and they are endeavoring to labor as the Master Workman and His disciples labored. Connected with the divine Healer, they are going forth in the power of His might to teach and to heal. They realize that the gospel is the only antidote for sin, and that as Christ's witnesses they are to bear testimony to its power. As they point the afflicted ones to the Lamb of God, who taketh away the sin of the world, His transforming grace and miracle-working power are causing many to accept the message of truth that is borne. His healing power, united with the gospel message, is bringing success in emergencies. The Holy Spirit is working upon hearts, and the salvation of God is being revealed.

But the world's need today cannot be met fully by the ministry of God's servants who have been called to preach the everlasting gospel to every creature. While it is well, so far as possible, for evangelical workers to learn how to minister to the necessities of the body as well as of the soul, thus following the example of Christ, yet they cannot spend all their time and strength in relieving those in need of help. The Lord has ordained that with those who preach the word shall be associated His medical missionary workers—Christian physicians and nurses who have received special training in the healing of disease and in soul winning.

Medical missionaries and workers in the gospel ministry are to be bound together by indissoluble ties. Their work is to be done with freshness and power. By their combined efforts the world is to be prepared for the second advent of Christ. Through their united labors the Sun of Righteousness is to rise, with healing in His wings, to lighten the benighted regions of the earth, where the people have long lived in gross darkness. Many who are now dwelling in the shadow of sin and death, as they see in God's faithful servants a reflection of the Light of the world, will realize that they have a hope of salvation, and they will open their hearts to receive the healing beams, and will in turn become light bearers to others yet in darkness.

So great are the world's needs, that not all who are called to be medical missionary evangelists can afford to spend years in preparation before beginning to do actual field work. Soon doors now open to the gospel messenger will be forever closed. God calls upon many who are prepared to do acceptable service, to carry the message now, not waiting for further preparation; for while some delay, the enemy may take possession of fields now open.

I have been instructed that little companies who have received a suitable training in evangelical and medical missionary lines should go forth to do the work to which Christ appointed His disciples. Let them labor as evangelists, scattering our publications, talking of the truth to those they meet, praying for the sick, and, if need be, treating them, not with drugs, but with nature's remedies, ever realizing their dependence on God. As they unite in the work of teaching and healing they will reap a rich harvest of souls.

And while God is calling upon young men and women who have already gained a practical knowledge of how to treat the sick, to labor as gospel medical missionaries in connection with experienced evangelical workers, He is also calling for many recruits to enter our medical missionary training schools to gain a speedy and thorough preparation for service. Some need not spend so long a time in these schools as do others. It is not in harmony with God's purpose that all should plan to spend exactly the same length of time, whether three, four, or five years, in preparation, before beginning to engage in active field work. Some, after studying for a time, can develop more rapidly by working along practical lines in different places, under the supervision of experienced leaders, than they could by remaining in an institution. As they advance in knowledge and ability, some of these will find it much to their advantage to return to one of our sanitarium training schools for more instruction. Thus they will become efficient medical missionaries, prepared for trying emergencies.

Much may be learned by visiting the hospitals. In these hospitals not a few of our consecrated young people should be learning to be successful medical missionaries. Observation, and the practice of that which has been learned, will enable our youth to become efficient nurses, with superior skill, fitted to stand upon the highest eminence. Every physician, every nurse, every helper, who has anything to do in God's service, must aim at perfection. Nothing short of this standard is pleasing to Him who has called us to be colaborers with Him. And especially should those who are in training to act as His medical missionaries turn resolutely from every temptation to be satisfied with a superficial knowledge of their profession. Let them rather reach upward to perfection. Theirs is a most exacting calling, and their preparation must be painstaking and thorough.

The cause of God today would have been far in advance of what it is, had we in former years been more active in the training of nurses who, in addition to their acquirement of more than ordinary skill in the care of the sick, had also learned to labor as evangelists in soul-winning service.

It is for the training of such workers, as well as for the training of physicians, that the school at Loma Linda has been founded. In this school many workers are to be qualified with the ability of physicians, to labor, not in professional lines as physicians, but as medical missionary evangelists. This training is to be in harmony with the principles underlying true higher education. The cause is in need of hundreds of workers who have received a practical and thorough education in medical lines, and who are also prepared to labor from house to house as teachers, Bible workers, and colporteurs. Such students should come out of the school without having sacrificed the principles of health reform or their love for God and righteousness.

Those who take advanced training in nursing, and go forth into all parts of the world as medical missionary evangelists, cannot expect to receive from the world the honor and rewards that often come to fully accredited physicians. Yet as they go about their work of teaching and healing, and link up closely with God's servants who have been called to the ministry of His word, His blessing will rest upon their labors, and marvelous transformations will be wrought. In a special sense they will be His helping hand.

The duties of the physician are arduous. Few realize the mental and physical strain to which he is subjected. Every energy and capability must be enlisted with the most intense anxiety in the battle with disease and death. Often he knows that one unskilled movement of the hand, even but a hairbreadth in the wrong direction, may send a soul unprepared into eternity. How much the faithful physician needs the sympathy and prayers of the people of God! His claims in this direction are not inferior to those of the most devoted minister or missionary worker. Deprived, as he often is, of sufficient rest and sleep, he needs a double portion of grace, a fresh supply daily, or he will lose his hold on God and will be in danger of sinking deeper in spiritual darkness than men of other callings. And yet often he is made to bear unmerited reproaches and is left to stand alone, the subject of Satan's fiercest temptations, feeling himself misunderstood, betrayed by his friends.

Many, knowing how trying are the duties of the physician and how few opportunities physicians have for release from care, even upon the Sabbath, will not choose this for their lifework. But the great enemy is constantly seeking to destroy the workmanship of God's hands, and men of culture and intelligence are called for to combat his cruel power. More of the right kind of men are needed to devote themselves to this profession. Painstaking effort should be made to induce suitable men to qualify themselves for this work. They should be men whose characters are based upon the broad principles of the word of God—men who possess a natural energy, force, and perseverance that will enable them to reach a high standard of excellence.

It is not everyone who can make a successful physician. Many have entered upon the duties of this profession in every way unprepared. They have not the requisite knowledge; neither have they the skill and tact, the carefulness and intelligence, necessary to ensure success. A physician can do much better if he has physical strength. If he is feeble, he cannot endure the wearing labor incident to his calling. A man who has a weak constitution, who is a dyspeptic, or who is lacking in self-control cannot become qualified to deal with all classes of disease. Great care should be taken not to encourage persons who might be useful in some less responsible position, to study medicine at a great outlay of time and means, when there is no reasonable hope that they will succeed.

I have been instructed that in view of the trying nature of medical missionary work, those who desire to take up this line should first be thoroughly examined by competent physicians to ascertain whether or not they have the strength necessary to endure the course of study through which they must pass in the training school.

We have a work to do in securing the best talent and in placing these workers in positions where they can educate other workers. Then when our sanitariums and mission fields call for physicians, we shall have young men who, through their experience gained by practical work, have become fitted to bear responsibilities.

THE MEDICAL STUDENT

While seeking a preparation for his lifework, the medical student should be encouraged to attain the highest possible development of all his powers. His studies, taxing though they are, need not necessarily undermine his physical health or lessen his enjoyment of spiritual things. Throughout his course of study he may continually grow in grace and in a knowledge of truth, while at the same time he may be constantly adding to the store of knowledge that will make him a wise practitioner.

To medical students I would say, Enter upon your course of study with a determination to do right and to maintain Christian principles. Flee temptation, and avoid every influence for evil. Preserve your integrity of soul. Maintain a conscientious regard for truth and righteousness. Be faithful in the smaller responsibilities, and show yourselves to be close, critical thinkers, having soundness of heart and uprightness, being loyal to God and true to mankind.

Opportunities are before you; if studious and upright, you may obtain an education of the highest value. Make the most of your privileges. Be not satisfied with ordinary attainments; seek to qualify yourself to fill positions of trust in connection with the Lord's work in the earth. United with the God of wisdom and power, you may become intellectually strong and increasingly capable as soul winners. You may become men and women of responsibility and influence if, by the power of your will, coupled with divine strength, you earnestly engage in the work of securing a proper training.

Exercise the mental powers, and in no case neglect the physical. Let not intellectual slothfulness close up your path to greater knowledge. Learn to reflect as well as to study, that your minds may expand, strengthen, and develop. Never think that you have learned enough and that you may now relax your efforts. The cultivated mind is the measure of the man. Your education should continue during your lifetime; every day you should be learning and putting to practical use the knowledge gained.

In order for you to become men and women that can be depended upon, there must be a growth of the powers, the exercise of every faculty, even in little things; then greater power is acquired to bear larger responsibilities. Individual responsibility and accountability are essential. In putting into practice that which you are learning during your student days, do not shrink from bearing your share of responsibility because there are risks to take, because something must be ventured. Do not leave others to be brains for you. You must train your powers to be strong and vigorous; then the entrusted talents will grow, as a steady, uniform, unyielding energy is exercised in bearing individual responsibility. God would have you add, day by day, little by little, to your stock of ideas, acting as if the moments were jewels, to be carefully gathered and discreetly cherished. You will thus acquire breadth of thought and strength of intellect.

God will not require of man a more strict account of anything than of the way in which he has occupied his time. Have its hours been wasted and abused? God has granted to us the precious boon of life not to be devoted to selfish gratification. Our work is too solemn, our time to serve God and our fellow men too short, to be spent in seeking for fame. Oh, if men would stop in their aspirations where God has set the bounds, what different service would the Lord receive!

There are many who are in such haste to climb to distinction that they skip some of the rounds of the ladder and in so doing lose experience which they must have in order to become intelligent workers. In their zeal the knowledge of many things looks unimportant to them. They skim over the surface and do not go deep into the mine of truth, thus by a slow and painstaking process gaining an experience that will enable them to be of special help to others. We want our medical students to be men and women who are most thorough and who feel it their duty to improve every talent lent them, that they may finally double their entrusted capital.

The light that God has given in medical missionary lines will not cause His people to be regarded as inferior in scientific medical knowledge, but will fit them to stand upon the highest eminence. God would have them stand as a wise and understanding people because of His presence with them. In the strength of Him who is the Source of all wisdom, all grace, defects and ignorance may be overcome.

Let every medical student aim to reach a high standard. Under the discipline of the greatest of all teachers our course must ever tend upward to perfection. All who are connected with the medical missionary work must be learners. Let no one stop to say, "I cannot do this." Let him say instead, "God requires me to be perfect. He expects me to work away from all commonness and cheapness, and to strive after that which is of the highest order."

There is only one power that can make medical students what they ought to be and keep them steadfast— the grace of God and the power of the truth exerting a saving influence upon life and character. These students, who intend to minister to suffering humanity, will find no graduating place this side of heaven. That knowledge which is termed science should be acquired, while the seeker daily acknowledges that the fear of God is the beginning of wisdom. Everything that will strengthen the mind should be cultivated to the utmost of their power, while at the same time they should seek God for wisdom; for unless they are guided by the wisdom from above they will become an easy prey to the deceptive power of Satan. They will become large in their own eyes, pompous, and self-sufficient.

God-fearing physicians speak modestly of their work, but novices with limited experience in dealing with the bodies and souls of men will often speak boastingly of their knowledge and attainments. These need a better understanding of themselves; then they would become more intelligent in regard to their duties and would realize that in every department where they have to labor they must possess a willing mind, an earnest spirit, and a hearty, unselfish zeal in trying to do others good. They will not study how best to preserve their dignity, but by thoughtfulness and caretaking will earn a reputation for thoroughness and exactitude, and by sympathetic ministry will gain the hearts of those whom they serve.

In the medical profession there are many skeptics and atheists who exalt the works of God above the God of science. Comparatively few of those who enter worldly medical colleges come out from them pure and unspotted. They have failed to become elevated, ennobled, sanctified. Material things eclipse the heavenly and eternal. With many, religious faith and principles are mingled with worldly customs and practices, and pure and undefiled religion is rare. But it is the privilege of every student to enter college with the same fixed, determined principle that Daniel had when he entered the court of Babylon, and throughout his course to keep his integrity untarnished. The strength and grace of God have been provided at an infinite sacrifice, that men might be victorious over Satan's suggestions and temptations, and come forth unsullied. The life, the words, and the deportment are the most forcible argument, the most solemn appeal, to the careless, irreverent, and skeptical. Let the life and character be the strong argument for Christianity; then men will be compelled to take knowledge of you that you have been with Jesus and have learned of Him.

Let not medical students be deceived by the wiles of the devil or by any of his cunning pretexts which so many adopt to beguile and ensnare. Stand firm to principle. At every step inquire, "What saith the Lord?" Say firmly, "I will follow the light. I will respect and honor the Majesty of truth."

Especially should those who are studying medicine in the schools of the world guard against contamination from the evil influences with which they are constantly surrounded. When their instructors are worldly-wise men, and their fellow students infidels who have no serious thought of God, even Christians of experience are in danger of being influenced by these irreligious associations. Nevertheless, some have gone through the medical course and have remained true to principle. They would not continue their studies on the Sabbath, and they have proved that men may become qualified for the duties of a physician and not disappoint the expectations of those who have encouraged them to obtain an education.

It is because of these peculiar temptations which our youth must meet in worldly medical schools that provision should be made for preparatory and advanced medical training in our own schools, under Christian teachers. Our larger union conference training schools in various parts of the field should be placed in the most favorable position for qualifying our youth to meet the entrance requirements specified by state laws regarding medical students. The very best teaching talent should be secured, that our schools may be brought up to the proper standard. The youth, and those more advanced in years, who feel it their duty to fit themselves for work requiring the passing of certain legal tests, should be able to secure at our union conference training schools all that is essential for entrance into a medical college.

Prayer will accomplish wonders for those who give themselves to prayer, watching thereunto. God desires us all to be in a waiting, hopeful position. What He has promised He will do, and inasmuch as there are legal requirements making it necessary that medical students shall take a certain preparatory course of study, our colleges should arrange to carry their students to the point of literary and scientific training that is necessary.

And not only should our larger training schools give this preparatory instruction to those who contemplate taking a medical course, but we must also do all that is essential for the perfecting of the courses of study offered by our Loma Linda College of Medical Evangelists. As pointed out about the time this school was founded, we must provide that which is essential to qualify our youth who desire to be physicians, so that they may intelligently fit themselves to stand the examinations required to prove their efficiency as physicians. They should be taught to treat understandingly the cases of those who are diseased, so that the door will be closed for any sensible physician to imagine that we are not giving in our school the instruction necessary for properly qualifying young men and women to do the work of a physician. Continually the students who are graduated are to advance in knowledge, for practice makes perfect.

The medical school at Loma Linda is to be of the highest order, because those who are in that school have the privilege of maintaining a living connection with the wisest of all physicians, from whom there is communicated knowledge of a superior order. And for the special preparation of those of our youth who have clear convictions of their duty to obtain a medical education that

will enable them to pass the examinations required by
law of all who practice as regularly qualified physicians,
we are to supply whatever may be required, so that these
youth need not be compelled to go to medical schools
conducted by men not of our faith. Thus we shall close a
door that the enemy would be pleased to have left open;
and our young men and women, whose spiritual interests
the Lord desires us to safeguard, will not feel compelled
to connect with unbelievers in order to obtain thorough
training along medical lines.

The teachers in our medical college should encourage
the students to gain all the knowledge they can in every
department. If they find any students deficient in caretaking, in a comprehension of their responsibilities, they
should lay the matter frankly before such ones, giving
them an opportunity to correct their habits and to reach
a higher standard.

The teachers should not become discouraged because
some are slow to learn. Neither should they discourage
the students when mistakes are made. As errors and
defects are kindly pointed out, the students in turn should
feel grateful for any instruction given. A haughty spirit
on the part of the students should not be encouraged. All
should be willing to learn, and the teachers should be
willing to instruct, training the students to be self-reliant,
competent, careful, painstaking. As the students study
under wise instructors, and unite with them in sharing
responsibilities, they may by the aid of the teachers climb
to the topmost round of the ladder.

Students should be willing to work under those of experience, to heed their suggestions, to follow their advice, and to go as far as possible in thought, training, and intelligent enterprise; but they should never infringe upon a rule, never disregard one principle, that has been interwoven with the upbuilding of the institution. The dropping down is easy enough; the disregard of regulations is natural to the heart inclined to selfish ease and gratification. It is much easier to tear down than to build up. One student with careless ideas may do more to let down the standard than ten men with all their effort can do to counteract the demoralizing influence.

Failure or success will be read in the course the students pursue. If they stand ready to question rules and regulations and order, if they indulge self, and by their example encourage a spirit of rebellion, give them no place. The institution might better close its doors than suffer this spirit to leaven the helpers and break down the barriers that it has cost thought, effort, and prayer to establish.

In training workers to care for the sick, let the student be impressed with the thought that his highest aim should always be to look after the spiritual welfare of his patients. He should learn to repeat the promises of God's word, and to offer fervent prayers daily, while preparing for service. Help him to realize that he is always to keep the sweetening, sanctifying influence of the great Medical Missionary before his patients. If those who are suffering can be impressed with the fact that Christ is their sympathizing, compassionate Saviour, they will have rest of mind, which is so essential to recovery of health.

Importance of Bible Study

If medical students will study the word of God diligently, they will be far better prepared to understand their other studies; for enlightenment always comes from an earnest study of the word of God. Nothing else will so help to give them a retentive memory as a study of the Scriptures. Let our medical missionary workers understand that the more they become acquainted with God and with Christ, and the more they become acquainted with Bible history, the better prepared will they be to do their work.

Faithful teachers should be placed in charge of the Bible classes, teachers who will strive to make the students understand their lessons, not by explaining everything to them, but by requiring them to explain clearly every passage they read. Let these teachers remember that little good is accomplished by skimming over the surface of the word. Thoughtful investigation and earnest, taxing study are necessary to an understanding of this word.

Christ, the great Medical Missionary, came to this world at infinite sacrifice, to teach men and women the lessons that would enable them to know God aright. He lived a perfect life, setting an example that all may safely follow. Let our medical students study the lessons that Christ has given. It is essential that they have a clear understanding of these lessons. It would be a fearful mistake for them to neglect the study of God's word for a study of theories which are misleading, which divert minds from the words of Christ to the fallacies of human production. God would have all who profess to be gospel medical missionaries learn diligently the lessons of the Great Teacher. This they must do if they would find rest and peace. Learning of Christ, their hearts will be filled with the peace that He alone can give.

Make the Bible the man of your counsel. Your acquaintance with it will grow rapidly if you keep your minds free from the rubbish of the world. The more the Bible is studied, the deeper will be your knowledge of God. The truths of His word will be written in your soul, making an ineffaceable impression.

These things God has been opening before me for many years. In our medical missionary training schools we need men who have a deep knowledge of the Scriptures, men who can teach these lessons to others clearly and simply, just as Christ taught His disciples that which He deemed most essential.

And the needed knowledge will be given to all who come to Christ, receiving and practicing His teachings, making His word a part of their lives. The Holy Spirit teaches the student of the Scriptures to judge all things by the standard of righteousness and truth and justice. The divine revelation supplies him with the knowledge that he needs. Those who place themselves under the instruction of the great Medical Missionary, to be workers together with Him, will have a knowledge that the world, with all its traditionary lore, cannot supply.

SPIRITUAL GROWTH

To every student who is seeking a medical education I would say, Look beyond the present. Turn away from the transitory things of this life, from selfish pursuits and gratifications. For what purpose are you seeking an education? Is it not that you may relieve suffering humanity? As the mind is enlarged by true knowledge, the heart is warmed by a sense of the goodness, compassion, and love of God. The soul is filled with an earnest longing to tell others how they may co-operate with the great Master Worker. You will do much for yourselves as you impart the knowledge you receive. Thus you will gain more knowledge to impart, and your ability to work for God will increase.

There are those who will suggest to you that in order to be successful in your profession you must be a policy man; you *must* at times depart from strict rectitude. These temptations find a ready welcome in the heart of man; but I speak that which I know. Do not be deceived or deluded. Do not pamper self. Do not throw open a door through which the enemy may enter to take possession of the soul. There is danger in the first and slightest departure from the strictest rectitude. Be true to yourself. Preserve your God-given dignity in the fear of God. There is great need that every medical worker get hold and keep hold of the arm of Infinite Power.

The policy principle is one that will assuredly lead into

difficulties. He who regards the favor of men as more desirable than the favor of God will fall under the temptation to sacrifice principle for worldly gain or recognition. Thus fidelity to God is constantly being sacrificed. Truth, God's truth, must be cherished in the soul and held in the strength of heaven, or the power of Satan will wrest it from you. Never entertain the thought that an honest, truthful physician cannot succeed. Such a sentiment dishonors the God of truth and righteousness. He *can* succeed; for he has God and heaven on his side. Let every bribe to dissimulate be sternly refused. Hold fast your integrity in the strength of the grace of Christ, and He will fulfill His word to you.

The medical student, however young, has access to the God of Daniel. Through divine grace and power he may become as efficient in his calling as Daniel was in his exalted position. But it is a mistake to make a scientific preparation the all-important thing, while religious principles which lie at the very foundation of a successful practice are neglected. Many are lauded as skillful men in their profession who scorn the thought that they need to rely upon Christ for wisdom in their work. But if these men who trust in their knowledge of science were illuminated by the light of heaven, to how much greater excellence might they attain! How much stronger would be their powers! with how much greater confidence could they undertake difficult cases! The man who is closely connected with the Great Physician has the resources of heaven and earth at his command, and he can work with a wisdom, an unerring precision, that the godless man cannot possess.

Like Enoch, the physician should be a man who walks with God. This will be to him a safeguard against all the delusive, pernicious sentiments which make so many infidels and skeptics. The truth of God, practiced in the life and constantly guiding in all that concerns the interest of others, will barricade the soul with heavenly principles. God will not be unmindful of our struggles to maintain the truth. When we place every word that proceeds out of the mouth of God above worldly policy, above all the assertions of erring, failing man, we shall be guided into every good and holy way.

The Christian physician, in his acceptance of the truth by his baptismal vows, has pledged himself to represent Christ, the Physician in chief. But if he does not keep strict guard over himself, if he allows the barriers against sin to be broken down, Satan will overcome him with specious temptations. There will be a blemish in his character that by its evil influence will mold other minds. The moral palsy of sin will not only destroy the soul of the one who departs from strict principles, but will have the power to reproduce in others the same evil.

It is not safe to be occasional Christians. We must be Christlike in our actions all the time. Then, through grace, we are safe for time and for eternity. The experimental knowledge of the power of grace received in times of trial is of more value than gold or silver. It confirms the faith of the trusting, believing one. The assurance that Jesus is to him an ever-present helper gives him a boldness that enables him to take God at His word and trust Him with unwavering faith under the most trying circumstances.

Our only security against falling into sin is to keep ourselves constantly under the molding influence of the Holy Spirit, at the same time engaging actively in the cause of truth and righteousness, discharging every God-given duty, but taking no burden that God has not laid upon us. Physicians and medical students must stand firm under the banner of the third angel's message, fighting the good fight of faith, perseveringly and successfully, relying not on their own wisdom, but on the wisdom of God, putting on the heavenly armor, the equipment of God's word, never forgetting that they have a Leader who never has been and never can be overcome by evil.

To every medical student who desires to be an honor to the cause of God during the closing scenes of this earth's history, I would say: Behold Christ, the Sent of God, who, in this world and in human nature, lived a pure, noble, perfect life, setting an example that all may safely follow. The Lord is reaching out His hand to save. Respond to His invitation, "Let him take hold of My strength, that he may make peace with Me; and he shall make peace with Me." Isaiah 27:5. . . . How eagerly the Saviour will take the trembling hand in His own, holding it with a warm, firm grasp, until the feet are placed on vantage ground! . . .

Trust in Him who understands your weakness. Keep close to the side of Christ; for the enemy stands ready to take captive everyone who is off his guard. . . .

It is young men whom the Lord claims as His helping hand. Samuel was a mere child when the Lord used him to do a good and gracious work. . . .

Gather to your soul the light of the word of God. Remember that day by day you are building character for time and for eternity. The teaching of the Bible in regard to character building is very explicit. "Whatsoever ye do in word or deed, do all in the name of the Lord Jesus." Colossians 3:17. Place yourself under His control, and then ask for His protecting power. He gave His life for you. Do not cause Him sorrow. Be guarded in all that you say and do. Christ wants you to be to other young men His representative, His delegated gospel medical missionary.

Remember that in your life, religion is not merely one influence among others; it is to be an influence dominating all others. Be strictly temperate. Resist every temptation. Make no concessions to the wily foe. Listen not to the suggestions that he puts into the mouths of men and women. You have a victory to win. You have nobility of character to gain. . . .

Jesus loves you. . . . His great heart of infinite tenderness yearns over you. . . . You may stand where you regard yourself, not as a failure, but as a conqueror, in and through the uplifting influence of the Spirit of God. Take hold of the hand of Christ, and do not let it go.

You may be a great blessing to others if you will give yourself unreservedly to the Lord's service. Power from on high will be given you if you will take your position on the Lord's side. Through Christ you can escape the corruption that is in the world through lust, and be a noble example of what He can do for those who co-operate with Him. . . .

God's purpose for us is that we shall ever move upward. Even in the smaller duties of common life we are to make continual growth in grace, supplied with high and holy motives, powerful because they proceed from One who gave His life to furnish us with the incentive to be wholly successful in the formation of Christian character. . . . You are to be strong in the strength of God, grounded in the hope of the gospel. . . .

Arise in your God-given dignity, living the truth in its purity. Christ is ready to pardon you, to take away your sins and make you free. He is ready to purify your heart and give you the sanctification of His Spirit. As you commit yourself to His service, He will be at your right hand to help you. Day by day you will be strengthened and ennobled. Looking to the Saviour for help, you will be a conqueror, yes, more than a conqueror, over the temptations that beset you. You will become more and more like Christ. The angels of heaven will rejoice to see you standing on the Lord's side, in righteousness and true holiness. . . .

Become all that the Lord desires you to be—a gospel medical missionary. You are to be not only an increasingly skillful physician, but one of the Lord's appointed missionaries, in all your work placing His service first. Let nothing mar your peace. Give your heart's best and holiest affections to Him who gave His life that you might be among the redeemed family in the heavenly courts. Striving for the crown of life will not make you dissatisfied or less useful. The Great Teacher desires to acknowledge you as His helping hand. He calls for your co-operation. Will you not now give Him all that you have and are? Will you not consecrate your talents to His service?

This life is your sowing time. Will you not pledge yourself to God, that your seed sowing shall be that which will produce, not tares, but a harvest of wheat? God will work with you; He will increase your usefulness. He has entrusted to you talents that in His strength you may use to produce a precious harvest.

To those who with steadfast perseverance strive to reveal the attributes of Christ, angels are commissioned to give enlarged views of His character and work, His power and grace and love. Thus they become partakers of His nature, and day by day grow up to the full stature of men and women in Christ. The sanctification of the Spirit is seen in thought, word, and deed. Their ministry is life and salvation to all with whom they associate. Of such ones it is declared, "Ye are complete in Him." Colossians 2:10.

The physician's example, no less than his teaching, should be a positive power on the right side. The cause of reform calls for men and women whose life practice is an illustration of self-control. It is our practice of the principles we inculcate that gives them weight. The world needs a practical demonstration of what the grace of God can do in restoring to human beings their lost kingship, giving them mastery of themselves. There is nothing that the world needs so much as a knowledge of the gospel's saving power revealed in Christlike lives.—*The Ministry of Healing*, pages 132, 133.

FOR FURTHER STUDY

A MISSIONARY TRAINING

With such an army of workers as our youth, rightly trained, might furnish, how soon the message of a crucified, risen, and soon-coming Saviour might be carried to the whole world!

EDUCATION A FITTING FOR SERVICE

The true object of education is to fit men and women for service by developing and bringing into active exercise all their faculties. The work at our colleges and training schools should be strengthened year by year, for in them our youth are to be prepared to go forth to serve the Lord as efficient laborers. The Lord calls upon the youth to enter our schools and quickly fit themselves for active work. Time is short. Workers for Christ are needed everywhere. Urgent inducements should be held out to those who ought now to be engaged in earnest effort for the Master.

Our schools have been established by the Lord; and if they are conducted in harmony with His purpose, the youth sent to them will be quickly prepared to engage in various branches of missionary work. Some will be trained to enter the field as missionary nurses, some as canvassers, some as evangelists, and some as gospel ministers. Some are to be prepared to take charge of church schools, in which the children shall be taught the first principles of education. This is a very important work, demanding high ability and careful study.

(493)

Satan is trying to lead men and women away from right principles. The enemy of all good, he desires to see human beings so trained that they will exert their influence on the side of error, instead of using their talents to bless their fellow men. And multitudes who profess to belong to God's true church are falling under his deceptions. They are being led to turn away from their allegiance to the King of heaven.

The signs which show that Christ's coming is near are fast fulfilling. The Lord calls upon our youth to labor as canvassers and evangelists, to do house-to-house work in places where the truth has not yet been proclaimed. He speaks to our young men, saying, "Know ye not that . . . ye are not your own? for ye are bought with a price: therefore glorify God in your body, and in your spirit, which are God's." 1 Corinthians 6:19, 20. Those who go forth into the work under the Master's direction will be wonderfully blessed.

The Lord calls for volunteers who will take their stand firmly on His side and will pledge themselves to unite with Jesus of Nazareth in doing the work that needs to be done now, just now. The talents of God's people are to be employed in giving the last message of mercy to the world. The Lord calls upon those connected with our schools and sanitariums and publishing houses to teach the youth to do evangelistic work. Our time and money must not be so largely employed in establishing sanitariums, food factories, food stores, and restaurants that other lines of work shall be neglected. Young men and women who should be engaged in the ministry, in Bible work, and in the canvassing work should not be bound down to mechanical employment.

It is to fortify the youth against the temptations of the enemy that we have established schools where they may be qualified for usefulness in this life and for the service of God throughout eternity. Those who have an eye single to God's glory will earnestly desire to fit themselves for special service; for the love of Christ will have a controlling influence upon them. This love imparts more than finite energy, and qualifies human beings for divine achievement.

Christ's Labor for Humanity

The work of those who love God will make manifest the character of their motives, for the saving of those for whom Christ has paid an infinite price will be the object of their efforts. All other considerations—home, family, enjoyment—will be made secondary to the work of God; they will follow the example of Him who showed His love for fallen man by leaving a heaven of bliss and the homage of the angels, to come to this world. The Saviour worked with unwearied effort to help human beings. He stopped at no sacrifice, hesitated at no self-denial; for our sakes He became poor, that through His poverty we might be made rich. His sympathy for the lost led Him to seek them wherever they were. And His colaborers must work as He worked, hesitating not to seek for the fallen, deeming no effort too taxing, no sacrifice too great, if they may but win souls to Christ. He who would be an efficient worker for God must be willing to endure what Christ endured, to meet men as He met them.

That education alone which brings the student into close relation with the Great Teacher is true education. The youth are to be taught to look to Christ as their guide. They are to be taught lessons of forbearance and trust, of true goodness and kindness of heart, of perseverance and steadfastness. Their characters are to answer to the words of David: "That our sons may be as plants grown up in their youth; that our daughters may be as cornerstones, polished after the similitude of a palace." Psalm 144:12.

The converted student has broken the chain which bound him to the service of sin, and has placed himself in right relation to God. His name is enrolled in the Lamb's book of life. He is under solemn obligation to renounce evil and come under the jurisdiction of heaven. Through earnest prayer he is to cleave to Christ. To neglect this devotion, to refuse this service, is to become the sport of Satan's wiles.

While cultivating the mind the student should also cultivate uprightness of heart and loyalty to God, that he may develop a character like that of Joseph. Then he will scorn the thought of yielding to temptation, fearing to sully his purity. Like Daniel, he will resolve to be true to principle and to make the very best use of the powers with which God has endowed him.

Long Courses of Study

There are many who think that in order to be fitted for acceptable service they must go through a long course of study under learned teachers in some school of the world. This they must do, it is true, if they desire to secure what the world calls education. But we do not say to our youth, Study, study, keeping your mind all the time on books. Nor do we say to them, You must spend your time in school in acquiring the so-called "higher education." The cause of God needs experienced workers. But we should not think that we must climb to the highest round of knowledge in every science. Time is short, and we must labor earnestly for souls. If students will study the word of God diligently and prayerfully, they will find the knowledge that they need.

It is not necessary that all know several languages; but it is necessary that all have an experience in the things of God. I do not say that there should be no study of the languages. The languages should be studied. Before long there will be a positive necessity for many to leave their homes and go to work among people of other tongues; and those who have some knowledge of these languages will be able to communicate with those who do not know the truth.

The Character of Teachers

The well-being, the happiness, the religious life, of the families with which the youth are connected, the prosperity and piety of the church of which they are members, are largely dependent upon the religious education that they receive in our schools. Because our schools have been established for so high and holy a purpose, the teachers should be men and women whose lives are purified by the grace of Christ, who are cultured in mind and refined in manners. And they should have a vivid sense of the perils of this time, and the work that must be accomplished to prepare a people to stand in the day of God. They should ever pursue a course that will command the respect of their students. The youth have a right to expect that a Christian teacher will reach a high standard, and they will pass severe judgment upon him if he does not.

The teachers in our schools will need to manifest Christlike love, forbearance, and wisdom. Students will come to school who have no definite purpose, no fixed principles, no realization of the claim that God has upon them. These are to be led to awake to their responsibilities. They must be taught to appreciate their opportunities, and to become examples of industry, sobriety, and helpfulness. Under the influence of wise teachers, the indolent may be led to arouse, the thoughtless to become serious. Through painstaking effort, the most unpromising student may be so trained and disciplined that he will go forth from the school with high motives and noble principles, prepared to be a successful light bearer in the darkness of the world.

Patient, conscientious teachers are needed to arouse hope and aspiration in the youth, to help them to realize the possibilities lying before them. Teachers are needed who will train their students to do service for the Master; who will carry them forward from one point to another in intellectual and spiritual attainment. Teachers should strive to realize the greatness of their work. They need enlarged views; for their work, in its importance, ranks with that of the Christian minister. With persevering faith they are to hold to the Infinite One, saying as did Jacob, "I will not let Thee go, except Thou bless me." Genesis 32:26.

Offering to God Our Best

Students are to offer to God nothing less than their best. Mental effort will become easier and more satisfactory as they set themselves to the task of understanding the deep things of God. Each should decide that he will not be a second-rate student, that he will not allow others to think for him. He should say, "That which other minds have acquired in the sciences and in the word of God, I will acquire through painstaking effort." He should rally the best powers of the mind and, with a sense of his accountability to God, do his best to conquer difficulties. And as far as possible, he should seek the society of those who are able to help him, who can detect his mistakes, and put him on his guard against indolence, pretense, and surface work.

The true motive of service is to be kept before students. The training they receive is to help them to develop into useful men and women. Every means that will uplift and ennoble them is to be employed. They are to be taught to use their powers in harmony with God's will. The influence exerted by a true, pure life is ever to be kept before them. This will aid them in their preparation for service. Daily they will grow stronger, better prepared, through the grace of Christ and a study of His word, to put forth aggressive efforts against evil.

No other knowledge is so firm, so consistent, so far-reaching, as that obtained from the study of God's word. Here is the fountain of all true knowledge.

GAINING EFFICIENCY

The third angel is represented as flying in the midst of heaven, showing that the message is to go throughout the length and breadth of the earth. It is the most solemn message ever given to mortals, and all who propose to connect themselves with the work should first feel their need of an education, of the most thorough training. Plans should be made and efforts put forth for the improvement of those who anticipate entering any branch of the work.

Ministerial labor should not be entrusted to boys, neither should the work of giving Bible readings be entrusted to young girls, because they offer their services and are willing to take responsible positions, while they are wanting in religious experience and lack a thorough education and training. They must be proved; for unless they develop a firm, conscientious principle to be all that God would have them be, they will not correctly represent His cause. All who are engaged in the work, in every mission, should gain a depth of experience. Those who are young in the work should have the help of such as have had experience and understand the manner of working. Missionary operations are constantly embarrassed for want of workers of the right class of mind—workers who have devotion and piety that will correctly represent our faith.

There are many who ought to become missionaries, but who never enter the field because those who are united with them in church capacity or in our colleges do not feel the burden to labor with them, to open before them the claims of God upon all their powers, and do not pray with and for them. The eventful period which decides the course of life passes, their convictions are stifled, other influences and inducements attract them, and temptations to seek positions that will, they think, bring them financial gain, take them into the worldly current. These young men might have been saved to the cause.

Our schools are to be training schools. If men and women come forth from them fitted in any sense for the missionary field, they must be led to realize the greatness of the work; practical godliness must be brought into their daily experience if they would be fitted for any place of usefulness in the cause of God. . . .

The School to Continue the Work of the Home

Those who attend our colleges are to have a training different from that given by the common schools of the day. Our youth generally, if they have wise, God-fearing parents, have been taught the principles of Christianity. The word of God has been respected in their homes, and its teachings have been made the law of life. They have been brought up in the nurture and admonition of the gospel. When they enter school, this same education and training is to continue. The world's maxims, the world's customs and practices, are not the teaching that they need. Let them see that the teachers in the school care for their souls, that they have a decided interest in their spiritual welfare. Religion is the great principle to be inculcated; for the fear of God is the beginning of wisdom. . . .

Pleasure in Religion

Wherever a school is established, there should be warm hearts to take a lively interest in the youth. Fathers and mothers are needed who will give warm sympathy and kindly admonitions. All the pleasantness possible should be brought into the religious exercises. Those who prolong these exercises to weariness are leaving wrong impressions upon the minds of the youth, leading them to associate religion with that which is dry, unsocial, and uninteresting. . . . Ardent, active piety in the teacher is essential. Unless constant care is exercised, and unless vitalized by the Spirit of God, the morning and evening service in the chapel and the Sabbath meetings will become dry and formal, and to the youth the most burdensome and the least attractive of the school exercises. The social meetings should be managed in such a way as to make them seasons not only of profit, but of positive pleasure.

Let those who teach the youth study for themselves in the school of Christ, and learn lessons to communicate to their students. Sincere, earnest, heartfelt devotion is needed. All narrowness should be avoided. Let the teacher so far unbend from his dignity as to be one with the children in their exercises and amusements, without leaving the impression that they are being watched. His very presence with them will give a mold to their actions, and will cause his heart to throb with new affection.

The youth need sympathy, affection, and love, or they will become discouraged. A spirit of "I care for nobody and nobody cares for me" takes possession of them. They may profess to be followers of Christ; but they have a tempting devil on their track, and they are in danger of becoming disheartened and lukewarm, and of backsliding from God. Then some feel it a duty to blame them and to treat them coldly as if they were a great deal worse than they really are. Few, perhaps none, feel it their duty to make personal efforts to reform them and to remove the unhappy impressions that have been made upon them.

The teacher's obligations are weighty and sacred, but no part of his work is more important than that of looking after the youth with tender, loving solicitude. Let the teacher once gain the confidence of his students, and he can easily lead and control and train them. The holy motives that underlie Christian living must be brought into the life. The salvation of his pupils is the highest interest entrusted to the God-fearing teacher. He is Christ's coworker, and his special and determined effort should be to win them to Christ. God will require this at his hands.

Every teacher should lead a life of piety, of purity, of painstaking effort. If the heart is glowing with the love of God, there will be seen in the life that pure affection which is essential; fervent prayers will be offered and faithful warnings given. When these are neglected, the souls under his care are endangered. . . .

And yet, after all these efforts have been made, teachers may find that some will develop unprincipled characters. They are lax in morals, the result, in many cases, of vicious example and lack of parental discipline. Though teachers may do all they can, they will fail to lead these youth to a life of purity and holiness. After patient discipline, affectionate labor, and fervent prayer, they will be disappointed by those from whom they have hoped for much. In addition to this they will meet the reproaches of the parents because they have not had power to counteract the influence of the wrong example and unwise training received in the home. But in spite of these discouragements the teacher must work on, trusting in God to work with him, standing at his post manfully and laboring in faith. Others will be saved to God, and their influence will be exerted in saving still others. . . .

Setting a High Standard

What is worth doing at all is worth doing well. While religion should be the prevailing element in every school, it will not lead to a cheapening of the literary attainments. It will make all true Christians feel their need of thorough knowledge, that they may make the best use of the faculties bestowed upon them. While growing in grace and in knowledge of our Lord Jesus Christ, they will seek constantly to put to the stretch their powers of mind, that they may become intelligent Christians.

The Lord is dishonored by low ideas or designs on our part. He who does not perceive the binding claims of God's law, who neglects to keep its every requirement, violates the whole law. He who is content to meet only partially the standard of righteousness, and who does not triumph over every spiritual foe, will not fulfill the purpose of Christ. He cheapens the whole plan of his religious life and weakens his character. Under the force of temptation his defects of character gain the supremacy, and evil triumphs.

To meet the highest standard possible, we need to be persevering and determined. In many cases established habits and ideas must be overcome before we can make advancement in the religious life. . . . The essential work is to conform the tastes, the appetites, the passions, the motives, the desires, to the great standard of righteousness. The work must begin in the heart. Unless the heart is wholly conformed to Christ's will, some master passion, or some habit or defect, will become a power to destroy.

Piety and religious experience lie at the very foundation of true education. God wants the teachers in our schools to be efficient. If they advance in spiritual understanding, they will see how important it is that they should not be deficient in a knowledge of the sciences. While teachers need piety, they also need a thorough knowledge of the sciences. . . .

The Christian aims to reach the highest attainments for the purpose of doing others good. Knowledge harmoniously blended with a Christlike character will make a man a light in the world. God works with human efforts. Those who give all diligence to make their calling and election sure will feel that a superficial knowledge will not fit them for a position of usefulness. Education balanced by a solid religious experience fits the child of God to do his appointed work steadily, firmly, understandingly. He who is learning of the greatest Educator the world ever knew, will have not only a symmetrical Christian character, but a mind trained for effective labor. . . .

God does not want us to be content with lazy, undisciplined minds, dull thoughts, and loose memories. He wants every teacher to feel dissatisfied with simply a measure of success and to realize his need of constant diligence in acquiring knowledge. Our bodies and souls belong to God, for He has bought them. He has given us talents and has made it possible for us to acquire more, that we may be able to help ourselves and others in the way of life. It is the work of each one to develop and strengthen the gifts that God has lent him. If all realized this, what a vast difference we should see in our schools, in our churches, and in our missions! But the larger number are content with a meager knowledge, a few attainments, content just to be passable. The necessity of being men like Daniel, men of influence, men whose characters have become harmonious by working to bless humanity and glorify God—such a need few feel, and the result is that there are few fitted for the great want of the times.

God does not ignore ignorant men; but if such are connected with Christ, if they are sanctified through the truth, they will be constantly gathering knowledge. By exerting every power to glorify God, they will have increased power with which to glorify Him. Those who are willing to remain in a narrow sphere because God condescended to accept them when they were there, are very foolish. Yet there are hundreds and thousands who are doing this very thing.

EFFICIENCY THROUGH SERVICE

God will accomplish a great work through the truth if devoted, self-sacrificing men will give themselves unreservedly to the work of presenting it to those in darkness. Those who have a knowledge of the truth and are consecrated to God should avail themselves of every opportunity to proclaim the message for this time. Angels of God are moving upon the hearts and consciences of the people of other nations, and honest souls are troubled as they witness the signs of the times in the unsettled state of the nations. The inquiry arises in their hearts, What will be the end of all these things?

But while God and angels are working to impress hearts, the servants of Christ seem to be asleep. Few are working in unison with the heavenly messengers. All who are Christians should be workers in the vineyard of the Lord. They should be wide-awake, zealously laboring for the salvation of their fellow men, and should follow the example that the Saviour has given them in His life of self-denial, sacrifice, and earnest effort.

God has honored us by making us the depositaries of His law, and if ministers and people were sufficiently aroused they would not rest in indifference. We have been entrusted with truths of vital importance which are to test the world, and yet in our own country there are cities, villages, and towns that have never heard the warning message.

Young men are aroused by the appeals that are made for help in the great work of God, and they make some advance moves; but the burden does not rest upon them with sufficient weight to lead them to accomplish what they might. They are willing to do a small work which does not require special effort. Therefore they do not learn to place their whole dependence upon God and by living faith draw from the great Source of light and strength, that their efforts may prove wholly successful.

Young men should be qualifying themselves for service by becoming familiar with other languages, that God may use them as mediums through which to communicate His saving truth to those of other nations. These young men may obtain a knowledge of other languages even while engaged in laboring for sinners. If they are economical of their time they can improve their minds and qualify themselves for more extended usefulness.

It will make our young men strong to go into new fields and break up the fallow ground of human hearts. This work will draw them nearer to God. It will help them to see that of themselves they are altogether inefficient, that they must be wholly the Lord's. They must put away their self-esteem and self-importance, and put on the Lord Jesus Christ. When they do this, they will be willing to go without the camp and bear the burden as good soldiers of the cross. They will gain efficiency and ability by mastering difficulties and overcoming obstacles. Men are wanted for responsible positions, but they must be men who have given full proof of their ministry, in willingness to wear the yoke of Christ.

THE EDUCATION MOST ESSENTIAL FOR GOSPEL WORKERS

There are Christian workers who have not received a collegiate education because it was impossible for them to secure this advantage, but God has given evidence that He has chosen them and ordained them to go forth and labor in His vineyard. He has made them effectual co-workers with Himself. They have a teachable spirit; they feel their dependence upon God; and the Holy Spirit is with them to help their infirmities. It quickens and energizes the mind, directs the thoughts, and aids in the presentation of truth.

When the laborer stands before the people to hold forth the words of life, there is heard in his voice the echo of the voice of Christ. It is evident that he walks with God, that he has been with Jesus and learned of Him. He has brought the truth into the inner sanctuary of the soul; it is to him a living reality; and he presents the truth in demonstration of the Spirit and of power. The people hear the joyful sound; God speaks to their hearts through the man consecrated to His service.

As the worker lifts up Jesus through the Spirit, he becomes really eloquent. He is earnest and sincere, and is beloved by those for whom he labors. What a sin would rest upon anyone who would listen to such a man merely to criticize, to notice bad grammar or incorrect pronunciation, and hold these errors up to ridicule! . . .

The speaker who has not a thorough education may sometimes fall into errors of grammar or pronunciation;

he may not employ the most eloquent expressions or the most beautiful imagery; but if he has himself eaten of the bread of life, if he has drunk of the fountain of life, he can feed hungry souls and give of the water of life to him that is athirst. His defects will be forgiven and forgotten. His hearers will not become weary or disgusted, but will thank God for the message of grace sent them through His servant.

Self-Improvement in Workers

If the worker has consecrated himself fully to God and is diligent in prayer for strength and heavenly wisdom, the grace of Christ will be his teacher, and he will overcome his defects and become more and more intelligent in the things of God. But let none take license from this to be indolent, to squander time and opportunities, and neglect the training that is essential in order to become efficient. The Lord is not pleased with those who, having had opportunities to obtain knowledge, neglect to improve the privileges placed within their reach. . . .

Above all other people on earth the man whose mind is enlightened by the word of God will feel that he must give himself to greater diligence in the perusal of the Bible and to a diligent study of the sciences, for his hope and his calling are greater than any other. The more closely man is connected with the Source of all knowledge and wisdom, the more he can be helped intellectually as well as spiritually. The knowledge of God is the essential education, and this knowledge every true worker will make it his constant study to obtain.

"ACCORDING THAT A MAN HATH"

God can and will use those who have not had a thorough education in the schools of men. A doubt of His power to do this is manifest unbelief. Our Saviour did not ignore learning or despise education, yet He chose unlearned fishermen for the work of the gospel because they had not been schooled in the false customs and traditions of the world. They were men of good natural ability and of a humble, teachable spirit, men whom He could educate for His great work.

In the common walks of life there is many a toiler patiently treading the round of his daily tasks, unconscious of latent powers that, roused to action, would place him among the world's great leaders. The touch of a skillful hand is needed to arouse and develop those dormant faculties. It was such men whom Jesus connected with Himself, and He gave them the advantages of three years' training under His own care. No course of study in the schools of the rabbis or the halls of philosophy could have equaled this in value.

A life devoted to God should not be a life of ignorance. Many speak against education because Jesus chose uneducated fishermen to preach the gospel. They assert that He showed preference for the uneducated. But there were many learned and honorable men who believed the teaching of Christ. Had these fearlessly obeyed the convictions of their consciences, they would have followed Him. Their abilities would have been accepted and employed in the service of Christ, had they offered them. But they had not moral power, in face of the frowning priests and jealous rulers, to confess Christ and venture their reputation in connection with the humble Galilean.

He who knows the hearts of all understood this. If the educated and noble would not do the work they were qualified to do, Christ would select men who would be obedient and faithful in doing His will. He chose humble men and connected them with Himself, that He might educate them to carry forward the great work on earth when He should leave it.

Christ was the light of the world. He was the fountain of all knowledge. He was able to qualify the unlearned fishermen to carry out the high commission He would give them. The lessons of truth given these lowly men were of mighty significance. They were to move the world. It seemed but a simple thing for Jesus to connect these humble persons with Himself, but it was an event productive of tremendous results. Their words and their works were to revolutionize the world.

God will accept the youth with their talent and their wealth of affection, if they will consecrate themselves to Him. They may reach to the highest point of intellectual greatness; and if balanced by religious principle, they can carry forward the work which Christ came from heaven to accomplish.

The students at our colleges have valuable privileges, not only of obtaining a knowledge of the sciences, but also of learning how to cultivate and practice virtues which will give them symmetrical characters. They are

God's responsible moral agents. The talents of wealth, station, and intellect are given of God in trust to man for his wise improvement. These varied trusts He has distributed proportionately to the known powers and capacities of His servants, to every man his work.

And the Giver expects returns according to the gifts. The humblest gift is not to be despised. Everyone has his peculiar sphere and vocation. He who makes the most of his God-given opportunities will return to the Giver, in their improvement, an interest proportionate to the entrusted capital.

The Lord does not reward the large amount of labor. He does not regard the greatness of the work so much as the fidelity with which it is done. The good and faithful servant is rewarded. As we cultivate the powers God has given us, we shall increase in knowledge and perception.

Perseverance in the aquisition of knowledge, controlled by the fear and love of God, will give the youth increased power for good in this life; and those who make the most of their opportunities to reach high attainments will take these attainments with them into the future life. They have sought and obtained that which is imperishable. The ability to appreciate the glories that "eye hath not seen, nor ear heard" (1 Corinthians 2:9), will be proportionate to the attainments reached.

Those who empty their hearts of vanity and rubbish, through the grace of God may purify the mind and make it a storehouse of knowledge, purity, and truth. And it will be continually reaching beyond the narrow boundaries of worldly thought, into the vastness of the infinite.

YOUNG MEN AS MISSIONARIES

Young men who desire to enter the field as ministers, colporteurs, or canvassers should first receive a suitable degree of mental training, as well as a special preparation for their calling. Those who are uneducated, untrained, and unrefined are not prepared to enter a field in which the powerful influences of talent and education combat the truths of God's word. Neither can they successfully meet the strange forms of error, religious and philosophical combined, to expose which requires a knowledge of scientific as well as Scriptural truth.

Those especially who have the ministry in view should feel the importance of the Scriptural method of ministerial training. They should enter heartily into the work, and while they study in the schools, they should learn of the Great Teacher the meekness and humility of Christ. A covenant-keeping God has promised that in answer to prayer His Spirit shall be poured out upon these learners in the school of Christ, that they may become ministers of righteousness.

There is hard work to be done in dislodging error and false doctrine from the head, that Bible truth and Bible religion may find a place in the heart. It was as a means ordained of God to educate young men and women for the various departments of missionary labor that colleges were established among us. It is God's will that they send forth not merely a few, but many laborers. But Satan, determined to overthrow this purpose, has often secured the very ones whom God would qualify for places of usefulness in His work. There are many who would work if urged into service, and who would save their souls by thus working. The church should feel her great responsibility in shutting up the light of truth, and restraining the grace of God within her own narrow limits, when money and influence should be freely employed in bringing competent persons into the missionary field.

Hundreds of young men should have been preparing to act a part in the work of scattering the seeds of truth beside all waters. We want men who will push the triumphs of the cross; men who will persevere under discouragements and privations; who will have the zeal and resolution and faith that are indispensable in the missionary field. . . .

Foreign Languages

There are among us those who, without the toil and delay of learning a foreign language, might qualify themselves to proclaim the truth to other nations. In the primitive church, missionaries were miraculously endowed with a knowledge of the languages in which they were called to preach the unsearchable riches of Christ. And if God was willing thus to help His servants then, can we doubt that His blessing will rest upon our efforts to qualify those who naturally possess a knowledge of foreign tongues, and who, with proper encouragement, would bear to their own countrymen the knowledge of truth? We might have had more laborers in foreign missionary fields had those who entered these fields availed themselves of every talent within their reach. . . .

It may in some cases be necessary that young men learn foreign languages. This they can do with most success by associating with the people, at the same time devoting a portion of each day to studying the language. This should be done, however, only as a necessary step preparatory to educating such as are found in the missionary fields themselves, and who, with proper training, can become workers. It is essential that those be urged into the service who can speak in their mother tongue to the people of different nations. It is a great undertaking for a man of middle age to learn a foreign language, and with all his efforts it will be next to impossible for him to speak it so readily and correctly as to render him an efficient laborer.

Young Men Wanted for Hard Places

We cannot afford to deprive our home missions of the influence of middle-aged and aged ministers, to send them into distant fields to engage in a work for which they are not qualified, and to which no amount of training will enable them to adapt themselves. The men thus sent out leave vacancies which inexperienced laborers cannot supply.

But the church may inquire whether young men can be entrusted with the grave responsibilities involved in the establishing and superintending of a foreign mission. I answer, God designed that they should be so trained in our colleges and by association in labor with men of experience that they would be prepared for departments of usefulness in this cause. We must manifest confidence in our young men. They should be pioneers in every enterprise involving toil and sacrifice, while the overtaxed servants of Christ should be cherished as counselors, to encourage and bless those who strike the heaviest blows for God. Providence thrust these experienced fathers into trying, responsible positions at an early age, when neither physical nor intellectual powers were fully developed. The magnitude of the trust committed to them aroused their energies, and their active labor in the work aided both physical and mental development.

Young men are wanted. God calls them to missionary fields. Being comparatively free from care and responsibilities, they are more favorably situated to engage in the work than are those who must provide for the training and support of a large family. Furthermore, young men can more readily adapt themselves to new climates and new society, and can better endure inconveniences and hardships. By tact and perseverance they can reach the people where they are.

Strength comes by exercise. All who put to use the ability which God has given them will have increased ability to devote to His service. Those who do nothing in the cause of God will fail to grow in grace and in the knowledge of the truth. A man who would lie down and refuse to exercise his limbs would soon lose all power to use them. Thus the Christian who will not exercise his God-given powers not only fails to grow up into Christ, but he loses the strength which he already had; he becomes a spiritual paralytic. It is those who, with love for God and their fellow men, are striving to help others, that become established, strengthened, settled, in the truth. The true Christian works for God, not from impulse, but from principle; not for a day or a month, but during the entire life. . . .

The Master calls for gospel workers; who will respond? Not all who enter the army are to be generals, captains, sergeants, or even corporals. Not all have the care and responsibility of leaders. There is hard work of other kinds to be done. Some must dig trenches and build fortifications; some are to stand as sentinels, some to carry messages. While there are but few officers, it requires many soldiers to form the rank and file of the army; yet its success depends upon the fidelity of every soldier. One man's cowardice or treachery may bring disaster upon the entire army. . . .

He who has appointed "to every man his work" (Mark 13:34) according to his ability, will never let the faithful performance of duty go unrewarded. Every act of loyalty and faith will be crowned with special tokens of God's favor and approbation. To every worker is given the promise, "He that goeth forth and weepeth, bearing precious seed, shall doubtless come again with rejoicing, bringing his sheaves with him." Psalm 126:6.—*Testimonies,* vol. 5, pp. 390-395.

A familiarity with the languages of the different nations is a help in missionary work. An understanding of the customs of those who lived in Bible times, of the location and time of events, is practical knowledge; for it aids in making clear the figures of the Bible and in bringing out the force of Christ's lessons.

CO-OPERATION BETWEEN SCHOOLS AND SANITARIUMS

There are decided advantages to be gained by the establishment of a school and a sanitarium in close proximity, that they may be a help one to the other. Instruction regarding this was given to me when we were making decisions about the location of our buildings in Takoma Park. Whenever it is possible to have a school and a sanitarium near enough together for helpful cooperation between the two institutions, and yet separated sufficiently to prevent one from interfering with the work of the other, our brethren should give most careful consideration to the benefits that would accrue through placing the institutions where they can help each other. One institution will give influence and strength to the other; and, too, money can be saved by both institutions, because each can share the advantages of the other.

Medical Evangelistic Work

In connection with our larger schools there should be provided facilities for giving students thorough instruction regarding gospel medical missionary work. This line of work is to be brought into our colleges and training schools as a part of the regular instruction. The students should learn how to care for the sick, for many of them will have to engage in this kind of work when they take up missionary labor in the fields to which they shall be called. They are to be taught how to use nature's remedies in the treatment of disease. While gaining a knowledge of present truth, they should learn also how to be ministers of healing to those whom they go forth to serve. They should be given wise instruction regarding the principles of healthful living. This should be looked upon as an important part of their education, even though they may never be missionaries in foreign lands. Even in the primary schools the children should be taught to form habits that will keep them in health.

Those in training to be nurses and physicians should daily be given instruction that will develop the highest motives for advancement. They should attend our colleges and training schools; and the teachers in these institutions of learning should realize their responsibility to work and to pray with their students. Students should learn to be true medical missionaries, firmly bound up with the gospel ministry. . . .

Whenever a well-equipped sanitarium is established near a school, it may add greatly to the strength of the medical missionary course in the school if there is cooperation between the two institutions. The teachers in the school can help the workers in the sanitarium by their advice and counsel, and by sometimes speaking to the patients. And, in return, those in charge of the sanitarium can assist in training for field service the students who are desirous of becoming medical missionaries. Circumstances, of course, must determine the details of the arrangements that it will be best to make. As the workers in each institution plan unselfishly to help the other, the blessing of the Lord will surely rest upon both institutions.

No one man, whether a teacher, a physician, or a minister, can ever hope to be a complete whole. God has given to every man certain gifts and has ordained that men be associated in His service in order that the varied talents of many minds may be blended. The contact of mind with mind tends to quicken thought and increase the capabilities. The deficiencies of one laborer are often made up by the special gifts of another; and as physicians and teachers thus associated unite in imparting their knowledge, the youth under their training will receive a symmetrical, well-balanced education for service.

The Benefit to the Patients

The benefits of hearty co-operation extend beyond physicians and teachers, students and sanitarium helpers. When a sanitarium is built near a school, those in charge of the educational institution have a grand opportunity of setting a right example before those who all through life have been easygoing idlers and who have come to the sanitarium for treatment. The patients will see the contrast between their idle, self-indulgent lives and the lives of self-denial and service lived by Christ's followers. They will learn that the object of medical missionary work is to restore, to correct wrongs, to show human beings how to avoid the self-indulgence that brings disease and death.

The words and actions of the workers in the sanitarium and in the school should plainly reveal that life is an intensely solemn thing in view of the account which all must render to God. Each one should now put his talents out to the exchangers, adding to the Master's gift, blessing others with the blessings given him.

Unity Among Workers

That the best results may be secured by the establishment of a sanitarium near a school there needs to be perfect harmony between the workers in both institutions. This is sometimes difficult to secure, especially when teachers and physicians are inclined to be self-centered, each considering as of the greatest importance the work with which he is most closely connected. When men who are self-confident are in charge of institutions in close proximity, great annoyance might result were each determined to carry out his own plans, refusing to make concessions to others. Those at the head of the sanitarium and those at the head of the school will need to guard against clinging tenaciously to their own ideas concerning things that are really nonessentials.

Consecrated Service

There is a great work to be done by our sanitariums and schools. Time is short. What is done must be done quickly. Let those who are connected with these important instrumentalities be wholly converted. Let them not live for self, for worldly purposes, withholding themselves from full consecration to God's service. Let them give themselves, body, soul, and spirit, to God, to be used by Him in saving souls. They are not at liberty to do with themselves as they please; they belong to God, for He has bought them with the lifeblood of His only-begotten Son.

And as they learn to abide in Christ, there will remain in the heart no room for selfishness. In His service they will find the fullest satisfaction.

Let this be taught and lived by medical missionary workers. Let these laborers tell those with whom they come in contact that the life that men and women now live will one day be examined by a just God, and that each one must now do his best, offering to God consecrated service. Those in charge of the school are to teach the students to use for the highest, holiest purpose the talents God has given them, that they may accomplish the greatest good in this world. Students need to learn what it means to have a real aim in life, and to obtain an exalted understanding of what true education means. They need to learn what it means to be true gospel medical missionaries—missionaries who can go forth to labor with the ministers of the word in needy fields.

Wherever there is a favorable opportunity, let our sanitariums and our schools plan to be a help and a strength to one another. The Lord would have His work move forward solidly. Let light shine forth as God designed that it should from His institutions, and let God be glorified and honored. This is the purpose and plan of Heaven in the establishment of these institutions. Let physicians and nurses, teachers and students, walk humbly with God, trusting wholly in Him as the only one who can make their work a success.

Nov. 14, 1905.

A BROADER VIEW

In carrying forward the Lord's work at home and abroad, those in positions of responsibility must plan wisely so as to make the best possible use of men and of means. The burden of sustaining the work in many of the foreign lands must be largely borne by our conferences in the homeland. These conferences should have means with which to assist in opening new fields, where the testing truths of the third angel's message have never yet penetrated. Within the past few years, doors have been thrown open as if by magic, and men and women are needed to enter these doors and begin earnest work for the salvation of souls.

Our educational institutions can do much toward meeting the demand for trained workers for these mission fields. Wise plans should be laid to strengthen the work done in our training centers. Study should be given to the best methods for fitting consecrated young men and women to bear responsibility and to win souls for Christ. They should be taught how to meet the people and how to present the third angel's message in an attractive manner. And in the management of financial matters they should be taught lessons that will help them when they are sent to isolated fields where they must suffer many privations and practice the strictest economy.

Earning Scholarships

The Lord has instituted a plan whereby many of the students in our schools can learn practical lessons needful to success in afterlife. He has given us the privilege of handling books that have been dedicated to the advancement of our educational and sanitarium work. In the very handling of these books the youth will meet with many experiences that will teach them how to cope with problems that await them in the regions beyond. During their school life, as they handle these books they may learn how to approach people courteously and how to exercise tact in conversing with them on different points of present truth. And as they meet with a degree of success financially, some will learn lessons of thrift and economy, which will be of great advantage to them when they are sent out as missionaries.

The students who take up the work of selling *Christ's Object Lessons* and *The Ministry of Healing* will need to study the book they expect to sell. As they familiarize their minds with the subject matter of the book in hand and endeavor to practice its teachings they will develop in knowledge and spiritual power. The messages in these books are the light that God has revealed to me to give to the world. The teachers in our schools should encourage the students to make a careful study of every chapter. They should teach the truths there presented and seek to inspire the youth with a love for the precious thoughts the Lord has entrusted to us to communicate to the world.

Thus the preparation for handling these books, and the daily experiences gained while bringing them to the attention of the people, will prove an invaluable schooling to those who take part in this line of effort. Under the blessing of God the youth will obtain a fitting up for service in the Lord's vineyard.

There is a special work to be done for our young people by those bearing responsibility in local churches throughout the conferences. When the church officers see promising youth who are desirous of fitting themselves for usefulness in the Lord's service, but whose parents are unable to send them to school, they have a duty to perform in studying how to give help and encouragement. They should take counsel with parents and youth, and unite in planning wisely. Some youth may be best fitted to engage in home missionary work. There is a wide field of usefulness in the distribution of our literature and in bringing the third angel's message to the attention of friends and neighbors. Other youth should be encouraged to enter the canvassing work to sell our larger books. Some may have qualifications that would make them valuable helpers in our institutions.

In many instances if promising youth were wisely encouraged and properly directed, they could be led to earn their own schooling by taking up the sale of *Christ's Object Lessons* or *The Ministry of Healing*. In selling these books they would be acting as missionaries, for they would be bringing light to the notice of the people of the world. At the same time they would be earning money to enable them to attend school where they could continue their preparation for wider usefulness in the Lord's cause. In the school they would receive encouragement and inspiration from teachers and students to continue their work of selling books; and when the time came for them to leave school, they would have received a practical training, fitting them for the hard, earnest, self-sacrificing labor that has to be done in many foreign fields, where the third angel's message must be carried under difficult and trying circumstances.

How much better is this plan than for students to go through school without obtaining a practical education in field work, and at the end of their course leave under a burden of debt, with but little realization of the difficulties they will have to meet in new and untried fields! How hard it will be for them to meet the financial problems that are connected with pioneer work in foreign lands! And what a burden someone will have to carry until the debts incurred by the student have been paid!

On the other hand, how much might be gained if the self-supporting plan were followed! The student would often be enabled to leave the educational institution, nearly or wholly free from personal indebtedness; the finances of the school would be in a more prosperous condition; and the lessons learned by the student while passing through these experiences in the home field would be of untold value to him in foreign fields.

Let wise plans now be laid to help worthy students to earn their own schooling by handling these books, if they so desire. Those who earn sufficient means in this way to pay their way through a course at one of our training schools will gain a most valuable practical experience that will help fit them for pioneer missionary work in other fields.

A great work is to be done in our world in a short time, and we must study to understand and appreciate, more than we have in past years, the providence of God in placing in our hands the precious volumes, *Christ's Object Lessons* and *The Ministry of Healing,* as a means of helping worthy students to meet their expenses while in training, as well as a means of liquidating the indebtedness on our educational and medical institutions.

Great blessings are in store for us as we wisely handle these precious books given us for the advancement of the cause of present truth. And as we labor in accordance with the Lord's plan we shall find that many consecrated youth will be fitted to enter the regions beyond as practical missionaries, and at the same time the conferences in the home field will have means with which to contribute liberally to the support of the work undertaken in new territory.

May 17, 1908.

The word of God is to stand on its own eternal merits; to be accepted as the word of God; to be obeyed as His voice, which declares His will to the people. The will and voice of finite man are not to be interpreted as the voice of God.

Those who teach the most solemn message ever given to the world should discipline the mind to comprehend its significance. The theme of redemption will bear the most concentrated study, and its depths will never be fully explored. Do not fear that you will exhaust the wonderful theme. Go to the fountain for yourself, that you may be filled with refreshment. Drink deep at the well of salvation, that Jesus may be in you a well of water, springing up unto everlasting life.

AN ENCOURAGING EXPERIENCE

At one of our conference schools the teachers led out in reviving an interest in the sale of *Christ's Object Lessons*. Bands of students, after prayerful study of the book, visited a large city near the school, in company with their teachers, and in their work gained a sound, solid experience that they prize above silver and gold. This kind of work is, in fact, one of the means that God has ordained for giving our youth a missionary training, and those who neglect to improve such opportunities lose out of their lives a chapter of experience of the highest value. By entering heartily into this work, students can learn how to approach with tact and discretion men and women in all the walks of life, how to deal with them courteously, and how to lead them to give favorable consideration to the truths contained in the books that are sold.

Students, your voice, your influence, your time—all these are gifts from God and are to be used in winning souls to Christ. As teachers and students engage heartily in selling *Christ's Object Lessons,* they will gain an experience that will fit them to do valuable service in connection with camp meetings. Through the instruction that they can give to the believers in attendance, and through the sale of many books in the places where such meetings are held, those who have been in the school will be able to do their part in reaching the multitudes who need to be given the third angel's message. Let teachers and students bear their share of the burden in showing our people how to communicate the message to their friends and neighbors.

When we follow plans of the Lord's devising we are "laborers together with God." Whatever our position—whether presidents of conferences, ministers, teachers, students, or lay members—we are held accountable by the Lord for making the most of our opportunities to enlighten those in need of present truth. And one of the principal agencies He has ordained for our use is the printed page. In our schools and sanitariums, in our home churches, and particularly in our annual camp meetings, we must learn to make a wise use of this precious agency. With patient diligence, chosen workers must instruct our people how to approach unbelievers in a kindly, winning way, and how to place in their hands literature in which the truth for this time is presented with clearness and power.

———

Only by the aid of that Spirit who in the beginning "was brooding upon the face of the waters;" of that Word by whom "all things were made;" of that "true Light, which lighteth every man that cometh into the world" (Genesis 1:2, R.V., margin; John 1:3, 9), can the testimony of science be rightly interpreted. Only by their guidance can its deepest truths be discerned. Only under the direction of the Omniscient One shall we, in the study of His works, be enabled to think His thoughts after Him.

A MISSIONARY EDUCATION

In the work of soul saving, the Lord calls together laborers who have different plans and ideas and various methods of labor. But with this diversity of minds there is to be revealed a unity of purpose. Oftentimes in the past the work which the Lord designed should prosper has been hindered because men have tried to place a yoke upon their fellow workers who did not follow the methods which they supposed to be the best.

No exact pattern can be given for the establishment of schools in new fields. The climate, the surroundings, the condition of the country, and the means at hand with which to work must all bear a part in shaping the work. The blessings of an all-round education will bring success in Christian missionary work. Through its means souls will be converted to the truth.

"Ye are the light of the world," Christ declares. "Let your light so shine before men, that they may see your good works, and glorify your Father which is in heaven." Matthew 5:14, 16. God's work in the earth in these last days is to reflect the light that Christ brought into the world. This light is to dissipate the gross darkness of ages. Men and women in heathen darkness are to be reached by those who at one time were in a similar condition of ignorance, but who have received the knowledge of the truth of God's word. These heathen nations will accept eagerly the instruction given them in a knowledge of God.

Very precious to God is His work in the earth. Christ and heavenly angels are watching it every moment. As we draw near to the coming of Christ, more and still more of missionary work will engage our efforts. The message of the renewing power of God's grace will be carried to every country and clime, until the truth shall belt the world. Of the number of them that shall be sealed will be those who have come from every nation and kindred and tongue and people. From every country will be gathered men and women who will stand before the throne of God and before the Lamb, crying, "Salvation to our God which sitteth upon the throne, and unto the Lamb." Revelation 7:10. But before this work can be accomplished, we must experience here in our own country the work of the Holy Spirit upon our hearts.

Worldly Plans Not to Be Followed

God has revealed to me that we are in positive danger of bringing into our educational work the customs and fashions that prevail in the schools of the world. If teachers are not guarded, they will place on the necks of their students worldly yokes instead of the yoke of Christ. The plan of the schools we shall establish in these closing years of the message is to be of an entirely different order from those we have instituted.

For this reason, God bids us establish schools away from the cities, where, without let or hindrance, we can carry on the education of students upon plans that are in harmony with the solemn message committed to us for the world. Such an education as this can best be worked out where there is land to cultivate and where the physical exercise taken by the students can be of such a nature as to act a valuable part in their character building and fit them for usefulness in the fields to which they shall go.

God will bless those schools that are conducted according to His design. When we were laboring to establish the educational work in Australia, the Lord revealed to us that this school must not pattern after any schools that had been established in the past. This was to be a sample school. It was organized on the plan that God had given us, and He has prospered its work.

New Methods

I have been shown that in our educational work we are not to follow the methods that have been adopted in our older established schools. There is among us too much clinging to old customs, and because of this we are far behind where we should be in the development of the third angel's message. Because men could not comprehend the purpose of God in the plans laid before us for the education of workers, methods have been followed in some of our schools which have retarded rather than advanced the work of God. Years have passed into eternity with small results, that might have shown the accomplishment of a great work. If the Lord's will had been done by the workers in earth as the angels do it in heaven, much that now remains to be done would be already accomplished, and noble results would be seen as the fruit of missionary effort.

The usefulness learned on the school farm is the very education that is most essential for those who go out as missionaries to many foreign fields. If this training is given with the glory of God in view, great results will be seen. No work will be more effectual than that done by those who, having obtained an education in practical life, go forth to mission fields with the message of truth, prepared to instruct as they have been instructed. The knowledge they have obtained in the tilling of the soil and other lines of manual work, and which they carry with them to their fields of labor, will make them a blessing even in heathen lands.—*Special Testimonies,* Series B, No. 11, pp. 27-30.

The teacher should not divorce himself from the church work. Those who conduct church schools and larger schools should regard it as their privilege, not only to teach in the school, but to bring into the church with which they are connected the same talents that are used in the school. Through their work and influence, power is to be brought into the church. They are to strive to bring the church to a higher standard.

All through our ranks are young men and women who should be trained for positions of usefulness and influence. Education is necessary both for the proper fulfillment of the domestic duties of life and for success in every field of usefulness. Under the guidance of the Holy Spirit these youth may be educated and trained so that all the powers will be given to God's service.

THE YOUTH TO BE BURDEN BEARERS

"I have written unto you, young men, because ye are strong, and the word of God abideth in you, and ye have overcome the wicked one." 1 John 2:14.

In order that the work may go forward in all its branches, God calls for youthful vigor, zeal, and courage. He has chosen the youth to aid in the advancement of His cause. To plan with clear mind and execute with courageous hand demands fresh, uncrippled energies. Young men and women are invited to give God the strength of their youth, that through the exercise of their powers, through keen thought and vigorous action, they may bring glory to Him and salvation to their fellow men.

In view of their high calling, the youth among us should not seek for amusement, or live for selfish gratification. The salvation of souls is to be the motive that inspires them to action. In their God-given strength they are to rise above every enslaving, debasing habit. They are to ponder well the paths of their feet, remembering that where they lead the way, others will follow. No one lives to himself; all exert an influence for good or for evil. Because of this, the apostle exhorts young men to be sober-minded. How can they be otherwise when they remember that they are to be co-workers with Christ, partakers with Him of His self-denial and sacrifice, His forbearance and gracious benevolence?

To the youth of today, as surely as to Timothy, are spoken the words, "Study to show thyself approved unto God, a workman that needeth not to be ashamed, rightly dividing the word of truth." "Flee also youthful lusts: but follow righteousness, faith, charity, peace." 2 Timothy 2:15, 22. "Be thou an example of the believers, in word, in conversation, in charity, in spirit, in faith, in purity." 1 Timothy 4:12.

The burden bearers among us are falling in death. Many of those who have been foremost in carrying out the reforms instituted by us as a people are now past the meridian of life and are declining in physical and mental strength. With the deepest concern the question may be asked, Who will fill their places? To whom are to be committed the vital interests of the church, when the present standard-bearers fall? We can but look anxiously upon the youth of today as those who must take these burdens, and upon whom responsibilities must fall. These must take up the work where others leave it, and their course will determine whether morality, religion, and vital godliness shall prevail, or whether immorality and infidelity shall corrupt and blight all that is valuable.

Those who are older must educate the youth, by precept and example, to discharge the claims that society and their Maker have upon them. Upon these youth must be laid grave responsibilities. The question is, Are they capable of governing themselves, and standing forth in the purity of their God-given manhood, abhorring everything that savors of wickedness?

Never before was there so much at stake; never were there results so mighty depending upon a generation as upon these now coming upon the stage of action. Not for one moment should the youth think that they can acceptably fill any position of trust without possessing a good character. Just as well might they expect to gather grapes of thorns, or figs of thistles.

A good character must be built up brick by brick. Those characteristics which will enable the youth to labor successfully in God's cause must be obtained by the diligent exercise of their faculties, by improving every advantage Providence gives them, and by connecting with the Source of all wisdom. They must be satisfied with no low standard. The characters of Joseph and Daniel are good models for them to follow; and in the life of the Saviour they have a perfect pattern.

All are given an opportunity to develop character. All may fill their appointed places in God's great plan. The Lord accepted Samuel from his very childhood, because his heart was pure. He was given to God, a consecrated offering, and the Lord made him a channel of light. If the youth of today will consecrate themselves as did Samuel, the Lord will accept them and use them in His work. Of their life they may be able to say with the psalmist, "O God, Thou hast taught me from my youth: and hitherto have I declared Thy wondrous works." Psalm 71:17.

The youth must soon bear the burdens that older workers are now carrying. We have lost time in neglecting to give young men a solid, practical education. The cause of God is constantly progressing, and we must obey the command, Go forward. There is need of young men and women who will not be swayed by circumstances, who walk with God, who pray much, and who put forth earnest efforts to gather all the light they can.

The worker for God should put forth the highest mental and moral energies with which nature, cultivation, and the grace of God have endowed him; but his success will be proportionate to the degree of consecration and self-sacrifice in which his work is done, rather than to either natural or acquired endowments. Earnest, continuous endeavor to acquire qualifications for usefulness is necessary; but unless God works with humanity, nothing good can be accomplished. Divine grace is the great element of saving power; without it all human effort is unavailing.

Whenever the Lord has a work to be done, He calls not only for the commanding officers, but for all the workers. Today He is calling for young men and women who are strong and active in mind and body. He desires them to bring into the conflict against principalities and powers and spiritual wickedness in high places their fresh, healthy powers of brain, bone, and muscle. But they must have the needed preparation. Some young men are urging their way into the work who have no real fitness for it. They do not understand that they need to be taught before they can teach. They point to men who with little preparation have labored with a measure of success. But if these men were successful, it was because they put heart and soul into the work. And how much more effective their labors might have been if at the first they had received suitable training!

The cause of God needs efficient men. Education and training are rightly regarded as an essential preparation for business life; and how much more essential is thorough preparation for the work of presenting the last message of mercy to the world! This training cannot be gained by merely listening to preaching. In our schools our youth are to bear burdens for God. They are to receive a thorough training under experienced teachers. They should make the best possible use of their time in study, and put into practice the knowledge acquired. Hard study and hard work are required to make a successful minister or a successful worker in any branch of God's cause. Nothing less than constant cultivation will develop the value of the gifts that God has bestowed for wise improvement.

A great injury is often done our young men by permitting them to begin to preach when they have not sufficient knowledge of the Scriptures to present our faith in an intelligent manner. Some who enter the field are novices in the Scriptures. In other things also they are incompetent and inefficient. They cannot read the Scriptures without hesitating, mispronouncing words, and jumbling them together in such a manner that the word of God is abused. Those who cannot read correctly should learn to do so, and should become apt to teach, before they attempt to stand before the public.

The teachers in our schools are obliged to apply themselves closely to study, that they may be prepared to instruct others. These teachers are not accepted until they have passed a critical examination, and their capabilities to teach have been tested by competent judges. No less caution should be used in the examination of ministers; those who are about to enter upon the sacred work of teaching Bible truth to the world should be carefully examined by faithful, experienced men.

The teaching in our schools is not to be the same as in other colleges and seminaries. It is not to be of an inferior order; the knowledge essential to prepare a people to stand in the great day of God is to be made the all-important theme. The students are to be fitted to serve God, not only in this life, but in the future life. The Lord requires that our schools shall fit students for the kingdom to which they are bound. Thus they will be prepared to blend in the holy, happy harmony of the redeemed.

Many teachers are in danger of making their training mechanical. There is danger that a ceremonial service will take the place of genuine heart work. Thus religion will become little more than a form. The students in our schools, the members of our churches, need something deeper than this. An intellectual religion will not satisfy the soul. Intellectual training must not be neglected, but it is not sufficient. Students must be taught that they are in this world to do service for God. They must be taught to place the will on the side of God's will.

Let those who have been trained for service now take their places quickly in the Lord's work. House-to-house laborers are needed. The Lord calls for decided efforts to be put forth in places where the people know nothing of Bible truth. Singing and prayer and Bible readings are needed in the homes of the people. Now, just now, is the time to obey the commission, "Teaching them to observe all things whatsoever I have commanded you." Matthew 28:20. Those who do this work must have a ready knowledge of the Scriptures. "It is written" is to be their weapon of defense. God has given us light on His word, that we may give this light to our fellow men. The truth spoken by Christ will reach hearts. A "Thus saith the Lord" will fall upon the ear with power, and fruit will appear wherever honest service is done.

1882.

LITERARY SOCIETIES

It is often asked, Are literary societies a benefit to our youth? To answer this question properly, we should consider not only the avowed purpose of such societies, but the influence which they have actually exerted, as proved by experience. The improvement of the mind is a duty which we owe to ourselves, to society, and to God. But we should never devise means for the cultivation of the intellect at the expense of the moral and the spiritual. And it is only by the harmonious development of both the mental and the moral faculties that the highest perfection of either can be attained. Are these results secured by literary societies as they are generally conducted?

Literary societies are almost universally exerting an influence contrary to that which the name indicates. As generally conducted they are an injury to the youth, for Satan comes in to put his stamp upon the exercises. All that makes men manly or women womanly is reflected from the character of Christ. The less we have of Christ in such societies, the less we have of the elevating, refining, ennobling element which should prevail. When worldlings conduct these meetings to meet their wishes, the spirit of Christ is excluded. The mind is drawn away from serious reflection, away from God, away from the real and substantial, to the imaginary and the superficial. Literary societies—would that the name expressed their true character! What is the chaff to the wheat?

The purposes and objects which lead to the formation of literary societies may be good; but unless wisdom from

God shall control these organizations, they will become a positive evil. The irreligious and unconsecrated in heart and life are usually admitted and are often placed in the most responsible positions. Rules and regulations may be adopted that are thought to be sufficient to hold in check every deleterious influence; but Satan, a shrewd general, is at work to mold the society to suit his plans, and in time he too often succeeds. The great adversary finds ready access to those whom he has controlled in the past, and through them he accomplishes his purpose. Various entertainments are introduced to make the meetings interesting and attractive for the worldlings, and thus the exercises of the so-called literary society too often degenerate into demoralizing theatrical performances and cheap nonsense. All these gratify the carnal mind, which is at enmity with God; but they do not strengthen the intellect nor confirm the morals.

The association of the God-fearing with the unbelieving in these societies does not make saints of sinners. When God's people voluntarily unite with the worldly and the unconsecrated, and give them the pre-eminence, they will be led away from Him by the unsanctified influence under which they have placed themselves. For a short time there may be nothing seriously objectionable; but minds that have not been brought under the control of the Spirit of God will not take readily to those things which savor of truth and righteousness. If they had had heretofore any relish for spiritual things they would have placed themselves in the ranks of Jesus Christ. The two classes are controlled by different masters and are opposites in their purposes, hopes, tastes, and desires. The followers of Jesus enjoy sober, sensible, ennobling themes, while those who have no love for sacred things cannot take pleasure in these gatherings, unless the superficial and unreal constitute a prominent feature of the exercises. Little by little the spiritual element is ruled out by the irreligious, and the effort to harmonize principles which are antagonistic in their nature proves a decided failure.

Efforts have been made to devise a plan for the establishment of a literary society which shall prove a benefit to all connected with it—a society in which all the members shall feel a moral responsibility to make it what it should be, and to avoid the evils which often make such associations dangerous to religious principles. Persons of discretion and good judgment, who have a living connection with heaven, who will see the evil tendencies and, not deceived by Satan, will move straight forward in the path of integrity, continually holding aloft the banner of Christ—such ones are needed to control in these societies. Such an influence will command respect and make these gatherings a blessing rather than a curse.

If men and women of mature age would unite with the youth to organize and conduct such a literary society, it might become both useful and interesting. But when such gatherings degenerate into occasions for fun and boisterous mirth, they are anything but literary or elevating. They are debasing to both mind and morals.

Bible reading, the critical examination of Bible subjects, essays written upon topics which would improve the mind and impart knowledge, the study of the prophecies or the precious lessons of Christ—these will have an influence to strengthen the mental powers and increase spirituality. A familiar acquaintance with the Scriptures sharpens the discerning powers and fortifies the soul against the attacks of Satan.

Few realize that it is a duty to exercise control over the thoughts and imaginations. It is difficult to keep the undisciplined mind fixed upon profitable subjects. But if the thoughts are not properly employed, religion cannot flourish in the soul. The mind must be preoccupied with sacred and eternal things, or it will cherish trifling and superficial thoughts. Both the intellectual and the moral powers must be disciplined, and they will strengthen and improve by exercise.

In order to understand this matter aright, we must remember that our hearts are naturally depraved, and we are unable of ourselves to pursue a right course. It is only by the grace of God, combined with the most earnest effort on our part, that we can gain the victory.

The intellect, as well as the heart, must be consecrated to the service of God. He has claims upon all there is of us. The follower of Christ should not indulge in any gratification, or engage in any enterprise, however innocent or laudable it may appear, which an enlightened conscience tells him would abate his ardor or lessen his spirituality. Every Christian should labor to press back the tide of evil and save our youth from the influences that would sweep them down to ruin. May God help us to press our way against the current.

STUDENT MISSIONARY WORK

It is not enough to fill the minds of the youth with lessons of deep importance; they must learn to impart what they have received. Whatever may be the position or possession of any individual who has a knowledge of the truth, the word of God teaches him that all he has is held by him in trust. It is lent him to test his character. His worldly business, his talents, his means, his opportunities for service, are all to be accounted for to Him to whom by creation and redemption he belongs. God bestows His gifts upon us that we may minister to others and thus become like Him. He who strives to obtain knowledge in order that he may labor for the ignorant and perishing is acting his part in fulfilling God's great purpose for mankind. In unselfish service for the blessing of others he is meeting the high ideal of Christian education.

Among the students in our schools there are those who have precious talents, and these talents they should be taught to put to use. Our schools should be so conducted that teachers and students will constantly become more and more efficient. By faithfully putting to a practical use that which they have learned they will increase in ability to use their knowledge.

It is necessary to their complete education that students be given time to do missionary work—time to become acquainted with the spiritual needs of the families in the community around them. They should not be so loaded

(545)

down with studies that they have no time to use the knowledge they have acquired. They should be encouraged to make earnest missionary effort for those in error, becoming acquainted with them and taking to them the truth. By working in humility, seeking wisdom from Christ, praying and watching unto prayer, they may give to others the knowledge that has enriched their lives.

The teachers and students in our schools need the divine touch. God can do much more for them than He has done, because in the past His way has been restricted. If a missionary spirit is encouraged, even if it takes some hours from the program of regular study, much of heaven's blessing will be given, provided there is more faith and spiritual zeal, more of a realization of what God will do.

There are many lines in which the youth can find opportunity for helpful effort. Companies should be organized and thoroughly educated to work as nurses, gospel visitors, and Bible readers, as canvassers, ministers, and medical missionary evangelists.

When school closes, there is opportunity for many to go out into the field as evangelistic canvassers. The faithful colporteur finds his way into many homes, where he leaves reading matter containing the truth for this time. Our students should learn how to sell our books. There is need of men of deep Christian experience, men of well-balanced minds, strong, well-educated men, to engage in this branch of the work. Some have the talent, education, and experience that would enable them to educate the youth for the canvassing work in such a way that much more would be accomplished than is now being done. Those who have this experience have a special duty to perform in teaching others.

The canvassing work is one of the Lord's appointed agencies for extending the knowledge of the truth for this time. The effort made in some schools to circulate *Christ's Object Lessons* has demonstrated what can be accomplished in the canvassing field by the students. The Lord has blessed the efforts put forth to relieve our schools from debt, and those who have engaged in the work have obtained an excellent experience. As they have taken up the work disinterestedly, great blessing has come to them. Many have thus gained a knowledge of how to handle our larger books.

Wherever possible, students should, during the school year, engage in city mission work. They should do missionary work in the surrounding towns and villages. They can form themselves into bands to do Christian help work. Students should take a broad view of their present obligations to God. They are not to look forward to a time, after the school term closes, when they will do some large work for God, but should study how, during their student life, to yoke up with Christ in unselfish service for others.

There is power in the ministry of song. Students who have learned to sing sweet gospel songs with melody and distinctness can do much good as singing evangelists. They will find many opportunities to use the talent that God has given them in carrying melody and sunshine into many lonely places darkened by sorrow and affliction, singing to those who seldom have church privileges.

Students, go out into the highways and hedges. Endeavor to reach the higher as well as the lower classes. Enter the homes of the rich as well as the poor and, as you have opportunity, ask, "Would you be pleased to have us sing some gospel hymns?" Then as hearts are softened, the way may open for you to offer a few words of prayer for the blessing of God. Not many will refuse to listen. Such ministry is genuine missionary work.

Students, educate yourselves to speak in the language of Canaan. Put away all foolish talking and jesting, all foolish amusements. By faith grasp God's promises and determine that you will be Christians here below while preparing for translation. If you strip yourselves of every hindrance to progress in the Christian life, your minds will be worked by the Holy Spirit, and you will become fishers of men. The salvation of God will go forth from you as a lamp that burneth. If your own hearts are filled with light from above, wherever you may be you will shed light upon others. He will bless you in your service, and you will see of His salvation.

The third angel was seen flying in the midst of heaven, heralding the commandments of God and the faith of Jesus. The message loses none of its power in its onward flight. John saw the work increasing until the whole earth was filled with the glory of God. With intensified zeal and energy we are to carry forward the work of the Lord till the close of time.

In the home, in the school, in the church, men, women, and youth are to prepare to give the message to the world.

Our schools are to be more and more efficacious and self-reliant from a human standpoint, more like the schools of the prophets. The teachers should walk very near to God. The Lord calls for strong, devoted, self-sacrificing young men and women who will press to the front and who, after a short time spent in school, will go forth prepared to give the message to the world.

From our colleges and training schools missionaries are to be sent forth to distant lands. While at school let the students improve every opportunity to prepare for this work. Here they are to be tested and proved, that it may be seen what their adaptability is and whether they have a right hold from above. If they have a living connection with heaven they will have an influence for good on those with whom they come in contact.

A Valuable Experience

While we were living at Cooranbong, where the Avondale school is established, the question of amusements came up for consideration. "What shall we do to provide for the amusement of our students?" the faculty inquired. We talked matters over together, and then I came before the students and said to them:

"We can occupy our minds and our time profitably without trying to devise methods for amusing ourselves. Instead of spending time in playing the games that so many students play, strive to do something for the Master.

"The very best course for you to pursue is to engage in missionary work for the people of the neighborhood and in the nearby settlements. Whenever you are listening to an interesting discourse, take notes and mark down the passages that the minister uses, so that you can review the subject carefully. Then after faithful study you will soon be able to give a synopsis of the discourses, in the form of Bible readings, to some who do not come to our meetings."

The older students decided to follow this suggestion. They had evening meetings for studying the Scriptures together. They worked first of all for one another, and as a result of the Bible studies among themselves, a number of the unconverted were won to the truth. And the effort in behalf of the neighbors was a blessing not only to themselves, but to those for whom they labored.

Those who went out to work for the neighbors were instructed to report any case of sickness they might find; and those who had had training in giving treatment to the sick were encouraged to use their knowledge in a practical way. To work for the Master came to be regarded as Christlike recreation.

After a time the Sunday labor question came up for consideration. It seemed as if the lines were soon to be drawn so tightly about us that we should not be able to work on Sunday. Our school was situated in the heart of the woods, far from any village or railway station. No one was living near enough to be disturbed in any way by anything we might do. Nevertheless we were watched. The officers were urged to observe what we were doing on the school premises; and they did come, but they did not appear to notice those who were at work. Their confidence and respect for our people had been so won by the work we had done for the sick in that community that they did not wish to interfere with our harmless labor on Sunday.

At another time when our brethren were threatened with persecution and were questioning in regard to what they should do, I gave the same advice that I had given in answer to the question concerning the use of Sunday for games. I said, "Employ Sunday in doing missionary work for God. Teachers, go with your students. Take them to the homes of the people, near and far, and teach them how to talk in a way to do good. Let the people know that you are interested in their souls' salvation." The blessing of God rested upon the students as they diligently searched the Scriptures in order to learn how to present the truths of the word in such a way that these truths would be received with favor.

Let the teachers in our schools devote Sunday to missionary effort. Let them take the students with them to hold meetings for those who know not the truth. Sunday can be used for carrying forward various lines of work that will accomplish much for the Lord. On this day house-to-house work can be done. Open-air meetings and cottage meetings can be held. Make these meetings intensely interesting. Sing genuine revival hymns, and speak with power and assurance of the Saviour's love. Speak on temperance and on true religious experience. You will thus learn much about how to work, and will reach many hearts.

Those students who get the most good out of life are those who live by the word of God in their connections and dealings with their fellow men. Those who receive to give, experience the greatest satisfaction in this life. Those who live for themselves are always in want, for they are never satisfied. There is no Christianity in shutting up our sympathies in our own selfish hearts. The Lord has ordained channels through which He lets flow His goodness, mercy, and truth; and we are to be co-workers with Christ in communicating to others practical wisdom and benevolence. We are to bring brightness and blessing into their lives, thus doing a good and holy work.

Helpful Effort in the School

The student has a special work to do in the school itself. In the schoolroom and in the school home there are missionary fields awaiting his labors. Here a variety of minds are gathered, many different characters and dispositions. By proving himself a help and blessing to these, the student has the privilege of showing the genuineness of his love for Christ and his willingness to improve the opportunities for service that come to him. By helpful, kindly words and deeds he may impart to his associates the grace of God bestowed on him.

God wants the youth to be a help to one another. Each has trials to bear, temptations to meet. While one may be strong on some points, he may be weak on others, having grave faults to overcome. God says to all, "Bear ye one another's burdens, and so fulfill the law of Christ." Galatians 6:2.

Not all the youth are able to grasp ideas quickly. If you see a fellow student who has difficulty in understanding his lessons, explain them to him. State your ideas in clear, simple language. Often minds apparently stolid will catch ideas more quickly from a fellow student than from a teacher. Be patient and persevering, and by and by the hesitancy and dullness will disappear. In your efforts to help others, you will be helped. God will give you power to advance in your studies. He will co-operate with you, and in heaven the words will be spoken of you, "Good and faithful servant."

Let every student realize that he is in the school to help his fellow students to co-operate with God, to co-operate with the prayers that are rising in their behalf. In sympathy and love he should help his associates to press heavenward.

Students, co-operate with your teachers. As you do this, you give them hope and courage, and at the same time you are helping yourselves to advance. Remember that it rests largely with you whether your teachers stand on vantage ground, their work an acknowledged success. They will appreciate every effort made by you to co-operate with their work.

Students should have their own seasons of prayer, when they may offer fervent petitions in behalf of the principal and teachers of the school that they may be given physical strength, mental clearness, moral power, spiritual discernment, and be qualified by the grace of Christ to do the work with fidelity and fervent love. They should pray that the teachers may be agents through whom God shall work to make good prevail over evil. Every day the student may exert a silent, prayerful influence, and thus co-operate with Christ, the Missionary in chief.

We are far behind what we should be in Christian experience. We are backward in bearing the testimony that should be given through sanctified lips. Even when sitting at the meal table, Christ taught truths that brought comfort and courage to the hearts of His hearers. When His love abides in the soul as a living principle, there will come forth from the treasure house of the heart words suitable to the occasion—not light, trifling words, but uplifting words, words of spiritual power.

Let teachers and students watch for opportunities to confess Christ in their conversation. Such witness will be more effective than many sermons. There are few who represent Christ truly. He needs to be formed within, the hope of glory; then He will be acknowledged as the giver of every good and perfect gift, the author of all our blessings, the one in whom is centered our hope of eternal life.

Students, make your school life as perfect as possible. You will pass over the way but once, and precious are the opportunities granted you. You are not only to learn but to practice the lessons of Christ. While obtaining your education, you have the opportunity to tell of the wonderful truths of God's word. Improve every such opportunity. God will bless every minute spent in this way. Maintain your simplicity and your love for souls, and the Lord will lead you in safe paths. The rich experience you gain will be of more value to you than gold or silver or precious stones.

You know not to what position you may be called in the future. God may use you as He used Daniel, to take the knowledge of the truth to the mighty of the earth. It rests with you to say whether you will have skill and knowledge to do this work. God can give you skill in all your learning. He can help you to adapt yourself to the line of study you take up. Make it your first interest to gather up right, noble, uplifting principles. God desires you to witness for Him. He does not want you to stand still; He wants you to run in the way of His commandments.

Christ desires to use every student as His agent. You are to co-operate with the One who gave His life for you. What rich blessings would come to our schools if teachers and students would consecrate themselves, heart, mind, soul, and strength, to God's service as His helping hand! His helping hand—that is what you may be if you will yield yourselves to His keeping. He will lead you safely, and enable you to make straight paths for yourselves and for others. He will give you knowledge and wisdom, and a fitness for fuller service.

With such an army of workers as our youth, rightly trained, might furnish, how soon the message of a crucified, risen, and soon-coming Saviour might be carried to the whole world! How soon might the end come—the end of suffering and sorrow and sin! How soon, in place of a possession here, with its blight of sin and pain, our children might receive their inheritance where "the righteous shall inherit the land, and dwell therein forever;" where "the inhabitant shall not say, I am sick," and "the voice of weeping shall be no more heard." Psalm 37:29; Isaiah 33:24; 65:19.—*Education,* page 271.

FOR FURTHER STUDY

Index to Scripture References

(557)

GENERAL INDEX